The Rehnquist Court and the Constitution

The Rehnquist Court and the Constitution

Tinsley E. Yarbrough

OXFORD
UNIVERSITY PRESS

OXFORD
UNIVERSITY PRESS

Oxford New York
Athens Auckland Bangkok Bogotá Buenos Aires
Cape Town Chennai Dar es Salaam Delhi Florence
Hong Kong Istanbul Karachi Kolkata Kuala Lumpur
Madrid Melbourne Mexico City Mumbai Nairobi Paris
São Paulo Shanghai Singapore Taipei Tokyo Toronto Warsaw

and associated companies in

Berlin Ibadan

Copyright © 2000 by Oxford University Press, Inc.

First published by Oxford University Press, Inc., 2000
198 Madison Avenue, New York, New York 10016

First issued as an Oxford University Press paperback, 2001

Oxford is a registered trademark of Oxford University Press.

Library of Congress Cataloging-in-Publication Data
Yarbrough, Tinsley E., 1941–
The Rehnquist Court and the Constitution / Tinsley E. Yarbrough.
p.   cm.
Includes index.
ISBN 0-19-510346-7 (Cloth); ISBN 0-19-514603-4 (Pbk.)
1. United States. Supreme Court. 2. Rehnquist, William H., 1924–
3. Judicial review—United States. 4. Law and politics. I. Title.
KF8742.Y37 2000
347.73'26—dc21   99–18538

10 9 8 7 6 5 4 3 2 1
Printed in the United States of America
on acid-free paper

To
Sarah and Todd

Contents

Preface

William Hubbs Rehnquist, appointed chief justice of the Supreme Court by President Reagan in 1986, has now served nearly a decade and a half in the Court's center seat. Reagan's selection of Rehnquist, the Burger Court's most conservative-activist member following his appointment as an associate justice by President Nixon in 1971, was hardly accidental. More than any of his predecessors, including Nixon, President Reagan and his administration challenged the federal human rights orthodoxy of the post–World War II era—a legacy forged in significant ways by Congress and the presidency but primarily through the work of the federal courts, especially the Supreme Court during the tenure of Chief Justice Earl Warren, 1953–69. Honing to a fine art the "southern strategy" that GOP presidents and would-be presidents had pursued with varying degrees of enthusiasm since President Eisenhower's day, candidate Reagan made an early appearance in his 1980 campaign at the Neshoba County Fair in Philadelphia, Mississippi, site of the 1964 murders of three civil rights workers at the hands of Ku Klux Klansmen and local police. There, he proclaimed his support for "states' rights" and vowed to "restore to states and local governments the powers that properly belonged to them."[1] As candidate and president, moreover, he defended restoration of tax exemptions for segregated private schools while opposing affirmative action programs and the implementation of school desegregation through "forced" busing.

Nor were embittered white southerners the only target of Reagan's conservative appeals. Through support for a school prayer amendment and opposition to Supreme Court decisions banning devotional exercises from public schools, recognizing rights of sexual privacy, expanding constitutional protections for erotic expression, and guaranteeing women a right of abortion, Reagan forged deep ties with the religious right and their followers. With even greater success than President Nixon, he also campaigned for the hearts of a more amorphous, yet larger, constituency incensed at Supreme Court rulings expanding the rights of suspects and defendants in criminal cases.

Whatever the extent to which the Reagan administration's challenges to postwar civil liberties doctrine reflected the president's personal philosophy rather than mere political strategy, such positions appeared clearly consistent with the philosophical leanings of key administration officials, especially his second attorney general, Edwin

Meese III, and William Bradford Reynolds, his assistant attorney general for civil rights. In various settings, they and other administration figures repeatedly and vigorously affirmed their opposition to race- and gender-conscious hiring and college admissions, the application of Bill of Rights safeguards to the states through the Fourteenth Amendment, bans on public school devotional exercises, the exclusion of illegally seized confessions and evidence from criminal proceedings, expansive concepts of constitutionally protected sexual privacy, abortion rights, and safeguards for erotic expression. They also regularly scorned judicial interpretations of the Constitution going beyond what, in their eyes, was the almost inevitably narrow "original intent" of its framers, accusing liberal-activist judges of creating rights under the guise of constitutional construction.

The administration's assaults on prevailing civil rights policies and constitutional doctrine took a variety of forms. Certain initiatives were directed at Congress, such as the attempt early in President Reagan's first term to secure repeal of the "preclearance" provisions of the 1965 Voting Rights Act, which required federal approval of new election regulations and were upheld by the Warren Court as a reasonable weapon against future enactment of discriminatory voter devices.[2] Executive agencies also pursued the administration's conservative rights agenda. Although ultimately rebuffed by the Supreme Court,[3] for example, Treasury Department officials, under pressure from the White House, reinstated tax exemptions for segregated private schools. Primarily, however, the administration's challenge to modern civil rights trends centered on the federal courts. It proposed constitutional amendments designed to overturn objectionable judicial interpretations of the Constitution. It supported legislation to restrict federal court jurisdiction over abortion and other civil liberties claims. As litigant and *amicus curiae* (friend of the court), it urged the Supreme Court to reverse and modify its own precedents. In an effort that led to the resignation of Solicitor General Rex Lee, the administration even attempted to convert that office, traditionally considered a representative of the rule of law rather than presidential policy goals, into a vigorous advocate for the Reagan human rights agenda.[4]

Most significant in terms of potential long-term impact, though, was the administration's use of presidential control over judicial appointments to perpetuate and expand its conservative human rights legacy. To a greater degree arguably than all his predecessors, President Reagan closely reviewed the ideological leanings of prospective judicial nominees and maximized White House control over judicial selection, substantially modifying the selection process toward his administration's policy goals.[5] With slight changes in emphasis and procedure, President Bush continued his predecessor's efforts to transform the judiciary. Together, they filled nearly three-quarters of all seats on the federal courts. In addition to elevating William Rehnquist to the Supreme Court's center seat, President Reagan appointed Sandra Day O'Connor, Antonin Scalia, and Anthony Kennedy to seats on the high bench, while George Bush chose David H. Souter and Clarence Thomas for the Court.

The Reagan-Bush judicial choices have had an undoubted influence on the direction of constitutional law, but not, to date, the sort of fundamental impact for which the Reagan White House had hoped. Chief Justice Rehnquist and Justices Scalia and Thomas have generally assumed positions consistent with the Reagan-Bush policy agenda, particularly in their intense opposition to abortion rights and affirmative action. But Justice O'Connor, whose selection was based more on gender than ideology and whose ambivalent position on the abortion issue as an Arizona state legislator provoked pro-life opposition to her confirmation, has become a classic swing voter in a number of issue areas. So, too, has Justice Kennedy, whose lack of an ideological "paper trail" made him a politically acceptable third choice to replace Justice Lewis Powell after Robert Bork's nomination went down to defeat in the Senate and President Reagan's second choice, Douglas Ginsburg, quickly succumbed to conflict of interest allegations and revelations the nominee had smoked marijuana while a member of Harvard's law faculty. Justice Souter, President Bush's first appointee to the Court, has become an articulate exponent of the sort of flexible, case-by-case approach to constitutional construction that led his jurisprudential mentor, the second Justice John Marshall Harlan, in liberal as well as conservative directions during his distinguished tenure on the Court. President Clinton's first-term appointments of two moderate legal pragmatists, Justices Ruth Bader Ginsburg and Stephen Breyer, to replace Justices Byron R. White and Harry A. Blackmun further undermined the Reagan-Bush judicial agenda. Since the departures of Justice Blackmun and Justices William J. Brennan and Thurgood Marshall, moreover, Justice John Paul Stevens, President Ford's lone appointment to the Court, has become the justice generally most likely to embrace civil liberties claims. It is hardly surprising, therefore, that much scholarly research on the Rehnquist Court to date has emphasized doctrinal continuity rather than change—the extent to which constitutional decision making in the Rehnquist era has largely kept faith in many fields of litigation with Burger Court, if not Warren Court, precedent,[6] just as Richard Nixon's appointments of "strict constructionists" to the Burger Court failed to produce the constitutional counterrevolution Warren Court critics had anticipated.[7]

Such centrist forces are clearly evident on the Rehnquist Court. They may tend to obscure, however, important developments on the Court with enormous potential for exerting a substantial impact on future decisional trends. Nor are such trends confined to issues that are most commonly the concern of modern constitutional cases, such as abortion and sexual privacy rights, religious liberty, the use of affirmative action programs to remedy past discrimination against minorities and women, and criminal procedure guarantees. In a number of important recent cases, for example, a majority has raised serious doubts about the continued viability of long-standing precedents regarding the scope of congressional authority over the states in the federal system; converted the Constitution's takings clause requiring just compensation for government takings of property for public uses into a meaningful and potentially limitless restriction on "regulatory takings" created by state environmental, zoning, and related controls; and perhaps begun to resurrect substantive due process as a meaningful restriction on what the Court considers unreasonable government interferences with economic liberty. Such rulings cast doubt on the current status of the constitutional "double standard," under which the post-1936 Supreme Court has presumed the validity of economic regulations, leaving the definition and protection of property rights largely to the political arena rather than the judicial process, while closely scrutinizing governmental interferences with noneconomic personal rights.[8]

They may also reflect an economic conservatism even more fundamental to the philosophy of traditional Republican elites than the social agenda Presidents Reagan and Bush pursued in broadening the party's voter base.

But constitutional developments on the Rehnquist Court have by no means been entirely compatible with the Reagan-Bush social agenda or more traditional Republican economic concerns. Justice Kennedy's rationale for the Court in *Romer v. Evans* (1996)[9] purported, for example, to apply a lenient, rational basis standard of review in striking down a Colorado constitutional amendment prohibiting governmental action protecting homosexuals from discrimination based on sexual preference. But Justice Scalia made a convincing argument in dissent that the Court was actually subjecting disfavorable treatment of homosexuals to heightened scrutiny, contrary to the Burger Court's 1986 decision in *Bowers v. Hardwick*,[10] rejecting meaningful constitutional protection for homosexual sodomy. And although the Court in 1997 unanimously upheld statutes prohibiting physician-assisted suicides, a bare majority of the justices suggested in separate opinions that, under certain circumstances, terminally ill persons were entitled to a right to die.[11] A majority on the Rehnquist Court thus appears unwilling to limit constitutional rights to enumerated guarantees or even to those unenumerated interests firmly entrenched in American tradition.

This book examines such decisional developments on the Rehnquist Court. It considers to some extent the backgrounds of the justices, controversies surrounding their appointments, elements in the Court's daily operations, and the justices' relations with each other and staff. My focus, however, is on doctrinal trends in constitutional law on the Court: the forces of continuity and change, the positions of the justices on specific constitutional issues, and their competing conceptions of the proper role of judges in constitutional adjudication. Such an analysis, it is hoped, will shed further light on a deliberative body that mirrors in many ways the complicated, turbulent state of contemporary American politics.

What follows, of course, is solely my responsibility. This book was possible, however, only through the assistance of a number of individuals and institutions. Generous grants from Earhart Foundation provided critical financial support, as did grants from the Research/Creative Activity Committee and Chancellor's Discretionary Fund at East Carolina University. The Thurgood Marshall Papers at the Library of Congress were an invaluable source of material regarding the inner workings of the Court; and the Lewis F. Powell, Jr., Papers at Washington and Lee University were also consulted for the one term Justice Powell remained on the bench following Chief Justice Rehnquist's elevation to its center seat. I am especially indebted to David Wigdor of the Library of Congress's manuscript division and to John N. Jacob, archivist of the Powell Papers, for their assistance with my research in those fine collections.

Sincere thanks are also extended, as always, to Cynthia Manning Smith for invariably flawless clerical assistance; to Oxford's superb editorial staff; and to Mary Alice, our son Cole, daughter Sarah and her husband Todd Ratner for their love and encouragement. As Sarah and Todd embark upon careers in the law, I dedicate this book to them with complete confidence that they will always maintain the noblest traditions of their chosen profession.

The Rehnquist Court and the Constitution

1

The Justices

In a White House ceremony on the morning of September 26, 1986, Chief Justice Burger administered his successor the oath of office required by the Constitution. That afternoon at the Supreme Court, Chief Justice Rehnquist took the judicial oath, promising to "administer justice without respect to persons, and do equal right to the poor and to the rich." Earlier, William Bradford Reynolds, President Reagan's assistant attorney general for civil rights, had denounced the "radical egalitarianism" of Rehnquist's colleague and the Court's senior associate justice, William J. Brennan, Jr., who, Reynolds charged, had "allowed his liberal orthodoxy to shape his jurisprudence." During the White House ceremony, by contrast, the president praised Rehnquist as a "brilliant" jurist who understood that "government by the people requires judicial restraint."[1] By that point, however, the new chief justice's critics had raised serious questions regarding Rehnquist's commitment to the Constitution and his judicial oath, as well as concerns about his personal candor and integrity.

The Rehnquist Confirmation

Opposition to Chief Justice Rehnquist's confirmation by the U.S. Senate covered a wide-ranging array of issues, but several were subjected to extensive scrutiny in the Senate judiciary committee[2] and the press. First, there were the memoranda he had written as a clerk to Justice Robert H. Jackson from 1952 to 1953. In the most publicized, entitled "A Random Thought on the Segregation Cases," Rehnquist had written that in *Brown v. Board of Education* and companion school desegregation cases the Warren Court was "being asked to read its own sociological views into the Constitution" and to adopt a position "palpably at variance with precedent and probably with legislative history."[3] The pre-1937 Court—the Old Court—and such justices as James McReynolds had erred, Rehnquist asserted, in writing their personal laissez-faire economic views into the Constitution. He added,

> If this Court, because its members individually are "liberal" and dislike segregation, now chooses to strike it down, it differs from the McReynolds court only in the kinds of litigants it favors and the kinds of special claims it protects. To those who would argue that "personal" rights are more sacrosanct than "property" rights, the short answer is that the Constitution makes no such distinction.

The memorandum appeared equally unsympathetic to the role of the Constitution and Court as protectors of minority rights.

> One hundred and fifty years of attempts on the part of the Court to protect minority rights of any kind—whether those of business, slaveholders, or Jehovah's Witnesses—have all met the same fate. One by one the cases establishing such rights have been sloughed off, and crept silently to rest. If the present Court is unable to profit by this example, it must be prepared to see its work fade in time, too, as embodying only the sentiments of a transient majority of nine men.

And what of *Plessy v. Ferguson* (1896)[4] and its "separate but equal doctrine"?

> I realize that it is an unpopular and unhumanitarian position, for which I have been excoriated by "liberal" colleagues, but I think *Plessy* . . . was right and should be re-affirmed. If the Fourteenth Amendment did not enact [Herbert] Spencer's *Social Statics*, it just as surely did not enact Myrdahl's [*sic*] *American Dilemma.*[5]

Two other Rehnquist memoranda pertained to *Terry v. Adams* (1953),[6] in which the Court struck down an unusual version of the white primary.[7] In one, he recommended that Justice Jackson vote to grant certiorari review of the case, but confessed to difficulty in "being detached about this case, because several of the [Yale law professor Fred] Rodell school of thought among the clerks began screaming as soon as they saw this that 'Now we can show those damn southerners, etc.'" He added, "I take a dim view of this pathological search for discrimination, a la [NAACP leader] Walter White, [Justice Hugo L.] Black, [Justice William O.] Douglas, Rodell, etc., and as a result I now have something of a mental block against the case."

In the second of the *Terry* memoranda, Rehnquist suggested what approach might be taken should Justice Jackson decide to dissent in the case. He recommended, for example, that the justice include "ideas" Jackson had recently expressed that "the constitution does not prevent the majority from banding together, nor does it attaint success in the effort." Elaborating, Rehnquist wrote,

> It is about time the Court faced the fact that the white people [in] the South don't like the colored people; the constitution restrains them from effecting this

dislike thr[ough] state action, but it most assuredly did not appoint the Court as a sociological watchdog to rear up every time private discrimination raises its admittedly ugly head. To the extent that this decision advances the frontier of state action and "social gain," it pushes back the frontier of freedom of association and majority rule. Liberals should be the first to realize, after the past twenty years, that it does not do to push blindly through towards one constitutional goal without paying attention to other equally desirable values that are being trampled on in the process.

This is a position that I am sure ought to be stated; but if stated by [Chief Justice Fred M.] Vinson, [Sherman] Minton, or [Stanley] Reed it just won't sound the same way as if you state it.

In a December 8, 1971, letter to Senate judiciary committee chairman James Eastland (D-Miss.) following hearings on his nomination as an associate justice, Rehnquist recalled that his *Brown* memorandum "was intended as a rough draft of a statement of" Justice Jackson's views, rather than his own position on the school segregation cases. During hearings on his confirmation as chief justice, he persisted in that explanation, although also suggesting that time may have blurred his memory. He asserted, too, that at the time the school segregation cases were before the Supreme Court, he thought that *Plessy* had been "wrongly decided . . . , that it was not a good interpretation of the equal protection clause to say that when you segregate people by race, there is no denial of equal protection."[8] Noting, however, that *Plessy* had been "on the books" for sixty years and that the same Congress that developed the Fourteenth Amendment had required segregation in District of Columbia schools, Rehnquist also testified that he did "not think I reached a conclusion" as Justice Jackson's clerk whether *Plessy* should be overruled.

Senate Democrats pressed the nominee to clarify his position. At one point, for example, Senator Joseph R. Biden, Jr. (D-Del.) cited a recent newspaper article[9] claiming that Rehnquist had strongly defended *Plessy* in luncheon debates with other clerks during Supreme Court review of the segregation cases. Rehnquist conceded that he was "sure" he had defended *Plessy* "around the lunch table," but insisted that he did not think he "ever really finally settled in my own mind" whether *Plessy* should be overruled.[10] Senator Howard Metzenbaum (D-Ohio) seemed especially impatient with portions of the Rehnquist memoranda and the nominee's efforts to suggest that they were a reflection of Justice Jackson's, rather than his own, views. "You, as a clerk, said," Metzenbaum observed, "'I take a dim view of this pathological search for discrimination a la Walter White, . . . etc.' . . . Is it not the fact that at the time you did not have to have a pathological search for discrimination in order to find it because it was such a reality of life?" "I think it probably was," Rehnquist responded.[11] Later, in another reference to Rehnquist's *Terry* memorandum, Metzenbaum asked, "Did you, in all of the time you worked with Justice Jackson, ever hear him say something like the following: It is about time that the Court faced the fact that the white people of the South do not like the colored people?" "I simply cannot recall at this time," the nominee replied.

Conservative Republicans on the judiciary committee sought to minimize the

Brown memorandum's potential impact. Not surprisingly perhaps, given his own history as a rabid segregationist and 1948 Dixiecrat presidential candidate, committee chairman Strom Thurmond (R-S.C.) took little part in that effort. But Utah Republican Orrin Hatch vigorously defended the nominee.

During Senate consideration of Rehnquist's 1971 nomination as associate justice, his coclerk Donald Cronson, then an executive in the Mobil oil company's London office, had cabled a message to Rehnquist later reprinted in the *Congressional Record.* In that cablegram, Cronson recalled that the *Brown* memorandum was "my work at least as much as it is yours and that it was prepared in response to a request from Justice Jackson." Prior to preparation of the memorandum, which bore only Rehnquist's initials, Cronson asserted, the two had collaborated in preparing another memorandum contending that *Plessy* had been wrongly decided, but also arguing that the Court should leave to Congress any change in segregation policy. Later, according to Cronson, Justice Jackson had asked for a second memorandum "supporting the proposition that *Plessy* was correctly decided." Rehnquist typed that memorandum, Cronson remembered, "but a great deal of the content was the result of my suggestions."[12]

During his questioning of Rehnquist, Senator Hatch first expressed reluctance to bring up "matters that have occurred 34 or 35 years ago" and bemoaned the committee's preoccupation with "these ancient events as though they are important today." Then, seizing on Cronson's recollections and published assertions that both he and the nominee thought that *Plessy* was wrong, the senator defended Rehnquist's version of the origins and nature of the Rehnquist *Brown* memorandum, declaring, "It is significant that the only other person with a firsthand knowledge about this segregation memorandum agrees with your account that it was drafted at Justice Jackson's request to reflect a particular point of view. . . . It is not a reflection of your own views according to the only other person who had firsthand knowledge or recollection of the memorandum. In fact, your co-clerk has stated that he collaborated with you on the drafting of the memo and that it may have been more a product of his own than of your own. That answers that question."[13]

But hardly, of course, to everyone's satisfaction. Soon, Massachusetts Democrat Edward M. Kennedy placed in the record the detailed analysis of the Rehnquist memorandum that journalist Richard Kluger had compiled for *Simple Justice*, his exhaustive study of *Brown.*[14] "Taking the careers and judicial assertions of both [Rehnquist and Jackson] in their totality," Kluger had concluded, "one finds a preponderance of evidence to suggest that the memorandum in question—the one that threatened to deprive William Rehnquist of his place on the Supreme Court—was an accurate statement of his own views on segregation, not those of Robert Jackson, who, by contrast, was a staunch libertarian and humanist."[15]

The evidence that led Kluger to his conclusion was very persuasive. With respect to Cronson's recollections, for example, he questioned why Rehnquist, in his 1971 letter to the Senate, had not mentioned the first memorandum; why, if Jackson requested two memoranda taking opposite positions on *Plessy*, Rehnquist had claimed that the second memorandum, the one bearing his initials, represented Jackson's views; why, if Rehnquist and Cronson collaborated on both memoranda, each carried the initials of just one of them and their styles were quite different; and why Rehnquist had not informed the Senate that Cronson coauthored the controversial memorandum and even considered it more his work than Rehnquist's, if indeed its preparation had been a joint effort. Justice Jackson's secretary Elsie Douglas, Kluger added, had "sharply denied" Rehnquist's account, calling it "incredible on its face" and charging that Rehnquist had "smeared the reputation of a great Justice."

Kluger cited other concerns as well. He doubted that the memoranda would have carried such "strikingly inappropriate" titles as "A Few Expressed Prejudices on the Segregation Cases" or "A Random Thought on the Segregation Cases" if intended for Justice Jackson's use at a conference of the justices and as an expression of his personal views. He seriously questioned, too, whether Jackson would have been at all inclined to deliver "so crude and elementary" an attack on the pre-1937 Court's protection of business interests as that contained in the memorandum bearing Rehnquist's initials, especially since all the members of the Court but one were veteran New Dealers "entirely familiar with the . . . Court's pre-1937 biases." Or that Jackson would have "disparaged," as Rehnquist's memorandum did, the Court's attempt to protect the interests of minority groups, "when Jackson himself wrote many a decision protect-ing minority rights," including his memorable opinion for the Court in *West Virginia Board of Education v. Barnette*,[16] upholding the rights of Jehovah's Witnesses—one of the very minority groups referred to in Rehnquist's memorandum. Or that Jackson would have shared with other justices "anything remotely approaching" the assertion in Rehnquist's memorandum that he had been "excoriated by 'liberal' colleagues" for his position on segregation. "A far more plausible explanation," wrote Kluger, "might be that the 'I' of the memo is Rehnquist himself, referring to the obloquy to which he may have been subjected by his fellow clerks, who discussed the segregation question over lunch quite regularly, who were almost unanimous in their belief that *Plessy* ought to be reversed, and who were, for the most part, 'liberal.'"

In support of this interpretation, Kluger cited an article Rehnquist had written for a 1957 issue of *U.S. News & World Report*, in which the future justice complained of the "liberal" biases of Supreme Court clerks, including "extreme solicitude for the claims of Communists and other criminal defendants, expansion of federal power at the expense of State power, [and] great sympathy toward any government regulation of business," enclosing the word "liberal" in the same "telltale quotation marks" he had used in the *Brown* memorandum.[17] As evidence that Rehnquist was "ideologically a pole apart" from other clerks, Kluger also quoted a fellow clerk, who, at the time of Rehnquist's initial appointment to the Court, characterized him as "a reactionary," adding, "I would expect him to be a reactionary today, but you never know what a person will do once appointed." Kluger questioned, too, why, if both the Rehnquist and Cronson memoranda were intended to state Justice Jackson's views, the latter memorandum was clearly from a clerk to his justice, with Cronson noting at one point, "One of the main characteristics of *your* work on this Court is a reluctance to overrule existing constitutional law" (emphasis added).

Kluger found equally convincing other evidence that Rehnquist's *Brown* memo-randum reflected his views rather than Justice Jackson's. In a 1959 article, Rehnquist cited *Brown* in bemoaning the "absence of *stare decisis* in constitutional law." An "unabashedly liberal" Stanford law school classmate termed Rehnquist "brilliant" but "so far-out politically that he was something of a joke." As a Phoenix lawyer, Rehnquist had given a 1957 speech denouncing Justices Black and Douglas, among others, as "left-wing," had been an ardent supporter of conservative Arizona senator Barry Goldwater, had opposed a local antidiscrimination ordinance, and had attacked a 1967 Phoenix school desegregation program. As assistant attorney general in charge of the Office of Legal Counsel in the Nixon Justice Department, he was the department's "most ardently prosecutorial advocate of wiretapping, government surveillance, preventive detention, and other so-called law-and-order techniques of a totalitarian cast." He had also drafted the administration's 1970 constitutional amendment proposal opposing busing as a school desegregation tool. His Supreme Court record to date, added Kluger, had been overwhelmingly conservative, with the justice regularly voting to restrict civil rights and liberties, to retain the death penalty, and to side with business in antitrust cases and against unions in labor litigation. Such a professional, political, and judicial record was entirely consistent, in Kluger's judgment, with the conclusion that Rehnquist's *Brown* memorandum reflected his own views, not those of the justice he served.

Rehnquist's roles as government lawyer and justice in disputes over military surveillance of civilian dissidents were another source of intense interest and concern to the judiciary committee. Shortly after his initial appointment to the Supreme Court, Rehnquist had participated in *Laird v. Tatum* (1972),[18] in which a five-four majority dismissed on standing grounds a challenge to Army surveillance of civilians, claimed to impose a chilling effect on the First Amendment rights of those opposed to U.S. military policies. Following announcement of the Court's decision, the American Civil Liberties Union (ACLU), which had furnished counsel for the *Laird* plaintiffs, filed a petition for rehearing and a motion that Justice Rehnquist recuse, or disqualify, himself from further participation in the case. As assistant attorney general in the Nixon administration, ACLU lawyers contended, Rehnquist had appeared as an expert witness in Senate hearings on military surveillance practices; he had intimate knowledge of the evidence in the *Laird* case and had made public statements questioning the merits of the *Laird* plaintiffs' allegations. Rehnquist refused to recuse himself and, in a highly unusual move, issued a memorandum denying that his prior connection with the case constituted a conflict of interest; noting that Justices Black and Frankfurter, among others, had participated in cases involving legislation they had helped to draft; and emphasizing that one justice's disqualification could produce an affirmance of the ruling below by an equally divided Court.[19]

Reacting editorially at the time, the *New York Times* observed that the government had won the *Laird* case only as a result of Justice Rehnquist's decision to furnish the fifth vote to overturn a federal appeals court decision invalidating the Army's surveillance program. His claim that he had a duty to participate to assure a decision in the case, asserted the *Times,* "seems only to underscore the impropriety of a former representative of Government to continue the Government's case on the Supreme Court—the court of last resort."[20]

Judiciary committee members examining Rehnquist's fitness to be chief justice found his participation in *Laird* equally disturbing, especially since congressional testimony the nominee had given while a member of the Nixon administration suggested that he had prejudged the *Laird* case prior to his appointment to the Court. As a witness before the Senate subcommittee on constitutional rights, chaired by North Carolina Democrat Sam J. Ervin, Jr., Rehnquist rejected Senator Ervin's assumption that the *Laird* plaintiffs had standing to challenge the military surveillance program in the courts. "My only point of disagreement with you," Rehnquist told the senator at that time, "is to say whether as in the case of *Tatum v. Laird* that has been pending in the Court of Appeals here in the District of Columbia that an action will lie by private citizens to enjoin the gathering of information by the executive branch where there has been no threat of compulsory process and no pending action against any of those individuals on the part of the Government."[21] That was precisely the rationale the Supreme Court, with Rehnquist participating, would use in overturning the lower court ruling that had invalidated the surveillance program.

Senator Kennedy entered portions of the Ervin hearing transcript into the record, quoted the part cited above, and asserted, "You had basically made up your mind on that issue, had you not, Mr. Rehnquist?" When the nominee objected to being obliged to defend action he had taken as a justice, Kennedy charged that Rehnquist "basically resented those [antiwar] demonstrators [against whom the surveillance program was directed]," adding, "You made up your mind evidently that those demonstrators were not going to get their way in the Supreme Court, even if you had to sit on the case to break a tie, even if you had to violate the ABA [American Bar Association] rules [regarding judicial ethics] and the fundamental principles of justice to do it."[22] Citing research that had reached the same conclusion,[23] Kennedy asked the nominee for his reaction to such claims. "That I was performing a judicial act," Rehnquist replied, "and that I ought not to be called upon somewhere else to justify this."[24]

Judiciary committee members also heard from witnesses who complained that between 1958 and 1964 Rehnquist had harassed blacks and Hispanics at Phoenix polling places. When such charges were raised in 1971 following Rehnquist's appearance before the committee for hearings on his nomination as associate justice, Senator Eastland, the committee chair, had declined to reconvene the committee. But Rehnquist wrote Eastland a letter denying the accusations and asserting that "[i]n none of these years did I personally engage in challenging the qualifications of any voters."[25] During Senate deliberations on his nomination as chief justice, witnesses opposing his confirmation again raised such charges. One witness described a "shoving match" involving the nominee that erupted at a Phoenix polling place when a black voter became angry when Rehnquist, the witness alleged, challenged the voter's credentials. "[Rehnquist] had two cards in his hand," the witness recalled. "One was the state constitution and the other was the U.S. Constitution. And if he thought you were down and out, and illiterate, he would challenge that vote." James S. Brosnahan, a former federal prosecutor in Phoenix who by 1986 was a senior partner in a San Francisco law firm, testified that he had gone to a polling place during one election to investigate allegations that Republican workers were harassing minority voters. Until 1964, Brosnahan noted, it had been legal to challenge voters if there was reason to believe they were illiterate, but not to stop persons in a voting line without reason to believe they were unqualified. "At that polling place, I saw William Rehnquist, who was known to me. He was serving on that day, as a challenger of voters. That is to say, the complaints had to do with his conduct." Another witness testified that he observed a Republican official, whom he later identified from a newspaper photograph as Rehnquist, questioning the voter qualifications of "everybody" at one precinct in 1964. The two, he added, had a long and tense exchange, at one point going "eyeball to eyeball." Yet another witness charged that in 1960 and 1962 he had seen Rehnquist at a precinct, telling other Republicans they should challenge "illiterates" and others unqualified to vote.[26]

Noting that all such witnesses had been Democratic activists, Republicans on the judiciary committee complained of partisan bias against the nominee. When Senator Hatch questioned the accuracy of James Brosnahan's memory, however, the former federal prosecutor's response drew loud applause from the audience. Had he not been "absolutely" certain he had interviewed Rehnquist that day, an indignant Brosnahan countered, "I would be home having my Friday afternoon lunch at Jack's [a San Francisco restaurant] and I would not be here in front of you."[27] And when Rehnquist stated that he did not "believe" he had ever personally challenged a voter during his years in Phoenix, Senator Metzenbaum shot back, "Mr. Justice, I am not talking about your being able to remember where you were on the third day of June 1952, I am talking about whether you ever confronted people and said to them: 'Can you read this Constitution?' 'What educational background do you have?' Challenge them in their right to vote. And you are saying that you do not remember. And I am saying to you, is it possible that a man as brilliant as you, could not remember if he had done that?" "Senator," Rehnquist replied, "challenging was a perfectly legitimate thing." "But you told the Senate that you never challenged anybody," an exasperated Metzenbaum rejoined. "I believe I told the Senate . . . I did not think I had challenged" voters, Rehnquist responded.[28]

Yet another target of concern for committee Democrats was the nominee's willingness to sign deeds containing racial and religious restrictions. A deed for a house Rehnquist had purchased in Maricopa County, Arizona, in 1961 and another for a Greensboro, Vermont, summer home, purchased in 1974, contained such covenants. Neither deed bore Rehnquist's signature, and Senator Hatch took his colleagues and the press to task for assigning any weight to the matter. Calling the issue "the biggest 'red herring' I have seen in the whole hearing," Hatch emphasized that the Supreme Court's 1948 decision in *Shelley v. Kraemer*[29] had made such covenants unenforceable and scorned committee Democrats for making "a big brouhaha about something this ridiculous."[30] For his part, Justice Rehnquist testified that he had first learned of the covenants "[t]he last couple days" and assured the committee that he "plan[ned] to do something about it."[31] Several days after the hearings adjourned, however, Rehnquist informed the committee that his lawyer had told him in 1974 that the deed to his Vermont property had contained a restriction against ownership by "members of the Hebrew race,"[32] yet the justice had taken no action.

When the hearings ended on August 1, Democratic senators were attempting to secure internal memoranda Rehnquist had written from 1969 to 1971, when he was in the Nixon Justice Department. Initially President Reagan invoked executive privilege and refused to turn over the memoranda to Congress, prompting Senator Kennedy to accuse the administration of "stonewalling" to conceal advice Rehnquist might have given President Nixon and Attorney General John Mitchell in the years leading to the Watergate scandal and Nixon's resignation from the presidency.[33]

Ultimately, Reagan gave up the documents sought,[34] but charges continued to surface regarding the nominee's fitness for the Court's center seat. One set of concerns focused on a medical report submitted to the judiciary committee on August 11 regarding Rehnquist's dependency for nearly a decade on a powerful painkilling drug. Dr. Freeman H. Cary, who had recently retired as the attending physician for Congress, prescribed the hypnotic drug Placidyl from 1972 to 1981 for Rehnquist to relieve his chronic back pain. According to the medical report, compiled by Dr. William Pollin, a former federal drug abuse official, Justice Rehnquist's daily dosage had been increased from 500 milligrams in the early 1970s to 1500 milligrams, somewhat above the maximum legal dosage, by 1976, where it remained in 1981, when Rehnquist was admitted to George Washington University hospital for drug-dependency treatment. During the FBI's background check of the nominee, Dr. Cary had told agents that he was concerned about the dosage and had made that clear to Rehnquist on several occasions. Dr. Pollin's report indicated that the nominee was no longer using the drug on a daily basis and suffered no drug "dependency," while Senator Hatch characterized Rehnquist as simply "a very compliant patient" who had been "overly prescribed by the doctors"; when asked, Hatch said that, in his judgment, the report should not be made public. But another committee member, Democrat Paul Simon of Illinois, called for the report's release and announced his decision to oppose confirmation, although emphasizing that his opposition was based on concerns about the veracity of the nominee's testimony before the committee and poor record on civil rights, not any fear that Rehnquist remained addicted to Placidyl.[35]

On August 14, the judiciary committee voted thirteen-five, with Democrats casting the negative votes, to recommend Rehnquist's confirmation to the full Senate. That same day, however, the nominee's disabled brother-in-law accused Rehnquist of unethical conduct in the management of a family trust fund. Rehnquist had drawn up the trust in 1961 at the request of his dying father-in-law, San Diego physician Harold Davis. Established for Harold Dickerson Cornell, the brother of Rehnquist's wife Natalie, the document stipulated that Cornell, a victim of multiple sclerosis, was to receive funds from the $25,000 trust whenever he "was unable to provide for himself in the manner to which he was accustomed." A year after the trust was established, Cornell, then forty-nine and a San Diego lawyer earning about $50,000 a year, was forced to retire as a result of his debilitating illness. In an interview with a *New York Times* reporter, Cornell claimed that he was poverty-stricken soon after retiring, making stew from bones, living off a $96 monthly Social Security check. At one point, he said, his financial condition became so desperate that he asked his family at an annual reunion if he could obtain funds from another trust established by his parents for emergencies and educational expenses. "Bill [Rehnquist] was at that meeting," Cornell recalled. "He certainly knew about my trust and he knew I was disabled and in serious financial straits. Bill and the others decided I didn't have the right to the emergency trust fund even though I was 100 percent disabled. And they never said, 'Hey, you have your own trust.'" Not until 1982, when one of his sisters became a trustee and her lawyer advised her to inform Cornell, did he first learn of the trust.[36]

Justice Rehnquist was teaching at Pepperdine University in Malibu, California, when his brother-in-law's interview appeared in the press, and a spokesperson at the Court indicated that it was the justice's policy not to discuss matters relating to his confirmation with the media. Several other members of Cornell's family suggested that Rehnquist and others had followed his father-in-law's wishes in concealing the trust from Cornell because he spent money carelessly. But an exasperated Cornell asked, "How could I squander trust money? It's ridiculous." Legal ethics scholar Stephen Gillers contended, moreover, that Rehnquist's "failure to act when he [through his wife] personally stands to gain by the failure is especially wrong."[37] Four Senate Democratic opponents of Rehnquist's nomination asked judiciary committee chairman Strom Thurmond to reopen the FBI investigation of the nominee's background. Thurmond passed the request on to the Justice Department, but Senate Republican leader Robert Dole opposed the petition, noting that Cornell's claims and the results of the FBI's investigation were already known to the judiciary committee when it voted to recommend confirmation to the full Senate.[38]

Mindful that two of President Nixon's Supreme Court nominees, Clement F. Haynsworth and G. Harrold Carswell, had been rejected by the Senate after receiving a positive judiciary committee recommendation, a coalition of civil rights groups scheduled a public forum in opposition to confirmation at the Dirksen Senate Office Building. Organizers of the forum also circulated a Louis Harris survey, conducted in August, indicating that the public opposed confirmation 58 to 30 percent nationwide.[39] Women's groups circulated a nine-page memorandum Rehnquist had signed in 1970 opposing the Equal Rights Amendment on the ground that its adoption would "hasten the dissolution of the family," turning "'holy wedlock' into 'holy deadlock.'" Judith Lichtman, executive director of the Women's Legal Defense Fund, contended that the memorandum "reflect[ed] a deep-seated animus to women's basic rights as partners in families." But the nominee's partisans dismissed it as a routine summary of possible legal objections to the proposed amendment, rather than a reflection of Rehnquist's personal views.[40]

As the full Senate prepared to consider the nomination, opponents also raised again the ethical concerns connected with Justice Rehnquist's refusal to recuse himself from participation in *Laird v. Tatum* as well as other matters. Opponents made public a letter Yale law professor Geoffrey C. Hazard, Jr., a Republican and a principal drafter of the ABA's Code of Judicial Conduct, had written to the judiciary committee, in which Hazard had suggested that the nominee's participation in *Laird* may have been unethical and that he also may have violated "a duty of candor to the Senate" in testimony regarding his role in the case. One hundred ten other law professors also joined in a statement indicating that he may have acted unethically or testified untruthfully on a variety of issues, including his testimony that he was not aware of the restrictive covenant in the deed to his Vermont summerhouse.[41]

When the debate moved to the Senate floor on September 11, Rehnquist's opponents reiterated such charges, while Senator Hatch characterized their arguments as "much ado about very little" and Senator Dole reasoned "that the people voted for

Ronald Reagan by landslide proportions in 1980 and 1984," adding that "they expect the President to carry their mandate all the way to the Supreme Court."[42] When it was over after five days of debate, Rehnquist won confirmation by a comfortable sixty-five–thirty-three vote, with forty-nine Republicans and sixteen Democrats favoring, and thirty-one Democrats and two Republicans opposing, confirmation. Even so, the nominee received more negative votes than any previous justice confirmed by the Senate.[43] Asked whether he had any regrets about the intense controversy his nomination had provoked, Rehnquist responded that the debate was simply part of the constitutional process, but added, "I'm not going to address myself really to the past. That's over, that chapter is closed, and I'm looking forward to the future and to trying to be a good Chief Justice." For his part, President Reagan praised the Senate's action and privately, according to Senator Dole, termed his new chief justice's opponents a "lynch mob."[44]

The Scalia Appointment

Almost forgotten in all the furor over Chief Justice Rehnquist's confirmation was the president's choice to succeed the new chief as associate justice. Antonin Scalia, fifty-year-old New Jersey native and son of a Sicilian immigrant who became a literary scholar and professor of Romance languages at Brooklyn College, was to be the first Italian-American justice. Product of a strict Roman Catholic family and education and characterized by a classmate as an archconservative Catholic even in high school, Scalia was a history major at Georgetown University and joined a Cleveland-based corporate law firm following completion of a Harvard law degree in 1960. Considered by colleagues to be outspokenly and deeply conservative, even in a firm whose principal clients were such major business interests as TRW and Republic Steel, he remained with the firm until 1967, when he joined the law faculty at the University of Virginia. Beginning in 1972, he held a variety of positions in the Nixon administration, ultimately becoming head of the Justice Department's Office of Legal Counsel, the post Justice Rehnquist had earlier held, shortly before the president's resignation.

Scalia remained with the Justice Department until the end of the Ford administration in January 1977, often championing the executive against judicial and congressional authority, including the position, eventually rejected by the Supreme Court,[45] that Nixon, not the government, had title to tapes and documents relating to the Watergate controversy. During the Carter years, Scalia returned to academics and conservative intellectual pursuits, becoming a visiting professor at Georgetown University's law school, a scholar-in-residence at the American Enterprise Institute, a University of Chicago law professor, and coeditor of two scholarly journals promoting federal and state deregulation of the market. He also lectured and published widely and critically on judicial activism and controversial Supreme Court decisions, especially the Court's recognition of an abortion right in *Roe v. Wade*[46] and partial acceptance of affirmative action programs in *Regents of the University of California v. Bakke*,[47] which had in 1978 overturned the use of racial quotas in university admissions but also permitted use of racial, gender, and other nonmerit factors to promote a university's important interest in a diverse student body. When lawyers and law students disturbed by what they considered a liberal bias in the nation's law schools formed the Federalist Society in 1981 to combat that supposed trend, they selected Scalia as the organization's faculty adviser. One of the society's founders was Steven G. Calabresi, who would become a special assistant to Attorney General Edwin Meese III in the Reagan Justice Department. One of the society's financial benefactors was a foundation endowed by Richard Mellon Scaife,[48] archconservative Pittsburgh newspaper publisher and heir to the Mellon fortune, who would later finance a variety of schemes to discredit President and Mrs. Clinton; partially funded a deanship at Pepperdine University initially offered to Kenneth Starr, the Bush administration solicitor general and independent counsel investigating the Clintons; and reputedly paid Starr's chief prosecution witness against the president and first lady for his cooperation in the Whitewater proceedings. Scalia's record and connections hardly damaged his standing with the Reagan administration, and in 1982 he was awarded a seat on the Court of Appeals for the District of Columbia. His circuit decisions in homosexual rights, libel, and other issue areas further enhanced his conservative credentials, leading ultimately to his nomination to succeed William Rehnquist as associate justice.[49]

Reaction to Scalia's nomination in the press and scholarly commentary was mixed and not always predictable. Columnist and Nixon administration apologist William Safire scorned Scalia's narrow interpretation of the First Amendment, terming it "Agnewism with a scholarly face," in a reference to President Nixon's first, and disgraced, vice president, but found "curiously reassuring" the assertion of a Reagan administration insider that "[i]t's more important [to Scalia's selection] that he's an Italian Catholic with nine kids."[50] Former Columbia University law dean and Yale president-designate Benno C. Schmidt, Jr., inaccurately predicted that the nominee's "gregarious, winning personality" would win him "tremendous" influence on the Rehnquist Court,[51] while journalist Anthony Lewis attempted to console liberals left "in a state of numbed foreboding" by Scalia's selection with the impression that he was "not a judge who willfully distorts precedents and hides difficulties in order to reach a predetermined result."[52]

How judiciary committee Democrats might have treated Scalia's nomination had the hearing on his confirmation not followed the often intense Rehnquist proceedings is difficult to assess. Harvard law professor Laurence E. Tribe had editorialized that the conservative credentials of both Rehnquist and Scalia were well-known, that President Reagan "quite properly took them into account," and that "[t]he Senate should do likewise."[53] By the time the committee got to Scalia, however, the members, as one reporter put it, "seemed worn out and distracted."[54] While the nominee had developed a lengthy paper trial of publications and speeches detailing his judicial and constitutional views, moreover, he was spared the charges of ethical impropriety, racial bias, and lack of candor that had dominated the Rehnquist hearings.

In his opening statement at the Scalia hearings, Montana Republican Alan Simpson sarcastically recalled the unfairly harsh treatment he thought Democrats on the committee had given Justice Rehnquist. Beginning by welcoming Scalia "to the pit," Simpson launched into a tirade against "the 'great hunters' [who] have been out to tack the 'pelt' of Bill Rehnquist on the wall of the den." When he went on to complain of the charges raised by Rehnquist's detractors, declaring, "[s]tonewalling, wiretapping, 'cover-up.' Lord sake, there is not one of us here at this table that has not dabbled in all that mystery,"[55] some in the audience wondered aloud, according to one journalist, "where personal confession left off and poetic license began."[56] Courtly Alabama Democrat Howell Heflin, although praising Scalia as a "fine jurist" with a "brilliant mind," expressed concern that the nominee "had been elusive, evasive, and had perhaps overly hidden behind some concepts of separation of powers" in declining to respond to certain questions put to him about his judicial and constitutional philosophy.[57] But in the main, the committee gave Scalia an easy run. In his opening statement, Senator Heflin joked "that my great grandfather married a widow who was married first to an Italian American."[58] As part of a contingent of senators presenting the nominee to the committee, New York Republican Alfonse D'Amato told Scalia that "Mama D'Amato . . . sends her best."[59] And even Senator Metzenbaum, the nominee's most persistent interrogator, good-humoredly reproached Scalia for showing "bad judgment in whipping me on the [tennis] court," to which the quick-witted nominee, foreshadowing the reputation for biting rhetoric he was to establish on the supreme bench, promptly responded, "It was a case of my integrity overcoming my judgment."[60]

For his part, Judge Scalia adroitly avoided presenting the image of an inflexible conservative ideologue. At one point, for example, he even testified that he was a "little wishy-washy" on whether he accepted a "strict constructionist" or "evolutionary" interpretation of the Constitution's more general language.[61] While conceding that he should not be regarded "as someone who would be likely to use the phrase, living Constitution," he also asserted that he attempted to following the "original meaning" of constitutional provisions rather than the "original intent" of their framers and thus might accept some degree of evolutionary development in the meaning of general constitutional language. A "strict original intentist," he explained, would contend, for example, "that even such a clause as the cruel and unusual punishment clause would have to mean precisely the same thing today that it meant in 1789 . . . so that if lashing was fine then, lashing would be fine now. I am not sure I agree with that. I think that there are some provisions of the Constitution that may [have] a certain amount of evolutionary content within them." At the same time, he thought the Constitution was "obviously not meant to be evolvable so easily that in effect a court of nine judges can treat it as though it is a bring-along-with-me statute and fill it up with whatever content the current times seem to acquire."[62]

At times Scalia had difficulty defending what skeptical senators considered his extreme earlier statements and writings. Senator Metzenbaum quoted the nominee's assertion that "[i]t would seem to be a contradiction in terms to suggest that a State practice engaged in and widely regarded as legitimate from the early days of the Republic down to the present time, is unconstitutional. I do not care how analytically consistent with analogous precedents such a holding might be, nor how socially desirable in a judge's view. If it contradicts long and continuing understanding of the society, as many of the Supreme Court's recent Constitutional decisions referred to earlier, in fact, do, it is quite simply wrong."[63] Metzenbaum found such language comparable to contending that "the Constitution means what the majority says it means" and wondered how it could be squared with the Court's decisions outlawing segregated schools despite their long tradition. Scalia's response was hardly convincing. Ignoring the Fourteenth Amendment's general language and the fundamental question whether segregation constituted discrimination, he replied that racial discrimination would be unconstitutional, even if practiced in all the states, because it was "facially contrary to the [Fourteenth Amendment's] language." Scalia added that he did "not know how a judge intuits that a particular practice is contrary to our most fundamental beliefs, to the most fundamental beliefs of our society, when it is one that was in existence when the Constitutional provision in question was adopted and is still in existence. . . . I worry about my deciding that [such an unenumerated right] exists. I worry that I am not reflecting the most fundamental, deeply felt beliefs of our society, which is what a constitution means, but rather, I am reflecting the most deeply felt beliefs of Scalia, which is not what I want to impose on the society."[64]

Nor did he always seek to avoid confrontation with committee members. Asked about his membership from 1976 to late 1985 in the Cosmos Club, which excluded women from membership, he stated that he "certainly would not belong to a club that practiced racial discrimination," but added, "I do not consider [a single-sex organization] an invidious discrimination. I think there are a lot of other people who likewise do not consider it invidious discrimination."[65] Asked about his assertion in a law review article that Justice Powell's mixed judgment on affirmative action in the *Bakke* case was "thoroughly unconvincing as an honest, hard-minded, reasoned analysis of an important provision of the Constitution,"[66] he insisted that he harbored "absolutely no racial prejudices," but "disagreed with affirmative action . . . as the way to eliminate" racial discrimination.[67]

Whatever misgivings his testimony may have created, however, Scalia's confirmation was never in doubt. Committee members who had divided thirteen-five in favor of Justice Rehnquist voted unanimously to approve Scalia's nomination. Senate floor debate on Rehnquist's confirmation had taken five days, Scalia's barely five minutes. Rehnquist received more negative votes than any previously confirmed justice, while Scalia won unanimous floor approval.

The First Woman Justice

Rehnquist and Scalia were not, of course, President Reagan's first selections to the supreme bench. With his nomination of Sandra Day O'Connor during his first year in the White House, Reagan became the first president to name a woman to the Court. Product of a prosperous southeastern Arizona ranching family whose holdings comprised 155,000 acres at the time of her nomination, Sandra Day completed an undergraduate degree in economics at Stanford University, then attended its law school, from which she and Justice Rehnquist graduated third and first, respectively, in the class of 1952. As a woman, however, she had no luck obtaining the sort of enviable position usually awarded even mediocre graduates of elite law schools. Although she interviewed with several firms in Los Angeles and San Francisco, she received only one offer, to be a legal secretary in the Los Angeles firm of William French Smith, Reagan's attorney general at the time of her appointment to the Court. Following work from 1952 to 1953 as a county deputy attorney in San Mateo, California, and a three-year stint as an attorney with the Army's quartermaster corps while her husband, John O'Connor, served with the judge advocate general's office in Frankfort, West Germany, the couple settled in suburban Phoenix, where she established a small practice; held several administrative posts, including four years as assistant state attorney general; became active in Republican Party affairs; was appointed in 1969 to fill an unexpired term in the Arizona senate; and in 1972 won election to the same seat, winning handily over her Democratic opponent, also a woman. The same year she was elected senate majority leader. In 1974, however, she moved to the judicial branch of Arizona government, winning a hard-fought election to a superior court judgeship. Then, in 1979, newly elected Democratic governor Bruce Babbitt made O'Connor his first appointee to the state court of appeals.

During five years in the senate, O'Connor developed a mainstream Republican, moderate to conservative record on most issues. But four votes she cast as a state legislator conflicted with the general pattern of her legislative voting. In 1970, she voted in the Arizona senate's judiciary committee to send to the floor a bill repealing the state's unusually restrictive abortion laws. Three years later, she co-signed a bill to make contraceptive information more widely available, and in 1974, she opposed a resolution urging Congress to propose an anti-abortion amendment to the Constitution and also voted against a University of Arizona stadium construction bill that limited the availability of abortions, albeit later defending that vote as part of her policy, as majority leader, of discouraging nongermane riders to legislation. On the other hand, she also supported restrictions on state abortion funding and legislation recognizing the right of hospital employees not to assist in performing abortions. Her judicial record was equally mixed, combining comparatively strict sentencing practices with concern about prison conditions.

Not surprisingly given her legislative record in Arizona, anti-abortion leaders opposed O'Connor's Supreme Court nomination. During confirmation proceedings from September 9 to 11, 1981, Dr. John C. Willke, president of the National Right to Life Committee, compared *Roe v. Wade* with the "civil rights outrage" the *Dred Scott* decision[68] had inflicted on the nation and contended that any person refusing to recognize the fundamental "right to life of the unborn child . . . should be disqualified from sitting on the Federal court."[69] Dr. Carolyn F. Gerster, a vice president of the organization, who had known the nominee since 1972, suggested, moreover, that O'Connor was guilty of "misrepresentation, evasion, and distortion of fact" in her testimony to the committee regarding abortion rights; and Dr. Willke asserted that if the nominee did "not repudiate *Roe v. Wade*, . . . that fact alone . . . should deny her the nomination."[70] When Senator Metzenbaum questioned the wisdom of confirming or defeating a candidate "based upon any one single issue," calling such an attitude an affront to democratic principles, the witnesses stood their ground, with Willke asserting that "the killing of 1.5 million unborn babies a year is such an intolerable evil that it is that once-in-a-century issue . . . [that] does in our minds disqualify a person from holding public office."[71]

The religious right joined forces with pro-life groups in opposing confirmation. Evangelist Jerry Falwell of the Moral Majority urged "good Christians," for example, to express concern over the president's choice. But the nominee assured the judiciary committee that she was personally "opposed to [abortion] as a matter of birth control or otherwise."[72] Women's rights groups and prominent liberals, moreover, obviously endorsed confirmation of the first woman to the Court, and one of the nominee's staunchest supporters, Senator Goldwater, characteristically recommended that "[e]very good Christian ought to kick Falwell right in the ass." In mid-September, every member of the judiciary committee but one voted to approve the nomination, while conservative Alabamian Jeremiah Denton, a supporter of mandatory chastity-belt legislation, voted present. Six days later, the full Senate endorsed the committee's recommendation without a dissenting vote.[73]

The Powell Seat

The O'Connor and Scalia nominations had sailed through the Senate, and Rehnquist had also survived the confirmation process despite serious questions regarding his political views and candor. President Reagan's fourth selection to the high Court was to be, of course, a different matter. Disregarding the recommendations of Barry Goldwater and other conservatives, President Ford had passed over former Yale law professor and Nixon solicitor general Robert H. Bork for Judge John Paul Stevens, a Nixon appointee to the Court of Appeals for the Seventh Circuit. When President Reagan appointed Scalia rather than Bork, columnist James Reston expressed surprise, noting that while Scalia was "articulate and personable," Bork had developed a "more brilliant career."[74] The 1987 retirement of Justice Powell, one of the Court's most influential members, gave President Reagan what was to be his last chance to fill a vacancy on the high bench, with the nod going this time to Bork, whom Reagan in 1982 had chosen for a seat on the Court of Appeals for the District of Columbia. But an exceptionally well-organized opposition, fueled in part by bitter memories of Bork as the Nixon official who had fired Watergate special prosecutor Archibald Cox, combined with the nominee's professorial, condescending tone and a jurisprudence many senators found unacceptably rigid, led to Bork's October 23, 1987, defeat in the Senate by a fifty-eight–forty-two vote.[75]

Reagan's next nominee, former Harvard law professor Douglas H. Ginsburg, who had been appointed to the D.C. court of appeals the previous year, also went down in flames, or at least smoke. Ginsburg was considered perhaps even more conservative than Bork. But in their haste to get the Bork debacle behind them, administration officials had sent the Ginsburg nomination to the Senate before thorough background checks had been completed. Soon, allegations surfaced in the press of a financial conflict of interest, reports of misrepresentations about the extent of the nominee's courtroom experience, and, most damaging of all for a conservative Republican nominee, revelations of marijuana use as a member of the Harvard law faculty. Ginsburg's nomination was hastily withdrawn.

In November, President Reagan made his third, and this time successful, attempt to fill the Powell seat, nominating federal appeals court judge Anthony M. Kennedy to the post. A fifty-one-year-old Sacramento native with an undergraduate degree from Stanford and LL.B. from Harvard, Kennedy had practiced with a San Francisco firm from 1961 to 1963, then took over his deceased father's Sacramento practice and, that same year, began a twenty-three-year stint as a part-time professor at the University of the Pacific's McGeorge School of Law. In the early 1970s, then Governor Reagan and his executive secretary, Edwin Meese, secured the assistance of Kennedy, a tax law specialist, in drafting a precursor to California's Proposition 14, the controversial tax-cutting measure that the state's voters adopted in 1978. On Reagan's recommendation, President Ford appointed Kennedy to a seat on the Court of Appeals for the Ninth Circuit in 1975.

Although sufficiently conservative to have attracted the likes of Edwin Meese, Kennedy was no ideologue of the Bork mold. Introducing the nominee to members of the Senate judiciary committee at the beginning of three days of hearings in mid-December, California senator Pete Wilson described Kennedy's constitutional philosophy as "reasonable balance,"[76] and the nominee's testimony before the committee reflected that characterization, as well as the sort of moderately conservative record Kennedy was to develop on the Court. Unlike Judge Bork, whose professed loyalty to original intent as the sole legitimate source of constitutional meaning helped to doom his chances for confirmation, Kennedy refused to commit himself to a single, over-arching theory of interpretation. Yet he also praised Hugo Black, the Court's most systematic practitioner of a jurisprudence based on text and historical intent, as "simply a magnificent justice."[77] Then, when asked to comment on the contours of the potentially limitless Ninth Amendment, for which Black favored a narrow construction,[78] Kennedy seemed unconcerned that "the Court [was] treating it as something of a reserve clause, to be held in the event that the phrase 'liberty' [in the due process guarantees] and other spacious phrases in the Constitution appear to be inadequate for the Court's decision."[79]

Such jurisprudential flexibility had a positive effect on Kennedy's chances for confirmation. In his opening statement at the hearings, for example, Senator Metzenbaum observed that he did "not necessarily agree" with all of the nominee's court of appeals decisions and "would have been pleased" had he resigned more speedily from all-male private clubs to which he had belonged. In an obvious reference to Judge Bork, the Ohio senator also noted that the "Senate and the American people rejected a nominee who believed individual freedoms can be found only in the fine print of the written Constitution," instead "reaffirm[ing] the value of broad constitutional protections for individual liberties and strong guarantees of equal protection." But Metzenbaum also assured committee members that if the hearing "demonstrates that Judge Kennedy does support these fundamental values—and I fully expect that it will—these months of struggle will pay rich dividends far into the future of our country."[80]

Not that the Kennedy hearings were entirely uneventful. At one point early in the proceedings, committee chairman Joseph Biden asked Kennedy about a recent newspaper column by conservative columnist Cal Thomas. Republican North Carolina senator Jesse A. Helms, an ultraconservative and staunch defender of the interests of prenatal, if not postnatal, children, had told Thomas, according to the column, that he and Judge Kennedy had met privately in the White House on November 12. "I think you know where I stand on abortion," Helms had reportedly remarked to Kennedy.

"Indeed I do," a smiling Kennedy had replied, "and I admire it. I am a practicing Catholic." Thomas detected in Senator Helms "a certain collegiality with what he believes to be Judge Kennedy's views" and a conviction that the nominee would oppose what Helms called "this 'privacy garbage'—recent Supreme Court decisions involving not only abortion but civil rights, protections for homosexuals."[81]

In his response to Biden's query, Kennedy, a devout Roman Catholic, conceded that he had a "wide-ranging" conversation with Senator Helms. But he disputed the accuracy of the remark Thomas, and presumably Helms, had attributed to him and insisted not only that he had no "such views with reference to privacy, or abortion, or the other subjects there mentioned," but also that he "was not attempting, and would not attempt to try to signal, by inference, or by indirection, my views on those subjects." In his judgment, Kennedy declared, "it would be highly improper for a judge to allow his, or her, own personal or religious views to enter into a decision respecting a constitutional matter. There are many books that I will not read, that I do not let, or these days do not recommend, my children read. That does not prohibit me from enforcing the first amendment because those books are protected by the first amendment."[82]

Spokespersons for various liberal organizations, including the National Organization for Women (NOW) and the Americans for Democratic Action (ADA), also testified in opposition to Kennedy's confirmation. Opponents particularly called the committee's attention to his position in a number of controversial discrimination cases, including one upholding a Navy regulation terminating homosexuals,[83] another in which he dissented from an *en banc* decision declaring facially unconstitutional an airline's weight limit for flight hostesses that did not apply to male employees, even directors of passenger services,[84] and a case terminating a school desegregation order.[85] In his opening statement for the ADA, Joseph Rauh conceded that Kennedy, "yes and even Judge Bork, might have been acceptable risks on the Court with a majority clearly devoted to the Bill of Rights." But citing the close divisions on the current Court in abortion and other controversial civil liberties cases, Rauh asserted that "we cannot afford to play Russian Roulette with our own dedication to the Bill of Rights" and warned that "[a] vote for the confirmation of Judge Kennedy is a vote to take risks with the very fabric of our society."[86]

Some committee Republicans, on the other hand, used the Kennedy hearings to criticize the treatment accorded Judge Bork. When Harold Tyler, chairman of the American Bar Association (ABA) committee on federal judiciary, reported that his committee had given Judge Kennedy its highest evaluation, Senator Orrin Hatch attacked Bork's treatment by the ABA committee, which had unanimously accorded Bork its highest rating when he was selected for the court of appeals, but was divided on its evaluation of his fitness for the Supreme Court, with ten committee members voting "well qualified," one "not opposed," and four "not qualified." After grilling Judge Tyler at length with respect to the committee's procedures for evaluating nominees and accusing four ABA committee members of "very partisan, political reasons" for their opposition to Bork's confirmation, Hatch declared, "I will tell you this. If we see another repeat of what happened to Judge Bork, this Senator is going to do everything in his power to make sure that there will be explanations given in full, fair, and open hearings. Fair to you, fair to the nominee." Judge Tyler reminded Hatch that in the past the ABA committee's unanimous evaluations had drawn the wrath of senators, then took issue with Hatch's call for committee members to individually explain and defend their ratings of nominees. "I do not see what good it would do—and indeed, I can see a lot of harm that would be done—realizing that we are not a public group, that we suddenly become 15 separate lawyers who, if we should vote one way as opposed to another, would have to come in here and individually explain ourselves. I think that would make no sense at all, and I do not see how anybody would want to be a member of this committee [under those circumstances]. I certainly would not."[87]

Whatever the weight of opposition to Bork, Kennedy's confirmation was secure. Even Harvard professor Laurence Tribe, one of Bork's severest critics, agreed that Kennedy was a "conservative," but found "much worth conserving in our constitutional tradition" and predicted that the nominee "would serve with distinction, and would work to preserve and protect basic constitutional values."[88] In fact, his "most salable quality," as judicial scholar Henry Abraham has noted, "was a negative one: he wasn't Bork." Comparing Kennedy to the "open-minded, fair, and independent" Justice Powell, a unanimous judiciary committee approved his nomination, and on February 18, 1988, ninety-seven senators present concurred.[89]

The Stealth Candidate

Anthony Kennedy was President Reagan's final appointee to the Court. But eighteen months into his tenure as Reagan's successor, President George Bush received his first opportunity to fill a vacancy on the high bench with the retirement on July 20, 1990, of William J. Brennan. A Democrat with nearly thirty-four years on the Court—seventh longest tenure of any justice—Brennan was considered the principal architect of the massive body of civil liberties law about which Republican presidents from Nixon to Bush had been complaining. In fact, Chief Justice Earl Warren's tenure (1953-69), the most liberal-activist period in the Court's history, was increasingly referred to as the Brennan rather than the Warren era.

President Bush was not about to place another William Brennan on the Court. But he was equally determined not to select a controversial nominee likely to meet Bork's fate. On the recommendation of his chief of staff, former New Hampshire governor John Sununu, the president selected a nominee who had made President Reagan's short list when Bork was chosen, but was so little known outside his home state that the press quickly dubbed him the "stealth" candidate. A Massachusetts native, David Hackett Souter was raised in Weare, New Hampshire, and still lived in the same house his family occupied in his youth. A Harvard undergraduate and law school product, as well as a Rhodes Scholar at Oxford, Souter possessed impeccable educational credentials; his career to date, while hardly distinguished, had been respectable and uneventful. Following law practice in Concord, he held several posts in New Hampshire's justice department, culminating in a two-year stint (1976–78) as the state's attorney general. In 1978, he was named to a superior court seat; five years later, Governor Sununu appointed him to the New Hampshire supreme court. And just three months before his nomination to the U.S. Supreme Court, President Bush had chosen him for a seat on the Court of Appeals for the First Circuit.

Whatever the limitations of his professional record, Souter was hardly controversial. Unlike Bork, he had left no paper trail of potentially damaging pronouncements, his sole publication a bland tribute to a state jurist. Initially, in fact, Souter seemed more a concern to the far-right core of President Bush's constituency than to liberals, especially his lifestyle and likely position on abortion and other volatile issues. One conservative warned Sununu, for example, that a fifty-one-year-old bachelor who rarely dated and, until recently, lived with his mother must be a homosexual! White House staffers assured conservatives that such gossip was nonsense and apparently convinced them that Souter would also keep the conservative faith on abortion and other controversial matters. Pat McGuigan of the Coalition for America, a conservative lobbying group headed by Paul Weyrich, its national chairman, met with Sununu to express the right's concerns about Souter. Then, McGuigan distributed a confidential memorandum, later leaked to the press, in which he indicated that although "[t]here were no words exchanged that would constitute any specific assurances on any specific issue, . . . the general thrust of the discussion definitely made me feel better."[90] Naturally, Souter's nomination also distressed liberals, who wondered how a person with the nominee's lifestyle could relate to the problems of modern families and who feared his stance in abortion and other controversial cases, despite President Bush's public assurances that he had subjected Souter to no abortion "litmus test" and had not even asked the nominee his position on the issue.[91]

Early in the five days of judiciary committee hearings devoted to the nomination, Senator Metzenbaum confronted Souter with the possible implications of Pat McGuigan's meeting with John Sununu. "At that meeting," Metzenbaum noted, quoting from the leaked McGuigan memorandum, "it was stated that Sununu asked, how are you doing? I [McGuigan] replied, well, John, you guys could have hit a home run if you had picked Edith Jones, a Texas judge. Instead, you hit a blooper single which has barely cleared the mitt of the first baseman who is backpedaling furiously and almost caught the ball. Sununu smiled and replied, Pat, you are wrong. This is a home run and the ball is still ascending; in fact, it is just about to leave Earth orbit." The memorandum, added Metzenbaum, "specifically provided that there were to be absolutely no leaks allowed"; shortly after it was written, "the Coalition for America announced they were fully supporting your nomination." The senator wanted the nominee to explain "what . . . John Sununu know[s] about you that we do not know."[92]

But Souter had done a thorough job preparing for the confirmation proceedings—staying out of the public eye, reviewing videotapes of recent hearings, and becoming especially familiar with the sorts of questions and responses that had contributed to Judge Bork's defeat. Skillfully deflecting Metzenbaum's thrust, Souter assured the committee that he and Sununu had not "discuss[ed] any substantive issue" referred to in the McGuigan memorandum. "The only discussion that I had with anyone at the White House in connection with this nomination or, for that matter the circuit nomination," he stated, "was my conversation with the President which I think lasted about a half an hour on the afternoon that he announced his intent to nominate me. He asked for no assurance on any subject."[93] Other elements of his appearance before the committee were equally effective. Unlike Bork, who had conceded his opposition to *Roe v. Wade,* Souter repeatedly refused to comment on the abortion issue, citing the impropriety of expressing views on matters likely to come before the Court. But his reluctance was selective, and his comments on other legal issues generally pleased his most likely committee critics. While Bork had outraged Senate liberals by scorning as judicial lawmaking the Court's recognition of an unenumerated right of marital privacy in the landmark *Griswold* case,[94] Souter avoided that trap. Like his jurisprudential role model, the second Justice John Marshall Harlan, who frequently registered conservative dissents from Warren Court decisions, but joined the *Griswold* decision and embraced a flexible, potentially open-ended conception of constitutional rights, Souter agreed that the Constitution includes protection for marital privacy and other unenumerated rights. In fact, he testified that his "argument" with the incorporation process, through which the modern Court had applied most Bill of Rights safeguards to the states through judicial construction of the Fourteenth Amendment,[95] was with Justice Black's contention in his *Griswold* dissent that incorporation was largely "meant to exhaust the meaning of enforceable liberty,"[96] thereby limiting the ultimate scope of constitutional safeguards for individual liberty. He also described the Warren Court's controversial 1966 decision in *Miranda v. Arizona,*[97] which established strict standards for police interrogation of suspects and became the rallying cry for law-and-order conservatives, as a "pragmatic" safeguard against coerced confesssions. He had kind words for other expansive civil liberties rulings as well. He even applauded Justice Brennan, archtypical practitioner of the "judicial activism" Reagan-Bush conservatives abhorred, as "one of the most fearlessly principled guardians of the American Constitution that it has ever had and ever will have."[98]

The nominee proved reasonably effective, too, in deflecting liberal concerns about his record. As New Hampshire's attorney general in 1976, Souter had filed a brief in the U.S. Supreme Court defending, unsuccessfully, the state's failure to comply with a federal law obliging employers to maintain statistics on the racial composition of their workforce. Earlier, as assistant attorney general, he had signed a brief supporting literacy tests for voters—a requirement Congress eventually banned nationwide. Senator Edward M. Kennedy cited such instances as evidence of Souter's insensitivity to "the weakest and most powerless in our society."[99] But Souter reminded Kennedy that the Supreme Court itself had upheld the constitutionality of fairly administered literacy tests. He questioned, moreover, the power of Congress "to require the assembly of racial data by a governmental entity with respect to whom there was absolutely no historical indication of any discrimination."[100]

When Senator Kennedy challenged Souter's commitment to gender equality, citing the nominee's argument in a 1978 case that the Supreme Court should "reexamine and perhaps eliminate" the heightened scrutiny to which it had begun to subject sexually discriminatory laws, Souter questioned the "looseness" of the Court's standard. In the 1970s, the Court had ultimately declined to characterize gender as a constitutional "suspect," vulnerable to the strict, "compelling interest" standard of review that invariably doomed racial and related forms of discrimination. But the justices had also refused to relegate gender classifications to the extremely lenient, "rational basis" equal protection scrutiny under which economic and certain other forms of discrimination routinely survived challenge. Instead, the Court opted to subject gender and related "quasi-suspect" classifications to varying degrees of intermediate scrutiny under which the discrimination at issue had to be closely related to a legitimate and substantial governmental interest.[101] "What is unfortunate about that standard of review," Souter told Kennedy, "is that it leaves an enormous amount of leeway to the discretion of the court. . . . [T]hat has nothing to do with the question of whether sex discrimination should receive heightened scrutiny. I think that to compare sex discriminations with common economic determinations seems to me totally inappropriate. The question is, what is a workable and dependable middle-standard for scrutiny." "In your brief," Kennedy observed, "you talk about even eliminating that test." "Well," shot back Souter, "I also talked about making the test more clear and eliminating this kind of protean quantity to it."[102]

Senator Kennedy was unimpressed with Souter's performance. When the nominee defended some of his actions in the state attorney general's office as those of a lawyer for New Hampshire's governor, Kennedy reminded Souter of "the fact that you are sworn to an oath of office [to uphold] the Constitution."[103] But the Massachusetts senator stood alone on the committee in opposing Souter's confirmation. And on October 2, 1990, the full Senate voted ninety-nine to confirm, enabling Souter to take his seat on the high bench during the second week of the Court's 1990-91 term.

The Best-Qualified Man

By choosing Souter, an obscure, stealth candidate with no paper trail, as his first nominee to the Supreme Court, George Bush had avoided the controversy aroused by the Bork nomination. He had good reason to assume that his second choice would not be "Borked." When Thurgood Marshall—pioneering figure of the modern civil rights movement and the first black justice—retired in 1991, President Bush named another African American, Clarence Thomas, to the Marshall seat. "An unwritten plank in the [current Republican] party's strategy," as Andrew Hacker has observed, "is that it can win the offices it wants without black votes. More than that, by sending a message that it neither wants nor needs ballots cast by blacks, it feels it can attract even more votes from a larger pool of white Americans who want a party willing to represent their racial identity."[104] The ever-cautious Bush was hardly so bold as to refuse to replace Thurgood Marshall with another African American justice. But in Thomas, he found one of the exceedingly rare black Republicans whose views and record were bound to please the conservative core of the Reagan-Bush constituency.

Clarence Thomas's triumph over his humble roots would inspire liberals and conservatives alike. Thomas was born poor in tiny Pin Point, Georgia, in 1948 of a father who deserted the family when Clarence was still a toddler and a mother who picked crab for five cents a pound to support the future justice, his brother, and his sister. Through the efforts of his stern, hardworking grandfather, with whom he and his brother went to live when he was seven, Clarence secured an education at St. Benedict's, a Roman Catholic school whose nuns had a tremendous impact on his life. To the bitter disappointment of his grandfather, who wanted his grandson to become a priest, Thomas dropped out of a Missouri seminary, disillusioned at the bigotry of white seminarians. But he soon received an undergraduate degree from Holy Cross College, then entered Yale Law School, from which he graduated in 1974. Following stints as an assistant to Missouri attorney general and future senator John Danforth, as attorney for a chemical company, and as Senator Danforth's legislative assistant, Thomas secured positions in the Reagan administration as assistant secretary of education and later as chairman of the Equal Employment Opportunity Commission (EEOC). In March of 1990, President Bush had named him to a seat on the Court of Appeals for the District of Columbia.[105]

As another black, retired chief judge A. Leon Higginbotham, Jr., of the U.S. Court of Appeals for the Third Circuit, would later detail in a devastating published letter to the nominee, Thomas had been an obvious beneficiary of the civil rights movement and affirmative action programs. Moreover, his connection with Yale, which he had entered under such a program, had led to his long association with Senator Danforth, his primary sponsor.[106] Yet as a member of the Reagan and Bush administrations, Thomas had been a vehement critic of the movement, its leaders, and the legislation it had spawned. He derided those civil rights activists who would, in his words, "bitch, bitch, bitch" about the administration he served.[107] When Justice Marshall asserted that black Americans had little reason to celebrate the Constitution's adoption, Thomas dismissed the justice's concerns as "an exasperating and incomprehensible . . . assault on the Bicentennial, the Founding, and the Constitution itself."[108] Affirmative action programs, he charged, "create a narcotic of dependency [among minorities and women], not an ethic of responsibility and independence. They are at best an irrelevance, covering up some real problems, and inevitably a stigma."[109] In his judgment, social welfare measures yielded the same result. His sister had been gainfully employed most of her life, often at more than one job. At one point, however, she quit work to care for an elderly aunt, obliging her to seek public assistance. Her lapse did not escape her brother's contempt, although Thomas's detractors wondered why he had not also attempted to help. "She gets mad when the mailman is late with her welfare check," he informed a conservative black audience in 1980. "That's how dependent she is."[110]

His official actions reflected such attitudes. As EEOC chairman, he had eliminated the use of minority hiring goals and employer timetables as devices for correcting racial and ethnic disparities in the workplace. He also largely abandoned class action lawsuits that had relied on statistical evidence to prove widespread discrimination by major corporations, preferring instead to have his agency intervene merely on behalf of individuals who could prove that they personally had been the victims of discrimination. In 1990, moreover, he acknowledged that over nine hundred age discrimination cases had been allowed to lapse under a law requiring EEOC investigation of such complaints within two years of their filing. Critics charged that, in fact, nine thousand such cases had been permitted to lapse, by accident or design.[111]

Thomas's EEOC record and statements obviously offended liberals, and his lifestyle likely disturbed them too. Following his divorce from his first wife, he had married a conservative white woman. They attended a suburban Virginia Episcopal church that reportedly mixed the politics of the religious right with speaking in unknown tongues and other elements of charismatic religious ritual.[112]

Thomas's views on "natural law" offended liberals as much as his EEOC tenure. In a 1987 speech to the conservative Heritage Foundation, he had praised an article in which businessman Lewis Lehrman urged a construction of the Constitution based on appeals to divine or natural-rights principles, condemned *Roe v. Wade* as legitimizing a continuing "holocaust" fundamentally at odds with natural law, and equated the pro-life movement with the campaign to abolish slavery.[113] Thomas termed Lehrman's essay "a splendid example of applying natural law."[114] He had also served on a White House task force that called for *Roe*'s dismantling, and he termed the right of marital privacy recognized in *Griswold* a judicial "invention."[115]

Nor were Thomas's lifestyle and views a concern only for liberals. The nominee had begun sprinkling references to natural law in his public pronouncements only after he hired two former students of Harry Jaffa, a Claremont College political theorist who had asserted that the *Griswold* decision could be defended on the basis of natural-law theory and whose views on the relationship of natural law to constitutional meaning closely resembled those reflected in Thomas's speeches and writings.[116] His pronouncements thus could have embodied more of the views of Professor Jaffa and his students than Thomas's own thoughts. Thomas's complete rejection, as a Supreme Court justice, of substantive due process, perhaps the principal vehicle for grafting natural-law principles onto the Constitution, makes his commitment to a natural-law approach to constitutional construction equally doubtful.[117] At the time of his appointment, however, his suggestion that judges should construe the Constitution in the light of higher law may have alarmed conservatives who agreed with Robert Bork that the Constitution's meaning should turn largely on the framers' intentions rather than judicial conceptions of justice or social utility. The Supreme Court of the late nineteenth and early twentieth centuries had used such rhetoric to protect business interests from government regulations in a line of laissez-faire decisions modern conservatives might applaud. But that same sort of thinking arguably underlay the modern Court's recognition of abortion and other privacy rights—rulings conservatives regularly condemn.[118]

When Senate confirmation proceedings began on September 10, judiciary committee Democrats were primed for a thorough inquiry into Thomas's record and views. Flanked by Senator Danforth and White House handlers, however, the nominee developed a powerful portrait of his humble origins and the indignities he and his family had endured because of their race. "I watched as my grandfather was called 'boy,'" he told committee members in his opening statement. "I watched as my grandmother suffered the indignity of being denied the use of a bathroom. But through it all they remained fair, decent, good people. Fair in spite of the terrible contradictions in our country."[119]

Thomas also moved quickly to distance himself from elements of his more recent past. In a move that prompted one frustrated journalist to label him a "liar or boob,"[120] he not only would venture no opinion on the constitutionality of abortion, but even declared that he had never taken a position on that most controversial of modern civil liberties issues. When an incredulous Patrick Leahy of Vermont probed him about whether he had formed an opinion on *Roe v. Wade* while at Yale Law School, for example, Thomas replied, "I was a married student and I worked, I did not spend a lot of time around the law school doing what the other students enjoyed so much, and that is debating all the current cases and all of the slip opinions. My schedule was such that I went to classes and generally went to work and went home."[121] Leahy assured Thomas that he, too, had worked his way through law school, "but also found, at least between classes, that we did discuss some of the law, and I am sure you are not suggesting that there wasn't any discussion at any time of *Roe v. Wade*?" "I cannot remember personally engaging in those discussions," Thomas responded. Had the nominee *ever* stated his views about *Roe*? "I can't recall saying one way or the other, Senator," replied Thomas.[122]

The nominee assured committee members, however, that he recognized a constitutional guarantee to marital privacy. His praise of Lewis Lehrman, he claimed, was merely a stratagem to reach conservatives whom, he said, he "had spent almost a decade of my life battling." To the extent that Lehrman "uses natural law to make a constitutional adjudication, in that sense, or to provide a moral code of some sort," declared Thomas, "I disagree with it."[123] He even acknowledged his personal debt to the man he hoped to replace on the Court and to the civil rights movement Justice Marshall had helped to lead.

Numerous liberal and civil rights groups, including the Leadership Conference on Civil Rights, the NAACP, NOW, and the AFL-CIO, had announced their opposition to Thomas's confirmation. Ralph G. Neas, the Leadership Conference's executive director, accused Thomas of "sprinting," rather than merely "running," from his record and ridiculed his Senate testimony as "the earliest confirmation conversion we've witnessed."[124] The ABA's judiciary committee assigned Thomas the lowest rating of any rating given a confirmed justice, with no member rating him well-qualified, twelve considering him qualified, two terming him not qualified, and one ABA committee member not voting. The nominee's responses to the general questions of senators regarding landmark Supreme Court decisions revealed, moreover, a limited knowledge of constitutional law—adding fuel to complaints that Thomas, the antiquota choice of an antiquota president, was himself a quota choice unfit for a seat on the nation's highest tribunal.

Even so, Thomas's race made a "no" vote extremely difficult, especially for Senate Democrats facing reelection. Yet when the judiciary committee voted on September 27, members split 7-7, with moderate Arizona Democrat Dennis DeConcini, who would later switch to the Republican Party, joining the six committee Republicans in support of nomination. Four days before a scheduled October 8 floor vote on the nomination, Senator Danforth was predicting sixty affirmative votes and a clear confirmation.

Thomas would be confirmed, of course, but not by the margin Senator Danforth had predicted. In its Sunday, October 6, issue, *Newsday* published charges raised against the nominee by Anita Hill, a black conservative Republican, Yale law graduate, and law professor at the University of Oklahoma. The same day, Professor Hill also aired her allegations in an interview with Nina Totenberg of National Public Radio. During her years as Thomas's counsel at the Department of Education and EEOC,

Hill claimed, he had repeatedly subjected her to graphic, grossly offensive sexual remarks and detailed descriptions of scenes from pornographic movies.

The conduct alleged, if true, violated EEOC guidelines for compliance with federal laws forbidding sexual harassment in the workplace. Even so, President Bush claimed he was "not the least" concerned about Professor Hill's charges and assured the public that Thomas still had his "full confidence."[125] Senator Danforth and other congressional supporters of Thomas's confirmation condemned the allegations as a desperate, last-minute smear of the nominee. Judiciary committee members, who were aware of Hill's assertions before their vote on Thomas, had chosen not to make them public when Hill initially declined to permit her name to be associated with the allegations. And for a time after she went public with the charges, the Senate leadership seemed inclined to go forward with a floor vote on the nomination. But a firestorm of public outrage by leaders of women's groups and allied organizations quickly derailed their plans. Floor action was delayed a week so that the judiciary committee could hold additional hearings.

Nothing in Professor Hill's background suggested any basis for questioning her credibility. Other women came forward with claims that Thomas had also harassed them, and witnesses testified that Hill had shared with them her distress at Thomas's behavior at the time it was allegedly occurring.

But the White House, Thomas, and judiciary committee Republicans pursued a brilliant strategy of making the nominee the victim and putting Professor Hill, the committee, the confirmation process, and the entire Congress on the defensive. Playing the race card and conveniently ignoring the race of his accuser, an indignant, emotional Thomas scorned Hill's charges as a "travesty" and the hearings as a "high-tech lynching for uppity-blacks who in any way deign to think for themselves, to do for themselves, to have different ideas," with the message "that, unless you kow-tow to an old order, this is what will happen to you, you will be lynched, destroyed, caricatured by a committee of the U.S. Senate, rather than hung from a tree."[126] In response to a query from Senator Leahy early in his testimony, moreover, Thomas shrewdly insisted that he would "not get into any discussions that I might have [had] about my personal life or my sex life with any person outside of the workplace."[127]

For their part, committee Republicans sought to discredit Hill. In a generally flattering profile of Thomas, the most conservative of the nation's mainstream weekly news magazines had reported in its September 16 issue, well before Hill's charges surfaced, that while at Yale the nominee could "sometimes [be heard] regaling other early risers with hilarious descriptions of the X-rated movies he liked to watch for relaxation."[128] Several books on the nomination have also drawn on interviews with Thomas's friends and the proprietor of a Washington, D.C., video rental store, from which he rented hundreds of pornographic and other videotapes, in documenting Thomas's enthusiasm for pornography and detailed descriptions of their contents, including some of the most graphically offensive titles in the genre.[129] But an apparently incredulous Senator Orrin Hatch ridiculed Professor Hill's claim that such an upstanding citizen as Judge Thomas could have described such distasteful films to her, in the language she alleged he used. Any person who had made such "graphic and . . . crude" statements, Hatch told the nominee, "would not be a normal person.

That person, it seems to me, would be a psychopathic sex fiend or a pervert."[130] Thomas readily agreed. With coaching from the White House, Hatch also came close to asserting that Professor Hill had actually based her accounts on passages from the horror novel *The Exorcist* and the record of a recent sexual harassment lawsuit.[131]

Nor was Hatch alone. In McCarthyesque style, Wyoming Republican Alan Simpson declared that his office was being flooded with warnings that Hill was not to be trusted. Yet Simpson cited no specific evidence, preferring instead simply to assure committee members and the television audience that "I really am getting stuff over the transom about Professor Hill. I have got letters hanging out of my pockets. I have got faxes. I have got statements from her former law professors, statements from people that know her, statements from Tulsa, OK, saying, watch out for this woman. But nobody has the guts to say that because it gets all tangled up in this sexual harassment crap."[132] Arlen Specter of Pennsylvania charged, moreover, that discrepancies in Professor Hill's testimony constituted perjury and hinted darkly at possible criminal charges against Thomas's accuser.

Committee Democrats, on the other hand, were as deferential to Thomas as Republicans were contemptuous of Professor Hill. Undoubtedly fearful of African American voter backlash, they acquiesced meekly when Thomas anticipated and rejected in advance any questions about his personal life, including his extensive acquaintance with the precise sorts of pornographic films Hill had accused him of describing to her. Nor did Democrats make more than a feeble effort to counter Thomas's remarkable charge that the Senate's investigation of allegations against one black by another black was somehow an exercise in racial bigotry.

The strategy obviously worked. By a two-to-one margin, a national survey of state and federal judges, conducted the day after the Senate vote on the nomination, found Professor Hill more credible than Judge Thomas.[133] A year later, 44 percent of participants in a national public opinion poll would report that they believed Hill, while only 34 percent thought Thomas truthful.[134] In a survey conducted at the time of the hearings, however, 40 percent of those polled found Thomas more credible, and 50 percent thought he should be confirmed, while only 24 and 29 percent, respectively, believed Hill and opposed confirmation.[135] On October 15, 1991, the full Senate followed those returns, voting fifty-two–forty-eight to approve the nomination. Even so, Thomas won his seat on the high Court by the smallest margin of approval in over a hundred years.

President Bush had termed Thomas the "best-qualified" person in the nation to replace Justice Marshall when he announced the nomination at the presidential summer home in Kennebunkport, Maine, the previous July 1. Thomas's first appearance before the judiciary committee prompted serious questions about the president's judgment. Professor Hill's allegations and Thomas's second appearance before the committee sparked further doubts about his moral fitness for the nation's highest tribunal, and postconfirmation research, however critical and partisan, has raised legitimate concerns about Thomas's candor before the committee.[136] As Justice Thomas's voting patterns on the Court quickly made clear, however, his selection was another victory for the Reagan-Bush judicial agenda.

The Clinton Appointments

Unlike Bush and especially Ronald Reagan, President Clinton had no desire to see the federal judiciary reject or weaken civil liberties precedents; to the contrary, he was from the beginning a strong supporter, for example, of the Supreme Court's abortion rulings and an opponent of congressional efforts to curb late-term abortions. At the same time, the centrist character of his successful campaign to break the Republican hold on the White House and a natural desire to avoid the "Borking" of his nominees clearly influenced his choices for federal judgeships, including seats on the Supreme Court. During his first term, Clinton named two justices to the high bench: Ruth Bader Ginsburg in 1993, to replace Byron White, and Stephen G. Breyer in 1994, to fill the vacancy left by the retirement of Nixon appointee Harry Blackmun. Especially as a result of the president's preference for bland, moderate, noncontroversial choices, neither appointment aroused much controversy, and both easily won confirmation. But Clinton's efforts to fill the two vacancies, especially the first, were plagued from the beginning with false starts and related problems, creating an image of White House ineptness and indecision.

Justice White announced his impending retirement only two months after President Clinton's inauguration. His decision was hardly unexpected; friends had long known that White, a Democrat, planned to leave the bench once a member of his party won the presidency. Finding White's replacement, however, was to be a protracted affair.

Speculation initially focused on New York governor Mario M. Cuomo, but in early April, the governor asked that his name be withdrawn from consideration. Clinton had described Cuomo as "a legal scholar who also understands the impact of the law on real people's lives." When the governor withdrew, the *New York Times* promptly editorialized that the Rehnquist Court needed "just those qualities," adding, "of all the shortcomings of the current Court, the most glaring is its myopia about real situations in the real world. This Court too often deals in abstract ideology with no appreciation of how people will actually behave under the force of its rulings."[137]

Personally, the president no doubt shared such sentiments. Politically, though, his goal was to select a nominee who would do the least damage to the centrist core of the constituency that provided his 1992 election victory, while not alienating traditional Democratic voters. Amidst concerns that he was unduly tied to sensitive political issues, interest in Clinton Interior Department Secretary Bruce Babbitt emerged and quickly faded. So, too, did the candidacies of Judges Stephen Breyer and Jon Newman of the U.S. Court of Appeals for the Second Circuit. Both were Jewish, and the so-called Jewish seat on the Court had been unoccupied since 1969, when Justice Abe Fortas resigned from the bench, and both also possessed distinguished professional credentials, including Supreme Court clerkships. But Judge Newman had angered conservatives with a *New York Times* Op-Ed piece during the Thomas confirmation proceedings in which he characterized the Bush Supreme Court nominee as "mediocre" and intimated that he believed Professor Hill's allegations.[138] White House aides reported, moreover, that the president was not fully satisfied with his first meeting with Breyer, while a number of interest-group leaders raised objections to his nomination. Consumer advocate Ralph Nader asserted, for example, that Clinton "could do better" and urged the president "not [to] rush to nomination before seriously pondering the judicial decisions and other writings of Judge Breyer on matters relating to corporate power, antitrust, consumer-regulatory policies and the scope of judicial review over health and safety agencies." Others cited Breyer's role in drafting controversial federal sentencing guidelines, which critics considered cumbersome and unduly rigid. Whatever the merits of such concerns, revelations Breyer had failed to pay social security taxes on the wages of a part-time housekeeper doomed his chances for a time, just as similar indiscretions had derailed the nominations of Clinton's first two choices for attorney general.[139]

When the White House had appeared to be moving toward Interior Secretary Babbitt as its choice, the *New York Times* published an editorial urging "Greater Diversity on the Supreme Court" and complaining that Clinton would be "squandering" such an opportunity with Babbitt's selection. The *Times* endorsed appointment of a Jewish woman to the high bench, mentioning Judge Patricia Wald of the Court of Appeals for the District of Columbia as an excellent prospect.[140] A month earlier, however, the newspaper had included among those being given serious consideration another Jewish woman on the same court, Ruth Bader Ginsburg.[141] Two days after revelations of Judge Breyer's social security difficulties, and a quickly arranged White House meeting, the president announced Judge Ginsburg's nomination.

A Columbia University law graduate and its first tenured woman law professor, Judge Ginsburg was denied a Supreme Court clerkship when Justice Frankfurter decided "he just wasn't ready to hire a woman." As a lawyer, she had won several major Supreme Court rulings supporting gender equality.[142] In a lecture at New York University the previous March, however, she had objected to the sweeping scope of the Supreme Court's majority opinion in *Roe* and suggested that its broad reach had contributed to the bitter two-decades national debate the ruling had provoked. Instead of imposing a detailed scheme prescribing the ways in which states could and could not regulate abortions during each trimester of a pregnancy, as Justice Blackmun's opinion for the *Roe* Court had, the Court, she contended, should simply have overturned the extreme Texas abortion law at issue in *Roe* and decided future cases in a similar manner.[143]

Women's groups voiced their concerns about Ginsburg's position on the abortion issue but also acknowledged her well-deserved reputation as the "Thurgood Marshall of the women's movement." By the same token, her centrist judicial record made her a difficult target for conservative and moderate senators. In contrast to the Thomas proceedings, Senate hearings on the Ginsburg nomination went smoothly. Senator Metzenbaum, a *Roe* defender, said that he was "puzzled" by Ginsburg's "often repeated criticisms" of the Court's decision and her assertion "that *Roe* curtailed a trend toward liberalization of State abortion statutes." Metzenbaum seriously doubted whether women "really were making real progress towards obtaining reproductive freedom" when *Roe* was decided.[144]

Ginsburg responded, however, by reminding the senator that she was merely quoting the *Roe* opinion itself in recalling the gradual liberalization of state abortion laws prior to the Court's decision. In her judgment, the intense controversy and aggressive anti-abortion movement *Roe* had provoked, combined with a post-*Roe* relaxation of efforts by pro-choice advocates who assumed "that the Court had taken care of the problem," had weakened the abortion reform movement. "[I]f the Court had simply done what courts usually do, stuck to the very case before it and gone no further," she reasoned, "then there might have been a change, gradual changes. We have seen it happen in this country so many times. We saw it with the law of marriage and divorce. In a span of some dozen years, we witnessed a shift from adultery as the sole ground for divorce to no-fault divorce in almost every State in the Union. Once the States begin to change, then it takes a while, but eventually most of them move in the direction of change."[145] *Roe*'s sweep, however, had stifled abortion reform through the political process.

As a vigorous defender of a broad construction of the First Amendment's establishment clause, Metzenbaum was no doubt more satisfied with Ginsburg's responses to questions he raised about *Lemon v. Kurtzman,* the 1971 case in which the Court had held that laws affecting religion must have a secular purpose and a primary effect neither advancing nor harming religion, while also avoiding excessive church-state entanglements.[146] Applauding Justice Black's assertion in the *Everson* case[147] that the establishment guarantee required a "wall between church and state that must be high and impregnable,"[148] the senator asked the nominee to comment on the ridicule to which Justices Scalia and Thomas, among others, had recently subjected the *Lemon* test, particularly in a 1993 Scalia opinion, joined by Justice Thomas, which compared the majority's periodic use of *Lemon* to "some ghoul in a late-night horror movie that repeatedly sits up in its grave and shuffles abroad, after being repeatedly killed and buried."[149] "My approach or attitude about criticism," Ginsburg replied, "is generally to ask: 'What is the alternative?' It is easy to tear down, to deconstruct. It is not so easy to construct. Some of my law school and judicial colleagues don't appreciate that sufficiently. It is much easier to criticize than to come up with an alternative."[150]

Conservative committee members naturally challenged Judge Ginsburg's acceptance of any sort of abortion right— "a right," Senator Hatch noted, "which many, including myself, think was created out of thin air by the Court."[151] But Hatch's comparison of the *Roe* Court's invocation of substantive due process as the basis for the abortion right with the earlier Court's use of essentially the same sort of formula to defend the rights of slaveholders in the *Dred Scott* case[152] gave the Utah senator more difficulty than his questions posed for Ginsburg. Interrupting Hatch, African American Illinois senator Carol Moseley-Braun termed Hatch's "line of questioning . . . personally offensive," adding, "it is very difficult for me to sit here and even to quietly listen to a debate that would analogize *Dred Scott* and *Roe v. Wade*."[153] Hatch attempted to explain that he was in no way defending *Dred Scott,* but instead was questioning the substantive due process basis for both decisions and the virtually unlimited authority with which that doctrine clothed judges. Senator Moseley-Braun was hardly impressed. "If there is another way that you can approach the criticism of judicial activism," she rejoined, "I would appreciate your taking it."[154]

Naturally, abortion opponents challenged Ginsburg's nomination. Disputing complaints of pro-choice spokespersons that the Reagan and Bush administrations had imposed an anti-*Roe* litmus test on all candidates for the federal bench, Paige

Cunningham of Americans United for Life complained that for "the first time in our history, a Supreme Court nominee has been required to pass a test, an abortion litmus test" and termed it "a tragedy that supporting an act which ends the life of one human being and scars the future of another should be considered the supreme test for the Supreme Court."[155] Howard Phillips, chairman of the Conservative Caucus, echoed Cunningham's sentiments, dismissing Judge Ginsburg as "simply . . . another vote for the proposition that our unborn children are less than human, and that their lives may be snuffed out without due process of law and with impunity."[156] There was never any doubt, however, that the committee would approve the nomination, and on August 3, the full Senate confirmed Judge Ginsburg's appointment by a vote of ninety-six–three.

President Clinton's second opportunity to name a justice came the following April, when *Roe*'s author, Harry Blackmun, announced that he was retiring from the bench at the end of the current term, explaining, "Eighty-five is pretty old. I don't want to reach a point where my senility level reached unacceptable proportions, and I don't want to be asked to retire like Oliver Wendell Holmes, Jr."[157]

Blackmun faced retirement with mixed emotions. Initially relatively conservative in most civil liberties fields following his 1970 appointment by President Nixon, he emerged in the mid-1970s as a strong member of a moderate-liberal faction on the Court in privacy and civil rights cases, including controversial affirmative action litigation.[158] He also was not only the author of *Roe*, but eventually reversed himself on the capital punishment issue as well, concluding late in his career that the death penalty, which he personally abhorred but had long considered within the reach of governmental power, was in fact unconstitutional.[159] With his retirement, the Court was losing its most liberal member—and one increasingly concerned about the conservative tenor of many of its decisions, a trend he was certain would continue well into the middle of the twenty-first century.[160]

President Clinton moved quickly to fill the vacancy left by Blackmun's retirement, but not without another false start. The president's initial choice for the seat, apparently, was George Mitchell, the Senate majority leader. Chief Justice Rehnquist, when first selected as an associate justice in 1971, had been the last appointee without prior judicial experience, and Mitchell's appointment would have fulfilled Clinton's desire to select a justice with extensive political experience rather than yet another lower court judge. Article I, Section 6, of the Constitution does forbid appointment of a member of Congress to a federal post for which the salary had been increased during the nominee's congressional term, but that provision was not a significant obstacle to Mitchell's selection. Although the salaries of justices had recently been increased, Congress could have simply lowered Mitchell's Supreme Court salary until his Senate term ended in 1995, just as it had to allow Senator Lloyd Bentsen (D-Tex.) to become Clinton's treasury secretary. As a member of the Senate, moreover, Mitchell was largely insulated from close congressional scrutiny of his credentials. Indeed, during an appearance with Mitchell on a television news interview program, Senate minority leader Robert Dole praised his colleague and assured viewers that he would "obviously" vote to confirm his nomination to the high bench.[161] But on April 12, Senator Mitchell withdrew his name from consideration after an informal offer of the position. The majority leader, reporters speculated, apparently was more interested in becoming the commissioner of major league baseball at an annual income of more than $1 million than a Supreme Court justice with a $164,000 yearly salary.

By early May, Secretary Babbitt and a federal appeals court judge, Richard S. Arnold of Little Rock, Arkansas, a long-time Clinton friend, were rumored to be frontrunners to fill the Blackmun seat. But women's groups expressed concerns about Arnold's vote with an appeals court majority in a 1984 case upholding the all-male membership policies of the Junior Chambers of Commerce—a decision the Supreme Court had later reversed[162]—as well as his vote in another case approving a law that required women under eighteen to notify both parents before obtaining an abortion or bypass the parental notification requirement by appeal to a judge—a decision the Supreme Court later affirmed.[163] And although at one point a White House official told a reporter that Babbitt's nomination was "95 percent" certain, Senator Hatch, among others, again warned that the interior secretary "would legislate from the bench laws that the liberal community doesn't have a tinker's chance of getting through the people's elected representatives."[164] Anxious to avoid a contentious confirmation battle, President Clinton again passed over the controversial Babbitt for Judge Stephen Breyer, whom Lloyd N. Cutler, the president's senior counsel, deemed "the one with the fewest problems."

A fifty-five-year-old San Francisco native, Judge Breyer was a member of a well-educated, middle-class Jewish family with a strong commitment to civic participation and intellectual pursuits. His father was legal counsel to the San Francisco school board for more than forty years, his mother active in Democratic Party politics, the League of Women Voters, and the local chapter of the United Nations Association. A graduate of Stanford and Marshall scholar at Oxford, Breyer clerked for Supreme Court justice Arthur J. Goldberg after law school at Harvard, then served for two years as a special assistant in the Justice Department's antitrust division. In 1967, he joined the law and government faculties at Harvard, where he became a full professor in 1970 and would continue teaching as an adjunct faculty member until his appointment to the Supreme Court. He also held a variety of government posts, including stints as an assistant special prosecutor in the Watergate investigation; special counsel to the Senate judiciary committee's subcommittee on administrative practices, where he developed a plan for deregulation of the airlines industry that became law during the Carter administration; and the judiciary committee's chief counsel from 1979 to 1980. Despite close ties with then committee chair Edward M. Kennedy, Breyer also earned the respect of influential congressional Republicans. Such connections later proved fortuitous when his nomination by President Carter to a seat on the Court of Appeals for the First Circuit was the only one of several Carter federal court choices to survive the confirmation process after the GOP took control of the White House and Senate in the 1980 elections.

As a member of the U.S. Sentencing Commission, to which he was appointed in 1985, Breyer played a key role in the development of the controversial standards designed to reduce disparities in sentencing and ensure that defendants would serve at least a mandatory portion of their sentences. On this occasion, however, neither harsh criticism of the sentencing guidelines nor his earlier social security difficulties would deny Breyer his seat on the Supreme Court.

In his appearance before the judiciary committee in mid-July, Judge Breyer, like Justice Ginsburg, made clear his acceptance of a flexible, pragmatic approach to the Constitution's meaning. Asked by Senator Leahy to discuss the nature and source of unenumerated constitutional rights, the nominee responded,

> You look back into history. You try to determine what are the basic values that underlay those things that are enumerated and that gives you a key to other basic values. You look to what Frankfurter and Harlan and Goldberg and others talked about as the traditions of our people, always trying to understand what people historically have viewed as traditional, and the values being there, you look to history in the past, to history in the present, and to the meaning, to what life is like today, to try to work out how—maybe an idea a little bit into the future, too—to get an idea of what are those things that are fundamental to a life of dignity.[165]

In offering her "enthusiastic support" of Judge Breyer's confirmation, Stanford law professor Kathleen Sullivan, among others, praised the nominee's commitment to "judicial pragmatism," a "flexible, undogmatic" approach to constitutional and statutory construction in which Breyer, like Holmes and the second Justice Harlan before him, "would look to text and structure and history and tradition and precedent and the way we live today and the way we might live in the future as his guides to meaning. He would not rigidly limit himself to any of these tools alone." Did this mean that the judge was "just going to do what he thinks is best according to his own light, what he thinks is practical or good?" she asked. "Absolutely not," she replied to her own question. Instead, like his mentor Justice Goldberg in his *Griswold* concurrence,[166] Breyer would look to "[t]radition, our people, our conscience, our experience, outside himself. . . . Pragmatism is a philosophy of judicial humility, not judicial arrogance. It holds that, as Holmes said, general propositions cannot decide concrete cases, and that adjudication between two competing legal claims is necessarily a matter of degree."[167]

During his questioning of Professor Sullivan, committee chairman Joseph Biden cited the work of Daniel A. Farber, a major critic of pragmatic jurisprudence.[168] But Biden agreed with Sullivan that legal pragmatism had been the dominant tradition on the twentieth-century Supreme Court and that most recent appointees (only Scalia and Thomas were not mentioned) embraced such a philosophy. Biden also made the questionable suggestion that acceptance of a pragmatic, flexible approach to legal issues would somehow help to reduce the degree and intensity of "ideological warfare" that recent judicial appointments had sometimes provoked.[169]

Somewhat ironically, given his professed commitment to text and the framers' intent as the primary legitimate guides to constitutional meaning, Senator Hatch took no part in the questioning of Breyer, termed him an "excellent nominee," and announced that Breyer's and Sullivan's testimony had "more than put to rest" any concerns that the nomination might have given him.[170] Senator Arlen Specter, on the other hand, expressed concern about legal pragmatism's policy implications and potentially limitless reach. Along the lines Justice Hugo Black had often pursued in attacking the constitutional philosophy of Justice Frankfurter and the second Justice Harlan, among other exponents of what more recently was being referred to as legal pragmatism, Specter suggested that judges applying such an approach were simply "Platonic Solons deciding what was good for the country in a change of constitutional doctrine," and he questioned whether, under such a formula, there was "any line, bright or dim, separating the Court's role from the legislative function." Professor Sullivan agreed that Specter had raised an "excellent" question, but insisted that a clear distinction could be made between "pragmatism on the one hand [and] personal opinion or popular opinion on the other," with the "pragmatic judge . . . look[ing] outside himself and to sources more lasting and deeper and enduring than the passions of the moment" in construing the law's meaning. But Specter was not convinced. "Well, Professor Sullivan," he countered, "that sounds good and makes sense to a substantial extent, but it is the judge who looks outside, starting from looking inside. And none of us can divorce ourselves from our own views, and it has to be significantly if not largely a personal decision as to what those outside forces are."[171]

As she had during the Ginsburg hearings, anti-abortion witness Paige Cunningham accused President Clinton again of imposing an abortion litmus test on the judicial process and charged that Breyer's selection "clearly implies that he has passed this political test."[172] A leader of the home schooling movement was also among witnesses testifying in opposition to confirmation. Breyer had spoken for an appeals court panel in a 1989 decision upholding a Massachusetts law requiring local school officials to approve home schools.[173] Many Massachusetts school districts were basing their approval of proposed home schools on specific objective criteria. But others, according to critics of the approval scheme, were applying unduly subjective, unwritten standards that, these critics alleged, violated the free exercise rights of home school parents, many of whom presumably saw home schooling as a way of providing religious instruction to their children and protecting them from the secular influences of public school systems. Speaking against Breyer's confirmation, Michael Farris, president of the Home School Legal Defense Association, who had served as lead counsel in an unsuccessful effort to secure Supreme Court review of the case, charged that Breyer ascribed a "very low opinion and value to the free exercise of religion."[174]

In *Employment Division v. Smith* (1990),[175] the Supreme Court had held that generally applicable, religiously neutral laws could be applied to religious practices, including the ritual use of peyote at issue in *Smith*, without a showing of the compelling interest long required of laws affecting religious liberty.[176] Congress attempted to restore the compelling interest standard in such cases with passage in 1993 of the Religious Freedom Restoration Act (RFRA). And while the Court in 1997 would overturn RFRA as an unconstitutional usurpation of ultimate judicial authority over the Constitution's meaning,[177] Farris cited RFRA in opposing the free exercise standard Breyer had applied in the home schooling case.

Senator Hatch naturally concurred with Paige Cunningham's criticisms of the Clinton administration's purported use of any single litmus test to determine judicial fitness. As a principal RFRA sponsor, he was also sympathetic to Farris's concerns about the courts' recent treatment of the free exercise guarantee in *Smith* and later cases. But Hatch assured Farris, based on his own questioning of Breyer, that the nominee seemed to have "an open mind" on the issue.[178]

Senator Biden questioned Judge Breyer about the Supreme Court's growing emphasis on property rights, especially in recent cases ascribing a broad construction to the Fifth Amendment's takings clause, requiring just compensation for government expropriation of private property for public uses.[179] The Court had concluded years ago that, beyond a point, government regulation of property could become so intrusive that it constituted a "taking" for which compensation was required,[180] but until the recent cases had given the regulatory takings notion a very narrow construction.[181] Carried to its "logical end," Senator Biden could see little difference between the current Court's approach to regulatory takings and the decisions of the *Lochner* era, in which the Court used substantive due process to invalidate economic controls it considered "unreasonable" or "arbitrary." Like many Supreme Court justices, Judge Breyer agreed that the Constitution embodied no particular economic theory. Noting that other takings cases were certain to come before the Court, however, he declined specific comment and refused to speculate on the concerns of Biden and others about "how far" the Court would go in converting the takings clause into a sort of potentially limitless due process formula.[182]

Judge Breyer also emerged largely unscathed from a potentially significant ethical challenge to his confirmation. Anticipating such questions in his opening statement to the judiciary committee, Breyer acknowledged "sitting on certain environmental cases in the first circuit at a time when I had an investment, an insurance investment in Lloyd's [of London]," an insurer of certain parties to the suits. Citing Breyer's holdings in Lloyd's and other companies regularly involved in pollution cases, legal ethics scholar Monroe H. Freedman accused the nominee, in a letter to Senator Biden, of violating legislation requiring federal judges to disqualify themselves from cases raising the appearance of a financial conflict of interest.[183] Ralph Nader and others criticized Breyer's record on health and safety issues, and Texas law professor Thomas O. McGarity, a Breyer acquaintance, suggested that his nomination could be "hazardous to our health" and asserted that Breyer's confidence in an unregulated marketplace "parallel[ed]" that of prominent Reagan appointees, including Justice Scalia, Judge Bork, and Judges Frank Easterbrook and Richard Posner of the Court of Appeals for the Seventh Circuit.

But ethics scholars Geoffrey Hazard and Stephen Gillers, among others, concluded that Breyer had properly participated in the cases in question, although Hazard did term Breyer's conduct "imprudent."[184] And both Democratic and Republican committee members generally sought to minimize any problem Breyer's ethics might pose for confirmation. When Breyer testified, for example, that others had "verified" his judgment that he had acted properly in one case,[185] Senator Metzenbaum interrupted. "You mean that the White House asked some ethics professors for their opinion, and one said it was imprudent, others said it was entirely proper, and some other professors apparently have said it was totally inappropriate." At that point, Senator Kennedy, chairman of the judiciary committee when Breyer was its chief counsel, asked that the letters to which Metzenbaum referred be entered into the record, adding, "I dare say they are not as described by the Senator from Ohio. I think in fairness to this nominee we ought to put into the record what [was written by] those legal scholars and ethicists that have been called on by this Committee under Republicans and Democrats alike and who are some of the most distinguished, thoughtful, and profound individuals that write on this subject matter." Senator Hatch then assured Breyer that "all but one found in your favor and said there was nothing unethical."[186]

Committee members and witnesses focused on many other elements of Breyer's background, record, and views as well. But with such bipartisan support, his confirmation chances were clear. Following enthusiastic committee approval, the full Senate endorsed his appointment on July 29, by an eighty-seven–nine vote.

By the mid-1990s, then, a variety of circumstances had combined to obstruct the Reagan administration's vision of a Supreme Court dominated by justices committed to a variety of "original intent," almost invariably invoked to narrow the reach of constitutional guarantees. William Rehnquist's elevation to the Court's center seat, like Justice Scalia's appointment, obviously fit the Reagan mold, as did, perversely enough, President Bush's selection of Clarence Thomas. But Justice O'Connor, whose appointment was primarily gender-based, proved to be more the judicial pragmatist Kathleen Sullivan had extolled in praising Stephen Breyer's nomination, and the Bork episode, along with Douglas Ginsburg's stillborn nomination, prompted President Reagan to select another legal pragmatist, Anthony Kennedy, as his final choice for the high bench. Not surprisingly, given the controversy Judge Bork's nomination aroused, Presidents Bush and Clinton also showed a preference for noncontroversial, "judicious choices,"[187] even if Bush erred in assuming that Thomas's race alone would insulate him from opposition. Bush's selection of Justice Souter, the protypical stealth candidate, placed another legal pragmatist on the Court, as did President Clinton's appointments of Ginsburg and Breyer.

The selection of noncontroversial, even obscure justices, does not necessarily promote judicial mediocrity. Justice Souter, in fact, has become a forceful defender of his positions and an articulate exponent of the constitutional philosophy his role model, the second Justice Harlan, embraced in an earlier era—even if certain admirers of Harlan's generally conservative voting record see Souter's record to date, in the words of one, a "total disaster." But the partial derailing of the Reagan judicial agenda has meant a much more complex pattern of Rehnquist Court decision making than the Reagan administration would have desired or expected in the early years of his White House tenure.

2

The Court

By all accounts, William Rehnquist was to be a more effective chief justice, especially in terms of his relations with his colleagues, than his predecessor. Warren Earl Burger had certainly looked the part, and his opinions were entirely workmanlike, readable efforts. But a preoccupation with Court pomp and his early grounds beautification campaign had hardly enhanced his image with Court veterans, including Justice Black, who once described the then new chief as "a good man—with flowers." No help either was Burger's irascible, overbearing personality—a manner reflected perhaps in his unsuccessful attempt at the beginning of his tenure to control the assignment of the Court's opinion not only when he was in the majority, consistent with long tradition, but even when he was in dissent in a case. As a result, most if not all their colleagues probably welcomed Burger's departure and the elevation of Rehnquist, who could be pompous and clearly was the justice most out of step with decisional trends on the Burger Court, but also was considered a diplomatic, considerate, generally unflappable colleague—even if some privately attributed his calm manner to the painkilling medications that had concerned senators who opposed his confirmation.

If their colleagues needed any reminder of the contrasts between the irascible Burger and the unflappable Rehnquist, moreover, they got it shortly after the new chief had taken his seat. Chief Justice Burger had retired primarily, he said, to devote his full attention to his activities as head of the commission planning the celebration of the Constitution's bicentennial. In a memorandum to the justices, Burger complained about a "fast-talk promoter" on Philadelphia's bicentennial committee who had recently announced to the press that the Court would sit in Philadelphia the following September. Burger assured his colleagues that "[n]o such statement was ever authorized by me." One such request, he reported, had been declined, another tabled. He had also informed "the Philadelphia people" that the Court could sit outside Washington only for "a purely ceremonial function [such as admission of lawyers to the Supreme Court bar] . . . if at all," but had later decided that even for such a ceremony "the selection of the admittees would present at least some 'sticky' problems—how many women, how many Hispanics, etc." Concluded Burger indignantly, "we have found on several occasions that some of the Philadelphia group are not wholly reliable and they have received no encouragement from me."[1]

Even when turning down the request of a colleague with whom his jurisprudential differences were pronounced, Rehnquist's tone and approach, on the other hand, were generally solicitous and diplomatic. At the time of Justice Marshall's retirement, for example, Marshall requested continuation of home-to-office transportation. In his reply, the chief justice reminded his colleague of the "brouhaha" with Congress that had developed five years earlier over such service for active justices, especially whether home-to-office trips constituted "official business." First through Rehnquist's negotiations with Senator William Proxmire (D-Wis.), who had raised the issue, and later through a change in the law, the justices, Rehnquist recalled, "were allowed to designate home-to-office transportation as official business where there was good reason for a Justice not to drive himself." Rehnquist stressed to Marshall, however, that "all of this was in the context of active members of the Court. The term 'official business,' in my view, just doesn't stretch to cover home-to-office transportation for retired Justices." No retired justice, he added, had previously received such assistance, and an attempt to press the issue might lead to an elimination of home-to-office transportation for active justices as well. "None of us would want that," wrote Rehnquist, "and so I think it best to let sleeping dogs lie."[2]

At the same time, Rehnquist acknowledged that he understood Marshall's concerns about the logical "incongruities" of denying retired justices home-to-office service while making the Court's cars available for transporting them from their chambers to other places, including the airport, during the day. Perhaps anticipating, inaccurately, George Bush's 1992 reelection and thus a Republican president to choose his successor, Rehnquist also expressed sympathy for Marshall's request "not merely in the abstract, but because in all probability I will be in the same boat you are within a couple of years."[3]

On at least one occasion, too, the chief justice displayed a willingness to confront the Senate Republican leadership in defending the judiciary against obstacles to the effective administration of justice. In his 1997 annual report on the state of the federal judiciary, Rehnquist warned that Senate delays in acting on scores of President Clinton's nominations to federal judgeships posed a serious threat to the nation's "quality of justice." Noting that 82 of 846 federal judgeships—nearly 1 of every 10 seats—were vacant and that 26 of the vacancies had existed for eighteen months or longer, he declared that both the White House and Senate must bear some responsibility for the backlog, but reserved his harshest criticism for the Senate. In 1996 and 1997, he noted, the Senate confirmed only 17 and 36 judges, respectively, well below the 101 confirmed in 1994, the year, he might have added, before Republicans assumed control of

Congress. Rehnquist conceded that the Senate was "surely under no obligation to confirm any particular nominee," but pointedly added that "after the necessary time for inquiry it should vote him up or down" so that "[i]n the latter case, the president can send up another nominee." Even if federal court jurisdiction had remained stable, but especially with its expanding scope over drug and firearms-related crimes, he asserted, "judicial vacancies will aggravate the problem of too few judges and too much work."[4]

Vermont senator Patrick Leahy of Vermont, ranking Democrat on the judiciary committee, naturally applauded the chief justice's assessment, expressing "hope his message will help shame the Senate into clearing the backlog early in [1998]."[5] Calling the figures cited by Rehnquist "pretty frightening," Leahy predicted a "constitutional crisis" if the stalemate continued. Just as predictably, judiciary committee chairman Orrin Hatch placed blame on the White House and on the judiciary itself. Pointing out that Clinton had submitted nominees for barely half the current vacancies (42 of 82), Hatch claimed that "[t]he president needs to do a better job," adding, "It has taken the president an average of 534 days to appoint a judge and the Senate 97 days to confirm. If he will give us good nominees, they will move quickly." Somewhat ironically, given the number of Reagan and Bush appointees in the federal courts and the findings of several studies that the voting records of Clinton judges were actually less liberal than those of President Carter and more comparable to those of Carter's Republican predecessor, President Ford,[6] Hatch also attempted to tie the backlog to the "activist" federal judiciary. "Every time we see another example of judicial activism, it makes my job harder. It increases the number [of senators] who want to scrutinize the next appointee even more closely." For Hatch, moreover, the Republican-controlled Senate's support for Clinton nominees had been stronger than that the Democrat-controlled Senate had given President Bush's judicial choices. "In May of 1991," he declared, ". . . there were 148 vacancies—66 more than now—and no one was writing articles about a crisis in the judiciary."[7]

In a *Washington Post* Op-Ed piece, Senator Hatch elaborated on his position. Renewing his attack on judicial activists, he insisted that "[j]udges must understand their role in our constitutional system as impartial magistrates, not Monday-morning legislators." He further noted that most judges responding to a recent congressional survey had said they were handling their current caseloads without difficulty and needed no additional help. Finally, he argued that the Supreme Court itself must share "some responsibility for increasing the federal bench's workload because it has dramatically expanded the federal courts' reach and ignored many important constitutional principles to force the courts into areas in which they should not be."[8]

In fairness to Hatch, he and Senator Charles Grassley of Iowa, a senior Republican on the judiciary committee, had blocked an effort in the Republican conference early in 1997 to require President Clinton to draw half of his nominees from lists submitted by Republican senators. In her reaction to Chief Justice Rehnquist's report, however, Nan Aron of the liberal Alliance for Justice accused three conservative Republicans on the judiciary committee—John Ashcroft of Missouri, Jon Kyl of Arizona, and Jefferson Sessions of Alabama—of using delaying tactics to prevent Senate votes on President Clinton's nominees. Senator Hatch had insisted that the "blue slip" process through which individual senators were entitled to put temporary holds on nominations was functioning no differently than when the Democrats controlled the Senate, but he also acknowledged that he had intervened to block tit-for-tat moves against Clinton nominees by, as he put it, a "handful" of Republicans. And the three senators Nan Aron cited seemed likely prospects for such tactics, especially Alabamian Jefferson Sessions, whose own nomination by President Reagan to a district judgeship had died in the Senate in the wake of reports Sessions had called the National Association for the Advancement of Colored People (NAACP) and American Civil Liberties Union (ACLU) "un-American" and "Communist-inspired," thought the Ku Klux Klan was "O.K." until learning some of its members were "pot smokers," and had called a white civil rights lawyer "a disgrace to his race."[9] Whatever the merits of the argument on each side, moreover, Senate Democrats and the White House had found in Chief Justice Rehnquist an unlikely, but valuable, ally in the continuing struggle with Senate Republicans over judicial appointments.

Nine Scorpions in a Bottle

Chief Justice Rehnquist's skill in running the Court has in no way eliminated, of course, the inevitable interpersonal clashes that have periodically developed throughout the history of an institution often described as "nine scorpions in a bottle." In his later years on the bench, Justice Harry Blackmun became increasingly outspoken in public discussions of his colleagues and trends in the Court's decisions. Blackmun remained solicitous of the other justices' feelings, however. In its report of Blackmun's address to the Eighth Circuit's annual judicial conference in St. Louis, in July of 1988, the *New York Times* incorrectly informed readers that the justice had described his colleague Justice Stevens as "unimaginative."[10] When Blackmun learned of the error, which the *Times* later corrected,[11] he immediately wrote Justice Stevens.

In a portion of his remarks suggesting to young lawyers what they should expect on going to the Court for the first time, Blackmun was quoted as having said that Justice White's writing was "hard to understand," that Marshall could be "sullen and at times overbearing," and that recent arrival Justice Kennedy had "settled right in. He takes positive positions, is firm, doesn't equivocate." The justice had reserved what one newspaper termed his "most scathing comments" for Antonin Scalia, calling him "the professor at work," and explaining, "He asks far too many questions [in oral argument]. He takes over the case from the counsel. He will argue with counsel. He can't get out of the courtroom." Justice O'Connor, he added, also asked a lot of questions, but Scalia "exasperated" even O'Connor in his domination of oral argument.[12] In his letter to Stevens, Blackmun assured his colleague that he had described him "as 'imaginative,'" not unimaginative, "perhaps the most imaginative of all of us, and as one who wanted to know counsel's theory. In other words, counsel had better be aware of his basic theory. . . . Where the AP got the word 'unimaginative' is beyond me. . . . I regret that this has happened."[13] Justice Blackmun's secretary also sent Stevens a note pointing out the *Times*'s correction of the error.[14]

In his letter to Stevens, Blackmun also sought to correct inaccurate impressions that press reports might have created regarding his remarks about Justices White and

Marshall. "I described Byron as asking penetrating questions," he wrote, "and said that if the attorney did not understand them he should not hesitate to say so and ask that they be repeated." Of Marshall, "I said that he would appear formidable on the bench and almost sullen and would ask leading and positive questions, and that one should not be overwhelmed by them; he usually ends up with humor."

Although his office issued a statement denying press reports that Blackmun had criticized his colleagues in his St. Louis speech, the justice clearly had used the conference as a forum for bemoaning what he considered the loss of philosophical balance brought on by the Reagan appointments to the high bench and for predicting that George Bush's election to the presidency would assure conservative domination of the third branch of government well into the next century. Such comments also received prominent play in the media, prompting judicial scholars David M. O'Brien and Ronald Collins, among others, to express concern that Blackmun had made the Court an election issue. While applauding such openness as a means of improving public understanding of the Court, O'Brien and Collins worried that the phenomenon of justices' pleading their cases in public might damage the institution's power and prestige.[15]

Blackmun's remarks undoubtedly also disconcerted at least some of his colleagues. Within the Rehnquist Court, however, the mild-mannered, gentle Blackmun was by no means the justice most likely to ruffle the feelings of others. Instead, Justice Scalia has enjoyed that dubious reputation. When the Rehnquist and Scalia nominations were pending in the Senate, Yale president-designate Benno C. Schmidt, in a newspaper profile of the nominees, questioned whether Rehnquist's "reactionary constitutional vision [was] so out of touch with that of his colleagues and the temper of the times that all his powers of intellect and personality cannot overcome the essential isolation that has been the overriding characteristic of his service [as an associate justice] on the Court to date." Emphasizing Scalia's outgoing personality, however, Schmidt predicted that Scalia, Rehnquist, and President Reagan's first appointee to the Court, Justice O'Connor, would make "a formidable trio" on the bench.[16] Stressing Scalia's zest for life and considerable people skills, other profiles also suggested that he would enjoy tremendous influence on the Rehnquist Court.[17]

Schmidt had also noted, however, that Justice Scalia possessed a "powerful intellect with a biting and effective pen." Others mentioned that he was the first academic selected to the Court since Felix Frankfurter, without considering that Justice Frankfurter was also at the center of a number of the most intense ideological and personal struggles in the Court's history.[18] Once on the Court, Scalia quickly subjected his colleagues to that same biting and effective pen in opinions that were expertly crafted and clearly demonstrated their author's rapier wit, as later chapters will show, yet also dripped with sarcasm and scorn toward not only application of the *Lemon* test in establishment cases, substantive due process, and other judicial doctrines he deplored, but his fellow and sister justices as well. On the bench, moreover, he could be a terror, dominating the questioning, debating with colleagues and lawyers alike, and once so alarming the chief justice with his rudeness during oral argument that a "scowling Rehnquist leaned over and shook his finger at Scalia while gesturing with his other hand at [Justice] Kennedy" to continue his questioning of counsel in the case.[19] Such behavior has been thoroughly documented in various sources, as has its impact on other justices.[20]

Nor did such behavior subside following Justice Blackmun's pointed remarks at the St. Louis judicial conference. During oral argument of a case during the 1996-97 term, Justice Scalia grew visibly impatient with one of the attorneys, appearing ready at one point, according to a journalist's account, "to leap from the bench, push the lawyer aside and argue the case himself." As counsel struggled to make his point, Chief Justice Rehnquist interrupted Scalia's questioning. "I think he's capable of answering himself," Rehnquist asserted. "[B]ut he's not capable," Scalia rejoined.[21] On another occasion, Rehnquist suggested to an attorney Scalia was grilling that he could "object to the question as leading"—to which Scalia retorted, "I'm leading him where he doesn't want to go." Reacting to concerns that he might be unduly harsh on his colleagues, he once contended that "bad ideas" deserve "clunking on the head."

One reporter described thusly Scalia's approach to attorneys during oral argument: "Unlike his colleagues, who no doubt enter the courtroom predisposed toward one side or the other, making points to the lawyers before them or to each other, Scalia rides rough, sometimes firing a series of questions with no pause for answers. His hypotheticals become hyperbole.... Scalia, a former law professor, will say to a lawyer, 'Shouldn't your answer be ...?' Or, when he wants to shoot down another justice's line of questioning, he will interrupt and ask the lawyer whether such questions are even relevant." During arguments, for example, over the constitutionality of the Brady handgun statute, which a five-four Court, speaking through Justice Scalia, struck down at the end of the 1996-97 term,[22] Justice O'Connor questioned counsel regarding the burden the law imposed on local sheriffs temporarily obliged by its provisions to run background checks of would-be gun purchasers. When Stephen P. Halbrook, the lawyer representing the sheriffs who had challenged the law as an undue intrusion on state authority, referred to testimony in the record indicating the number of hours the law required of local officers, O'Connor pressed for more detail and even urged Halbrook to file additional information with the Court's clerk. At that point, Scalia interrupted, coaxing the lawyer to the broad argument that Congress lacked the power to require local officials to administer federal gun-control provisions, whatever the degree of burden created. Later, during arguments over statutes forbidding physician-assisted suicide, which the Court would uphold at the end of the term, [23] Scalia became so embroiled in an exchange with Harvard law professor Laurence Tribe, representing those challenging the statutes at issue, that for an extended period neither one permitted the other to complete a question or response.

Scalia's colleagues, of course, have not been altogether defenseless in coping with his behavior on the bench. Justice Souter, despite early concerns over his fitness for the bench, has not only become an effective challenger to Scalia in the crafting of judicial opinions; his mild-mannered personality has also been an effective counterpoint on the bench to Scalia's bombast. During arguments in a Maryland case over whether police can order passengers to leave a vehicle stopped for speeding, a practice later affirmed by a divided Court,[24] Justice Souter raised a hypothetical question: "Let's assume that [a] bright line [constitutional rule] allowed nothing more than requiring the passenger to get out of the car so that if the passenger then said, 'I've had enough of this, I'm leaving,' the passenger, so far as the bright line rule is concerned, would be allowed to go." At that point, Scalia interrupted. "In fact, the passenger says, 'Thank goodness. This guy was speeding. I am so glad to get out of this car. Let me catch the nearest cab and go.'" "You can see," Souter joked, "what Justice Scalia's passengers tend to feel like."

Scalia concedes, apparently apologetically, his tendency to dominate oral arguments and the harsh tone of his opinions, explaining, "It is the academic in me. I fight against it. The devil makes me do it."[25] He was even moved to assure one Washington audience, "I am not a nut," to greater effect, one can hope, than Richard Nixon's earlier assurances to the nation that he was "not a crook." Nor is he the only justice with an overbearing personality. Justice Ginsburg is also an aggressive inquisitor, who so frequently interrupts other justices that some of her colleagues simply cut her off and continue their questioning of lawyers. In the end, the unusually harsh tone of Scalia's opinions and his domineering courtroom demeanor have undoubtedly damaged rather than strengthened his influence on the Court. Even without such tendencies, moreover, Justices O'Connor and Kennedy, the key swing votes on the current Court, are the most influential justices, to such a degree that some question whether the Rehnquist Court should not more aptly be dubbed the "Kennedy Court."[26] But Scalia's opinions and courtroom style, combined with what the *New Republic*'s Jeffrey Rosen has contended is the justice's "intellectual contempt for most of his colleagues,"[27] have further isolated him on the Court, minimizing his influence.

Justice O'Connor has found Scalia's conduct particularly offensive. In 1989, when O'Connor filed a concurrence in *Webster v. Reproductive Services*,[28] terming premature Scalia's proposal in a separate opinion that *Webster* should have been used to reexamine and overrule *Roe v. Wade*, Scalia charged that O'Connor's analysis of the abortion issue "cannot be taken seriously."[29] From that point on, according to another justice, O'Connor has been "deeply wounded" by what she deemed Scalia's insults in opinions and on the bench. Indeed, a former Scalia clerk acknowledged, by one account, that Scalia had "completely alienated" O'Connor and "lost her forever." During a Ninth Circuit judicial conference, O'Connor reminded her audience of the adage that "sticks and stones will break my bones but words will never hurt me," yet added, "That probably isn't true."[30] Since she, like Justice Kennedy, is pivotal to consensus building on the Court, O'Connor's alienation from Scalia has probably worked to undermine further whatever influence he might otherwise have enjoyed among the justices. Scalia, on the other hand, seems decidedly more interested in aggressively defending his positions than in developing voting blocs to assure he prevails in cases before the Court.

Nor, in all likelihood, has Justice Scalia's close association with Justice Thomas, the member of the Court with whom Scalia is most regularly aligned, enhanced the standing of either justice with his colleagues. Thomas assumed his seat amid public concerns, probably shared by at least some of his new colleagues, that he was unprepared for the tasks ahead. At least a few of their number, moreover, probably also believed Anita Hill and her supporters, thus considering Thomas a perjurer as well.

Even with the most positive attitude toward his new post, Thomas's assimilation into the Court would have been difficult at best.

Edward Lazarus, who clerked for Justice Blackmun during the Court's 1988 term, has concluded in a recent study, however, that "[f]rom the moment Thomas crossed the Court's threshold, he carried an aura of partisanship as well as indifference to the institutional culture to which he had ascended." Thomas, for example, shocked his new colleagues and others by posing for the cover of *People* magazine with his wife and a Bible. He made public appearances on behalf of the conservative political organizations that supported his nomination. He surrounded himself, according to Lazarus, "with uniformly archconservative clerks—including . . . a hand-me-down from Scalia who had found even his boss insufficiently pure ideologically." He gave his clerks broad discretion, enabling them, "with typical narrow-gauged zeal, [to create] drafts [of opinions] remarkably provocative in result and dismissive of any point of view other than their own." His chambers "exuded a sense of score settling," while his wife "spoke ominously about the Justice feeling that he 'doesn't owe any of the groups who opposed him anything.'" During confirmation proceedings, he "had assured the Senate, almost meekly, that 'I have no agenda.'" Now, he liked "to tell his clerks, 'I ain't evolving.'" During oral argument, he "not only remained unvaryingly silent but looked uninterested, often not even bothering to remove the rubber band from his stack of briefs."[31]

Lazarus found none of this suprising. Even Thomas's mentor, Senator Danforth, had observed that during the confirmation proceedings, "Thomas was reduced to uncontrollable fits of weeping, vomiting, hyperventilating, and writhing on the floor." Even before Professor Hill's allegations surfaced, he suspected that people were trying to kill him. "If Anita Hill told the truth, Thomas's enemies had humiliated him, exposed him, forced him into lying. If she lied, all the worse." Such an experience would have had a tremendous impact on anyone, and certainly on one at the extreme edge of politics, who, if innocent of Hill's charges, had a right to consider himself as having been "grievously wronged" or, if culpable, had brought to the Court "not only ideology but an inner rage, a willingness to sacrifice every inch of his personal dignity to satisfy his own ambition." In either case, Thomas's appointment, Lazarus asserted, had denied the Court the addition of a jurist committed to "balanced, impartial, collegial judgment."[32] Presumably, certain of Thomas's colleagues have found his demeanor and extreme conservatism, like Scalia's, irritating or at least frustrating.

In general, however, changes in the Rehnquist Court's membership over time have probably led to greater philosophical homogeneity and improved relations among the justices. With the departure of Marshall, Brennan, and Blackmun, the Court lost its liberal wing. Its conservative bloc of Rehnquist, Scalia, and Thomas now requires, moreover, the votes of pragmatic conservatives O'Connor and Kennedy to prevail, just as the Court's pragmatic moderates, Stevens, Souter, Ginsburg, and Breyer, need O'Connor or Kennedy to win any close case. And while the collapse of the liberal bloc and rise of the legal pragmatists has by no means inhibited Justice Scalia's penchant for biting dissents and concurrences or aggressive courtroom behavior, one suspects that the atmosphere in the Court is generally more congenial than at earlier times in Chief Justice Rehnquist's tenure. Largely perhaps because the justices have been drawn mainly from the federal courts of appeals, they have also adapted to the Court's routine with relative ease, vulnerable to little, if any, of the "freshman effect" long considered a typical fate of new appointees to the high bench.[33]

Even during its most turbulent times, moreover, it is likely that at least most members of the Rehnquist Court, like the justices of previous eras, have attempted to place the interests of the institution over philosophical and personal disagreements as well as the petty jealousies and conflicts that afflict any collegial body. The outspoken Justice Scalia would be included in that number. Following the defeat of his Supreme Court nomination in the Senate, Robert H. Bork resigned his federal appeals court seat, took an office in the American Enterprise Institute, a conservative think tank, and began writing and lecturing on social and political problems confronting the nation. In *Slouching Towards Gomorrah*,[34] a bitter Bork vehemently attacked most of the nation's institutions, including the Supreme Court, which he termed one of the most destructive influences in contemporary society. The remedy, he recommended, was a constitutional amendment authorizing Congress to overrule any federal court decision by a majority vote.

Although confirming the worst fears of those who opposed Bork's nomination to the Supreme Court, and no doubt convincing certain of his supporters that he lacked the temperament and judgment critical to effective membership, conservatives generally applauded Bork's analysis and recommendations. In remarks to members of the Jewish Anti-Defamation League, Justice Scalia also implicitly acknowledged the connection between his views and Judge Bork's judicial and constitutional philosophy, calling himself an "originalist" who sought to be "faithful to the [Constitution's] text" and declaring that he, like Bork, did "not believe in the living Constitution, this document that morphs from generation to generation. I favor what some might call the dead Constitution, but I prefer to call it the enduring Constitution." He insisted, too, that there was no room in his judicial philosophy for his personal beliefs and noted his unhappiness at casting the controlling vote when the Supreme Court invalidated state and federal flag-burning statutes on First-Fourteenth Amendment grounds.[35] "I came down to breakfast the next morning," he jokingly added, "and my wife is humming 'Stars and Stripes Forever.' This does not make for a happy camper." He made equally clear his opposition to judges who read their personal preferences into the Constitution's meaning.

But Scalia has also displayed his ultimate, if conflicted, loyalty to his institution and the legal traditions it embodied. Disagreeing with Judge Bork's proposal to permit Congress to override unpopular rulings, he observed, "Bork essentially has given up. I'm not so pessimistic. I'm not ready to throw in the towel. . . . We can get back."[36]

Nor have most Rehnquist Court justices been lacking in the sense of humor so necessary to the harmonious functioning of a collegial body. In 1990, for example, Justice Blackmun circulated a memorandum indicating that he was the "acting Chief Justice" during the absence from Washington of the chief justice, as well as Justices Brennan, White, and Marshall. "It occurs to me," he continued, "that in this happy state of affairs things ought to be done, such as reassigning cases, striking some as too difficult to decide, setting July and August argument sessions, closing the building now for a week or two, scheduling square dancing in the Great Hall, and obtaining a

Court cat to chase down the mice and 'Boris,' who, I am told, is the rat upstairs. . . . I might as well make some use of my newly found status. We juniors on the Court seem to be the only members who are doing any work these days."[37] "By all means sign me up for the square dancing," Justice O'Connor quickly responded. "And I might offer some suggestions for those cases which are too difficult to decide."[38]

More recently, a tennis-shoe manufacturer shipped Justice O'Connor a boxed pair of sneakers in black plastic wrap, which was placed label-side down on her front porch. Security personnel took no chances. Five O'Connor neighbors were promptly ordered from their Chevy Chase, Maryland, homes and the street roped off while an FBI terrorism task force, Maryland state bomb squad, and local fire and rescue units solved the mystery. In an anguished letter, a company official assured the justice that during thirty years of operation, that was the first time it had "been linked with a potential act of terrorism. . . . We're as wholesome as apple pie." When asked about the incident, Justice O'Connor, who had undergone a mastectomy in 1988, reported that she had worn "my $30,000, museum-quality tennis shoes" in a recent fund-raiser race for breast cancer research—the estimated cost, she told a reporter, for security agencies to respond to the bomb scare at her home.[39]

Earlier, when Chief Justice Rehnquist began appearing on the bench sporting four gold stripes on each sleeve of his judicial robe, patterned after one worn by a character in a recent local Gilbert and Sullivan production, Justice Ginsburg decided something was missing. At a dinner given in the Court's Great Hall honoring the twenty-fifth anniversary of the establishment of the National Center for State Courts, she introduced the chief justice, then presented him with a formal white wig of the sort worn by British judges. Rehnquist placed the wig over his bald pate, then quickly removed it.[40] The justices' clerks, not surprisingly, are not invariably serious either. In 1988, for example, a previously disbarred lawyer, who had pled guilty to 114 counts of theft by deception in the late 1970s, petitioned for reinstatement to the Supreme Court bar. One of Justice Marshall's clerks agreed that the petition should be denied, adding, "I'm a softie, but I'm not *this* soft!"[41] Despite their lofty positions, moreover, the justices also shared the frustrations of modern life. "You are quite right," Justice White once wrote Justice Blackmun. "These word processors just aren't reliable."[42]

The Law Clerks

Whatever the tensions among the justices during the early years of Rehnquist's tenure as chief justice, Edward Lazarus has laid some of the difficulty at the feet of clerks for the Court's most conservative members. When Rehnquist's 1957 article accusing clerks of that era of a liberal bias first appeared,[43] Yale law professor Alexander Bickel, who had recently clerked for Justice Frankfurter, promptly objected, minimizing the clerks' influence, asserting that "as a group the law clerks will no more fit any single political label than will any other eighteen young Americans who are not picked on a political basis," and pointedly declaring that "[o]nly those who cannot conceive of intellectual disinterestedness, those who, having despaired of our system of higher education, having totally despaired also of the nation's future—only those have cause to be uneasy that there are clerks at the Court."[44]

Although declining to speculate about the influence of clerks on the Court in the 1950s, Lazarus suspected Bickel of "excessive protest" and suggested that the Yale scholar's views may have been influenced by his service as a clerk in the chambers of Justice Frankfurter, "who, as much as any judge ever, knew his own mind." Lazarus was certain, however, that Rehnquist's portrait of a liberal bias on the Warren Court did "not even begin to capture either the very significant power that clerks wielded at the Court during my time (and in the several years subsequent) or the very conscious and abusive manner in which clerks wielded that power for partisan ends."[45] When Lazarus arrived at the Court for the beginning of the October 1988 term, he found the clerks divided into "two well-entrenched and hostile camps," which included "a critical mass of ideological conservatives": four had previously clerked for Robert Bork; another had helped research Bork's *Tempting of America*,[46] which Lazarus described as the defeated Supreme Court nominee's "best-selling, score-settling diatribe against his political and jurisprudential opponents";[47] and several others were proteges of such leading Reagan lower court appointees as court of appeals judges J. Harvie Wilkinson and Ralph Winter. Ten of the thirty-six clerks that term, he noted, were members of the conservative Federalist Society, which Antonin Scalia had once served as adviser. Styling themselves "the Cabal," the conservatives, Lazarus quickly concluded, had come to the Court with a "desire for revenge" against "numerous perceived wrongs, most notably the tarring of Robert Bork." Indeed, one of their number had e-mailed his fellow conservatives shortly before the term began, "Every time I draw blood I'll think of what they did to Robert H. Bork."[48]

Some of the more liberal clerks also objected to aspects of Court routine. That same term, for example, sixteen clerks objected to aspects of the Christmas party held annually in the Great Hall. In a November 21 letter to the chief justice, all of Brennan's, Stevens's, and Marshall's clerks; three from Blackmun's chambers; and two O'Connor clerks expressed their concern "regarding the Court's celebration of Christmas." Noting that in the past, such events had included a large Christmas tree, a tape recorder playing Christmas music, wreaths around the busts of former chief justices, and the singing of carols, the clerks conceded that "[s]ome of us do not object to all these observances," but added that all were "concerned that members of the public as well as Court employees may be offended by them. We request an opportunity for a small group of us to discuss this matter with you at your convenience."[49] Justice Marshall was more to the point. "As usual, I will not participate," he had written the chief justice a week earlier. "I still prefer to keep church and state apart."[50]

The clerks' plea had no discernible effect, and Justice Marshall persisted in his refusal to attend the annual Christmas parties. Perhaps grateful, however, that contributions from the justices went to defray certain of the expenses connected with the affair, thereby obviating somewhat the establishment clause problems he considered inherent in government-funded religious celebrations on public property, the justice offered to "pay my share of the bill."[51]

In contrast to the feeble efforts of mostly liberal clerks to effect some modifications of the Court's annual Christmas rituals, Edward Lazarus found the conservative clerks the term he served "brash, snide, dimissive, and [confident] . . . they were ascendant— likely to have enough votes among the Justices to 'win' most of the time."[52] Whatever their actual influence, however, the moderating impact of the Clinton nominations and certain of the Reagan-Bush appointees, especially Justice Souter, has limited somewhat the impact of conservative ideologues on the Court, whether clerks or justices. Even so, the growing role of the clerks in the Court's work and product remains a significant concern to students of the judicial process.

The initial use of law clerks by American judges is generally traced to Horace Gray of Massachusetts, who first began the practice in 1875 as chief justice of his state supreme court, then took a clerk with him to the Supreme Court when he was appointed in 1882. The hiring of top recent law graduates as clerks in the higher federal judiciary became a general practice in the 1930s, and federal district judges were first authorized to appoint them in the 1940s. Initially each federal judge was entitled to a single clerk. Supreme Court justices received a second in 1947, and district court and court of appeals judges in 1965 and 1970, respectively. In 1970, Supreme Court justices were authorized a third clerk, and since 1978, each justice has been entitled to a fourth, while court of appeals judges have been allowed a third since 1980. At this writing, Chief Justice Rehnquist and Justice Stevens have three clerks each, the remaining justices four clerks.

Typically, Supreme Court justices rely heavily on favored faculty at elite law schools in securing talented clerks. Professor Paul M. Bator, who began teaching at Harvard after clerking for Justice Harlan during the 1956 term, was a major source, for example, of Harlan's clerks. In fact, after interviewing one of Bator's clerkship prospects, Harlan informed the candidate that his "ultimate selection . . . [was] entirely in [Bator's] hands."[53] As Edward Lazarus has indicated, moreover, justices and their surrogates seek to find clerks who are philosophically compatible with the chambers they will serve—whatever those leanings might be. In 1985, for example, Judge Frank M. Johnson, Jr., the veteran Alabama federal judge long praised and reviled for his courageous civil rights rulings, recommended Glen M. Derbyshire, one of his clerks on the Court of Appeals for the Eleventh Circuit, for a clerkship with Justice Marshall. In his formal letter, Judge Johnson praised Derbyshire's professional competence and moral character. But in an attached, handwritten note, Johnson also assured the justice, "You will find that this young man's philosophy is thoroughly compatible with ours," adding, "I would not recommend him to you if it were otherwise."[54]

At times, selection of clerks has also raised the sorts of questions the Court regularly confronts in affirmative action cases. When African American Harvard law professor Derrick Bell submitted a recommendation to Justice Marshall in behalf of Sheryll D. Cashin, one of his African American students, he noted that during the twenty years he had been writing clerkship letters for his black students, his references had spoken "honestly of the many talents these students possess but, sadly, seldom are these abilities measurable by the standards of traditional grades and honors." Bell happily informed Marshall on that occasion, however, that the candidate was "an impressive young woman in all the ways one would hope of a Harvard Law Student AND her spectacular performance is measurable in all the traditional ways: top undergraduate and law school grades, a prestigious . . . Marshall Scholar[ship] . . . , and a Harvard Law Review editorship with a very well-written Note completed and published in her second year." Cashin's law review note had dealt with affirmative action in the granting of public contracts. Earlier that term, the Court, in *City of Rich-mond* v. *Croson Co.* (1989),[55] with Justice Marshall among the dissenters, had struck down that city's minority set-aside program for the awarding of city construction contracts, largely on the ground that the arrangement was not narrowly limited to remedy the effects of specific incidents of prior discrimination. Had the Richmond city council followed the advice in Cashin's note, Bell asserted, "the result in the recent *Croson Co.* case might have been a happier one for set-aside proponents. Ms. Cashin is a very self-assured person, and had she been a legal consultant to the City at the time of the plan's adoption, I have no doubt that she would have fought hard for her view that specific discriminatory practices, public or private, are the basic starting point for narrowly-tailored remedies."[56]

Cashin got the clerkship. So, the following year, did Crystal Nix, another of Bell's black students with an impressive record. In his letter supporting Nix's application, the professor reminded Justice Marshall of the time in the early 1970s when the jus-tice, during a visit to Harvard, met with black students, who asked why he had not hired more black clerks. "You responded," Bell recalled, "that the work of the Court and the quality of the other clerks was such that your clerks had to be able to hold their own with the best in the country." Now, added Bell, "[i]t must be gratifying to you as it is to me that today, many black law graduates can compare with the best of their white classmates."[57] Both Bell and Marshall probably derived some satisfaction also from the letter *New York Times* executive editor Max Frankel wrote in behalf of Nix, a *Times* staff member before she left the paper to attend law school. "I write," observed Frankel, "to commend to you our former colleague, Crystal Nix, whose defection to the law remains a painful wound at the *Times.*" The continuing absence of significant diversity in the selection of clerks remains a sore point, however, with certain members of Congress.[58]

Traditionally, Supreme Court clerks have assisted their justices primarily in the screening of writ of certiorari petitions by which most litigants seek the Court's review of their cases, by drafting bench memoranda summarizing cases and the ques-tions they raise prior to oral argument, and in the preparation of opinions. Given the massive growth in the number of petitions filed in the Court since the caseload explo-sion of the 1960s, most justices have increasingly delegated the function of screening petitions to their clerks. Since 1972, in fact, most of the Court's members have partic-ipated in a "cert pool," first suggested by Justice Powell. Under the pool arrangement, one clerk in the pool prepares a certiorari memorandum recommending for or against a grant of review, then circulates the memorandum to all members of the pool.

The pool procedure places an enormous responsibility on the single clerk respon-sible for preparing the cert memo in a given case. As long as several justices declined to participate in the pool, preferring instead to have each petition examined in their own chambers, the chances were relatively low that a case raising significant legal questions might be overlooked in the pool process. At the time of Justice Marshall's retirement in 1991, however, only he and Justice Stevens were not participating in the pool. If Marshall's successor chose to participate, Stevens would soon be the only member of the Court not participating in the pool. At that point, Justice Kennedy wrote the chief justice a letter in which he termed the pool "vital to our operations" and recommended that Marshall's successor be encouraged to participate. Noting, however, that the new justice's participation "would mean . . . that only John [Paul Stevens] would be reviewing the petitions without the use of the pool memo," Kennedy had a suggestion. "I propose we alter the system so that in each case one pool member does not receive the pool memo but instead performs an independent review of the petition by whatever in-chambers system he or she selects. To insure review isolated from the [pool] memo, perhaps the exclusion rotation should be designed so a clerk for the excluded judge has not prepared the memo for that case."[59]

In his reply to Kennedy, Chief Justice Rehnquist agreed that growing participation in the pool was an "obvious weakness" in the arrangment. As originally conceived by Justice Powell, the chief justice recalled, all members of the Court were expected to participate. When initially only five justices took part, the pool posed little threat to the integrity of the screening process. But "[b]y a process of accretion it has grown to seven, and . . . that number could increase to eight if our new colleague decides to participate." Rehnquist was uncertain at that point whether he agreed with Kennedy's proposal, but recommended that he circulate his memorandum to the other justices. Justice Blackmun concurred with Kennedy. "So long as there [were] four or three not in the Pool," Blackmun wrote Rehnquist, "there was a brake against errors that might be committed by Pool writers. Now John is the only non-participant."[60] Later, Blackmun informed the chief justice that he had his clerks do an independent review and annotation of all pool memoranda and that he thought several other chambers followed a similar procedure. Although extra work for his clerks, Blackmun considered such a review a useful safeguard against errors in the pool process. His clerks had reported, moreover, "that it enhances their understanding of the Court's entire docket and helps make them better Pool memo writers in the process."[61]

Characteristically, however, Justice Scalia approached the matter from a different perspective. Most of the cert pool's mistakes related, in Scalia's judgment, "not to cases that are improvidently denied [review] but to cases that are improvidently granted." He recommended that the Court's certiorari grants be announced the second rather than the first Monday after the Court's vote to grant review. During that intervening week, he proposed, the chambers of one of the justices favoring the grant of certiorari would review the case "to be sure there are no unseen obstacles." Such a procedure, Scalia concluded, "would be more effective in reducing our mistakes than dropping one or two of us from the cert pool."[62]

Ultimately, apparently, no change in the pool procedure was implemented, except in individual chambers, and Justice Stevens, who has long favored creation of a new court responsible for screening petitions to the Supreme Court,[63] remains the only justice who does not participate in the pool. Especially given the number of patently frivolous petitions filed each term, primarily by prison inmates, the influence that individual clerks exercise over the screening process is not nearly so significant a cause for alarm as the clerks' growing role in perhaps the most important part of the work of the Court and individual justices—the preparation of judicial opinions. In the early years of the Warren era, justices generally continued the tradition of personally preparing first drafts of their opinions. My research on Justice Black, for example, drew extensively on drafts of his opinions that were clearly the justice's handiwork, written in longhand in Black's distinctive scrawl, often on legal pads.[64] Research in the papers of Justice Douglas and other justices of that period and before revealed the same pattern.

Even during the Warren years, however, certain justices permitted their clerks to prepare the first drafts of opinions. As a former Wall Street lawyer accustomed to delegating the drafting of briefs and related duties to young associates, the second Justice Harlan gave his clerks the task of preparing first drafts of opinions, with the justice orally outlining beforehand what he expected, then reviewing drafts for possible revision. After Harlan's eyesight largely failed him in the 1960s, such a pattern became an obvious imperative, for which the justice was assigned an additional clerk. Thus, despite their distinctive style, much of the prose of Harlan's opinions, including the assertion for the Court in *Cohen v. California* (1971),[65] upholding a First-Fourteenth Amendment right to offensive public speech, that "one man's vulgarity [was] another's lyric," originated with Harlan clerks.[66]

As the number of clerks assigned to each justice has grown, the number of members of the Court delegating the responsibility for opinion drafts to their clerks has also increased. Indeed, as of this writing, only Justices Stevens and Scalia, apparently, produce their own first drafts. Judge Richard Posner of the Court of Appeals for the Seventh Circuit, among others, has detailed some of the costs of this growing reliance on law clerks and conversion of judges from authors into editors in an era in which, ironically, the number of cases decided by signed opinion in the Supreme Court has been declining precipitously—from 161 in 1985, to 121 in 1990, to 91 in 1994, even though the Court's overall caseload has increased from 5,158 to 8,100 over the same period.[67] In a study of the federal judiciary, Judge Posner, who clerked for Justice Brennan, cited several differences between opinions drafted by law clerks and those written by judges, none supportive of delegation of the opinion-writing function to clerks. Some have expressed concern that the delegation of opinion drafting to law clerks may result in a change in the judge's literary style with every change of clerks; Judge Posner argued, however, that "the dominant effect is stylistic uniformity rather than variety." Any variation in the opinions of the same judge, he explained, was "more than offset by the smaller variance between opinions of different judges," a phenomenon Posner traced to the tradition in which clerks have been drawn from a "far more homogenous" pool than judges: "young, academically gifted, recent graduates of the nation's leading law schools, which provide a pretty uniform legal education." Thus, the "strongly marked individuality that traditionally characterized English and American judges and that makes the opinions of a Holmes, a Cardozo, or a Learned Hand instantly recognizable as their author's personal work," Posner lamented, was "becoming a thing of the past."[68]

Not surprisingly, as Posner noted, the standard style common to clerk-drafted opinions is that of "the student-written sections of the law reviews"—"colorless and plethoric, . . . heavily given to euphemism."[69] Like law review notes and articles, they also tend to be longer than opinions written by judges, in part because the clerks have become accustomed to writing in law school, but primarily because they are uncertain what can be omitted. "Not being the judge, [the clerk] is unsure what facts and reasons are essential and he naturally tends to err on the side of inclusion. And since he is not an experienced lawyer, many things are new and fresh to him that are old hat to his judge, other judges, and other readers of the opinion."[70] Inexperience also leads to heavy reliance on "copious footnotes and abundant references to secondary literature," as well as efforts "to conceal novelty and to disguise imagination as deduction" on the part of clerks who "feel naked" without such "ostentatious display[s] of the apparatus of legal scholarship."[71]

Even more critical than such problems of style, prolixity, focus, and flow, Posner contended, was the impact of clerk-authored opinions on the credibility accorded the judicial product. "The less that lawyers and especially other judges regard judicial opinions as authentic expressions of what the judges think, the less they will rely on judicial opinions for guidance and authority. . . . The more the thinking embodied in opinions is done by law clerks rather than by judges, the less authority opinions will have."[72]

Posner acknowledged that his concerns were by no means "universally shared."[73] Judge Harry T. Edwards of the Court of Appeals for the District of Columbia had staunchly defended the existing clerkship system, for example, contending that "careful judges will not allow an opinion to issue in their name until the words constituting the opinion precisely reflect their views of the proper disposition of the case."[74] But Posner was not convinced. "The qualification implicit in the adjective 'careful' is surely important," he observed, adding, "and Judge Edwards does not address the temptation to judicial carelessness that comes from having a staff of eager young assistants quite willing to take responsibility from the judge's shoulders. More important, adoption is not creation. If it were, contemporary opinions would have the same feel as opinions written in the days when most judges wrote their own opinions. They do not."[75]

Judge Posner is very persuasive. But the influence of the law clerks on the Rehnquist Court is not the only probable explanation for growing concerns about the quality of the Court's opinions. The clerks' backgrounds and, arguably, their considerable egos, have obviously affected the style and quality of the Court's opinions, helping to account for the weaknesses Judge Posner has described. Compounding such problems, however, have been the increasing complexities of the issues that the Court has faced, combined with deep internal divisions among the justices over judicial philosophy and approach to specific legal issues—divisions only partially resolved by recent retirements from the bench.

The June Crunch

At work also may be what is termed at the Court the "June crunch"—end-of-term pressures to complete the writing and circulation of opinions, announce the final batches of decisions for the term, and adjourn for summer recess by the end of that critical month. Problems posed by the "spring pileup" and proposals for eliminating it have been a regular subject of intracourt memoranda and Court conferences throughout Chief Justice Rehnquist's tenure. Comparatively early in the 1989 term, for example, the chief justice sent his colleagues a memorandum urging them to complete assigned opinions in a timely fashion. Since moving to the Court's center seat, Rehnquist had attempted to assure that all justices be given responsibility for drafting approximately the same number of opinions for the Court each term. He noted in his memorandum, however, that such a policy did not take into account the difficulty a particular opinion might give its assignee. In the future, therefore, he planned to pay close attention to chambers to which one or more uncirculated majority opinions had been assigned more than four weeks earlier, to those with one or more uncirculated dissents for which a majority opinion had been circulated more than four weeks previously, and to any chamber that had not voted in a case in which both the majority and dissenting opinions had been circulated. Emphasizing that such situations cast "no negative reflection" on the chambers involved, he announced nevertheless that in the future he would give "some preference" in the assignment of additional majority opinions to those justices "who are 'current' with respect to past work."[76]

Given its obvious implications for future opinion assignments on the Court, which was at that time extremely divided, Rehnquist placed his new policy on the agenda for the justices' January 5, 1990, conference. Since Justice Stevens was to be absent from that session, he wrote the chief justice a lengthy letter summarizing his views, circulating copies to other justices. Stevens applauded Rehnquist's efforts to assure prompt completion of opinions, but questioned the wisdom of relying "too heavily" on the factors the chief justice had cited in his memorandum. First, Stevens argued, the quality of the Court's work product was more important than its "prompt completion." Undue emphasis on speed could have an adverse effect not only on quality, he added, but on "the orderly production of a group of opinions." The justice offered the following example: "If I am assigned three opinions, one of them requiring a study of the record and considerable research and two that can be written on the basis of little more than a careful review of the briefs, which should I work on first? To get my fair share of assignments [of obvious interest to any justice], I should probably do the easy cases right away and save the hard one until my desk is clear. But often all three will be finished more promptly if I write the first draft of the hardest case first so that a law clerk can be doing the editing, footnoting, and rewriting of that draft while I turn out the other two."[77]

Although agreeing that dissents were generally easier to write and should usually be ready for circulation within two or three weeks after the majority opinion was first circulated, Stevens also pointed out that justices could find themselves in dissent in several cases at once or a dissenting justice could find an issue that the majority considers routine "of exceptional importance to the dissenters," as had been the case, he noted, with Justice Scalia in *Morrison v. Olson* (1988),[78] upholding the constitutionality of the federal independent counsel statute. "I do not think a justice's share of majority opinions should be reduced because he is temporarily preoccupied with such an opinion, or because," he pointedly added, "he is out of step with the majority in a large number of cases." In fact, wrote Stevens, "The incorrect impression that the majority votes as a 'block' could be enhanced if a disproportionate number of Court opinions were written by those Justices."

Stevens was clearly concerned about the impact of Rehnquist's policy on his chambers. His secretary had reviewed the interval between the date Stevens received an opinion assignment and his first circulation of an opinion the previous term, finding that only five had met Rehnquist's four-week deadline. "Several others were circulated a few days later," Stevens conceded, "but this statistic persuades me that there is probably an arbitrary element in your use of a four-week deadline that may well distort the assignment process."

To whatever extent Rehnquist actually gave "some preference" to "current" chambers in opinion assignments, the June crunch has not been overcome. Later in the 1989-90 term, and the following term as well, he circulated additional memoranda suggesting ways of coping with the problem.[79] By June of 1991, however, he was expressing concern that despite a steady reduction in the number of cases decided each term, "we still have the same amount of congestion, flurry, and backup in June as we did in the earlier terms." His first reaction, he noted, was "to cast about and find some human fault that is causing all of this." Now, he had decided the problem "is probably endemic to the system."

During a term, the Court normally hears oral arguments two weeks each month. To cope with the June crunch, Rehnquist recommended that the justices eliminate the second week of arguments in April. While "frankly recognizing" that such a schedule would reduce the maximum number of cases heard from 152 to 140, the change would also mean that opinion assignments for cases decided in April could be made a week earlier and that there would be only half as many opinions to write. The term deadline for circulating majority opinions could be moved up to around May 15, and that for circulating dissents to about June 1. Thus, the justices would have four weeks, rather than two, following the dissent deadline within which to complete their work and recess.[80]

Despite such efforts, the June crunch persists. Meanwhile, the number of signed opinions of the Court each term has continued to decline, falling below a hundred cases annually, as noted earlier, by the 1994-95 term. Whatever the cause, the justices of the Burger and Rehnquist Courts have simply appeared more overwhelmed by their workload than their counterparts of an earlier era, even though they are giving full review to substantially fewer cases, have largely delegated the screening and opinion-writing functions to their clerks, and have more clerks on which to rely than justices of the past.

Other Procedural Issues

The Court faces other essentially procedural problems as well. In a letter written to the chief justice on one of the occasions Rehnquist was attempting to manage the end-of-term pileup of cases, Justice Blackmun suggested that the justices do away with Thursday conferences in May and June. The Court had begun holding Thursday conferences in addition to its traditional Friday sessions, Blackmun reminded Rehnquist, "during Chief Justice Burger's regime at a time when we had the hot-lead printshop and when [announcements of] opinions [in Court] were all confined to Mondays." Burger had established Wednesday and Thursday conferences in part to reduce the burden and expense of weekend printshop operations. Now that decisions were being announced on any day the Court was in session and printshop technology had changed, Blackmun recommended that the Thursday conferences be eliminated late in the term, freeing the justices for other work. At the same time, he praised Rehnquist's "expeditious handling" of the conferences, noting that he could not recall any May or June sessions going beyond noon.[81]

Although Justice Blackmun predicted there would be "little positive reaction" to his proposal, the Court has modified its conference schedule.[82] During the two weeks each month the Court usually sits to hear cases, the justices normally meet in conference on Wednesday afternoons to discuss cases argued the previous Monday, then hold their Friday conference to discuss cases argued on Tuesday and Wednesday. As Justice Blackmun noted in his letter, Chief Justice Rehnquist has been efficient in leading conference sessions. But the Court's caseload has quadrupled since the 1950s, from about two thousand petitions annually to around eight thousand. As in the past, nearly 80 percent of petitions are denied review without conference discussion. Thus, even though the Court devotes additional time to conferences and gives full review to considerably fewer cases annually than it once did, many more petitions are given at least some discussion at conference, leaving the justices less time to devote to argued cases.[83]

Perhaps not surprisingly, given the delay in filling Justice Powell's seat, the justices of the Rehnquist Court have also examined ways of coping with vacancies on the bench, as well as the disqualification of one or more justices from participation in particular cases. In 1988, for example, they discussed at conference the possibility of asking Congress to enact legislation permitting them to invite a retired justice to sit on cases in the absence of a full Court. Following reflection on the matter, Justice Stevens wrote the chief justice to suggest further discussion at conference. Such an arrangement, he asserted, would not only resolve the problems created by a prolonged illness or delay in filling a vacancy, but would also make the prospect of retirement more appealing to eligible jurists and would be "consistent with the congressional decision to continue paying retired judges and justices their full salaries in order to facilitate [their] retirement." Finally, of course, wrote Stevens, it would enable the Court to act in the admittedly rare case in which the necessary quorum of six justices could not otherwise be mustered.[84]

Opponents of the proposal at conference had cited two principal disadvantages. First, temporary changes in the Court's composition "might introduce an element of either actual or apparent inconsistency in the development of legal doctrine." Second, the problem of selecting cases on which a retired justice might sit, and of determining which justices should be invited to sit on particular cases, "might be awkward or divisive." Responding to the first concern, Stevens asserted that it would not be necessary to invite a retired justice to sit whenever such an opportunity arose. The Court might decide, for example, that only active justices hear "an especially important or controversial case," just as senior judges on the federal courts of appeals were ineligible to hear cases reviewed *en banc*, or by the entire court, rather than in the three-judge panels normally convened to hear appeals court cases. But even putting aside such cases, Stevens asserted, many significant cases involving statutory construction and conflicts among circuits over the proper disposition of similar cases would remain—cases "on which a definite answer would be more important than the particular make-up of the

Court." In Stevens's view, the public would be more likely to accept a decision by a nine-member Court than a four-three decision or affirmance of a lower court decision by an equally divided Court.

Stevens acknowledged, of course, that his experience on the Seventh Circuit Court of Appeals had made him more familiar with, and less apprehensive about, the use of changing panels than he might otherwise have been. Their successful use in the circuits had led Stevens to believe, however, that "the occasional use of a retired justice on this Court would not diminish its authority or prestige." Nor was Stevens concerned that the selection of justices for particular cases would create insurmountable problems. He suggested that the unanimous consent of the justices might be required, but thought selection by majority rule of the justices would also be feasible and similar to the procedures used to select masters in original cases. If several retired justices were available, moreover, selection could be made randomly or by rotation or invitation.

Stevens's proposal has not been adopted, and not surprisingly perhaps, given the deaths of certain retired justices and the precarious condition of others. Even so, it further reflects the continuing concern of Rehnquist Court justices with finding ways to manage their caseloads.

Fortunately, questions on the Rehnquist Court regarding the recusal of justices from participation in particular cases, which in part prompted Justice Stevens's proposal, have not provoked to date the outcry that Rehnquist's refusal to disqualify himself in the *Laird* case aroused during his first term on the bench. In 1990, however, Justice Rehnquist received a letter from an Indianapolis firm representing one of the parties in a case before the Court.[85] The letter indicated that a Rehnquist nephew was an associate in the firm, but had not been involved in the case at issue.[86] In the past, Rehnquist and other members of the Court had disqualified themselves in such situations. The justices used the case, however, to announce a new policy that the federal rules governing recusal did not require disqualification under such circumstances.[87] In another case that same year, television newsman Tim O'Brien reported that the petitioner—a mentally ill state inmate challenging treatment against his will with antipsychotic drugs—had written Justice O'Connor a threatening letter. O'Brien indicated that evidence was available that the justice was notified of the threat at the time it occurred. But O'Connor informed other justices that she had "no present recollection" of the matter and, in any event, had no plans to disqualify herself "unless my colleagues believe I should."[88]

Threats of the sort Justice O'Connor received are not uncommon for members of the Court, even if the records of the two most recent chief justices have not been of the sort likely to make them the targets of the sort of roadside billboard impeachment appeals to which Earl Warren was regularly subjected. As the author of *Roe v. Wade*, Justice Blackmun was a frequent object of death threats, presumably from anti-abortion extremists zealously, but selectively, committed to the sanctity of life. In 1985, someone fired into Blackmun's suburban Washington apartment. And while police, who recovered a bullet from a chair, speculated the shot was fired randomly or at a distant target, the incident occurred at the same time officials were investigating identical death threats mailed to Blackmun, Justice Powell, and New York Senator Alfonse D'Amato.[89]

Nor has Blackmun been the only Rehnquist Court justice subjected to threats. In March of 1988, for example, the Court's marshal at the time, Alfred Wong, indicated in a memorandum to the justices that during the past year his office had received direct information concerning sixteen threats to the Court and individual justices, while more than a hundred persons of the many investigated by the Secret Service for threats against the president or vice president that year had also shown at some point what Wong euphemistically termed "a direction of interest" toward Supreme Court justices. Many of them, Wong added, "were considered dangerous." Noting that his office was already calling on the U.S. marshals service to provide protection for justices participating in public events out of Washington, Wong also indicated that the Secret Service had frequently recommended that the justices receive protection whenever they left the capital and that cabinet officers already received such protection, even though the "threat" level against them, with the exception of the secretary of state, was "so low . . . as to be invisible."[90]

Following the mail-bomb murder of federal judge Robert Vance in Alabama the following year, Wong sent the justices a memorandum regarding suspicious packages received through the mail. Detailing the "Do's and Don't's" for such situations, he emphasized that bomb-sniffing dogs were available for the Court from capitol police or the Secret Service and that in serious cases his office could call on local bomb squads and the Army's explosive ordnance unit. Urging the justices not to lift, slide, or move any package found at their front doors, Wong also recalled his brief tenure with New York City's bomb squad many years earlier. "It was always helpful when the fire department was the first to respond to a suspicious package found in a public area," he remembered. "Despite many warnings not to do so, firemen invariably would pick up or move the package. We then knew it was safe for us to handle."[91] Wong obviously did not want the justices to provide such assistance to local bomb units.

Almost as frustrating for judges as threatening psychotics, if not so potentially dangerous, are what Chief Justice Rehnquist has termed "frequent filers"—litigants notorious for initiating frivolous suits—of which the Rehnquist Court has surely had its fair share. In a November 1990 memorandum to the conference, the chief justice identified three individuals who had filed 21, 43, and 11 petitions, respectively, with the Court, and nineteen litigants who had filed at least 6 claims, each relating to a single set of circumstances—a total of over 354 certiorari petitions, all of which had been rejected. Although conceding that such petitions consumed no conference time, Rehnquist expressed concern about their drain on the time of law clerks and the Court clerk's office, and suggested that restrictions be imposed on the repetitive claims of such litigants.[92]

Frivolous filings have hardly ceased, however. During the 1996-97 term, for example, the justices had before them various civil rights allegations and claims under the Racketeer Influenced and Corrupt Organizations Act (RICO) that one Eileen Vey had filed against President and Mrs. Clinton, numerous senators, judges (including the chief justice), foreign officials, and private citizens. Over the past six years, Vey had filed twenty-six such submissions with the Court, all of which had been denied and were patently frivolous. Only two months earlier, the Court had gone further, instructing the clerk of the Court not to accept any further petitions unless Vey paid the required fees.[93] Since even that action had failed to deter what the Court characterized as her "abusive" conduct, the clerk was instructed not to accept any further petitions from her in noncriminal matters unless Vey complied with the Court's rules.[94] On this occasion, the chief justice had recused himself.

Even here, however, the Court was not unanimous in its approach to such repetitive suits. Justice Stevens dissented, citing an earlier, similar case in which he had also filed a dissent. In that 1992 case, Stevens, joined by Justice Blackmun, had argued, as he had on earlier occasions, that the Court's resources could be better used by a simple denial of the litigant's frivolous petitions than "by drafting, entering, and policing the order the Court enters today." Any "theoretical administrative benefit" the Court's approach might offer, Stevens contended, was "far outweighed by the shadow it casts on the great tradition of open access that [previously] characterized the Court's history."[95]

Like certain of the suits brought before them, some of the disputes among the justices over the Court's internal operations have been, to put it charitably, relatively trivial. On assuming the Court's center seat in 1986, Chief Justice Rehnquist revised the docket sheets on which justices maintain vote talleys on actions taken in individual cases, as well as possible notes of conference discussions. Justice Blackmun soon protested, complaining in a memorandum to the conference that the columns on the new sheets were much too narrow and that two were essentially unnecessary. Justice Marshall was already using a revised docket sheet that Blackmun thought had "much merit" and attached to his memorandum for his colleagues' consideration. Justice Brennan had also begun using a docket sheet similar to Marshall's. "The Chief, I understand," added Blackmun, "prefers to have our names listed in order of juniority; the rest of us employ the seniority order so that we go down the page as the votes are cast." Based on an apparent poll of other chambers, Blackmun reported that if Justice Brennan were willing to accept Marshall's docket sheet, seven members of the Court would favor the same form. Justice Stevens's docket sheets could then be separately run, Blackmun proposed, to include additional material Stevens wished placed on the reverse side of the sheet; and the chief justice's sheets could also be run separately, "to list [our] names in order of juniority" rather than seniority.[96]

Justice Stevens concurred with Blackmun's suggestions for the front of the docket sheet, which the new chief justice also accepted. But his colleague's memorandum also prompted Stevens to suggest a change in the order of voting at conference. From the days of Chief Justice John Marshall, it had been customary for the chief justice to be the first to discuss a case in conference, followed by the other justices in descending order of seniority, and for the justices to vote on a case in reverse order. At some point during the Warren or early Burger period, however, the order had been changed, with justices discussing and immediately voting on a case in descending order of seniority.[97] In a memorandum to the conference, Justice Stevens reminded his colleagues "that there was once a time when the voting order on argued cases began with the junior justice and ended with the Chief Justice." Since as an associate justice Chief Justice Rehnquist had "experienced the disadvantage of speaking only after most of his colleagues had already voted," Stevens wondered whether Rehnquist "might be sympathetic to considering a return to the Court's old practice of having the discussion of argued cases proceed down the ladder but have the voting then go up the ladder."[98] As with Stevens's suggestion regarding retired justices, however, the Court did not return to the traditional pattern of conference discussion and voting.[99]

At times, of course, the justices' debates over judicial procedure have been intertwined with substantive disputes over legal issues. In 1990, while they were considering proposed changes in the federal rules of criminal procedure, Justice Scalia balked at a proposal that U.S. magistrate judges be authorized to issue warrants for searches abroad under certain circumstances.[100] Justice Brennan quickly responded, challenging an implication in Scalia's memorandum to the conference that under the Court's recent decision in *United States v. Verdugo-Urquidez*,[101] a search warrant, in Brennan's words, "was *never* required when the location of the search is outside the United States and its territories."[102] The *Verdugo-Urquidez* majority, over the dissents of Brennan, Marshall, and Blackmun, had held that the Fourth Amendment guarantee against unreasonable searches and seizures did not apply to a search by federal Drug Enforcement Administration (DEA) agents of the Mexican residence of a Mexican national who had no voluntary connection to the United States. But the case, Brennan insisted, had not decided whether the Fourth Amendment and its warrant clause "would apply to searches of overseas residences owned by United States citizens." Scalia had suggested that *Verdugo-Urquidez* had also decided that question when Chief Justice Rehnquist, speaking for the majority, asserted, while discussing the effects of applying Fourth Amendment safeguards to nonresident aliens, "Indeed, the Court of Appeals [had] held that absent exigent circumstances, United States agents could not effect a 'search or seizure' for law enforcement purposes without first obtaining a warrant—*which would be a dead letter outside the United States*—from a magistrate in this country."[103] Disputing Scalia's suggestion, Brennan declared, "Such an aside does not a holding make." Supporting retention of the proposed revision, he asserted that as long as the constitutionality of warrantless searches of the foreign residences of U.S. citizens remained an open issue, there was "much to be gained by providing a mechanism by which United States agents" could obtain a warrant in such cases. A majority ultimately decided, however, to send the proposed rules changes to Congress for final action without the disputed provision.[104]

The Veil of Secrecy

Traditionally, the justices of the Supreme Court have zealously guarded the confidentiality of their internal deliberations. Justices alone attend the Court's conferences. They regularly impose restrictions on access and use of the papers they choose to place with the Library of Congress or other archives. Some have severely edited their papers; as his death approached, for example, Justice Black insisted that family members burn his conference notes. Since 1987, law clerks have been given a Code of Conduct instructing them not to discuss the Court's work with outsiders, even after their clerkships have ended. In fact, a 1989 revision of the code admonishes clerks to be circumspect even with their counterparts from other chambers, avoiding, for example, any hint of a justice's likely vote in a pending case.[105] Radio and television coverage of the Court's proceedings are prohibited, and while the justices on rare occasions have appeared in unofficial photographs and television documentaries—Justice Blackmun even impersonated Joseph Story in the motion picture *Armistad* (1997) following his retirement—only one photograph of the Court in session—taken in 1935, the year the Court first moved to its present quarters—is known to exist. The justices are also constantly vigilant against improper news gathering connected with their work, even though clerks and even justices have occasionally leaked confidential information, including advance word of forthcoming rulings, to the press.

As college professors are well aware, members of the Rehnquist Court have been at least as insistent on maintaining the secrecy of their proceedings as justices of other periods. When in 1993, for example, political scientist Peter Irons produced "May It Please the Court," an excellent collection of edited audio recordings of the Court's oral arguments in twenty-three landmark cases, a majority on the Court vehemently protested. Contending that Irons had violated the agreement under which he had obtained access to the tapes, the justices initially threatened legal action and instructed the Court's marshal to deny Irons further access to the archives. Only in the face of considerable negative public reaction to its stance did the justices relent, instructing the National Archives to make audio recordings available for a nominal fee to interested researchers.[106]

During Chief Justice Rehnquist's first term in the Court's center seat, the justices also investigated a television reporter's apparent breach of the secrecy of the conference room. On June 11, 1987, Sheryl Farmer, secretary to the Court's information officer, had escorted Tim O'Brien of ABC News and a crew of two into the conference room for a brief filming session. Farmer soon noticed that O'Brien was looking in the fireplace, leaned over to pick up several sheets of paper, and began examining them. Emphasizing that he was a guest, Farmer asked O'Brien to return the papers to the fireplace. But a few minutes later, she spotted the newsman thumbing through a list she had not remembered his bringing with him into the conference room and also making notes. When she asked him about the notes, O'Brien assured her they related only to the filming. But when she showed the list to another member of the Court's staff, he and the film crew were ordered to return to the public information office. Asked if he had taken anything from the conference room or taken notes on any material he picked up there, O'Brien replied, according to a summary of the incident, that he had not, but that "even if he had seen anything confidential, he would not 'use' it because he had been a guest of the Court and his filming was allowed as a courtesy."[107]

On learning of the incident, Chief Justice Rehnquist informed his colleagues that if O'Brien "did what he appears to have done," he had "committed a rather gross breach at least of courtesy if not of ethics, and that something should be done about it." The reaction of other justices varied. Justice Stevens, the member of the Court most sympathetic to media requests for access to its proceedings, agreed that Rehnquist should talk with O'Brien, but also suggested that the Court's staff may have erred in permitting a film crew in the conference room on a conference day without first making certain no confidential materials were in "plain view." Stevens's guess was that O'Brien would decide the news value of anything he obtained was "not worth the loss of our good will and that no serious harm will come from the incident."[108] Noting that O'Brien had apparently seen a memorandum containing opinion-writing assignments, Justice Brennan recommended that the newsman be denied "any further privileges" if he made any use of the materials,[109] while Justice Blackmun, who like Rehnquist and Brennan was also offended, reported that he was not "too disturbed" by the incident. Blackmun suggested, in fact, that the justices and those responsible for cleaning the conference room "may tend to be a little careless in throwing complete papers into the fireplace," adding, "They ought to be torn up if they contain any information presumably confidential." Noting the steady "accumulation of material in the fireplace week after week," Blackmun also proposed that a fire in the fireplace "once in a while is probably a good thing."[110]

Justice Scalia's reaction was characteristically witty and pointed. "I am formally appalled—which means not really surprised but for the record wish to be noted as surprised—by the incident you describe." O'Brien apparently had "not only conducted a trash search in the Conference Room of the Supreme Court of the United States (an activity that we had some difficulty justifying in an apartment garage) but then lied about it and sought to remove material from the room contrary to authorized instructions." Obviously unsympathetic to the adage, as he put it, that "boys will be boys," Scalia did "not think [the] incident should be made light of, but should be regarded as (what it was) an entirely unacceptable breach of the terms on which members of the press are allowed into the public portions of this building." If the chief justice found Farmer's account more credible than O'Brien's "denial (if he persists in it)," Scalia recommended that Rehnquist exclude the reporter from the Court. "I think," he added, that "the incident and its outcome should also be made known to the other members of the press corps, so that they may know what we expect."[111] Justice White concurred. Although agreeing with O'Connor and Powell, among others, that he and his colleagues "should be more careful about permitting press access to the Conference room and about what papers we throw into the fireplace," White contended that "our own lack of care hardly excuse[d]" O'Brien's behavior and recommended that the justices "at the very least indicate our displeasure in a letter or statement that could be circulated among the press corps even if this might make O'Brien a hero in the minds of some."[112] Justice Marshall was more succinct. "This incident," he wrote Rehnquist, "enforces my original vote to keep the press out of the conference room (period)." The first black justice was equally protective of his own chambers. When one of his clerks invited a visitor to Marshall's chambers on the anniversary of the *Brown* decision, he promptly sent his clerks a curt memo: "This is to inform you that my policy has been and is that nobody gets invited to my Chambers by anybody but me. And I intend to continue that policy."[113]

Belatedly, a seemingly contrite O'Brien eventually wrote Chief Justice Rehnquist a letter of apology. He had indeed, he conceded, "removed from the fireplace and briefly examined what appeared to be a 'status report' of cases." He "shouldn't have done it," he added, but "[a]t the time," he wrote, "the invasion of the Court's privacy seemed both minimal and totally harmless. I had no plans to 'use' or discuss with anyone what I saw." O'Brien especially regretted, he noted, the loss of "trust and friendship of people I respect and admire and whose opinions I highly value" that the incident may have caused, as well as "the grossly incorrect impression" his actions may have created "that this is the way my network and I gather news."[114]

The ending to O'Brien's letter was maudlin at best. Noting that his work as a reporter had "exposed [him] to the vast beauty of our country and the unique greatness of our Constitution," he assured Rehnquist that covering the Court had been "one of the great joys" of his life, that the incident had left him "feeling simply awful," and that "it would never happen again." In a gracious response, the chief justice accepted O'Brien's apology and predicted his colleagues would also, adding, "We live and we learn."[115] In response to the incident as well as the Court marshal's growing concern about security, however, Rehnquist limited the size of tour groups visiting the justices' dining room and gymnasium and banned tour visits to the conference room.[116]

Media requests to photograph the justices or broadcast their proceedings have received short shrift on the Rehnquist Court. During production of the PBS documentary "This Honorable Court," the justices stipulated that there was to be no filming or photographing of any justice or group of justices in the conference room or on the bench, and none during the traditional handshaking ceremony among the justices immediately preceding oral argument. But they left to the judgment of individual justices whether they would be filmed or photographed in the courtroom or other places in the Court. Nor did they seek to set any limit to the number of justices the producers could interview, or where outside the Court building such interviews would be conducted.[117] Later, the Court denied the same production unit's request to televise Justice Kennedy's investiture,[118] as well as the request of former network television reporter and presidential press secretary Ron Nessen of the Mutual Broadcasting System for permission to cover the Kennedy ceremony on radio, despite Nessen's assurances that "Obviously, there would be no commercial announcements on the program."[119] Only Justice Stevens, apparently, favored radio coverage of the ceremony, "[u]nless Justice Kennedy feels otherwise."[120]

When Justice Thomas was appointed to the Court, a Washington attorney acting on behalf of various media organizations requested television, radio, and still camera coverage of the swearing-in ceremony at the Court. In memoranda to his colleagues, Justice Stevens recommended that media coverage be permitted, but also contended that the White House installation ceremony conducted in recent years on such occasions served "no useful purpose and should be avoided if possible. The fact that the President's political advisors regard it as a useful and important photo-opportunity," added Stevens, "emphasizes why I think we should do whatever we can to terminate the practice."[121] Stevens proposed that the Court advise the president that the only installation ceremony, in the justices' opinion, should take place in the courtroom and that Presidents Reagan, Ford, Nixon, Kennedy, and Eisenhower had attended past investitures. "I suspect," he added, "that if our preference were made known to the President, he might well overrule his political advisors because of his respect for the Court as an independent institution."

Concurring with Stevens, Justice Blackmun complained that White House ceremonies for newly appointed members of the Court simply meant further "politization of the appointment process." Blackmun thought the practice had probably begun during the Reagan administration and "certainly" had not taken place when he, Chief Justice Burger, and Justices Stevens and O'Connor were appointed. "I refused to attend the White House ceremony the last time," Blackmun declared, "and I shall not attend this time, if there is one." While noting that he would "defer to any strongly expressed wishes of the Chief Justice," Blackmun also found merit in Stevens's support of the media request to televise a "ceremonial occasion" at the Court.[122]

Warning against permitting the camel to get his nose under the tent, Justice Scalia opposed camera coverage of the Thomas investiture "unless there is some offsetting benefit," such as elimination of the White House ceremony. Scalia conceded that the "President's men are going to want good theater and attractive close-ups," but emphasized that an investiture, unlike oral argument, was "for show and not for go, and awareness of the cameras' presence is no problem." Unless the chief justice thought it appropriate to propose a single "in-Court ceremony," however, Scalia favored the continued exclusion of media coverage. Other justices generally appeared of the same mind or opposed media coverage of the event altogether.[123]

During his tenure as chief justice, Rehnquist had always inquired of presidents whether they would prefer to come to the Court or have a separate White House installation ceremony when new justices were appointed, with the response invariably in favor of the separate ceremony. The chief justice was also concerned about the "considerable say" a president would want were a televised investiture held at the Court, as well as with the security and logistical problems such an event would create. Nor was he certain the president would accept such an arrangement, and he found it "somewhat awkward to invite someone to your house on the condition that he not invite you to his house."[124] Since the Judicial Conference of the United States, which the chief justice headed, had recently begun a four-year pilot program of televising the proceedings of several district courts and courts of appeals, he also considered it unwise to lift the Court's ban on televised oral arguments pending the outcome of the pilot project; he doubted, in any event, that the televising of a ceremonial occasion attended by the president was the best way to introduce television to the Court. In a memorandum to the conference, Rehnquist agreed with Scalia that there were "too many imponderables to think that we would be happy with the result if we offer the White House some sort of trade-off." Even so, he put the issue of camera coverage of the Thomas investiture to a vote of the justices. Voting by letter, a majority opposed coverage.

Similar media requests have also been denied. In 1988 and 1989, the justices refused to allow National Public Radio and ABC News to provide radio coverage in *Morrison v. Olson*, the independent counsel case,[125] and *Webster v. Reproductive Health Services*.[126] When *Life* magazine proposed a group portrait of the justices for an issue celebrating the 200th anniversary of the 1789 Judiciary Act, a request the Court's information officer favored in part because it "sets no precedent the Court need follow except every 100 years,"[127] Justice Marshall questioned "[w]hat happens if one or more other magazines or papers make the same or similar requests,"[128] and Justice Scalia agreed, contending that it was "a bad idea to accede to such a request from a single commercial organization" and adding, "That is precisely why we have an official photograph."[129] And when the same magazine proposed that each justice contribute a historical profile of a provision of the Bill of Rights to a special issue commemorating the 200th anniversary of its adoption, the chief justice responded for a unanimous

Court "that it would not be appropriate for us to undertake [that] sort of writing," particularly since "[w]e are constantly engaged in deciding what the various provisions of the Bill of Rights mean in cases which come before us."[130]

On at least two occasions during Chief Justice Rehnquist's first decade in the Court's center seat, the decisions of retiring justices regarding the disposition of their papers have also provoked concerns among their colleagues relative to the confidentiality of the Court's deliberations. In 1980, Justice Brennan had taken the unprecedented step for a sitting justice of making his papers, on file in the Library of Congress's manuscript division, available to researchers, beginning with his years on the Warren Court and then gradually expanding access to include cases decided five years earlier. In 1990, the year of his retirement, the chief justice and Justice O'Connor discussed with Brennan their concern, and that of certain other members of the Court, that his liberal policy regarding access to his papers was jeopardizing the deliberative process. "They have suggested," wrote Brennan in a memorandum to the conference following the meeting, "that, to avoid embarrassment to any of our colleagues, I should not grant access to files that may include any written material from Justices who are still sitting on the Court." Since yielding to that suggestion at that point would have meant the closing of all Brennan's files for the years following 1962, when Justice White joined the Court, the justice was unwilling to comply with his colleagues' request. He emphasized, however, that access had been limited to academic researchers, typically law professors and political scientists, and also assured other justices that "[w]orks published by scholars who have used my papers . . . have been uniformly substantive and, on the whole, worthwhile. To my knowledge, there have been no irresponsible uses of this material." In an effort to appease his colleagues, Brennan also instructed the Library of Congress to secure more detailed information from researchers regarding the purpose of their research and to impose a time limit on the papers' use.[131] In addition, he largely limited access to papers covering the Rehnquist Court years to his official biographer.[132]

If Justice Brennan's policy regarding access to his papers concerned certain of his colleagues, the disposition of Justice Marshall's collection must have caused them extreme distress. Justice Marshall had outraged many Americans in 1987 with his conclusion, in a speech delivered in Hawaii, that there was little reason to celebrate the Constitution's bicentennial. In April of 1986, African American historian John Hope Franklin of Duke University sent Marshall materials that would provide the basis for his controversial address. "Thanks so much for the material on the Bicentennial celebration or whatever else it is," the justice soon responded. "You have given me just the materials I need which will be used when the appropriate time arrives. As of now, everything is so hush hush around here I don't know what is going on about the anniversary. I think I will wait to be asked to do something and then let them have it."[133]

When the opportunity arrived, the justice did not mince words. Rejecting the "complacent belief" that the vision of the Constitution's original framers had "yielded the 'more perfect Union' it is said we now enjoy," Marshall declared that he did not "find the wisdom, foresight, and sense of justice exhibited by the Framers particularly profound." Instead, the government they established "was defective from the start, requiring several amendments, a civil war, and major social transformations to attain the system of constitutional government and its respect for the freedoms and individual rights we hold as fundamental today." In his judgment, many Americans would understandably prefer to commemorate not the original Constitution, but "the suffering, struggle, and sacrifice that has triumphed over much of what was wrong with the original document now stored in a vault in the National Archives. They will observe the anniversary with hopes not realized and promises not fulfilled. With these citizens, I join. I will not celebrate the birth of a 200-year-old document. I will celebrate its life."[134]

Critics of Marshall's bicentennial remarks could legitimately complain that his preoccupation with the framers' failure to confront slavery and related issues in an enlightened manner had unduly affected his judgment regarding an otherwise masterly document. But much citizen reaction merely confirmed the justice's reference to "hopes not realized and promises not fulfilled." One letter writer purporting to be a Macon, Georgia, planter suggested that the justice was descended from slaves on his ancestors' plantation and invited Marshall to attend a family reunion "in costume of the occasion." The justice did not answer that letter. But when an Alabama insurance agent called him a "disgrace to your race" and declared that retirement would be the "best thing" Marshall could do "for the negro race . . . and the country as well," Marshall had a ready rejoinder. "I am not at all surprised," he wrote, "at hearing such comments from a person who as late as 1987 still spells 'negro' with a small 'n.'"[135]

Marshall's address also irritated certain of his colleagues, but not nearly so deeply as the access the justice decided to grant those wishing to examine his papers. In 1991, the justice signed an agreement with the Library of Congress for disposition of his papers. Two clauses in the deed provided, first, that "the Collection shall be made available to the public at the discretion of the library," and, second, that use would be limited to "researchers or scholars engaged in serious research." In May 1993, following Marshall's death in January, the library, giving the deed a broad construction, granted virtually unrestricted public access to his papers.

Beginning with articles in the *Washington Post* on May 23, the day before the collection was open to public inspection, various newspapers and magazines drew on the Marshall collection for revealing accounts of internal conflicts among the justices in abortion, homosexual rights, and other controversial issue areas. In an angry letter to library head James H. Billington, Chief Justice Rehnquist accused the library staff of misconstruing Marshall's wishes and warned that "[u]nless there is some presently unknown basis for the library's action, we think that future donors of judicial papers will be inclined to look elsewhere for a repository."[136]

Family members and close friends of the justice were equally incensed. William T. Coleman, Jr., a longtime friend who had been the first black Supreme Court clerk (to Felix Frankfurter) and had served in the Ford cabinet, told a reporter that the justice had initially wanted all his papers burned on his death and had relented only on the plea of Coleman and others that they should be preserved for history. Karen Hastie Williams, a lawyer and goddaughter of the late justice, reported that the library's action had dismayed Marshall's widow, Cecilia.[137] In an Op-Ed piece for the *Washington Post*, journalist Carl T. Rowan revealed that the justice had returned a $250,000 advance and the promise of more in royalties to a publisher rather than expose private Court discussions in a book Marshall and Rowan had planned to write. Marshall's decision, Rowan declared, reflected his revulsion at such disclosures.[138]

In a *New York Times* Op-Ed article entitled "Library of Congress—or School for Scandal?" two of Marshall's former clerks, Crystal Nix (1991-92) and Sheryll D. Cashin (1990-91), also expressed their shock and dismay. On numerous occasions in many separate conversations, even during the fall of 1991, when Marshall was supposedly granting "indiscriminate" release of his papers to the public, the justice had made clear to them, they asserted, his commitment to the Court's ethic of confidentiality. In fact, when a former clerk (probably Edward Lazarus) announced plans to write a book on the Court, Marshall had told the clerks that he did not believe anyone with inside knowledge of the Court's work "should discuss its inner workings, in any manner and under any circumstances." When he retired from the Court, he turned down hundreds of requests for books, interviews, and public speeches; and when Nix and Cashin urged him to write a memoir, not about his years on the Court but about his life as a civil rights lawyer, they felt "the brunt of his furor." As the first black justice, he was especially sensitive to any breach of Court confidentiality by his chambers. "I don't want people to be able to say, 'See, you can't trust those Negroes,'" they remembered his often saying. Nix and Cashin acknowledged that Marshall had indeed signed an agreement leaving access to the library's discretion. But they were equally certain the justice had not intended that documents concerning recent cases or active justices be released or that "reporters, litigators, and voyeurs" be granted access. The library's decision to the contrary "display[ed] arrogance, disrespect, and gross disregard for the truth," they declared. "Justice Marshall and the Court deserve better."[139]

But members of the library staff were equally confident that they were carrying out, as James Billington put it, Justice Marshall's "exact intentions in opening access to his papers." Nor would the librarian comply with William Coleman's request that access be suspended for two weeks while Marshall's wishes were further explored. Billington, assistant manuscript curator David Wigdor, and another member of the library staff had met with Justice Marshall at the Court when the agreement was signed. At that meeting, Billington recalled in a statement to the press, the justice was "in very good form intellectually and personally very expansive . . . . He made it very clear he wanted the collection available without restrictions after his death." Wigdor agreed. "It sounded to me like a very informed decision that [the justice] had thought about pretty carefully."[140] As for the clause limiting access to serious researchers or scholars, Billington stressed that the library had always included journalists—the principal object of Marshall family members' concern—in that category, excluding only such casual researchers as high school students in search of a term project and tourists. "It would be highly inappropriate," insisted Billington, "for somebody running a public institution in a democratic society, which I am, to set myself up as a dictatorial arbiter as to who is a serious researcher."[141]

In a few days, press attention to the controversy subsided. Nor for the near term at least did the dispute affect the decisions of retiring justices regarding their choice of an archive for their papers. Justice White, who retired the year of Marshall's death, had already made plans to donate his papers to the Library of Congress when the controversy over Marshall's papers arose. White not only made no change in his plans as a result of the controversy, but even wrote the library a letter disassociating himself from Chief Justice Rehnquist's letter and indicating that it was not clear the library had done anything inconsistent with his late colleague's wishes.[142] Justice Blackmun, the next justice to retire, also donated his papers to the library.

But the chief justice's letter did speak for a majority of the Court's membership. Like the Court's opposition to the public distribution of audio recordings of its oral arguments and to broadcast coverage of its proceedings, moreover, the letter suggests a Court concerned to the point of obsession with the secrecy of its deliberations—a concern that has apparently persisted to the present and calls to mind Justice Stewart's admonition in the *Pentagon Papers Cases* that "when everything is classified, then nothing is classified."[143]

3

Governmental Power

The Rehnquist Court, like other Courts of the post-1937 era, has focused largely on the scope and limits to noneconomic personal rights. Over the years of Chief Justice Rehnquist's tenure in the Court's center seat, however, the justices have also regularly confronted a variety of issues relating to the scope of national authority, separation of powers, interstate relations, federalism, and related questions of governmental power. More importantly perhaps, the Court's recent decisions expanding the reach of the Fifth Amendment's takings clause and its Fourteenth Amendment counterpart, as well as rulings involving challenges to congressional authority over the states, have suggested a weakening of the justices' commitment to the constitutional double standard, that is, the doctrine under which the protection of economic freedoms and the limits to Congress's power over the states have largely been left to the political arena rather than the judicial process since 1937. This chapter examines a variety of governmental power issues raised before the Court, while chapter 4 focuses on the current status of the double standard.

Judicial Authority

We turn first in this chapter to decisions and changes in the law that have affected the scope of federal judicial power and jurisdiction. With the unanimous support of his colleagues, Chief Justice Rehnquist campaigned vigorously early in his tenure for an end to the Court's congressionally mandated obligation to review certain categories of cases on appeal from lower courts. In a December 2, 1987, letter to a member of a subcommittee of the House judiciary committee, Rehnquist asserted that every justice for the previous ten years had supported the "virtual abolition" of the Court's mandatory appellate jurisdiction. Substantial elimination of the mandatory caseload, he argued, would maximize the time given to cases that "truly require[d]" the Court's attention and would also "reduce the importance of the highly artificial yet quite troublesome distinction that [had] emerged between certiorari and direct appeal"—a distinction in which the Court assigned "no precedential weight" to denials of petitions for writs of certiorari, while the summary dismissal of a mandatory appeal "constitute[d] technical precedent even though the Court gives no reason for the dismissal." Retention of mandatory jurisdiction, on the other hand, meant that litigants could continue to bring cases to the Court as a matter of right, without regard to their general public significance, and that the Court, given its heavy and growing caseload, would continue to dispose of many such cases through "the generally unsatisfactory device of summary dispositions."[1]

Ultimately, the Court's plea was successful. Under legislation effective September 25, 1988, the mandatory writ of appeal was largely confined to certain voting cases and other litigation required by Congress to be tried in a three-judge district court.[2] Apart from its few mandatory appeals, original cases, and cases certified to the high bench by a lower federal court, then, the Court has become "virtually an all-certiorari tribunal."[3]

In overlapping lines of decisions, combined with congressional legislation, the Court has also limited habeas corpus review of criminal convictions and the retroactive application of newly announced procedural rules. During the Warren era, the Court had generally applied a three-part formula in determining whether judicial changes in the constitutional rules of criminal procedure should be retroactively applied to pending cases. The formula involved consideration of the purpose of the newly announced rule, the extent of justified past reliance by law enforcement and courts on rules replaced by the new requirement, and the effect of retroactive application on the administration of criminal justice. Under that formula, retroactive application of a newly announced rule to cases pending on direct appeal or habeas corpus review was more likely if the purpose of the new rule was to enhance the truth-determining function of criminal justice in situations where officials could not reasonably have been expected to have anticipated the new rule and if retroactive application was unlikely to result in the release of many convicted felons.[4] Justice Harlan had argued, however, that while every new procedural requirement should apply fully to all cases still pending on direct appeal when it was announced, the rule should not be applicable in habeas corpus challenges to criminal convictions previously upheld on direct appeal.[5]

In *Teague v. Lane* (1989),[6] a plurality came close to embracing Justice Harlan's position. Speaking for herself, the chief justice, and Justices Scalia and Kennedy, Justice O'Connor concluded that new constitutional rules of criminal procedure should be applied retroactively to cases on collateral review only under two circumstances that Justice Harlan had delineated: first, if the new rule placed "certain kinds of primary, private individual conduct beyond the power of the criminal law-making authority to proscribe," and second, "if it requires the observance of 'those procedures that . . . are "implicit in the concept of ordered liberty." ' "[7] Such an approach,

O'Connor explained, was necessary to assure compliance with the principle of finality, "which is essential to the operation of the criminal justice system."[8] Although questioning the propriety of the Court's making such a significant change in the law without briefs and argument, as well as what he viewed as the plurality's unduly narrow construction of the fundamental fairness element of Justice Harlan's formula, Justice Stevens also argued that the Court should adopt Harlan's retroactivity analysis, creating a majority behind that position, which the Rehnquist Court has continued to embrace.[9]

The result, of course, has been to substantially reduce the impact of retroactivity on the criminal justice system. Under *Teague* and its progeny, habeas corpus relief is unavailable for persons whose convictions were upheld in state courts based on precedents in effect at the time the petitioner's conviction became final, even if the construction given such precedents were subject to reasonable debate. In *Butler v. McKellar* (1990),[10] for example, a man arrested on an unrelated assault charge for which he retained counsel was told that he was a suspect in a woman's murder. After receiving *Miranda* warnings, he signed a waiver of his rights and made incriminating statements about the murder. At trial the court denied his motion to suppress the statements, following which he was convicted and sentenced to death. After his conviction became final on direct appeal, he filed habeas corpus proceedings in federal district court. The district court dismissed, and the court of appeals affirmed, rejecting Butler's argument that the Supreme Court's decision in *Edwards v. Arizona* (1981)[11] required police to refrain from all further custodial questioning once an accused invokes his right to counsel on any offense. When the Supreme Court, in *Arizona v. Roberson* (1988),[12] later barred police-initiated interrogation following a suspect's request for counsel in a separate investigation, Butler sought a rehearing. But the court of appeals denied the request, concluding that the *Edwards-Roberson* restrictions on police interrogations were only marginally related to the truth-determining function of criminal justice and thus were not retroactively applicable to habeas proceedings. The Supreme Court affirmed on the ground that *Roberson* had announced a "new" procedural rule, even though a majority of the *Roberson* Court had concluded that *Roberson* was controlled by *Edwards*. "[T]he fact that a court says that its decision . . . is 'controlled' by a prior decision," Chief Justice Rehnquist concluded for the *Butler* majority, "is not conclusive for purposes of deciding whether the current decision is a 'new rule' under *Teague*." Reasonable minds could have differed over the proper outcome in *Roberson*, Rehnquist asserted; thus "*Roberson* announced a 'new rule.'"[13] Nor, he added, did *Roberson* fall within the two exceptions articulated by Justice Harlan and embraced in *Teague*.

In dissent, Justice Brennan, joined by Justice Marshall and in part by Justices Blackmun and Stevens, accused the majority, "under the guise of fine-tuning the definition of 'new rule,'" of stripping state inmates "of virtually *any* meaningful federal review of the constitutionality of their incarceration." According to the majority, Brennan declared, a legal ruling was to be deemed "new" as long as its correctness, "based on precedent existing when the petitioner's conviction became final, [was] 'susceptible to debate among reasonable minds.'" Under *Butler*, therefore, a state inmate could "secure habeas relief only by showing that the state court's rejection of the constitutional challenge was *so* clearly invalid under then-prevailing legal standards that the decision could not be defended by any reasonable jurist." Declaring that "[r]esult, not reason, propels the Court today," Brennan charged the majority with having precluded habeas corpus review "for all but the most indefensible state court rejections of constitutional challenges" and asserted that, with *Butler*, "the Court has finally succeeded in its thinly veiled crusade to eviscerate Congress' habeas corpus regime."[14]

Despite the protests of Brennan and others, a broad construction of *Teague* remains firmly entrenched in the Court's case law, especially in capital suits. In *Simmons v. South Carolina*,[15] a 1994 case, the Court held that a capital defendant must be permitted to inform his sentencing jury that he is parole-ineligible if the prosecution presents arguments to the jury regarding the defendant's potential future threat to society if given a life sentence rather than death. Speaking for the majority in a 1997 case, *O'Dell v. Netherland*,[16] Justice Thomas concluded that *Simmons* established a "new" rule that did not fall within the *Teague* exceptions. But the debate over the reach of the retroactivity doctrine in habeas cases also continues. *O'Dell* was a five-four decision. In a dissent joined by Justices Souter, Ginsburg, and Breyer, Justice Stevens characterized the rule announced in *Simmons* as a fundamental principle of procedural fairness squarely within the Harlan-*Teague* exception to nonretroactivity in habeas proceedings for rules "implicit in the concept of ordered liberty." Since *Teague*, Stevens conceded, the Court had never found a newly announced procedural rule to meet that exception. But, in his view, the *Simmons* rule was of that "bedrock" character.[17] Stevens further contended that, contrary to the Court's conclusion, *Simmons* had not announced a new rule. In a 1977 case, he noted, a plurality had concluded that a defendant's due process rights were violated when his death sentence was based in part on information he had no opportunity to deny or explain.[18] Nine years later, in *Skipper v. South Carolina* (1986),[19] all the justices had cited the earlier case with approval as establishing the "elemental due process requirement that a defendant not be sentenced to death" based on such information. Given those cases, Stevens could not understand how any "reasonable jurist" in 1988, when O'Dell's conviction became final, could "have thought that [he] did not have a right to rebut the prosecutor's future dangerousness arguments."[20]

Building on Burger Court precedents, the Rehnquist Court has also limited the scope of federal habeas review in other ways. In *Withrow v. Williams* (1993),[21] a closely divided Court refused to extend to the interrogation process its decision in *Stone v. Powell* (1976),[22] barring Fourth-Fourteenth Amendment exclusionary rule claims in the federal habeas proceedings of state defendants who had a full and fair opportunity to raise such arguments in the state courts. Overturning the conviction of a defendant whom police threatened to lock up if he did not cooperate, and who was not informed of his *Miranda* rights until forty minutes after questioning began, Justice Souter emphasized that the *Miranda* warnings, unlike the Fourth-Fourteenth Amendment claim at issue in *Stone*, "enhance[d] the soundness of the criminal process by improving the reliability of evidence introduced at trial." Although reluctantly embracing the position that *Miranda*, like the Fourth-Fourteenth Amendment exclusionary rule, was a judicially created prophylactic designed to deter police misconduct, rather than a personal constitutional right, Souter also asserted that *Miranda* "safeguards 'a fundamental *trial* right.'"[23]

But *Withrow* has hardly been typical of Rehnquist Court habeas rulings. In *Withrow* itself, Justice O'Connor, joined by Chief Justice Rehnquist, cited broad police acceptance of *Miranda* as sufficient reason for refusing to extend its safeguards to federal habeas proceedings and declared, "applying *Miranda*'s prophylactic rule on habeas does not increase the amount of justice dispensed; it only increases the frequency with which the admittedly guilty go free."[24] And Justice Scalia, joined by Justice Thomas, would have required the presence of "unusual equitable factors" in a case before permitting relitigation in habeas proceedings of issues state defendants had "already been afforded an opportunity for full and fair litigation in the [state] courts."[25] The Court has also limited the circumstances under which successive habeas corpus petitions can be filed in a case. In *McCleskey v. Zant* (1991), for example, a majority, per Justice Kennedy, held that a petitioner had the burden of explaining why newly raised challenges to his conviction were not raised in earlier proceedings and of establishing that further review was necessary to prevent a fundamental miscarriage of justice.[26] In dissent, Justice Marshall, joined by Justices Blackmun and Stevens, condemned the *Zant* Court's departure from earlier precedent[27] and what he termed its "unjustifiable assault on the Great Writ."[28] But under intense lobbying by Chief Justice Rehnquist, among others, Congress in 1996 enacted the Antiterrorism and Effective Death Penalty Act, which codified and expanded the restrictions on habeas review that the Court had imposed in *Zant* and related cases. The 1996 statute stipulated, among other things, that no claim raised in a second or successive habeas corpus petition could be decided unless based on a new constitutional rule that the Supreme Court had retroactively applied to habeas cases and that, but for the constitutional error alleged, no reasonable fact finder would have found the applicant guilty of the crime for which he was convicted. Before being permitted to file such a petition in a federal district court, moreover, petitioners were obliged to satisfy a court of appeals that the suit satisfied the statute's requirements, and the court of appeals decision was not reviewable in the Supreme Court.

Later that year, a unanimous Court, speaking through the chief justice, upheld the law against claims that it unconstitutionally limited the Court's appellate jurisdiction.[29] In separate opinions, however, Justices Stevens and Souter, joined by Justice Breyer, emphasized that the law did not foreclose all Supreme Court review in such cases—through, for example, original petitions filed with the Court or review under the All Writs Act.[30] In his opinion, moreover, Justice Souter noted that "if it should later turn out that statutory avenues other than certiorari for reviewing a gatekeeping determination [by a court of appeals under the law] were closed, the question whether the statute exceeded Congress's Exceptions Clause power [to regulate the Supreme Court's appellate jurisdiction] would be open. The question could arise if the Court of Appeals adopted divergent interpretations of the gatekeeper standard" for barring second or successive habeas petitions.[31] In a 1997 case, moreover, a narrow majority, speaking through Justice Souter over the dissents of the chief justice and Justices Scalia, Kennedy, and Thomas, held that the new law did not apply to noncapital cases pending at the time of its adoption.[32]

The Court's constructions of the Eleventh Amendment prohibition on federal lawsuits brought against states by citizens of other states, and citizens or subjects of foreign nations, have been equally mixed. In a 1994 case, a majority concluded that a railway owned by the Port Authority of New York and New Jersey, and created pursuant to the Constitution's interstate compact clause, lacked the immunity accorded states under the Eleventh Amendment. A number of elements relating to the compact in question, Justice Ginsburg observed for the Court, suggested a state intent to clothe the railway with immunity, as well as congressional concurrence in that judgment, particularly provisions establishing state control over port authority commissioners and state court decisions characterizing the authority as an agency of the parent states. But other, more powerful indicators, especially the states' lack of financial responsibility for the authority, Ginsburg concluded, pointed away from a conferral of immunity.[33] In an earlier case, however, Justice Scalia, the current Court's principal professed textualist, construed the Eleventh Amendment "to stand not so much for what it says" and held for a six-three majority, despite the amendment's reference to citizens or subjects of other states or foreign nations, that Indian tribes could not sue states without their consent.[34] When Scalia first circulated his opinion in the case, one of Justice Marshall's clerks reported that Scalia's effort "contains no surprises; in addition to denying Native Americans access to federal court, Justice Scalia describes the Eleventh Amendment in terms calculated to increase its scope generally."[35]

In *Seminole Tribe v. Florida*,[36] a 1996 case, a five-four majority went further, holding that Congress lacked the authority under its commerce power to authorize Indian tribes to sue states. Overruling a plurality's contrary judgment in an earlier case,[37] Chief Justice Rehnquist concluded for the Court that congressional abrogation of state sovereign immunity violated fundamental principles of federalism.

The majority rested its decision largely on *Hans v. Louisiana*,[38] the controversial 1890 decision that invoked general notions of sovereign immunity in construing the Eleventh Amendment to forbid lawsuits brought against states by their own citizens, as well as by the citizens of other states and foreign nations, to which the amendment's language referred. In powerful separate dissents, Justices Stevens and Souter, the latter joined by Ginsburg and Breyer, condemned *Hans* and what Stevens termed the majority's "shocking . . . affront to a coequal branch of our Government." The Court had acknowledged Congress's power to abrogate state sovereign immunity under its authority to enforce the Fourteenth Amendment, but Rehnquist left unanswered the obvious question why congressional authority under the Fourteenth Amendment should be treated differently from Congress's other powers for Eleventh Amendment purposes. Yet "with [that] narrow and illogical exception," Justice Stevens declared, the Court was now preventing "Congress from providing a federal forum for a broad range of actions against States, from those sounding to copyright and patent law, to those concerning bankruptcy, environmental law, and the regulation of our vast national economy."[39]

Nor was *Seminole* to be the Court's final recent expansion of the state sovereign immunity doctrine. In one decision at the conclusion of its 1998-99 term, a five-four majority held that state governments enjoy immunity from private damage suits brought in state as well as federal court to secure rights established in federal law. Finding such immunity inherent in statehood, state sovereignty, principles of federalism, and perhaps in a sort of natural or divine law more reminiscent, a dissenter thought, of James I than James Madison, the justices refused to permit Maine probation officers to sue the state over its failure to honor overtime provisions of the federal Fair Labor Standards Act of 1938 (FLSA). In another ruling, the Court invoked the immunity doctrine to shield Florida from the obligation to defend itself in federal court from lawsuits attacking a state college student educational financing scheme claimed to violate a private company's rights under federal patent and trademark laws. And in a companion to that case, the Court struck down a congressional statute that had expressly abrogated state sovereign immunity in patent infringement suits. Although reaffirming its position that Congress could revoke state immunity in laws enacted under its authority to enforce provisions of the Fourteenth Amendment, the majority, speaking through Chief Justice Rehnquist, rejected, strangely enough, the contention of the private plaintiff and the United States that a law enacted to protect patent rights from state infringement fell within Congress's Fourteenth Amendment authority to forbid state deprivations of property without due process of law, finding the statute instead to be an exercise of congressional lawmaking power under Article I of the Constitution. Congress could, of course, authorize federal officials to file suits against states to enforce the rights of individuals under such federal statututes. As Justice Souter, joined by Justices Stevens, Ginsburg, and Breyer, noted in his lengthy and cogent dissent, however, such relief was more apparent than real, given the limits of Justice Department resources. The Court, Souter observed, had thus "abandon[ed] a principle nearly as inveterate, and much closer to the hearts of the Framers [than the immunity doctrine]: that where there is a right, there must be [an adequate] remedy" to protect against its violation.[40]

While generally limiting the reach of civilian federal tribunals in habeas, Eleventh Amendment, and other cases, the Rehnquist Court has significantly expanded the jurisdiction of military tribunals. Since the Fifth Amendment's language makes the right of grand jury inapplicable to "cases rising in the land and naval forces," the Supreme Court has long held that most other procedural safeguards of the Bill of Rights also apply only to civilian proceedings.[41] In light of the obvious impact of such a stance on the reach of procedural rights guaranteed by the Constitution, the Warren Court handed down a number of decisions limiting the scope of military jurisdiction. The Court denied the military jurisdiction over the offenses of civilian dependents[42] and discharged soldiers, even for offenses committed during military service,[43] and, in its most controversial such ruling, *O'Callahan v. Parker* (1969),[44] a six-three majority limited court-martial proceedings only to the service-connected offenses of military personnel.

During the Burger era, the Court broadly construed the types of offenses that could be termed "service connected." In *Schlesinger v. Councilman* (1975),[45] for example, a majority concluded that the marijuana offense with which an Army captain was charged was service connected, even though it occurred in his off-post apartment while he was off duty and was otherwise consistent with the sorts of offenses the Court in *O'Callahan* and other cases[46] had characterized as non-service connected. In dissent, Justice Brennan, joined by Justices Douglas and Marshall, bemoaned what he considered the Court's departure from "an unbroken line of decisions" precluding "expansion of military jurisdiction at the expense of the constitutionally preferred civil jurisdiction."[47] Terming the crime at issue "a common everyday type of drug offense that [civilian] federal courts encounter all over the country every day," Brennan asserted that an offense could not be designated service connected "merely because the participants are servicemen."[48]

Ultimately, however, that was precisely what the Rehnquist Court concluded, overruling *O'Callahan* and holding that a person's status as a serviceperson was sufficient to invoke court-martial jurisdiction, whatever the nature of the offense involved. In *Solorio v. United States* (1987),[49] a general court-martial convened to try Solorio for the sexual abuse of fellow coast guardsmen's minor daughters in his private home dismissed the prosecution on *O'Callahan* grounds. After the Coast Guard Board of Military Review reinstated the charges and the Court of Military Appeals affirmed on the ground that the offenses charged were service connected, the Supreme Court upheld reinstatement of the prosecution, declaring that a court-martial's jurisdiction depended solely on the defendant's status as a member of the armed forces. Speaking for five members of the Court, Chief Justice Rehnquist cited the language of Article I, Section 8, Clause 14 of the Constitution, granting Congress power "[t]o make Rules for the Government and Regulation of the land and naval Forces," as the principal basis for its interpretation of court-martial jurisdiction and chided the *O'Callahan* Court's "less than accurate" reading of English and American history in reaching a contrary conclusion, while presenting his own version of that history in defending the majority's position.

In joining the chief justice's opinion, Justice O'Connor wrote Rehnquist that she had "enjoyed the history lesson,"[50] while Justice Powell indicated that he "was particularly interested in [Rehnquist's] reexamination of English history."[51] But not all members of the Court were impressed with the Court's decision or rationale. Concurring only in the Court's decision, Justice Stevens argued that the petitioner's offenses were sufficiently "service-connected" to confer military jurisdiction and attacked the majority for "reaching out to reexamine" *O'Callahan*. "I had thought," Stevens declared, "that we all could agree that such drastic action is only appropriate when essential to the disposition of a case or controversy before the Court. The fact that any five Members of the Court have the power to reconsider settled precedents at random, does not make that practice legitimate."[52]

The other dissenters' differences with the majority were more fundamental. In a bench memorandum prepared for Justice Marshall's reference when attorneys presented oral argument in *Solorio*, a Marshall clerk speculated that the government's "real concern" in seeking to have *O'Callahan* overturned was with "off-base use of drugs," but noted that the Court of Military Appeals had held that such offenses were "ordinarily service-related" and that, in any event, "these issues aren't before us."[53] Fearful perhaps that a majority might use *Solorio* as a vehicle for overruling *O'Callahan*, Marshall had voted to deny certiorari in the case. When it was decided, he, Brennan, and Blackmun found themselves in dissent. At Brennan's request, Marshall said he would "be delighted to take on [a *Solorio*] dissent."[54]

In his opinion for the Court, as noted earlier, Chief Justice Rehnquist had dealt at length with military history in concluding that the congressional authority to make rules and regulations for the military was intended to reach all actions of military personnel, whether service connected or not. For Marshall, however, the constitutional language most relevant to a proper resolution of the case was the Fifth Amendment provision denying the right to a grand jury only to those persons involved in "cases arising in the land or naval forces, or in the Militia, when in actual service in time of War or public danger." The text of that provision, argued Marshall, was inconsistent with the *Solorio* majority's conclusion that military status was the only relevant factor in a determination of court-martial jurisdiction. That language, he insisted, limited military jurisdiction in terms of the nature of the case, not the defendant's status; and the *O'Callahan* decision had turned not on whether Congress had Article I power to "create court-martial jurisdiction over all crimes committed by service members, but rather [on] whether Congress, in exercising that power, had encroached upon the rights of members of Armed Forces whose cases did not 'arise in' the Armed Forces."[55] If a case involving a member of the armed services was not service connected, it was not one within the only exception to the grand jury recognized in the Fifth Amendment and thus was not within the reach of court-martial jurisdiction. Were such a distinction not made, Marshall asserted, quoting from *O'Callahan*, military jurisdiction could "be expanded to deprive every member of the armed services of the benefits of an indictment by a grand jury and [by implication] a trial by a jury of his peers."[56]

In the same year the Court expanded court-martial jurisdiction, the justices also overturned a Civil War-era decision denying federal courts remedial power in extradition cases. In *Kentucky v. Dennison* (1861),[57] the Court held that states have an Article IV obligation to extradite fugitives back to the states from which they fled, but also ruled that the federal courts have no power to enforce that nondiscretionary, ministerial duty on states that refuse to extradite. For the next 125 years, state governors at times granted asylum to fugitives from other states, citing inhumane prison conditions, insufficient evidence of guilt, questionable jurisdiction, and related grounds for their decisions. When protracted negotiations for the extradition of a fugitive from Iowa to Puerto Rico failed in the 1980s, however, Puerto Rican officials filed suit in federal district court, contending that Iowa's inaction violated both Article IV and the federal extradition statute. Citing *Dennison*, the district court dismissed and the Court of Appeals for the Eighth Circuit affirmed. Speaking for the Supreme Court, with three justices concurring on narrow grounds, Justice Marshall rejected *Dennison*'s fundamental premise that the states and federal government were in all respects coequal sovereigns as flagrantly inconsistent with current law. Since the federal extradition statute clearly applied to Puerto Rico, Marshall also concluded for the Court that the commonwealth could seek federal court relief under the statute without regard to whether the Article IV extradition clause, the text of which referred only to states, had any application in a case involving a U.S. territory.[58]

Presidential Immunity

A number of Rehnquist Court cases dealing with the reach of judicial power have elaborated upon the Court's position regarding the nature and degree of immunity from civil damage suits to which government officials are entitled.[59] A related 1997 case involved a suit brought against an Alabama county and its sheriff by a death-row inmate whose conviction was overturned on a finding that the sheriff had intimidated prosecution witnesses into making false statements against the accused, while suppressing evidence of his innocence. A five-four majority concluded that Alabama sheriffs were state rather than county policymakers for law enforcement purposes and that the county was thus not liable under federal civil rights legislation for the actions of its sheriff. Justice Ginsburg, joined by Justices Stevens, Souter, and Breyer, registered a sharp dissent, declaring that "[a] sheriff locally elected, paid, and equipped, who automatically sets and implements law enforcement policies operative within the geographic confines of a county, is ordinarily just what he seems to be: a county official."[60]

But the most important, and some would say wrongheaded, Rehnquist Court decision to date regarding the scope of judicial authority grew out of the Paula Jones suit against President Clinton. In *Nixon v. Fitzgerald* (1982),[61] a five-four Burger Court majority, speaking through Justice Powell, held that presidents and former presidents are absolutely immune from damage suits arising from actions within the "outer perimeter" of their official duties. Citing the unique importance of the presidency, Powell concluded that such cases would unduly divert the president's energies from his official tasks and might inhibit him from exercising his powers and duties in a fearless and aggressive manner. "As is the case with prosecutors and judges—for whom absolute immunity now is established—a President," Powell reasoned, "must concern himself with matters likely to 'arouse the most intense feelings.' . . . Yet, as our decisions have recognized, it is in precisely such cases that there exists the greatest public interest in providing an official 'the maximum ability to deal fearlessly and impartially with' the duties of his office. . . . This concern is compelling where the officeholder must make the most sensitive and far-reaching decisions entrusted to an official under our constitutional system."[62]

Interestingly, in light of the position the Court was later to assume in *Clinton v. Jones* (1997),[63] Powell also based the *Nixon* ruling on the "sheer prominence of the President's office." Given the visibility of the presidency, the impact of the president's actions "on countless people," and the president's obligation to "make the most sensitive and far-reaching decisions entrusted to any official under our constitutional system," the majority thought it inevitable that "the President would be an easily identifiable target" for civil suits. "Cognizance of this personal vulnerability," Powell asserted, "frequently could distract a President from his public duties, to the detriment of not only the President and his office but also the Nation that the Presidency was designed to serve."[64]

Four years earlier, three members of the *Nixon* majority—Rehnquist, Burger, and Stevens—had favored absolute immunity for other executive officials as well. In *Butz v. Economu* (1978),[65] involving a member of President Nixon's cabinet, a five-four majority concluded that such officials are generally entitled only to qualified immunity from suit; they could be sued for damages, but only if they knowingly violated someone's rights or reasonably should have known their actions were illegal. In dissent, Justice Rehnquist, joined by Burger and Stevens as well as Justice Stewart, suggested that all federal officials were generally entitled to absolute immunity and argued that "an occasional failure to redress a claim of official wrong doing . . . result[ing] from the doctrine of absolute immunity" was "a lesser evil than the impairment of the ability of responsible public officials to govern."[66] Citing the steady growth in lawsuits against public officials, Rehnquist considered it contrary to "logic and common experience to suggest that officials will not have [the increase in such suits] in the back of their minds when considering what official course to pursue," adding, "It likewise strains credulity to suggest that this threat will only inhibit officials from taking action which they should not take in any event. It is the cases in which the grounds for action are doubtful, or in which the actor is timid, which will be affected by today's decision."[67]

In *Nixon v. Fitzgerald*, Rehnquist and the other *Butz* dissenters still on the Court obtained absolute immunity for the president by securing the votes of Justice O'Connor, who had been recently appointed to the high bench, and Justice Powell, who had joined the *Butz* majority but was willing to recognize an absolute immunity for presidents, if not for subordinate officials. Justice White, author of the Court's *Butz* opinion, registered a dissent joined by three other members of the *Butz* majority: Brennan, Marshall, and Blackmun. The *Nixon* case involved an Air Force management analyst fired from his position after he testified before a congressional subcommittee about cost overruns and unexpected technical difficulties in the development of an airplane. Such incidents eventually led to statutory protections for "whistle-blowers," and in his *Nixon* dissent, Justice White expressed concern that under the Court's decision a president would be able "deliberately [to] cause serious injury to any number of citizens even though he knows his conduct violates a statute or tramples on the constitutional rights of those who are injured. . . . He would be immune regardless of the damage he inflicts, regardless of how violative of the statute and of the Constitution he knew his conduct to be, and regardless of his purpose."[68] The majority had considered absolute immunity necessary to the effective functioning of the presidency. White could not agree "that if the Office of President is to operate effectively, the holder of the Office must be permitted, without fear of liability and regardless of the function he is performing, deliberately to inflict injury on others by conduct that he knows violates the law."[69]

Chief Justice Burger emphasized in a concurring opinion that *Nixon v. Fitzgerald* involved only official actions, but he also went further, declaring that "President[s], like Members of Congress, judges, prosecutors, or congressional aides—all having absolute immunity—are not immune for acts outside official duties."[70] In *Clinton v. Jones*,[71] a unanimous Court embraced Burger's position. In challenging Paula Jones's damage suit against President Clinton for "abhorrent" sexual advances he allegedly made toward her while Arkansas's governor, the president's counsel had not sought the absolute immunity the Court had granted former President Nixon. Instead, they claimed only a temporary immunity from further proceedings in the case until his tenure in the presidency had ended, citing as the primary basis for his claim the distractions such suits pose for sitting presidents. The Court, speaking through Justice Stevens, refused to recognize even a temporary presidential immunity from suits unrelated to the performance of official duties. Rejecting any basis in precedent for such a claim, Stevens noted that earlier immunity decisions had been rested primarily on the need to assure that officials can perform their duties vigorously and "without fear that a particular decision may give rise to personal liability."[72] Suits based on alleged private misconduct raised no such concerns. Nor would the Court accept the president's contention that suits for private conduct would "impose an unacceptable burden on the President's time and energy," particularly since only three presidents in the nation's entire history to that point had been the targets of suits based on their private actions.[73] Stevens also rejected any presumption on the president's part that executive-judicial interactions, "even quite burdensome interactions, necessarily rise to the level of constitutionally forbidden impairment of the Executive's ability to perform its constitutionally mandated functions." The courts had long held, Stevens asserted, that presidential actions were subject to judicial review and process.[74] "If the Judiciary may severely burden the Executive Branch by reviewing the legality of the President's official conduct, and if it may direct appropriate process to the President himself," wrote Stevens, "it must follow that the federal courts have power to determine the legality of his unofficial conduct. The burden on the President's time and energy that is a mere by-product of such review surely cannot be considered as onerous as the direct burden imposed by judicial review and the occasional invalidation of his official actions."[75]

Stevens was equally abrupt in rejecting the president's concern that a decision denying temporary immunity would "generate a large volume of politically motivated harassing and frivolous litigation" or that national security concerns might prevent a president from explaining the need for postponement of a given case. The justices considered neither risk "serious," assumed that courts would quickly terminate most "frivolous and vexatious litigation," predicted that few such cases would be filed in any event, and expressed confidence that trial courts would readily accommodate any scheduling and related problems the president might confront. "If Congress deems it appropriate to afford the President stronger protection," Stevens added, "it may respond with appropriate legislation. . . . Congress has enacted more than one statute providing for the deferral of civil litigation to accommodate important public interests."[76]

In a thoughtful opinion concurring in the judgment, Justice Breyer agreed that the Constitution did not "automatically grant" presidents immunity from civil lawsuits based on private conduct. Once a president had cited and explained conflicts between his participation in a particular proceeding and his public duties, however, a trial judge, in Breyer's judgment, should be permitted to schedule a trial in an "ordinary civil damages action (where postponement normally is possible without overwhelming damage to a plaintiff) only within the constraints of a constitutional principle—a principle that forbids a federal judge in such a case to interfere with the President's discharge of his public duties."[77] Since President Clinton had not made such a showing, the decision in the *Jones* case had not required an application of that principle. But Breyer was fearful that the majority's descriptions of the relevant precedents had so "de-emphasize[d] the extent to which they support[ed] such a principle" that they appeared to reject the president's considerable "independent authority to control his own time and energy." Were the majority "wrong in predicting the future infrequency of private civil litigation against sitting Presidents," he perceptively added, the Court's recognition and future delineation of the principle would "prove a practically necessary institutional safeguard."[78]

Nixon v. Fitzgerald and other case law, Breyer went on to contend, offered strong support for his proposition that judges hearing private damage suits against a sitting president could not issue orders that significantly distracted him from his official duties. Since President Nixon was no longer in office at the time of the *Fitzgerald* suit, the *Jones* Court had concluded that the grant of immunity there could hardly have been based on a concern that litigation would distract the president from his official duties, but instead rested entirely on concerns that a president's fear of civil lawsuits could distort his decisions—a factor not present in suits regarding private misconduct. Disputing that reasoning, Breyer pointed out that the immunity recognized in *Fitzgerald* clearly applied to both sitting and former presidents. In many other cases, moreover, the Court had "found the problem of time and energy distraction a critically important consideration militating in favor of a grant of immunity."[79] By the same token, in his judgment,

[a] Constitution that separates powers in order to prevent one branch of Government from significantly threatening the workings of another could not grant a single judge more than a very limited power to second guess a President's reasonable determination (announced in open court) of his scheduling needs, nor could it permit the issuance of a trial scheduling order that would significantly interfere with the President's discharge of his duties—in a private civil damage action the trial of which might be postponed without the plaintiff suffering enormous harm.[80]

The Court's disposition of President Clinton's immunity claim has largely escaped close scrutiny. Former Los Angeles prosecutor Vincent Bugliosi has faulted the justices, however, for not applying (and the president's counsel for not adequately urging) a balancing approach in the case of the sort used to resolve the presidential claims to executive privilege at issue in *United States v. Nixon* (1974).[81] In his *Jones* concurrence, Justice Breyer had supported considerable deference to presidents regarding the scheduling of such suits. But Justice Stevens had assumed for the Court that "the case at hand, if properly managed by the District Court, [was] ... highly unlikely to occupy any substantial amount of petitioner's time."[82] Bugliosi convincingly argued, however, that instead of flatly rejecting President Clinton's claim to temporary immunity and leaving the scheduling of such suits to the trial court's discretion, courts should first balance the public interests in postponement against the hardships delay would pose for a plaintiff, denying the president's claim for delay only where postponement would create extraordinary difficulties for the plaintiff.

Arguably, though, the principal weakness in the Court's resolution of *Jones* was its simplistic distinction between suits growing out of a president's official actions and those based on private misconduct in terms of their likely effect on a president's performance of official duties. To assume that presidents will fearlessly fulfill their official duties, Stevens reasoned, they must have absolute immunity from civil damage suits based on their official actions. Suits arising from private conduct, on the other hand, are not relevant to the performance of official duties, and there is thus no basis for concluding that fear of civil liability for private misconduct will inhibit a president's performance of official duties.

Whatever the weight of such a rationale as a general proposition, it is surely questionable in the context of the *Jones* case. One does not have to accept Mrs. Clinton's allegations of a vast right-wing conspiracy against her husband to agree that those providing financial support and legal representation for the plaintiff were staunch opponents of President Clinton's position on abortion and other controversial issues. Indeed, their opposition to the president's policy agenda was undoubtedly the overwhelming motivation behind their rush to Paula Jones's side. Presidential fears of civil liability in such cases would appear at least as likely to inhibit a president in the fearless and effective performance of his duties as a suit directed at official misconduct. With due respect, the Court also seems to have grossly underestimated the distracting effects of such suits, if events in the *Jones* case—and, for that matter, the Monica Lewinsky affair—are any indication of their general impact.

Separation of Powers

Although rejecting the claim to temporary immunity that President Clinton advanced in *Jones* and declining, during the 1998-99 term, to review lower court decisions rejecting claims of presidential privileges for government attorneys and secret service agents, a divided Court in 1998 supported the posthumous attorney-client privilege claims raised by counsel to Clinton White House aide Vincent W. Foster, Jr. During the early stages of various investigations into the 1993 dismissal of White House travel office employees, Foster met with Washington attorney James Hamilton to seek legal representation, during which Hamilton took handwritten notes of their conversation. Following Foster's suicide nine days later, a federal grand jury, acting on the request of Independent Counsel Kenneth Starr, issued subpoenas for Hamilton's notes and other materials. Hamilton's law firm moved to quash the subpoena, citing attorney-client privilege. A federal district court granted the motion, but the court of appeals reversed. Concluding that the risk of posthumous revelations of attorney-client communications, if confined to criminal cases, would have little or no chilling effect on such communications, while the costs of maintaining confidentiality would be high, the appeals panel subjected posthumous attorney-client privilege claims to a balancing test under which an exception to the privilege would be recognized for communications of substantial importance to a criminal investigation.[83]

Speaking through Chief Justice Rehnquist, a six-three Supreme Court majority reversed the court of appeals. Emphasizing the attorney-client relationship as "one of the oldest recognized privileges for confidential communications,"[84] and the extensive case law supporting its posthumous recognition, the chief justice rejected the independent counsel's suggestion that his proposed exception would have little effect on a client's willingness to confide in counsel. "He reasons," wrote Rehnquist, "that only clients intending to perjure themselves will be chilled by a rule of disclosure after death, as opposed to truthful clients or those asserting their Fifth Amendment privilege . . . because for the latter group, communications disclosed by the attorney after the client's death will reveal only information that the client himself would have revealed if alive."[85] In truth, though, Rehnquist asserted, clients consulted lawyers for many purposes, "only one of which involves possible criminal liability."[86] Nor would the Court embrace the balancing test the independent counsel had recommended, and the court of appeals adopted, for such cases. "Without assurance of the privilege's posthumous application," observed the chief justice, "the client may very well not have made disclosures to his attorney at all, so the loss of evidence [caused by posthumous recognition of the privilege] is more apparent than real. . . . [And] [b]alancing *ex post* the importance of the information against client interests, even limited to criminal cases, introduces substantial uncertainty into the privilege's application."[87] As for Starr's assertion, based on *United States v. Nixon* and on *Branzburg v. Hayes* (1972)[88] (rejecting a constitutional testimonial privilege for newspersons called before grand juries), that privileges should be strictly construed since they conflict with "the paramount judicial goal of truth seeking," Rehnquist replied that those cases dealt "with the creation of privileges not recognized by the common law, whereas here we deal with one of the oldest privileges in the law."[89]

In dissent, Justice O'Connor agreed that the attorney-client privilege should "ordinarily" survive a client's death, but also embraced the balancing approach advanced by the court of appeals in the case, concluding that "a criminal defendant's right to exculpatory evidence or a compelling law enforcement need for information may, where the testimony is not available from other sources, override a client's posthumous interest in confidentiality."[90] O'Connor emphasized, moreover, that a client's interests in confidentiality were "greatly diminished" after death and that the risk of criminal liability had, of course, "abated altogether," while the costs of an absolute posthumous privilege could be "inordinately high."[91]

Justices Scalia and Thomas joined O'Connor's dissent. Earlier, however, when the Court upheld the constitutionality of the federal independent counsel law in a case involving Reagan administration officials suspected of obstructing a congressional inquiry into possible Justice Department and Environmental Protection Agency misconduct in enforcing federal antipollution regulations, Justice Scalia had filed a lone dissent, contending that the independent counsel statute violated fundamental separation of powers principles.

Under the version of the law enacted in 1978, a special panel of federal judges was authorized to appoint an independent counsel at the attorney general's request. Those appointed were then free to investigate and prosecute crimes within the scope of the order authorizing their selection, functioned independently of the attorney general's supervision, and could be removed by the attorney general only for cause, not at will.[92] Speaking for the majority in *Morrison v. Olson* (1988),[93] Chief Justice Rehnquist characterized the independent counsel as an "inferior" federal officer who, under the Constitution's appointments clause, could be appointed by a court rather than the president. Even though the law granted counsel appointed under the law considerable independence from the attorney general, Rehnquist reasoned, the attorney general's removal power made the position of independent counsel to some degree inferior to that of the attorney general in rank and authority. Counsel were empowered, moreover, to perform only certain limited duties, were restricted in jurisdiction to functions specified by the appointing judicial panel, and held an office of "temporary" duration. Since the Constitution's language in no way limited Congress's discretion to vest the appointment of inferior officials in the courts, Rehnquist also rejected the contention that the appointments clause prohibited members of one branch of government from appointing officials to another branch or forbade the special panel from defining an independent counsel's jurisdiction, which the Court held to be incidental to the appointing power. Nor did Rehnquist attach much weight to various administrative duties given the special panel under the law. Most, such as the authority to receive, but not act upon, reports from the independent counsel, were similar to functions long performed by federal judges in other contexts. And while the panel could terminate an office once an independent counsel's work was completed, the attorney general had sole authority to remove counsel while an investigation or prosecution was pending.

Finally, Rehnquist rejected challenges to the statute resting on separation of powers doctrine. Restricting the attorney general's authority to remove counsel only for cause, in the majority's judgment, did not improperly interfere with executive power, especially since the removal power, while limited, was clearly in an executive's hands. Cases recognizing unlimited presidential authority to remove executive officers, moreover, were not intended to establish rigid categories of officials a president could and could not remove from office; instead, they were designed merely to assure that Congress did not improperly interfere with the president's exercise of executive power and duty to take care that the laws be faithfully executed. Congress's imposition of a good-cause limitation on the removal of an independent counsel did not, Rehnquist concluded, unduly trammel on executive power, but was merely essential to assure the counsel's independence. Nor was the statute, Rehnquist added, an attempt by Congress to increase its power at the expense of the executive. The law did permit members of Congress to request the attorney general to seek appointment of counsel, but the attorney general had no obligation to comply. Beyond that provision, moreover, Congress's role under the statute was limited to reviewing reports or other information submitted by counsel and generally overseeing the counsel's activities. The judicial panel's primary role involved the selection of counsel, and while those selected were somewhat independent of the executive, sufficient executive control was maintained to assure that the president could effectively perform his constitutional duties, especially since, Rehnquist asserted, an attorney general's decision *not* to request appointment of counsel was "committed to his unreviewable discretion."[94]

As the Court's strongest defender of executive authority, at least in cases arising in Republican administrations, Justice Scalia was biting in dissent. Often, he maintained, efforts to disrupt the Constitution's allocation of authority to the national government's three branches came to the Court "clad, so to speak in sheep's clothing:

the potential of the asserted [effort] to effect important change in the equilibrium of power is not immediately evident, and must be discerned by a careful and perceptive analysis." But not on this occasion, asserted Scalia; "this wolf comes as a wolf."[95] Emphasizing that the independent counsel's functions were entirely executive in nature and scorning the majority's efforts to minimize the impact of the challenged statute on executive independence, the justice contended that the Constitution had placed executive authority entirely in the president and declared, "It is not for us to determine, and we have never presumed to determine, how much of the purely executive powers of government must be within the full control of the President. The Constitution prescribes that they *all* are." To Scalia, therefore, it was "irrelevant *how much* the statute reduce[d] Presidential control" over the executive branch of the government. He found little consolation, moreover, in the attorney general's discretion to refuse to appoint a counsel in a given case since under the challenged statute the attorney general was obliged to appoint counsel unless there were "no reasonable grounds to believe" further investigation was warranted. Expressing a judgment that would later be confirmed by the intense political pressure brought to bear on Attorney General Janet Reno to recommend appointment and expanded jurisdiction for counsel during the Clinton presidency, Scalia also cited the "substantial" political consequences an attorney general and president would suffer in "seeming to break the law by refusing to" appoint counsel. Even more fundamentally, "decisions regarding the scope of [an independent counsel's] investigation, its duration, and, finally, whether or not prosecution should ensue, [were] likewise beyond the control of the President and his subordinates."[96] Given the office's autonomy and purely executive character, Scalia concluded that the independent counsel was a "principal" rather than inferior officer whose appointment thus should have been vested in the president rather than judges. To the charge that placing such power in the president, "even when alleged crimes by him or his close associates [were] at issue," would be "unthinkable," the justice responded,

> No more so than that Congress should have the exclusive power of legislation, even when what is at issue is its own exemption from the burdens of certain laws [for example, legislation prohibiting employment discrimination]. . . . No more so than that this Court should have the exclusive power to pronounce the final decision on justiciable cases and controversies, even those pertaining to the constitutionality of a statute reducing the salaries of the Justices. . . . A system of separate and coordinate powers necessarily involves an acceptance of exclusive power that can theoretically be abused. . . . While the separation of powers may prevent us from righting every wrong, it does so in order to ensure that we do not lose liberty.[97]

That did not mean, he added, that there were no controls over any branch's abuse of its exclusive powers: Congress could impeach, the executive could decline to prosecute under an unconstitutional statute, and the courts could dismiss malicious prosecutions. Most importantly, the people could replace those officials guilty of abuse.

When a modification of the legislative process supported primarily by congressional Republicans and presidents of both parties came before the Court in the 1997-98 term, Justice Scalia again defended executive power and was again in dissent. The Line Item Veto Act of 1996 empowered the president to cancel three types of legislation previously signed into law: any amount of discretionary funding, any item of new direct spending, and any tax benefit of particularly limited coverage. Congress could disapprove a cancellation by joint resolution, but such resolutions were subject to presidential veto, which could be overridden only by the usual two-thirds vote of each congressional chamber. Not surprisingly, given the vigorous constitutional debate that adoption of the statute provoked, the law also authorized any member of Congress adversely affected by its provisions to file suit in federal district court and also provided for direct, expedited appeal to the Supreme Court. Four representatives and two senators, including former Senate majority leader Robert Byrd (D-W.Va.), filed suit the day after the law went into effect. Since President Clinton had not yet exercised the power granted in the statute, the Supreme Court dismissed that suit on standing grounds.[98] Within two months of the decision, however, President Clinton cancelled a congressional waiver of the federal government's right to recoup $2.6 billion in taxes New York had levied against Medicaid providers, as well as a tax regulation permitting certain food refiners and processors to defer capital gains taxes if they sold their stock to eligible farmers' cooperatives. When hospital associations and two unions representing health care employees challenged the first cancellation, and a farmers' cooperative and one of its members the second, the Supreme Court held that the line item veto statute's cancellation provisions violated the Constitution's presentment clause.[99]

Under the presentment clause, Justice Stevens reasoned for a six-three majority, Congress was empowered to enact legislation subject to presidential veto. The amendment or repeal of laws was to follow the same process, with the president possessing no power to amend or repeal legislation. Yet, "[i]n both legal and practical effect" in the case before the Court, Stevens concluded, "the President [had] amended two Acts of Congress by repealing a portion of each."[100] Quoting extensively from the Constitution's text, Stevens found important differences between the president's constitutional power to return, or veto, a bill and the cancellation authority embodied in the challenged statute. "The constitutional return takes place," he observed, "*before* the bill becomes law; the statutory cancellation occurs after the bill becomes law. The constitutional return is of the entire bill; the statutory cancellation is of only a part. Although the Constitution expressly authorizes the President to play a role in the process of enacting statutes, it is silent on the subject of unilateral Presidential action that either repeals or amends parts of duly enacted statutes." Particularly since the procedures for enacting statutes were "the product of the great debates and compromises that produced the Constitution itself," Stevens concluded that such silences should be construed "as equivalent to an express prohibition" and that the power to enact laws, as the Court had earlier observed in striking down an arrangement under which proposed executive actions were subject to a legislative veto, could only "be exercised in accord with a single, finely wrought and exhaustively considered, procedure."[101]

The government had sought support for the legislation in two arguments drawn largely from the Court's ruling in *Field v. Clark*,[102] an 1892 case upholding the Tariff Act of 1890. The tariff statute exempted certain products from import duties, but empowered the president to suspend exemptions on the products of nations that imposed "unequal and unreasonable" import tariffs on U.S. products and also specified the duties to be imposed on the products of such nations during the suspension. The government argued that cancellations under the line item veto statute were very similar to the suspensions authorized for the president under the Tariff Act, that is, they were exercises of discretionary authority implicitly granted the president by federal laws read in the light of the line item veto statute, and thus, neither more nor less than the power to decline to spend specified sums of money or implement specified tax measures. In rejecting the analogy the government had attempted to draw, Stevens noted, among other things, that under the Tariff Act the president was simply executing policy Congress had specifically embodied in the statute; that the law at issue in *Field*, like other statutes cited by the government, had involved foreign affairs, an arena in which the president enjoyed "a degree of discretion and freedom from statutory restriction which would not be admissible were domestic affairs alone involved";[103] and that in *Field*, "Congress itself made the decision to suspend or repeal the particular provisions at issue upon the occurrence of particular events subsequent to enacting [the law, leaving] only the determination of whether such events occurred up to the President. The Line Item Veto Act authorizes the President himself to effect the repeal of laws, for his own policy reasons, without observing the procedures set out in the [presentment clause]."[104] Stevens readily conceded that Congress, by adopting the act, had anticipated that the president would cancel certain statutory provisions; but Congress could not, he asserted, alter the constitutional procedures for enacting, amending, or repealing legislation other than by constitutional amendment.

In a concurring opinion, Justice Kennedy conceded the importance of curbs on "persistent excessive [federal] spending" and eloquently declared that "[a] nation cannot plunder its own treasury without putting its Constitution and its survival in peril." Asserting nevertheless that "[f]ailure of political will does not justify unconstitutional remedies," President Reagan's final Supreme Court nominee joined the majority in striking down the line item veto statute. Reaching separation of powers issues Justice Stevens had largely avoided in deciding the case on presentment clause grounds, Kennedy maintained that government attempts to transgress the separation of powers were as great a threat to individual liberty as violations of the Bill of Rights and other civil liberties guarantees.

Separation of powers helps to ensure the ability of each branch to be vigorous in asserting its proper authority. In this respect the device operates on a horizontal axis to secure a proper balance of legislative, executive, and judicial authority. Separation of powers operates on a vertical axis as well, between each branch and the citizens in whose interest powers must be exercised. . . . By increasing the power of the President beyond what the Framers envisioned, the statute compromises the political liberty of our citizens, liberty which the separation of powers seeks to secure.[105]

In separate opinions joined by Justice O'Connor and each other, Justices Scalia and Breyer registered vigorous dissents. Although conceding that some of the parties, but not others, had standing to challenge the line item veto law, Scalia found the cancellations at issue "entirely in accord with the Constitution."[106] Since Congress and the president had clearly complied with the presentment clause in enacting the laws that President Clinton had later partially cancelled, Scalia contended, "the Court's problem with the Act [was] not that it authorizes the President to veto parts of a bill and sign others into law, but rather that it authorizes him to 'cancel'—prevent from 'having legal force or effect'—certain parts of duly enacted statutes."[107] Scalia found nothing in the Constitution preventing such cancellations if, as in the line item veto statute, Congress had authorized them. In fact, he saw "not a dime's worth of difference between Congress's authorizing the President to *cancel* a spending item, and Congress's authorizing money to be spent on a particular item at the President's discretion." The latter, he added, had of course "been done since the Founding of the Nation."[108] If carried too far, the discretion extended the president could amount to an unconstitutional delegation of legislative authority to the executive, but Scalia asserted that the president's discretion under the line item veto statute was "no broader than the discretion traditionally granted the President in his execution of spending laws" and routinely upheld by the courts.[109]

Justice Breyer prefaced his dissent with a discussion of three general background considerations. First, he pointed out that in an earlier, less complicated era, Congress could have achieved the goal underlying the line item veto statute by simply embodying each appropriation in a separate bill, each subject to separate presidential veto. Since it was no longer feasible for Congress to divide spending provisions into thousands of separate bills, the question for the current Court, Breyer contended, was whether "the Constitution permits Congress to choose a particular novel *means* to achieve this same, constitutionally legitimate, *end*." Second, the case required the Court to focus on constitutional provisions relating to separation of powers that the Court in the past "had interpreted . . . generously in terms of the institutional arrangements they permit." Finally, wrote Breyer, the case involved no interbranch dispute for the Court to referee. Application of such considerations, combined with the need to construe nonliteral separation of powers principles in a manner conducive to "workable government," convinced Breyer that the challenged statute was constitutional.[110]

In rejecting the majority's conclusion that the line item veto law infringed upon the Constitution's text, Breyer reasoned that in cancelling appropriations measures under the statute, the president was in no way repealing or amending any measure, but was instead simply following the line item veto law in the same way he would have been obliged to follow its requirements had the cancellation provisions been written directly into every spending provision in the form of a grant of discretionary power. "Literally speaking," observed Breyer, "the President has not 'repealed' or 'amended' anything. He has simply *executed* a power conferred upon him by Congress, which power is contained in laws that were enacted in compliance with the exclusive method set forth in the Constitution."[111] In Breyer's judgment, like Scalia's,

Congress had simply delegated discretion to the executive over the enforcement of laws, as it had done in numerous other contexts through grants of discretionary authority. Nor, he contended, did the statute violate unwritten separation of powers principles. The power granted—to enforce or cancel certain types of appropriations measures and tax benefits—was more clearly executive in nature than certain other delegations the courts had upheld in the past. Particularly since the statute included a provision allowing Congress, by simple majority vote, to exempt any future appropriation from its coverage, the line item veto statute clearly did not encroach upon congressional power or aggrandize the presidency.

> In sum, . . . the Act before us is novel. In a sense, it skirts a constitutional edge. But that edge has to do with means, not ends. The means chosen do not amount literally to the enactment, repeal, or amendment of a law. Nor, for that matter, do they amount literally to the "line item veto" that the Act's title announces. Those means do not violate any basic Separation of Powers principle. They do not improperly shift the constitutionally foreseen balance of power from Congress to the President. Nor, since they comply with Separation of Powers principles, do they threaten the liberties of individual citizens. They represent an experiment that may, nor may not, help representative government work better. The Constitution in my view authorizes Congress and the President to try novel methods in this way.[112]

As Scalia and Breyer indicated, the cancellation provisions of the line item veto statute bear many similarities to congressional grants of discretionary power to the executive that the Court has routinely upheld over the years. The findings presidents must make under the statute as a predicate to cancellation—that the cancellation will reduce the federal deficit, will not impair any "essential government functions," and will not harm the national interest—are no more nebulous, moreover, than guidelines limiting the executive's discretion under other legislation which the Court has regularly validated.[113] Indeed, the Court has struck down only two delegations of lawmaking power to the executive in its entire history to date.[114] Even so, it is difficult to avoid the conclusion that Congress intended the Line Item Veto Act to be precisely what its title says, an artfully worded attempt to confer on the president a type of veto power that the Constitution's text does not recognize and that could otherwise have been adopted only through constitutional amendment—a process in which states would be unlikely to ratify a proposal empowering presidents to limit congressional appropriations to them and their local governments, among other recipients of federal largesse. Provisions of the statute lend further credence to that conclusion. As with formal vetoes, for example, presidential cancellations of appropriated funds were subject to a strict time limit; under the challenged statute, the president was to transmit a special message to Congress notifying it of each cancellation, just as with vetoes, except that cancellation messages were to be submitted to Congress within five calendar days (excluding Sundays) after a provision's enactment, rather than the ten days allowed for vetoes. Such a deadline, and the close connection it requires between an appropriation and its cancellation, smacks of the veto, whatever its label.

Interstate Relations

Like earlier Courts, the Rehnquist Court has decided its share of interstate disputes, perhaps the most noteworthy of which to date was its 1998 resolution of the protracted debate between New York and New Jersey over ownership of Ellis Island. An 1834 compact, approved by Congress as required by the Constitution's provisions regarding interstate compacts, set the boundary between the two states as the middle of the Hudson River; provided that Ellis Island, which then consisted of three acres, was part of New York, although located on the New Jersey side of the river; and further stipulated that New York had exclusive jurisdiction over submerged lands and waters between the two states to the low-water mark on the New Jersey shore, but subject to certain exceptions, including New Jersey's right to submerged lands on its side of the boundary.

In the dispute over ownership of Ellis Island that the Supreme Court would ultimately decide, both states agreed that the compact gave New York sovereign authority over the island; and early in this century the Court had held that New Jersey retained sovereign rights over submerged lands on its side of the river.[115] But after 1891, when the island was first used as a receiving site for immigrants, the national government had begun adding landfill around the island's shoreline, gradually enlarging the original island by some 24.5 acres. After 1954, when the immigration process was moved from the island, the property was developed as a national historic site, while New York and New Jersey began asserting rival claims of sovereign authority over its filled land.

Finally, in 1993, New Jersey filed an original suit in the Supreme Court, asserting its claim to the substantial portion of the island created through landfill. After a trial, a special master appointed by the Court concluded that the middle of the Hudson River marked the boundary line between the two states and that New York retained some jurisdiction over Ellis Island as it existed in 1834, when the compact was adopted. He further held, however, that the compact did not reach the issue of control over the island's landfill portions. Instead, citing the common law doctrine of avulsion governing the addition of land to existing terrain, he found that the added portions of the island were under New Jersey's control and rejected New York's claim that it possessed authority by virtue of prescription, or long use and assertion of its authority over the island, an assertion in which, New York claimed, New Jersey had long acquiesced.

When both states registered exceptions to the master's report and recommendations, a six-three majority, speaking through Justice Souter, held that New Jersey had authority over the filled land added to the original island.[116] Souter attached no weight to the compact's failure to describe Ellis Island's dimensions; that simply meant, in the Court's view, that when the compact was adopted in 1834, "everybody knew what Ellis Island was."[117] The compact's failure to address the consequences of landfilling on the agreement merely reflected, moreover, its acceptance of the prevailing common law doctrine of the era—that landfill was avulsion and thus had no effect on a property's boundaries for legal purposes. Souter asserted, therefore, that the submerged lands surrounding the original island remained New Jersey's when the United States added landfill to them.

Nor would the Court agree that New York had acquired authority over the landfill through prescriptive acts in which New Jersey acquiesced. To establish ownership by prescription and acquiescence, New York was obliged to show by a preponderance of the evidence that it exercised control over the added land with New Jersey's consent from 1890, when the national government first began to add landfill to the original island, to 1954, when New Jersey first vigorously asserted its sovereignty. To make such a showing, Souter maintained, New York had to establish that whenever it referred to Ellis Island, it meant something other than the original territory, which concededly was New York's, and also that U.S. occupation of the land had adversely affected New York's opportunity to act more overtly in support of its claim to sovereignty, as well as any attention New Jersey reasonably would have given whatever acts New York claimed to have performed in asserting its jurisdiction. The evidence New York presented— such as its recording of the vital statistics of people on the island, including the island in New York voting districts and people there on voter registration lists, and the national government's understanding regarding the island's sovereignty—was insufficient, according to Souter, to support a finding of prescription, particularly since such acts occurred off the island and were either equivocal in indicating whether they were referring only to the original island or ill calculated to give notice to New Jersey of New York's claim. Nor did such evidence leave federal personnel, the island's actual occupants, with a clear understanding that the landfill might be subject to New York's control.

In a concurring opinion joined by Justice Ginsburg, Justice Breyer conceded his initial expectation that Ellis Island would be found to be "part and parcel of New York," especially since his own ancestors had landed as immigrants at "Ellis Island, New York." But Breyer ultimately joined the majority in concluding that the island's filled portion belonged to New Jersey. Breyer based his position primarily on the fact that the events on which New York primarily relied in attempting to establish its sovereignty by prescription, and New Jersey's acquiescence in that claim, had occurred during the period that the federal government controlled the island. During those years, Breyer reasoned, New Jersey could hardly have been reasonably expected to mount a major protest against New York's assertions of sovereignty, yet those were the years critical to New York's claim. Under such circumstances, Breyer asserted, any rule of prescription recognizing New York's authority over Ellis Island "would create serious problems of fairness in other cases."[118]

Justice Stevens was convinced, on the other hand, that the evidence clearly favored New York's claim. While conceding that the quantity of evidence supporting either state's claims was quite small, Stevens pointed out, among other things, that there was no evidence that any of the thousands of people who worked on the island, and the hundreds who resided there, during its years as an immigration center believed part of the island belonged to New Jersey. People living on the island were counted in state and federal census data as New York residents. New York officials had issued all discovered birth and death certificates of island residents; marriages on the island were entered into under New York law, and no evidence existed of any resident married under New Jersey law. Residents consistently listed a New York address. On the few occasions municipal police and fire protection became necessary during the period of federal control of the island, New York personnel invariably responded. Courts considering the question consistently assumed or decided the island was part of New York. Nor would Stevens agree that New Jersey had no notice of New York's assertions. Ellis Island, after all, was not some "remote atoll in the far Pacific";[119] instead, it was an enclave entirely within New Jersey's geographic boundaries. Under such circumstances, Stevens thought it highly likely that New Jersey would have been aware of official New York and federal acts reflecting an assumption that the entire island was under New York's control. To Stevens, moreover, the one isolated and unsuccessful attempt by a New Jersey official to convince the federal government to use New Jersey labor in construction work on the island merely demonstrated that people in New Jersey were aware of New York's assumption of control over the island and acquiesced in the federal government's acceptance of New York's sovereignty. Indeed, in Stevens's view, New York's claim was supported not merely by "a preponderance, but by clear, convincing, and uncontradicted evidence," and the Court's contrary conclusion rested on "a hypertechnical focus on detail that overlook[ed] the significance of the record as a whole."[120]

Justice Scalia, joined by Justice Thomas, supported New York's claim to sovereignty over the entire island, but not the state's reliance on a prescription argument, which carried with it a heavy burden of proof. Instead, Scalia characterized the 1834 compact on which Ellis Island's status was based as "poorly drafted and ambiguous," and based his defense of New York's claim on the familiar contract principle "that the practical construction of an ambiguous agreement revealed by later conduct of the parties [was] good indication of its meaning."[121] Following that approach, and tracking the sorts of factual data Stevens had compiled, Scalia pointed out that all parties to the compact, including the federal government, had behaved for a lengthy period "as though all of Ellis Island belonged to New York." New York had provided the island's residents with privileges and services a sovereign normally provides, while New Jersey offered none and otherwise behaved as though "it assuredly knew that *it* was *not*" the island's sovereign. The federal government treated the island as part of New York for census and other governmental purposes. For Scalia, "[t]hat practical construction suffice[d] . . . to establish what the Compact of 1834 meant."[122]

Earlier in the same term that the Ellis Island dispute was decided, the Court had before it a rare case calling for construction of the Article IV provision requiring states to give "full faith and credit" to the laws, records, and judicial decisions of other states. Normally, states routinely comply with the full faith and credit obligation with little difficulty, although a number of controversial disputes over its meaning had come before the Court at times in the past, especially in the once sensitive divorce field.[123] During the 1997-98 term, however, the justices faced the somewhat complicated question whether an injunction issued by a court in one state could control proceedings in a different case and state. That case involved Ronald Elwell, a General Motors researcher. Elwell had frequently aided his company in product liability cases, but as their relations deteriorated, testified over GM's objections for the plaintiffs in a

Georgia case involving a pickup truck equipped with a fuel tank that burst into flames following collisions. As settlement of a later suit for his wrongful discharge, General Motors gave Elwell an undisclosed sum of money and a Michigan court permanently enjoined him from testifying in future GM cases over the company's objections, except in the Georgia case cited above, which was still pending. Later, however, plaintiffs in a suit brought in a Missouri court, but removed by GM into federal court, subpoenaed Elwell to testify in support of their claim that a faulty GM fuel pump caused the fire that killed their mother. General Motors attorneys argued that the Michigan court's injunction barred Elwell from testifying in the Missouri federal suit. But the Supreme Court, speaking through Justice Ginsburg, concluded that while states were expected to honor the judicial decrees of courts in other states, such orders could not control proceedings in other cases, the merits of which the issuing court had not considered. By the same token, one state's decree could not determine evidentiary issues, such as what witnesses would be permitted to testify, in a suit brought in another state by parties who were not subject to the jurisdiction of the first state's court.[124]

Concurring in the judgment, Justice Scalia distinguished between the obligation of states under Article IV to accord general validity to the judgments of courts in other states and GM's assertion of a state court's obligation to execute the decrees of other state courts, declaring that only the former fell within the full faith and credit obligation under the long-established principle that "the judgment of a state court cannot be enforced out of the state by an execution issued within it."[125] Justice Kennedy, joined by Justices O'Connor and Thomas, also concurred with only the judgment. Kennedy agreed that a state court could not decline to enforce another state's judicial decisions based merely upon some disagreement with the other state's laws, even when the law in question contravened the public policy of the second state. But Kennedy questioned the wisdom of two exceptions to the principle that the Court's opinion had recognized: that a court in another state could decline to enforce a state court's judgment when that order purported to accomplish an act within the exclusive province of that other state or interfered with litigation over which the issuing state had no authority. Instead, Kennedy would have rested the decision more narrowly on the "undoubted principle that courts need give a prior judgment no more force or effect than the issuing State gives it."[126] Kennedy doubted that the Michigan court would have meant to extend its injunction against Elwell to any party not then before it or subject to its jurisdiction. That being the case, Kennedy reasoned, the court in the fuel pump case should not have been considered bound by the injunction and thus unable to subpoena Elwell.

In the current era as in the past, the Court has decided few cases based on Article IV's interstate privileges and immunities clause, which has traditionally been construed only to forbid states from unreasonably discriminating against visitors from other states in favor of their own citizens. In 1985, a Burger Court majority used the clause to invalidate a New Hampshire supreme court rule limiting bar admission to state residents. Relying heavily on precedent that strictly scrutinized under the equal protection guarantee laws limiting access to the legal profession and certain other positions to U.S. citizens only,[127] Justice Powell conceded for the Court in *Supreme*

Court of New Hampshire v. Piper (1985)[128] that lawyers were to some extent judicial officers, but rejected the claim that such a position, unlike that of government office-holders, could only be entrusted to a full-fledged member of a state's political community and thus limited to state citizens only. Nor could the majority agree that the state's discrimination against nonresidents at issue in the case bore a close relationship to a substantial governmental interest of the sort traditionally required to justify such regulations. In *Supreme Court of Virginia v. Friedman* (1988),[129] the Rehnquist Court used a similar rationale in striking down a state residency requirement for admission to the bar on motion rather than examination; the following year a majority invalidated a Virgin Islands regulation requiring applicants to reside there at least one year before applying for admission to the district court bar and to state an intent to be a territorial resident.[130]

In his opinion for the Court in the *Friedman* case, Justice Kennedy agreed that a state or territory might be justifiably concerned with assuring that its lawyers kept abreast of local legal requirements, but concluded that there were "equally or more effective means" available for promoting such interests, means that would "not themselves infringe constitutional protections."[131] In an early draft of the opinion, however, Kennedy had gone further, suggesting that state laws evaluated under Article IV's privileges or immunities clause might be subject to the "less restrictive means" analysis, under which laws subjected to strict scrutiny in certain equal protection and First Amendment cases were invalidated if other means than those embodied in a challenged law were available for accomplishing the important interests the law was claimed to promote. Justice O'Connor quickly responded, finding "strict application of less restrictive means to be troublesome" in such cases and adding, "Too ready a use of this approach would put courts in the position of constantly second guessing legislative judgments in a way which may not be wise or necessary."[132] On reading O'Connor's concerns, Justice Blackmun joined Kennedy's opinion, but expressed the "hope that you will not delete entirely the less-restrictive-means analysis, as Sandra has suggested."[133] In her letter, O'Connor had conceded that Justice Powell's *Piper* opinion had "clearly endorse[d] such an approach" and Blackmun considered its use "an important device to keep teeth in the Privileges and Immunities Clause."

When Kennedy modified his language, O'Connor joined his opinion, although she "continue[d] to have some concerns about such an analysis."[134] But Chief Justice Rehnquist dissented, as he had in *Piper* and would in the Virgin Islands case, and Justice Scalia joined him in both *Friedman* and the Virgin Islands case, while Justice O'Connor joined them in the latter litigation. As he had first asserted in *Piper*, Rehnquist did not believe that Article IV's privileges and immunities clause required states to ignore residency in admitting lawyers to practice in the same way they were required to ignore residency in other commercial fields, such as trading in foreign goods and commercial fishing.[135] The lawyers of a state, Rehnquist contended, would "in many ways . . . intimately deal with [its] self-governance," and the state should thus be allowed to limit law practice to its own residents, just as access to governmental positions could be so limited.[136] In the Virgin Islands case, Rehnquist reluctantly agreed that the territory's durational residency requirement was invalid under earlier cases "dealing with the 'right' of interstate travel."[137] Based on what he termed "the unique circumstances of legal practice in the Virgin Islands," however, Rehnquist favored remanding the rule limiting law practice to residents alone for further proceedings regarding "genuine factual disputes" indicated in the record "about the nature of these circumstances and their relationship to the challenged residency requirement."[138]

Federalism

While the number of cases brought before the Court regarding interstate relations has been relatively small, the justices of the Rehnquist Court have confronted a rather wide variety of disputes involving issues of federalism. In 1995, a five-four majority rebuffed Arkansas's attempt to impose term limits on that state's congressional delegation. By amendment to its constitution, the state prohibited the names of otherwise eligible congressional candidates from appearing on the ballot if they had already served three terms in the U.S. House of Representatives or two Senate terms. A state trial court held the provision contrary to the qualifications for service in Congress stipulated in Article I of the Constitution, and the Arkansas supreme court affirmed, concluding that a state had no authority to change, add to, or diminish the Constitution's age, citizenship, and residency requirements for membership in Congress and rejecting Arkansas's contention that since write-in voting was permitted, its term limits provision was merely a restriction on access to the ballot rather than an outright disqualification of certain congressional incumbents. Citing *Powell v. McCormack*,[139] its 1969 decision rejecting congressional authority to supplement the constitutional qualifications for membership in Congress, the Supreme Court upheld the state courts.

Rebuffing Arkansas's contention that states possessed reserved powers under the Tenth Amendment to supplement the qualifications stated in the Constitution, the majority, per Justice Stevens, reasoned that such authority was not within the states' original powers prior to the Tenth Amendment's adoption and thus could not be considered among the states' reserved powers. Even if the states possessed some degree of original power of the sort Arkansas was claiming, Stevens added, the Constitution's framers intended that it be the sole source of congressional qualifications—a conclusion compelled by the unanimous judgment of courts and commentators on the issue, by the records of the 1787 constitutional convention and debates in the state ratifying conventions, by the Constitution's structure and text, and especially, as the *Powell* Court had emphasized, by the "fundamental principle of our representative democracy . . . 'that the people should choose whom they please to govern them.'"[140] The states' formulations of diverse qualifications for their congressional representatives, Stevens asserted, would have resulted in a patchwork of requirements inconsistent with the framers' vision of a uniform national Congress representing the people of the United States. That many states imposed term limits and other qualifications on state officials immediately after the Constitution's adoption, while only one state adopted term limits for members of Congress, reflected, in Stevens's judgment, that national vision and its acceptance by the states. To Arkansas's representation of its term-limit provision as merely a limitation on ballot access, an argument based primarily on the challenged amendment's exemption of write-in candidates from its coverage, Stevens responded that, even so viewed, the regulation was still an indirect attempt to evade the constitutional qualifications for membership in Congress and thus an effort to trivialize the basic democratic principles underlying the Constitution's requirements. Nor could the majority find any support for the term limit provision in the Article I, Section 4, power given states to regulate the "times, places, and manner of holding [congressional] elections." Since Article I, Section 4, also gave Congress power to "make or alter such regulations," Stevens observed, acceptance of Arkansas's argument would mean that Congress could itself impose term limits, too, yet under *Powell* Congress was clearly denied authority to supplement the constitutional qualifications for congressional membership. The state's construction was fundamentally inconsistent, moreover, with the framers' intention that the states have power only to regulate congressional election procedures, not a substantive "license to exclude classes of candidates from federal office."[141] In short, any limits on congressional tenure, beyond the voters' obvious discretion to "turn the rascals out," required adoption of a constitutional amendment.

Justice Thomas spoke for the four dissenters in a wide-ranging and frequently penetrating critique of the majority decision and rationale. Joined by Rehnquist, O'Connor, and Scalia, Thomas began with a reference to what he considered to be a basic irony in the Court's assertion that its decision was based on regard for democratic principles. Even though voters clearly possess in the franchise itself the power to impose term limits without resort to formal regulations, Thomas scoffed at the notion that a judicial decision invalidating a constitutional amendment approved by nearly 60 percent of Arkansas's voters in all its congressional districts, could somehow be squared with democratic principles. Emphasizing that nothing in the Constitution's text specifically precluded states from supplementing the constitutional qualifications for a congressional seat, he also argued that "where the Constitution is silent, it raises no bar to action by the States or the people."[142] Nor did Thomas see any inconsistency between the holding in *Powell* that Congress could not add to the congressional membership qualifications prescribed in the Constitution and the authority of individual states to supplement those requirements with provisions of their own. "The logical conclusion," asserted Thomas, was "simply that the Framers did not want the people of the States and their state legislatures to be constrained by too many qualifications imposed at the national level." But that did not mean the "Framers intended to bar the people of the States and their state legislatures from adopting additional eligibility requirements to help narrow their own choices."[143] Thomas also turned historical circumstances to advantage. He noted, for example, that prior to the Fourteenth Amendment's adoption, the constitutional requirement that members of Congress be U.S. citizens meant different things in different states. Thus, the Constitution's qualifications clauses themselves initially embodied standards for service in Congress that varied from state to state. Against that historical background, Thomas was unwilling to accept the majority's insistence on uniform national qualifications.

Ultimately, however, it is difficult to join Thomas's contention that the framers' listing of specific qualifications for membership in Congress did not foreclose the states from supplementing those provisions with other eligibility restrictions. Had the framers not intended the listed qualifications to exclude others, they arguably would not have used language that appeared to limit states to regulating the "times, places, and manner" of conducting congressional elections, but instead would also have specifically authorized states to impose additional eligibility requirements. Had the framers not explicitly given the states power over time, place, and manner, their silence regarding state authority over qualifications would be easier to construe as permitting states to supplement the constitutional requirements with their own, as Justice Thomas has contended. That the framers considered it necessary to specify a state role over the time, place, and manner of congressional elections makes such a rationale more difficult, if not impossible, to embrace. Even so, many of Thomas's arguments in defense of state power over term limits are also difficult to ignore.

Under the supremacy clause and general principles of federalism, the federal and state governments have long been held to be immune from intergovernmental taxation.[144] For a time, income or interest derived from one level of government in the federal system, such as the salaries of government employees and income from government contracts, was also considered immune from taxation by the other level of government, on the theory that the burden of such taxes in effect extended to the government itself. The conservative Supreme Court of the 1920s carried such thinking to ridiculous limits.[145] In the 1930s, however, the Court began to reverse such precedents and reaffirm the traditional policy that only the governments themselves enjoyed intergovernmental tax immunities. The Court in 1938, for example, upheld nondiscriminatory federal taxation of the salaries of state employees[146] and the following year approved state authority to tax federal salaries.[147]

The Rehnquist Court has, of course, continued in that tradition, albeit not with complete unanimity. In *South Carolina v. Baker* (1988),[148] a majority rejected that state's challenge to a federal income tax provision denying an exemption for interest earned on unregistered long-term state and local bonds, with Justice Brennan holding for the Court that neither the Tenth Amendment nor general principles of federalism forbade a nondiscriminatory federal tax on the interest from state bonds. But Justice O'Connor dissented from the majority's reversal of long precedent, declaring that "constitutional principles do not depend upon the rise or fall of particular legal doctrines" and criticizing the majority for "shirk[ing] its responsibility [by] . . . fail[ing] to inquire into the substantial adverse effects on state and local governments that would follow from federal taxation" of state and local bond interest.[149]

O'Connor joined the Court the next year in holding that Michigan had violated principles of intergovernmental tax immunity by favoring retired state and local government employees over retired federal employees.[150] But, on that occasion, Justice Stevens filed a lone dissent. Under the tax provision at issue, Michigan exempted from taxation all retirement benefits paid by state and local governments, but taxed benefits paid by other employers, including the federal government. While the majority found forbidden discrimination in the arrangement, Justice Stevens pointed out that the state could have achieved the same result simply by increasing state and local retirement benefits and complained that the Court's approach "trivializes the Supremacy Clause."[151] Stevens readily agreed that the scheme discriminated against federal employees and all other Michigan taxpayers, but not in an unconstitutional manner. In his judgment, "[t]he fact that a State may elect to grant a preference, or an exemption, to a small percentage of its residents [did] not make the tax discriminatory in any sense that [was] relevant to the doctrine of intergovernmental tax immunity. The obligation of a federal judge to pay the same tax that is imposed on the income of similarly situated citizens in the State should not be affected by the fact that the State might choose to grant an exemption to a few of its taxpayers—whether they be state judges, other state employees, or perhaps a select group of private citizens."[152]

Just as the federal government's immunity from state taxation is based on the supremacy clause, as originally recognized in the *McCulloch* case,[153] principles of national supremacy also provide the basis for the federal preemption doctrine, under which the national government can preserve any power within its authority exclusively for its own exercise, entirely prohibiting or preempting state or local legislation. Modern preemption principles were established decades ago,[154] and Rehnquist Court preemption rulings to date have made only minor adjustments in existing case law.[155] The justices have vigorously disagreed at times, however, over the applicable principles in individual cases. Justice Scalia, for example, took sharp exception to the principal opinion's application of preemption doctrine in *Cipollone v. Liggett Group, Inc.* (1992).[156] A 1965 federal statute required the now familiar warning label placed on cigarette packages and preempted state imposition of other warning statements on packages and in cigarette advertising. A 1969 amendment to that requirement banned state smoking and health regulations with respect to the advertising or promotion of cigarettes with packaging carrying the federal label. In a wrongful death suit against cigarette manufacturers, a district court ruled, among other things, that the 1965 and 1969 regulations preempted the claims raised against the defendants to the extent that they relied on their advertising, promotional, and public relations activities after the effective date of the 1965 statute. After a court of appeals affirmed that portion of the district court's decision, the Supreme Court held that certain of the claims raised, but not others, had been preempted.

In the principal opinion in the case, Justice Stevens asserted at one point that the Court must construe provisions of federal law "in light of the presumption against the preemption of state police power regulations."[157] Justice Scalia, joined by Justice Thomas, objected. Scalia conceded that courts should find against a congressional intent to preempt state regulations in a field of federal control "absent convincing evidence of statutory intent" to the contrary. But he rejected the notion that in the face of such evidence courts should persist in rejecting preemption without a "plain statement" to that effect in the federal law, or a finding that it was not susceptible to a limiting construction foreclosing preemption. Recently, observed Scalia, the Court had held that a provision of federal legislation deregulating the airlines industry and preempting state laws relating to airline rates, routes, and services was also broad enough to forbid state regulation of fare advertising, despite the availability of plausible limiting constructions of the law to the contrary. "[W]e interpreted an express pre-emption provision broadly," he asserted, "despite the fact that a well-respected canon of statutory construction supported a narrower reading. . . . We said not a word about a 'presumption against . . . pre-emption' . . . that was to be applied to construction of the text. In light of our willingness to find pre-emption in the absence of *any* explicit statement of pre-emptive intent, the notion that such explicit statements, where they exist, are subject to a 'plain-statement' rule is more than somewhat odd."[158]

In a number of cases, the Rehnquist Court has invoked traditional constitutional principles in rejecting claims that challenged federal regulations interfered with the reserved powers of the states. In a 1990 case, for example, the Court upheld congressional power to authorize state national guard units ordered to active federal duty outside the United States without either the state governor's consent or a national emergency. Citing the broad military powers conferred on Congress under Article I's plain language, Justice Stevens spoke for a unanimous Court in rejecting Minnesota's assertion of states' rights claims usually invoked by southern states in civil rights disputes. In a note to Stevens, Justice Blackmun, who grew up in Minnesota, "well recall[ed]" the dual oath required of guardsmen and the Army instructors assigned to his unit when he was a "buck private in the rear ranks" in the early 1930s. "I might add," observed Blackmun, "that those instructors were not very impressed" with Minnesota's militiamen.[159]

Over the dissents of Justices Brennan and O'Connor, the Court also upheld Congress's use of its spending authority to induce states to raise the minimum age for purchasing liquor.[160] Under the regulations at issue, Congress conditioned the states' receipt of highway funds on their adoption of twenty-one as the minimum drinking age. Speaking for the majority, Chief Justice Rehnquist found the regulation clearly consistent with Congress's obligation to spend for the "general welfare" and further concluded that the states' broad powers under the Twenty-First Amendment did not prevent the federal government from achieving indirectly, through its taxing and spending power, what it might not have power to do directly. While conceding that the Court had long ago suggested that Congress's financial inducements of state action could at some point amount to unconstitutional coercion,[161] the chief justice also noted that a state's failure to comply with the drinking-age requirement resulted in only modest reductions in highway funding. "[T]he argument as to coercion," he concluded, was thus "more rhetoric than fact."[162]

In a brief dissent, Justice Brennan concurred with Justice O'Connor's view that federal regulation of the minimum age for purchasing liquor fell "squarely" within the reach of state authority under the Twenty-First Amendment, interfering with state reserved powers. In her more elaborate effort, Justice O'Connor agreed with the majority that Congress could attach conditions to state receipt of federal funds to assure state spending consistent with federal goals. O'Connor emphasized, however, that such restrictions must be reasonably related to those goals and found the majority's application of that standard "cursory and unconvincing."[163] In her judgment, the regulation was only marginally related to the reason for the funding, highway construction, and was actually an attempt to regulate intrastate liquor sales, a matter within state reserved powers. "The immense size and power of the Government of the United States," O'Connor declared, "ought not obscure its fundamental character. It remains a Government of enumerated powers. . . . Because [the minimum-age requirement] cannot be justified as an exercise of any power delegated to the Congress, it is not authorized by the Constitution."[164]

Whatever the merit of Justice O'Connor's argument, or the weight of the Twenty-First Amendment in such cases, the majority's decision in the drinking age case reflected the deference the post-1937 Court has usually accorded congressional authority in federal-state disputes. In a number of recent cases, however, the Rehnquist Court has seemingly begun to resurrect pre-1937 principles of federalism in striking down congressional use of the commerce power to regulate the policies and practices of state and local governments, and in other cases, a majority of the justices have demonstrated a solicitude for private property rights not seen on the Court since 1936. Such decisions have raised serious doubts about the continued viability of the constitutional double standard under which the post-1937 Court has left the scope of governmental power over the economy and definition of economic freedoms overwhelmingly to the political process. The following chapter explores the status of the double standard in the Rehnquist Court.

4

The Double Standard

The Old Court's impact on American law and the nation's social, economic, and political fabric is familiar to all students of constitutional politics. Imbued with the "survival of the fittest" tenets of Social Darwinism, a shifting majority of justices who served on the Supreme Court from the late 1880s to the late 1930s imposed a laissez-faire economic theory on the Constitution's text, converting its provisions into potent weapons against both federal and state controls over economic interests and the excesses of the Industrial Revolution.

The weapons chosen for this campaign were diverse, indeed. Congress had authority to regulate commerce "among the several states," the justices conceded, but that power extended only to commercial transactions, not to the production or manufacture of products intended for interstate trade. The Sugar Trust's monopolistic control of virtually all the nation's sugar production was thus beyond federal antitrust authority despite its obvious effect on the pricing of sugar in interstate commerce.[1] True, in the first Supreme Court case construing congressional commercial authority, Chief Justice John Marshall had extended the power's reach to local or intrastate activities that affected interstate commerce.[2] But such authority, the Court concluded in the Sugar Trust case and numerous other contexts, was limited only to those activities that exerted a *direct* effect on interstate trade, not those having only an *indirect* or *incidental* impact. Whether an activity exerted a direct effect on interstate commerce and was subject to federal regulation would depend, moreover, on the character of the effect rather than the degree of its impact on commerce. Thus, wages, hours, and related industrial policies were beyond federal control despite their enormous impact on pricing and other components of interstate trade.

Complementing the severe limits that the Old Court's highly technical and artificial production-commerce and direct-indirect distinctions placed on federal authority was its expansive construction of the Tenth Amendment's reservation to the states of all powers not delegated by the Constitution to the national government. Under the justices' "dual federalism" reading of the reserved powers clause, the national government was forbidden to use its express or implied constitutional powers to regulate matters traditionally controlled by the states. The Court permitted Congress to penalize interstate shipment of items that were intrinsically harmful to the public (diseased plants and livestock, impure food and drugs) or, though themselves harmless, that were transported interstate for injurious purposes (lottery tickets, women).[3] But when Congress forbade interstate shipment of goods produced with child labor, the justices balked, distinguishing the earlier cases and charging the nation's lawmakers with "invading" the states' traditional authority—however timidly exerted—to protect the health and safety of children.[4] When Congress next imposed a heavy tax on companies that used child labor, attempting to enforce through the tax power what it had been forbidden to require via its commercial authority, the Court again wielded the dual federalism ax. Citing the Child Labor Tax Act's regulatory features, the justices distinguished it from earlier federal taxes enacted to inhibit offensive business practices—taxes the Court had upheld.[5]

Substantive due process, however, was perhaps the most potent and expansive judicial weapon of the laissez faire era. Converting the Fifth and Fourteenth Amendments' historic guarantees of proper procedure into substantive limitations on federal and state power, the Court, in such cases as *Lochner v. New York (1905)*[6] and *Adkins v. Children's Hospital* (1923),[7] assumed a superlegislative authority to strike down regulations found to constitute an "unreasonable" or "arbitrary" interference with property and economic freedom on the ground that they violated the due process clauses. Far from presuming economic controls valid and placing a heavy burden on those challenging such laws, as the Marshall and later Courts had done, the justices held that (economic) freedom was to be the rule, regulation the exception, in such cases.

Depression, politics, the rise of the administrative state, and changing high Court membership left the laissez-faire majority's precedents and doctrines in shambles. Until recently, the Supreme Court had not invalidated a single economic regulation on substantive due process grounds since 1936. The sole precedent in which the post-1937 Court has overturned an economic control under the equal protection guarantee was later reversed as placing an undue burden on governmental discretion.[8] Rejected, too, were Old Court distinctions between production and commerce and direct and indirect effects on interstate trade, the modern justices holding instead that Congress can reach any activities that, individually or in the aggregate, exert a substantial effect on interstate commerce.[9]

The same lines of cases also relegated the Tenth Amendment, of course, to the status of truism, with the Court refusing to recognize a static, unchanging division between federal and state power. A statute falling within the ambit of Congress's enumerated or implied powers was valid, the justices concluded, whether or not it dealt with matters traditionally subject to state regulation.[10] Between 1937 and 1995, the

Court would strike down only one act of Congress as an unconstitutional interference with state residual powers. In *National League of Cities v. Usery* (1976),[11] a five-four majority struck down regulations extending federal wage and hour requirements to state and local government employees, Justice Rehnquist holding for the Court that the challenged legislation interfered with integral state functions and thus violated principles of federalism. That precedent proved so unworkable in practice, however, that a different five-four majority reversed it in 1985 in the *Garcia* case, reaffirming the traditional view that the remedy for federal laws that infringed upon no specific constitutional limitation on congressional authority lay with the political process, not the courts.[12]

While largely relegating the reach of government's economic power and the scope of property rights to the political arena, the post-1937 Court also forged a now historic commitment to vigorous protection of noneconomic rights. The justices first began to suggest their acceptance of this constitutional double standard, of course, in the otherwise unexceptional 1938 case of *United States v. Carolene Products Co.*,[13] which upheld a federal statute prohibiting the interstate shipment of adulterated (or "filled") milk against due process and other challenges. In his majority opinion, Justice Stone concluded for the *Carolene Products* Court that laws "affecting ordinary commercial transactions" were to be presumed constitutional and struck down only if lacking "some rational basis within the knowledge and experience of the legislators."[14] At that point, however, Stone inserted his now famous "Footnote Four," in which he suggested that "[t]here may be narrower scope for operation of the presumption of constitutionality" in cases involving laws claimed to violate "a specific prohibition of the Constitution," such as Bill of Rights guarantees and their Fourteenth Amendment counterparts; or regulations restricting access to the political process, including "restrictions upon the right to vote, . . . restraints upon the dissemination of information, . . . interferences with political organizations, . . . [and] prohibition of peaceable assembly"; or finally, those discriminating "against discrete and insular minorities." Such legislation, Stone intimated, might "be subjected to more exacting judicial scrutiny . . . than are most other types of legislation."[15]

For most of the Court's history since 1937, Justice Stone's "Footnote Four" has proven prophetic, indeed. In the Rehnquist Court, however, the double standard's continued vitality is doubtful at best. The current majority appears reasonably committed to the protection of recognized noneconomic rights, if generally reluctant to expand on the scope of unenumerated guarantees, the focus of the next chapter. But the Rehnquist Court has also given the Fifth Amendment's takings clause a remarkably broad and, arguably, unprecedented reach, while reviving the potential of state sovereignty and federalism concepts to significantly restrict otherwise valid exercises of congressional regulatory authority. In 1996, moreover, a majority invoked economic due process for the first time since 1936, holding in *BMW v. Gore*[16] that an Alabama jury's huge award of punitive damages to a luxury automobile purchaser whose "new" car was repainted without his knowledge prior to sale was "grossly excessive" and thus contrary to due process. More recent opinions suggest that *Gore* was hardly an isolated ruling. Instead, as suggested in this chapter, *Gore* and other recent economic decisions have provided a doctrinal basis for the meaningful erosion, if not demise, of the double standard, signaling a major rebirth of Supreme Court solicitude for propertied and commercial interests that may await only the election of another Republican president.

Congressional Power and State Sovereignty

Chief Justice Marshall's opinion for the Court in *Gibbons v. Ogden,*[17] it has been said, described congressional authority over interstate commerce "with a breadth never yet exceeded."[18] The commerce over which Congress was delegated power, the chief justice asserted, included navigation and every other form of commercial intercourse, and not merely the exchange of goods and commodities. The commerce "among the several states" that Congress was empowered to regulate *did not* reach the "completely internal commerce of a state"—commercial activities, that is, "which are completely within a particular state, which do not affect other states." By the same token, congressional authority *did* extend to "that commerce which concerns more states than one," to "all the external concerns of the nation, and to those internal concerns which affect the states generally."[19]

The chief justice's construction of the authority Congress could exert over such commerce was equally expansive: "It is the power to regulate; that is, to prescribe the rule by which commerce is to be governed. This power, like all others vested in Congress, is complete in itself, may be exercised to its utmost extent, and acknowledges no limitations, other than are prescribed in the constitution."[20] Marshall could have intended to include the Tenth Amendment among the limitations on the commerce power "prescribed in the constitution." Instead, he declared, "If, as has always been understood, the sovereignty of Congress, though limited to specified objects, is plenary as to those objects, the power over commerce with foreign nations, and among the several states, is vested in Congress as absolutely as it would be *in a single government.*"[21] That passage strongly suggests, if it does not conclusively demonstrate, that Marshall in no way considered notions of dual national and state sovereignty as barriers to otherwise valid exercises of congressional power. He also made it clear that perceived abuses of congressional authority that abridged no specific constitutional limitations on Congress's power were subject only to political, not judicial, remedy. "The wisdom and the discretion of Congress, their identity with the people, and the influence which their constituents possess at election," he maintained, "are . . . the sole restraints on which they have relied, to secure them from its abuse. They are the restraints on which the people must often rely solely, in all representative governments."[22]

Marshall agreed in *Gibbons,* of course, that states via their police powers might regulate activities also subject to federal control under the commerce clause. Taney Court decisions[23] recognized, moreover, a concurrent power relationship between the federal government and the states, subject only to the proviso that state laws conflicting with otherwise valid congressional statutes are unconstitutional. But such rulings dealt with the impact of congressional authority on state power, not with possible restrictions on national power that might be implicit in the Tenth Amendment and state sovereignty concepts. Thus, it was not until the era of laissez-faire on the Court (1888-1937), a century after the Constitution's adoption, that a shifting majority began regularly to invoke the Tenth Amendment, narrow constructions of national regulatory power, and substantive due process in a vigorous, if uneven, campaign against governmental efforts to control the excesses of the industrial revolution and the consequences of the Great Depression. Nor, even in that period, were the justices bent on the promotion of state power at the expense of federal prerogative. Instead, both state and federal statutes were repeatedly sacrificed on the altar of the Social Darwinian thought then dominating the Court.

The commerce clause and Tenth Amendment rhetoric of that era, some of it drawn out of context from passages in the opinions of the Marshall, Taney, and post-Civil War Courts, could be reduced to a few oft-repeated propositions. Production and commerce were distinct enterprises, with the former primarily subject to state control and the latter within the reach of congressional power. Congress's authority over commerce also extended to those intrastate or local activities directly affecting interstate commerce, but not to those exerting only an indirect or incidental impact on national trade. The extent of an activity's effect on interstate commerce, moreover, had no relationship to its direct or indirect character. As Justice Sutherland observed for the Court in *Carter v. Carter Coal Co.* (1936),[24] invalidating New Deal legislation designed to relieve conditions in the coal industry,

> The distinction between a direct and indirect effect turns, not upon the magnitude of either the cause or the effect, but entirely upon the manner in which the effect has been brought about. If the production by one man of a single ton of coal intended for interstate sale and shipment, and actually so sold and shipped, affects interstate commerce indirectly, the effect does not become direct by multiplying the tonnage, or increasing the number of men employed, or adding to the expense or complexities of the business, or by all combined. It is quite true that rules of law are sometimes qualified by considerations of degree, as the government argues. But the matter of degree has no bearing upon the question here.[25]

In short, a particular activity might be exerting a disastrous effect on interstate commerce; but if that impact were "indirect" rather than "direct," as determined by the courts, Congress was powerless to intervene. Failure to draw such distinctions, the Court had noted in overturning the National Industrial Recovery Act the previous year in the *Schechter* case, would mean that "the federal authority would embrace practically all the activities of the people and the authority of the State over its domestic concerns would exist only by sufferance of the federal government."[26]

A laissez-faire majority persisted on the Court through the early years of the Depression and President Roosevelt's first term. Early 1937, however, brought the Court-packing plan, the Court's "switch in time that would save nine," and an abrupt end to the era of judicial economic conservatism. As Justice Stone emphasized in *Carolene Products*, economic regulations were now to be presumed constitutional, upheld against due process and equal protection attack unless found to be totally lacking in any "rational basis." Judicial determinations with respect to the reach of the commerce clause would no longer "give controlling force to nomenclature such as 'production' and 'indirect' and foreclose consideration of the actual effects of the activity in question upon interstate commerce."[27] No longer would the Tenth Amendment block enforcement of an otherwise valid exercise of congressional power. "[That] amendment," Justice Jackson declared for the Court in *United States v. Darby Lumber Co.* (1941), "states but a truism that all is retained which has not been surrendered. There is nothing in the history of its adoption to suggest that it was more than declaratory of the relationship between the national and state governments as it had been established by the Constitution before the amendment or that *its purpose was other than to allay fears that the new national government might seek to exercise powers not granted, and that the states might not be able to exercise fully their reserved powers.*"[28] Like Chief Justice Marshall in *Gibbons*, moreover, the post-1937 Court "made emphatic the embracing and penetrating nature of [the commerce] power by warning that effective restraints on its exercise must proceed from political rather than from judicial processes."[29]

For most of the intervening years, the Court has kept faith with *Gibbons* and with the New Deal majority's broad construction of the commerce power and refusal to construe the Tenth Amendment as a restriction on otherwise valid federal statutes. A number of decisions arguably went even further, emphasizing, in the spirit of Marshall's broad construction of interstate commerce, that Congress's power reaches all interstate movement, commercial or noncommercial in nature;[30] holding that Congress can reach every class of activities it has a rational basis to believe is affecting interstate commerce;[31] and "put[ting] entirely to rest" the notion "that in Commerce Clause cases the courts have power to excise [from federal control], as trivial, individual instances falling within a rationally defined class of activities."[32] And *Usery*, the sole pre-Rehnquist Court, post-1937 ruling to invalidate an exercise of the commerce power on Tenth Amendment, state sovereignty grounds, did not, of course, survive a decade.

Several Rehnquist Court decisions suggest, however, that the era of judicial laissez-faire in commerce cases may be ending. Of them, *United States v. Lopez* (1995) is potentially the most significant. A five-four *Lopez* majority struck down the federal Gun-Free School Zones Act, prohibiting possession of any firearm in a school zone, on the ground that the proscribed offense was not economic activity that substantially affected interstate commerce. In defending the statute, the government argued that possession of firearms in schools may result in violent crime that in turn would affect the national economy through increased insurance costs and the reluctance of persons to travel to areas of the nation perceived to be unsafe. Also cited were the substantial threat that violence posed for the educational process and its impact on the nation's economic well-being.

Like the laissez-faire justices of the pre-1937 Court, the majority, speaking through the chief justice, found this connection between gun possession in schools and the national economy entirely too remote and speculative. "To uphold the Government's contentions here," declared Rehnquist, "we would have to pile inference upon inference in a manner that would bid fair to convert congressional authority under the Commerce Clause to a general police power of the sort retained by the States."[33] Rehnquist conceded that "some of our prior cases have taken long steps down that road, giving great deference to congressional action," and that "[t]he broad language" of such opinions had "suggested the possibility of additional expansion," but concluded that the Court "decline[d] .. to proceed any further."[34]

Rehnquist intimated that the challenged statute might have been upheld had it included a jurisdictional provision assuring that the offenses at issue in particular cases actually exerted a substantial effect on interstate commerce. But the law had not included such an element, Congress had made no formal findings regarding the effect of gun possession in schools on interstate commerce, and the school zone gun law represented "a sharp break with the long standing pattern of federal firearms legislation."[35] The chief justice came close to declaring, moreover, that only that firearm possession constituting in itself an "economic activity" would be subject to federal control, whatever its effect on interstate commerce.

Missing entirely was the repeated assertion of earlier opinions, including *Gibbons*, that the remedy for perceived abuses of the commerce power was political rather than judicial. Instead, Rehnquist focused on the judiciary's duty "to say what the law is,"[36] on the "judicially enforceable outer limits" of congressional authority,[37] and on the dire threat that the challenged statute and arguments in its behalf posed for state sovereignty. "[I]f we were to accept the Government's arguments," the chief justice exclaimed, "we are hard-pressed to posit any activity by an individual that Congress is without power to regulate."[38]

In a concurring opinion joined by Justice O'Connor, Justice Kennedy emphasized what he considered to be the "limited" nature of the Court's holding and urged the exercise of "great restraint before the Court determines that the [Commerce] Clause is insufficient to support an exercise of the national power."[39] But Kennedy refused to agree that the Court lacked the power and duty "in every instance . . . to review congressional attempts to alter the federal balance."[40] The challenged statute regulated an activity historically within the scope of state power and clearly "beyond the realm of commerce in the ordinary and usual sense of that term."[41] As such, it "contradict[ed] the federal balance the Framers designed and that this Court is obliged to enforce."[42]

Justice Thomas's concurring opinion was as sweeping in scope as the Kennedy concurrence was cautious. A jurisprudential soul mate, apparently, of Justice McReynolds and other pre-1937 laissez-faire justices, Thomas decried what he viewed as the unfortunate drift of the case law "far from the original understanding of the Commerce Clause."[43] Indeed, he appeared to assign the clause a more limited construction than the Old Court majority embraced. Giving *Gibbons* perhaps its most narrow reading ever, Thomas rejected the notion that Chief Justice Marshall's opinion there provided any basis for the view that Congress is empowered by the commerce clause to regulate local activities that substantially affect interstate commerce. When Marshall construed commerce "among the several states" to include that commerce that "extended to," "affected," or "concerned" more than one state, according to Thomas, the chief justice was simply "acknowledging that although the line between intrastate and interstate/foreign commerce would be difficult to draw, federal authority could not be construed to cover purely intrastate commerce."[44] Even if *Gibbons* were interpreted to embrace the "affects" language, he added, Congress would at most be permitted, as Chief Justice Rehnquist was suggesting, "to regulate only intrastate *commerce*" having that effect, not "*all* activities" with that impact on interstate commerce.[45] For Thomas, in fact, the model for construction of the commerce clause appeared to be *E.C. Knight, Schechter, Carter Coal*, and other narrow Old Court interpretations of the commerce power, not the rulings of the past half century or the liberal reading traditionally given Marshall's construction of congressional authority, which Thomas termed a "misreading" of *Gibbons*.

Three of the four *Lopez* dissenters filed opinions in the case. In his brief dissent, Justice Stevens largely endorsed the rationales of Justices Souter's and Breyer's more elaborate dissenting opinions. For Stevens, the relation of gun possession to interstate commerce was obvious. "Guns are both articles of commerce and articles that can be used to restrain commerce," he declared. "Their possession is the consequence, either directly or indirectly, of commercial activity. In my judgment, Congress' power to regulate commerce in firearms includes the power to prohibit possession of guns at any location because of their potentially harmful use; it necessarily follows that Congress may also prohibit their possession in particular markets. The market for the possession of handguns by school-age children is, distressingly, substantial. Whether or not the national interest in eliminating that market would have justified federal legislation in 1789, it does today."[46]

Justice Souter's dissent focused, in the words of Justice Stevens, on "the radical character of the Court's holding and its kinship with the discredited, pre-Depression version of substantive due process."[47] Unlike Justice Thomas, Souter saw the laissez-faire era as "one of this Court's most chastening experiences"[48] and the *Lopez* ruling a move back in the direction of that "untenable" period in the Court's history. Since 1937, the Court's review of commercial legislation had turned solely on "whether the legislative judgment is within the realm of reason."[49] The *Lopez* majority, by contrast, had probed the justifications underlying Congress's judgment, finding them inadequate to support the firearms statute. In Souter's judgment, there was "no reason to hope that [this] qualification of rational basis review will be any more successful than the efforts at substantive economic review made by our predecessors as the century began."[50] For Souter, the majority's construction of the commerce clause had a familiar ring. "The distinction between what is patently commercial and what is not," he declared, "looks much like the old distinction between what directly affects commerce and what touches it only indirectly."[51]

Justice Breyer, joined by Stevens, Souter, and Ginsburg, began his thoroughgoing dissent by reminding readers of three "basic principles" of commerce clause construction: that Congress's power reaches local activities that substantially or, under recent precedents, only "significantly" affect interstate commerce; that courts are to consider "cumulative" or aggregate effect rather than the impact of an "individual act (a single instance of gun possession)"; and that the delegation of commercial power to Congress, not the courts, meant that Congress was entitled to considerable deference in the exercise of that authority—a deference or "leeway" best captured in the "rational basis" standard. Applying these principles, as well as Justice Holmes's admonition that commerce is a "practical" conception rather than a "technical legal" one,[52] Breyer found it obvious that Congress "had a *rational basis* for finding a significant (or substantial) connection between gun-related school violence and interstate commerce."[53] Given the "inextricabl[e]" link between education and the national economy, "gun-related violence in and around schools," he declared, was a "commercial, as well as a human, problem."[54] By attempting to draw clear-cut lines between commercial and noncommercial activities, the majority had failed to heed Justice Jackson's warning in *Wickard* that questions of congressional power should not turn on "nomenclature"[55] but upon economic reality. The Court's decision to ignore Justice Jackson and strike the challenged statute down conflicted with precedents upholding congressional regulations of activities with a "less significant" connection to interstate and foreign commerce than the effect of school violence[56] and threatened "legal uncertainty" in a "reasonably well settled" area of law.[57] A decision affirming the statute, on the other hand, would have been consistent with traditional constructions of the commerce power, "with the exception of one wrong turn subsequently corrected."[58] Justice Thomas had contended in his *Lopez* concurrence that the Court's "wrong turn" in the commerce field had been taken in 1937 and should be corrected at "an appropriate juncture."[59] But Justice Breyer was referring, of course, to the laissez-faire era.

Although the cautious tone of the Kennedy-O'Connor concurrence limited somewhat the immediate precedential value of Chief Justice Rehnquist's *Lopez* opinion, the Rehnquist opinion and *Lopez* concurrences demonstrated a clear willingness on the part of a narrow majority of the current Court to significantly extend the reach of judicial review in commerce clause cases. Several decisions limiting congressional authority over state and local officials also suggest such a trend. In the *Garcia* case, decided a year before Rehnquist's appointment as chief justice, a majority had overruled Rehnquist's assertion for the *Usery* Court that congressional regulations conflicting with traditional, integral, or essential state functions unconstitutionally interfered with state sovereignty. Upholding application of federal wage and hour standards to state and local government employees, the *Garcia* majority held that the appropriate remedy for alleged abuses of federal regulatory authority was political rather than judicial.

In several cases decided before and after *Garcia*, however, the Court has recognized limits to Congress's power to force state and local officials to enact and administer federal regulatory policies. In the 1981 *Hodel* case, the Court upheld a congressional statute designed to protect against the adverse effects of surface coal-mining operations, even though the law at issue required states either to establish a regulatory scheme conforming to federal minimum standards or to adopt a federal regulatory program. Since the statute gave states a choice, Justice Marshall held for the Court, "there [could] be no suggestion that the Act commandeers the legislative processes of States by compelling them to enact and enforce a federal regulatory program."[60] Thus, the law did not conflict with state sovereignty under the Tenth Amendment.

The following year the Court upheld federal legislation directed at the nationwide energy crisis over the claims of Mississippi officials that the statute unduly invaded state sovereignty.[61] Challenged provisions of the law required state regulatory commissions and unregulated utilities to consider adoption of specific rate and regulatory standards and to follow federal notice and comment procedures when acting on the proposed federal standards. Other provisions, designed to encourage the development of cogeneration and small power facilities, directed the Federal Energy Regulatory Commission (FERC), in consultation with state regulatory authorities, to establish rules to carry out that goal; required state officials to implement them; and authorized the FERC to exempt qualified facilities from certain state and federal regulations. Noting that states were only required to "consider" adoption and enforcement of federal rate and regulatory standards and that federal requirements were consistent with congressional authority to preempt state regulations, the Court upheld the statute.

In *New York v. United States* (1992), however, the Court struck down the "take-title" provision of a 1985 congressional statute regulating the disposal of low-level radioactive waste. Under the take-title portion of the statute, a state or regional compact that failed to provide for the disposal of all such waste generated in the state by a particular date was required, at the request of the waste generator or owner, to take title and possession of the waste and assume liability for all damages suffered by the generator or owner as a result of the state's failure to take prompt possession. The "choice" offered states under the statute to either accept ownership and liability for waste or regulate it according to Congress's instructions was, Justice O'Connor held for the Court, unconstitutionally coercive and thus a violation of the Tenth Amendment.

> Whatever the outer limits of [state] sovereignty may be, one thing is clear. The Federal Government may not compel the States to enact or administer a federal regulatory program. The Constitution permits both the Federal Government and the States to enact legislation regarding the disposal of low level radioactive waste. The Constitution enables the Federal Government to preempt state regulation contrary to federal interests, and it permits the Federal Government to hold out incentives to the States as a means of encouraging them to adopt suggested regulatory schemes. It does not, however, authorize Congress simply to direct the States to provide for the disposal of the radioactive waste generated within their borders.[62]

Justice White, joined by Justices Blackmun and Stevens, dissented from the Court's decision striking down the take-title provision. Emphasizing the federal-state cooperation that had led to adoption of the challenged statute and Congress's power, had it wished, to preempt the field entirely, Justice White viewed the regulation as entirely consistent with the traditional view that limits on congressional regulatory authority were properly political rather than judicial in nature. For White, the "ultimate irony of the [Court's] decision [was] that in its formalistically rigid obeisance to 'federalism,' the Court gives Congress fewer incentives to defer to the wishes of state officials in achieving local solutions to local problems. This legislation was a classic example of Congress acting as arbiter among the states in their attempts to accept responsibility for managing a problem of grave impact."[63]

In a separate opinion, Justice Stevens went further, finding nothing in the Constitution denying Congress the authority to command states to implement congressional legislation. "Nor," he added, "does the structure of the constitutional order or the values of federalism mandate such a formal rule. To the contrary, the Federal

Government directs state governments in many realms. The Government regulates state-operated railroads, state school systems, state prisons, state elections, and a host of other state functions.... I see no reason why Congress may not also command the States to enforce federal water and air quality standards or federal standards for the disposition of low-level radioactive waste."[64]

Stevens's point was well-taken. The Tenth Amendment's text, standing alone, obviously does not incorporate some concept of state power interdicting an otherwise valid exercise of national authority. It simply reserves to the states powers not delegated to the United States. Congress clearly has been delegated power over interstate commerce, and that authority has long been held to include power to regulate local activities that substantially affect interstate commerce. Just as clearly, the policies and practices of state and local governments may exert such an impact on interstate commerce, and nothing in the language of the Tenth Amendment—or any other constitutional provision, for that matter—forbids Congress to impose its delegated authority on states and localities. The *New York* majority surmounted that obstacle to its ruling only by declaring that the restraints that the Tenth Amendment imposes on congressional power were "not" to be "derived from the [amendment's] text . . . , which is essentially a tautology," but from limits inherent in some "incident of state sovereignty."[65]

In its next decision of the *New York* variety, a majority drew on the *Federalist* essays and other sources in further defending state sovereignty restrictions on national power. The cases providing the Court's opportunity were *Printz v. United States* (1997) and *Mack v. United States* (1997),[66] companion cases invalidating provisions of the Brady handgun statute at the end of the 1996-97 term. Named for James Brady, the presidential aide seriously injured in the 1981 assassination attempt on President Reagan, the challenged statute authorized the attorney general to establish a national system of background checks on handgun purchasers and ordered local sheriffs to conduct such investigations and a number of related tasks until the national system was in operation. Finding no basis in the Constitution's text for striking down the handgun law, the majority, per Justice Scalia, sought its decision "in historical understanding and practice, in the structure of the Constitution, and in the jurisprudence of this Court."[67]

A number of early congressional regulations required state courts to perform certain duties related to citizenship proceedings, controversies between ship captains and crews, fugitive slaves, Revolutionary War claims, and the deportation of enemy aliens. But, according to Scalia, those laws established, "at most," an original understanding that the federal government could impose obligations on state *judges*. Scalia considered such obligations consistent with the framers' obvious assumption that state courts would be expected to hear certain federal cases and with the mandate of the supremacy clause that state judges are "bound" to obey federal law. But he rejected the notion that the imposition of certain duties on state judges implied a congressional authority "to impress the state executive into its office."[68] In fact, when the first Congress enacted legislation providing for the incarceration of federal prisoners in state jails, it merely "recommended" that states adopt enabling legislation. Nor, in Scalia's judgment, did passages from the *Federalist* bolster the government's case. Alexander Hamilton's assertion in No. 36 that Congress would probably "make use" of state officers and regulations in tax collections, like Madison's prediction to the same effect in No. 45, Hamilton's observation in No. 27 that the Constitution would "enable the [national] government to employ the ordinary magistracy of each [state] in the execution of its laws," and Madison's assumption in No. 45 that state officials would be "clothed" with federal authority in other contexts as well, suggested only that states might "consent" to assist the new government in meeting its responsibilities.[69]

In defending Congress's power to adopt the Brady Act, Justice Souter relied heavily in his *Printz* and *Mack* dissent on Hamilton's observation in No. 27 that under the Constitution, "the legislatures, courts, and magistrates, of the [states] . . . will be incorporated into the operations of the national government *as far as its just and constitutional authority extends*, and will be rendered auxiliary to the enforcement of its laws."[70] But Scalia read that passage as merely underscoring the obligation of all state officials "not to obstruct the operation of federal law."[71] If the passage meant more, supporting federal power to direct state officials, Scalia added, it conflicted with the Court's conclusion in *New York* "that state legislatures are *not* subject to federal direction."[72]

Scalia further noted that until recent years Congress had declined to enact statutes "commandeering" state and local officials to administer federal regulations. He agreed that a number of recent federal funding measures had required state and local participation in implementing federal regulations. But he concluded that those could "perhaps be more accurately described as conditions upon the grant of federal funding than as mandates to the States."[73] Whatever their constitutional status, moreover, they had "little relevance" to the issues raised by the handgun statute and were "of such recent vintage," in any event, that they were "no more probative than the statute before us of a constitutional tradition that lends meaning to the text."[74]

Nor was the "structure of the Constitution," in the majority's view, supportive of the government's position. The system of "dual sovereignty" established in the Constitution provided for a national government that acted upon individuals, not states. Federal laws "commandeering" state executive officials violated that principle and also conflicted with the president's authority to "faithfully execute" federal law. Since such "commandeering" statutes were inconsistent with the concept of "dual sovereignty," they were not within the reach of Congress's delegated or implied powers and thus violated the Tenth Amendment.

Turning finally to the Court's own precedents, Justice Scalia characterized statutes of the Brady variety as such a "novel phenomenon" that the justices did not first encounter them until the 1970s. Citing *Hodel* and *FERC*, he noted that the regulations at issue there had been upheld only because they did not "require" states to enforce federal law. When first confronted "squarely" with a statute "commandeering" state officials in the *New York* case, he added, the Court had invalidated it on Tenth Amendment grounds. No weight could be given, either, to the Court's decisions upholding federal laws that obliged state courts to apply federal regulations. Such rulings, like early congressional regulations imposing obligations on state courts, said "nothing about whether state executive officers must administer federal law."[75]

Justice Scalia concluded with the following summary of the Court's position:

We held in *New York* that Congress cannot compel the States to enact or enforce a federal regulatory program. Today we hold that Congress cannot circumvent that prohibition by conscripting the State's [executive] officers directly. The Federal Government may neither issue directives requiring the States to address particular problems, nor command the States' officers, or those of their political subdivisions, to administer or enforce a federal regulatory program. It matters not whether policymaking is involved, and no case-by-case weighing of the burdens or benefits is necessary; such commands are fundamentally incompatible with our constitutional system of dual sovereignty.[76]

In a brief concurrence, Justice O'Connor emphasized that local law officers could continue to participate voluntarily in the handgun program and that, in any event, the Brady statute's directives to local officials were merely interim measures scheduled to terminate in 1998. She also suggested that she would support directives tied to federal funding, but agreed that provisions "which directly compel state officials to administer a federal regulatory program, utterly fail[ed] to adhere to the design and structure of our constitutional scheme."[77]

Justice Thomas reiterated his view that the commerce clause did not reach "wholly *intra* state, point-of-sale transactions" and asserted that a Congress with no authority "to regulate the intrastate transfer of firearms" surely could not conscript state law enforcement officers to enforce such regulations. Even if congressional power extended to local activities substantially affecting interstate commerce, a proposition he had disputed in *Lopez*, Thomas questioned whether Congress could regulate the handgun transactions covered by the Brady Act, given not only the Tenth Amendment, but the Second as well. Although resting his vote on the Tenth Amendment, he noted that the Second Amendment also appeared to "contain an express limitation on the government's authority," one that went beyond safeguarding state power to maintain a militia.[78]

Justice Stevens, joined by Justices Souter, Ginsburg, and Breyer, dissented. As in the *New York* case, Stevens found nothing in the Constitution's text permitting local police to ignore a command imposed by Congress pursuant to its delegated powers. His reading of the *Federalist* convinced him, in fact, that the Constitution's framers intended to confer on the new national government "the power to demand that local [executive] officials implement national policy programs."[79] And the failure of the early Congress to exercise that power was in no way "an argument against its existence," particularly since such thinking "would undermine most of [the Court's] post-New Deal Commerce Clause jurisprudence."[80] The early Congress had imposed obligations, moreover, on state courts and their clerks; and many of the functions of such officials in that period were essentially executive in character. In Stevens's judgment, therefore, the majority's attempt to distinguish federal enlistment of state judges and other state personnel "rest[ed] on empty formalistic reasoning of the highest order."[81]

Finding the cases "closer than I had anticipated," Justice Souter joined Stevens's dissent, but not because of what he considered the few early instances "of federal employment of state officers for executive purposes."[82] Instead, he based his vote, as noted earlier, primarily on Hamilton's assertion in *Federalist* No. 27 that under the supremacy clause and related constitutional provisions, state officials would become "auxiliaries" to the national government, obligated to assist it in the enforcement of its laws. That passage and portions of Nos. 45 and 36 persuaded Souter that the national government was empowered "to require state 'auxiliaries' to take appropriate action,"[83] even though that authority could not be used to require a state legislature to enact a regulatory scheme of the sort at issue in the *New York* case and might be subject to other limitations as well. Congress should also be required, he added, to pay for administrative support required of state and local officials.

Justice Breyer, like Justice Souter, joined Stevens's dissent but also wrote a brief concurrence. Noting that certain other federal systems, including those of Germany and Switzerland, provided for state implementation of many federal laws, Breyer viewed that approach as perhaps a better device for preserving local control than "the principle the majority derives from the silence of the Constitution."[84] Like Justice Stevens, moreover, Breyer could not understand how creation of a purely federal "gun-law bureaucracy" would "better promote either state sovereignty or individual liberty" than the federal-state approach established in the Brady Act.[85]

At one level, of course, *Lopez, New York,* and the Brady Act cases can be viewed as only modest departures from the modern Court's traditional broad reading of the commerce clause and narrow construction of the Tenth Amendment. All dealt after all with relatively specialized situations, and all but one involved federal directives to state and local officials rather than private commercial concerns. Even so, it is difficult to square the recent decisions with most of the Court's relevant post-1937 case law or with *Gibbons v. Ogden.* In both rhetoric and substance, in fact, they resemble much more the Old Court's conception of the commerce power and dual federalism construction of the Tenth Amendment. They thus raise doubts about the continued vitality of that element of the double standard presuming the constitutionality of federal regulatory statutes and refusing to view the Tenth Amendment as a barrier to otherwise valid exercises of federal power.

Economic Due Process

The *Lopez* dissenters, especially Justice Souter, accused the majority of resurrecting substantive due process, the linchpin of the laissez-faire era, via a narrow construction of the commerce power and broad interpretation of the Tenth Amendment. It is somewhat ironic, therefore, that Souter and two other *Lopez* dissenters helped to form the majority in the Court's first decision in sixty years to invalidate a state economic action on substantive due process grounds.[86] In 1993, a federal district court invoked the doctrine to strike down a Chicago ordinance designed to curb the spread of graffiti through a ban on the sale of spray paint and jumbo indelible markers within the city limits. Noting that vandals could easily purchase spray paint and markers elsewhere, the court declared it "irrational" to deprive the law-abiding 99 percent of easy access to spray paint when the challenged ban did not accomplish its purpose.[87] But a federal appeals panel reversed the district court. Applying the lenient, rational basis standard of substantive due process, under which economic regulations had regularly been reviewed—and upheld—since 1936, the panel expressed amazement that even "the most wild-eyed radical's list of candidates for the status of 'fundamental rights' would include spray paint."[88] Under the rationality standard, the appeals court might have added, the Supreme Court presumably would uphold every economic measure.

Until, that is, *BMW v. Gore*.[89] When Dr. Ira Gore, a Birmingham, Alabama, physician, learned that his "new" BMW sports sedan had been repainted prior to sale, he sued the distributor for damages. At trial, BMW acknowledged a company policy under which vehicles damaged in manufacture or transportation were repaired and sold as new, without informing local dealers, if the repairs did not exceed 3 percent of the suggested retail price of the car. Gore sought $4,000 in actual damages and $4 million in punitive damages, which he considered an appropriate penalty for the company's having sold a thousand repaired cars for more than they were worth. On BMW's appeal of a jury award of the full damages sought, the Alabama Supreme Court reduced the punitive damages awarded by $2 million, refusing to allow punitive damages based on sales in other states. Speaking through Justice Stevens, a Supreme Court majority found the $2 million award grossly excessive and thus contrary to due process.

Given its pronouncements in two earlier cases, the Court's decision was hardly unexpected. In *Pacific Mutual Life Insurance Co. v. Haslip* (1991), the Court upheld a $1 million Alabama jury's punitive damages award against an insurance company whose agent had misappropriated premium payments even though the punitive damages awarded were more than four times the amount of compensatory damages sought. In a concurring opinion, Justice Scalia largely embraced the traditional "law of the land" conception of due process and asserted "that no procedure firmly rooted in the practices of our people can be so 'fundamentally unfair' as to deny due process of law."[90] Because the traditional American practice was to leave punitive damages to the discretion of the jury and Alabama procedures were both consistent with that tradition and violative of no specific provision of the Bill of Rights, Scalia favored approving the challenged procedure "without further inquiry into its 'fairness' or 'reasonableness.'"[91]

The majority, per Justice Blackmun, agreed that the traditional common law procedure used in Alabama to assess punitive damages was not "so inherently unfair as to be *per se* unconstitutional." Unlike Scalia, however, the majority construed due process to include substantive restraints on jury discretion in such cases. Emphasizing that unlimited discretion might "invite extreme results that jar one's constitutional sensibilities," Blackmun concluded for the Court that punitive damages awards must be reasonable. "We need not, and indeed we cannot," he observed, "draw a mathematical bright line between the constitutionally acceptable and the constitutionally unacceptable that would fit every case. We can say, however, that general concerns of reasonableness and adequate guidance from the court when the case is tried to a jury properly enter into the constitutional calculus."[92] Since the *Haslip* trial judge's instructions to the jury placed "reasonable constraints" on its discretion and the proceedings included other comparable safeguards, the majority concluded that the award challenged met the requirement of reasonableness.

Two years later, in *TXO Production Corp. v. Alliance Resources Corp.* (1993),[93] the Court upheld a jury's award of $19,000 in actual damages and $10 million in punitive damages, but reaffirmed its position in *Haslip* that such awards must be "reasonable." After reaching an agreement to pay Alliance a substantial amount for oil and gas development rights on Alliance's West Virginia property, TXO embarked upon a campaign of fraud and trickery in an effort to pressure Alliance into renegotiating the royalty arrangement. In light of the millions of dollars potentially at stake and TXO's malicious and fraudulent behavior, a plurality, speaking through Justice Stevens, concluded that the damages awarded did not exceed state authority. But Stevens also cited several early-twentieth-century Supreme Court decisions imposing substantive limits on jury awards and asserted, in response to a statement by Alliance counsel denigrating such rulings as "*Lochner*-era precedents," that justices who dissented in *Lochner* joined the jury award decisions.[94]

Justice Scalia, joined by Justice Thomas, who was appointed to the Court after the *Haslip* decision, agreed in an opinion concurring in the judgment that "traditional American practice" reflected in West Virginia law required state trial and appellate courts to review the reasonableness of jury damage awards. He was also willing to concede that the Fourteenth Amendment due process clause, "despite its textual limitation to procedure, incorporates certain substantive guarantees specified in the Bill of Rights" via the incorporation process. But Scalia disputed "the existence of a so-called 'substantive due process' right that punitive damages be reasonable" and the more general "proposition that [due process] is the secret repository of all sorts of other, unenumerated, substantive rights—however fashionable that proposition may have been (even as to economic rights of the sort here) at the time of the *Lochner*-era cases the plurality relies upon." Merely to conclude that state law requires some judicial review of the reasonableness of punitive damages awards, exclaimed Scalia, "is not to say that there is a federal constitutional right to a substantively correct 'reasonableness' determination."[95]

Like Justices Scalia and Thomas, Justice Kennedy joined only the Court's judgment. Kennedy maintained that the "reasonableness" formula was unduly vague, providing no standard by which to compare a challenged award to the malefactions on which it was based. He preferred an approach that focused on the reasons underlying an award rather than the amount of damages. Where an award reflected jury bias, passion, or prejudice, any judgment was unconstitutional, regardless of its size. Applying his formula in light of the clear evidence in the case of TXO's deliberate misconduct, Kennedy concluded that the challenged award was motivated by the jury's legitimate interests in deterrence and punishment rather than whim.

Although speaking only for a plurality in *TXO*, Justice Stevens secured a narrow majority, including Justice Kennedy, for the Court's decision overturning the $2 million in punitive damages at issue in *BMW v. Gore*. Along the lines Kennedy had recommended in *TXO*, Stevens focused on aggravating factors that might have justified the huge award at issue in *Gore*—specifically, the degree of reprehensibility of

BMW's conduct, the ratio of compensatory to punitive damages, and the difference between the size of the award and the severity of criminal or civil sanctions that could be imposed for comparable misconduct. None of these guideposts, he concluded, was present in *Gore*; hence, the Court's decision that the damages awarded were grossly excessive.

In a dissent joined by Justice Thomas, Justice Scalia again registered his opposition to substantive due process and derided the majority for finally taking the step, threatened in *Haslip* and *TXO*, "of declaring a punitive award unconstitutional simply because it was 'too big.'"[96] Justice Ginsburg, joined by the chief justice, also dissented, calling the majority's application of "a vague concept of due process . . . as its ultimate guide"[97] an unnecessary and unwise intrusion "into territory traditionally within the States' domain," particularly in view of legislative efforts to reform punitive damages proceedings then under way in various state legislatures.[98] Ginsburg and Rehnquist stopped short of an outright rejection of substantive due process, preferring instead to emphasize the "presumption of legitimacy" normally accorded such state decisions.[99] Given that presumption, they concluded that the Alabama Supreme Court ruling was consistent with the principles governing punitive damages awards.

The Court's opinion in *Gore*, along with the prevailing opinions in *TXO* and *Haslip*, make clear, however, that a narrow majority on the Rehnquist Court is now applying a stricter standard of substantive due process in economic cases than *Carolene Products* and other post-1937 cases embraced. Indeed, in his *TXO* plurality opinion Justice Stevens even specifically rejected application of a rational basis standard in punitive damages cases. Under such a standard, he warned, "apparently *any* award that would serve the legitimate state interest in deterring or punishing wrongful conduct, no matter how large, would be acceptable."[100] The Stevens plurality obviously favored closer judicial scrutiny of such awards, and the *Gore* majority clearly adopted a similar stance. So, in substantive due process cases as in commerce clause litigation, the current Court is subjecting economic controls to more stringent review than the double standard reflects.

The Takings Clause

Although Justices Scalia and Thomas adamantly oppose application of substantive due process, they have regularly joined the Court in decisions giving an expansive construction to the Fifth Amendment clause forbidding "private property [to] be taken for public use without just compensation," even though the 1897 decision extending that guarantee to state cases via the Fourteenth Amendment had itself been based on a substantive due process rationale.[101] For many years, application of the takings clause was limited to situations in which government took actual title to property through condemnation proceedings or engaged in action having essentially the same effect. In *United States v. Causby* (1946), for example, the Court ruled that bombers roaring to and from a government-leased airport only eighty-three feet above an adjacent chicken farm was "as much an appropriation of the use of the land as a more conventional entry upon it." But the Court later made clear the narrow scope of its ruling, declaring in 1963 that jet aircraft operations disturbing residents adjacent to airports, despite the obvious impact of such noise on property values, did not constitute a taking since the homes involved were still inhabitable.[102]

The Court of the laissez-faire era, however, had laid a foundation for a much broader construction of the takings clause. In *Pennsylvania Coal Co. v. Mahon* (1922),[103] the justices held that a statute prohibiting coal mining that endangered the stability of surface dwellings could not be applied, without compensation, in behalf of a property owner who attempted to secure the law's enforcement against a company that had sold him the property while reserving mining rights. Justice Holmes conceded for the majority that "Government hardly could go on if to some extent values incident to property could not be diminished without paying for every such change in the general law."[104] Holmes concluded, however, "that while property may be regulated to a certain extent [without compensation], if regulation goes too far it will be recognized as a taking."[105] The Pennsylvania law had gone too far.

Despite *Mahon's* potential as a basis for radical expansion of judicial authority in such cases, the Old Court seemed reluctant to give the notion of regulatory takings a broad reach. In 1928, for example, the justices upheld a Virginia law providing for the destruction of all ornamental red cedar trees that might infect neighboring apple orchards with cedar rust disease, even though owners were paid only for the cost of removing the trees, not for loss of market and land value.[106] Two years earlier, the Court upheld a zoning ordinance despite its effect on property values,[107] although it later struck down a particular application of a zoning regulation.[108]

The post-1937 Court was even more deferential to government in responding to takings claims. *Goldblatt v. Hempstead* (1962)[109] upheld a safety regulation applicable to sand and gravel pits, even though the Court recognized that the ordinance at issue prohibited a beneficial use to which such property had previously been devoted. In *Penn Central Transp. Co. v. New York City* (1978),[110] a majority rejected takings claims advanced against a historic preservation law used to prevent construction of an office building, and a five-four 1987 decision even upheld a modern version of the statute struck down in the *Mahon* case.[111]

Beginning the year after Chief Justice Rehnquist's elevation to the Court's center seat, however, a majority has regularly invoked the takings clause to expand judicial oversight of land use regulations. Building on the Holmes dictum in *Mahon*, the Court has concluded that a variety of zoning controls have imposed such a severe economic hardship on property that the regulation at issue amounted to a taking for which compensation was required. In one of the most significant of these rulings, *Nollan v. California Coastal Comm'n* (1987),[112] the state had granted the Nollans permission to replace their small beach bungalow with a larger home, provided that they permitted the public to pass across their stretch of private beach, an area situated between two public beaches. The Court, per Justice Scalia, held that the requirement constituted a taking for which the Nollans were entitled to compensation. Scalia conceded that the coastal commission could have denied the Nollans' request to build a larger home and could also have imposed other restrictions without incurring a taking, but only if the regulation at issue "substantially advanced" legitimate state interests. But the Court was skeptical of the commission's assertion that the easement required of the Nollans would promote public viewing of the beach and related goals. Scalia found it "quite impossible," for example, "to understand how a requirement that people already on public beaches be able to walk across the Nollans' property reduces any obstacle to viewing the beach created by the new house."[113]

Justice Scalia again spoke for the majority in *Lucas v. South Carolina Coastal Council* (1992),[114] upholding a challenge to the state's uncompensated refusal to allow a developer to construct beachfront housing that constituted a threat to the coastal environment or was built in an unsafe setting. Citing *Nollan* and other cases, Scalia concluded that compensation was automatically required whenever government physically "invaded" private property or a regulation denied a property owner "all economically beneficial or productive use of the land."[115] *Lucas* fell within the second restriction, in the majority's judgment. Compensation was thus required unless the state could establish on remand that South Carolina's property and nuisance law prohibited such development at the time Lucas purchased the property. "Where the State," Scalia declared, "seeks to sustain a regulation that deprives land of all economically beneficial use, we think it may resist compensation only if the logically antecedent inquiry into the nature of the owner's estate shows that the proscribed use interests were not part of his title to begin with."[116]

In the *Dolan* case, decided two years later, a five-four majority, per Chief Justice Rehnquist, reversed lower court rulings and struck down as an uncompensated regulatory taking a planning commission's decision to permit a store owner to expand her building and pave the parking lot, but only if she dedicated a portion of the land for a greenway designed to reduce flooding and for a pedestrian/bicycle path. Applying a standard of "rough proportionality," the chief justice required a showing of a close relationship between the challenged conditions and legitimate governmental interests. Although conceding that the state clearly had a legitimate interest in flood control and the reduction of traffic congestion, Rehnquist found an insufficient connection between these interests and the contested easement. Some evidence, not merely a conclusory statement, was necessary, the chief justice asserted, to justify the commission's action. In the 1998-99 term, moreover, the Court concluded that regulatory takings issues, unlike questions raised in a condemnation proceeding, could be submitted to a jury.[117]

Justice Stevens has been the Court's most persistent critic of an expansive takings doctrine. In his *Dolan* dissent, Stevens accused the majority of resurrecting economic due process. The very case in which the Court first construed the Fourteenth Amendment to embody the takings guarantee,[118] he noted, had made no mention of the Fifth Amendment takings clause or the argument that the Fourteenth Amendment absorbed provisions of the Bill of Rights, including the takings clause, making them applicable to the states. Instead, the Court invoked "the same kind of substantive due process analysis more frequently identified with" *Lochner* and other decisions of the laissez-faire era.[119]

The regulatory takings concept adopted by the *Mahon* Court during the same era, Stevens declared, also had "an obvious kinship" with the *Lochner* line of cases, and "both doctrines [were] potentially open-ended sources of judicial power to invalidate state regulations that members of this Court view as unwise or unfair."[120] In short, the current majority was using the eminent domain clause to subject regulatory takings to the same sort of heavy burden of justification that all economic legislation was obliged to surmount via substantive due process during the laissez-faire period.

Justice Stevens's analogy is perceptive. Arguably, the broad conception of the takings clause that Justice Scalia and a majority of the current Court have adopted embodies a strict form of substantive due process, albeit by another name—and one exclusively available for the protection of economic interests. A cynic might suspect, in fact, that a Court dominated by the appointees of conservative Republican presidents has simply hit on a device for extending broad protection to economic freedom, while largely excluding unenumerated noneconomic interests from meaningful constitutional protection. After all, where construed to forbid or require compensation for regulatory takings as well as the actual takings arguably contemplated by the Fifth Amendment's framers and by the courts for years after its adoption, the takings clause could assume the same open-ended role in economic cases that substantive due process played on the pre-1937 Court, without risking further expansion of the scope of due process as a vehicle for protecting noneconomic interests.

Such concerns have hardly dampened the enthusiasm of certain members of the Rehnquist Court for an expansive takings clause jurisprudence or the willingness of others to embrace economic due process. A pair of cases decided during the 1997 term, for example, accorded the takings clause an even broader construction than reflected in earlier decisions and also underscored the willingness of a number of justices, despite their protests to the contrary, to resurrect the substantive due process doctrine of the *Lochner* era.

In *Phillips v. Washington Legal Foundation* (1998),[121] a conservative interest group and other plaintiffs challenged a Texas Interest on Lawyers Trust Account (IOLTA) program, which used the client funds of attorneys. Funds that were unlikely to earn net interest income for a client after payment of service and related costs were put into a federally authorized pool of funds, the proceeds from which were used to finance legal services for low-income persons. A federal district court rejected a takings clause challenge to the arrangement, concluding that the plaintiffs had no property interest in the income generated from the pool; but the Court of Appeals for the Fifth Circuit reversed, holding that the interest belonged to the clients as holders of the principal, and the Supreme Court affirmed the appeals panel's decision. Applying the familiar legal principal that "interest follows principal" and asserting that property rights exist even when the property in question has no "economically realizable value to its owner," Chief Justice Rehnquist held for a five-four majority that any interest earned from the pool was the property of the clients, even though individually the income they would have earned would have been entirely offset by handling costs. He then remanded the case to the lower courts for further proceedings to determine whether that property had been "taken" by the state and what "just compensation," if any, was due the property holders.

Justice Souter, joined by Justices Stevens, Ginsburg, and Breyer, filed a dissent objecting to the majority's decision of the property question in the abstract and remanding only the taking and compensation questions to the lower courts. In

Souter's judgment, the appeals panel should have initially resolved the property issue "only in connection with what is a compensable taking"[122] since the respondents would ultimately be entitled to relief only on a finding that the property in question had been "taken" without "just compensation." And Souter thought it unlikely the respondents could prevail on all those questions. Under federal and state regulations, he observed, clients with funds in an IOLTA pool were effectively barred from receiving any net interest on their individual funds. Given that fact, it might ultimately be concluded that the IOLTA arrangement had not actually taken any respondent's property or that the "'just compensation' for any taking was zero." Were that the case, "there would be no practical consequence for purposes of the Fifth Amendment in recognizing a client's property rights in the interest [from the pool] in the first place" since "any such recognition would be an inconsequential abstraction."[123]

Souter was concerned as well that the Court's abstract analysis of the property question in the case might "skew" lower court resolution of the taking and compensation questions in the respondents' favor and might also "unsettle accepted governmental practice elsewhere." The Court's approach, he suggested, might encourage takings challenges whenever government held and made use of the funds of private parties—when, for example, government engaged in excessive tax withholding. He doubted such withholding practices would violate the takings clause, but thought "the Court's abstract ruling may encourage claims of just this sort."[124] To avoid such dangers, Souter favored vacating the appeals court judgment and remanding the case for plenary lower court consideration of all its takings clause issues.

Justice Breyer, joined by the other dissenters, went further, concluding that interest from IOLTA pools was, in fact, not a client's property. The majority's conclusion to the contrary had rested on the legal truism that "interest follows principal" and on the Court's decision in *Webb's Fabulous Pharmacies, Inc. v. Beckwith* (1980),[125] which had held violative of the takings clause a statute authorizing a state to confiscate the interest from funds deposited with a court clerk in interpleader cases. Challenging the relevance to the case of the general rule that interest follows principal, Breyer pointed out that

> [t]he most that Texas law here could have taken from the client is not a right to use his principal to create a benefit (for he had no such right [under federal and state IOLTA regulations]), but the client's right to keep the client's principal sterile, or right to prevent the principal from being put to productive use by others. . . . And whatever this Court's cases may have said about the constitutional status of such a right, they have *not* said that the Constitution forces a State to confer, upon the owner of property that cannot produce anything of value for him, ownership of the fruits of that property should that property be rendered fertile through the government's lawful intervention.

These interventions would include IOLTA pools, in which client funds that individually would not have generated any net interest income would become productive as part of the government-created pool. Breyer obviously did not agree that interest *"earned only as a result of IOLTA rules* and earned upon otherwise *barren* client principal 'follows principal.'"[126] Nor, in his judgment, was *Webb's* relevant, for there, "[b]ut for state intervention the principal . . . could have, and would have, earned interest." That case said "little about *this* kind of principal, principal that otherwise is barren."[127]

In defending the proposition that the respondents had a property right at stake in the IOLTA funds, even though no net interest would have been generated had each client's funds been deposited individually, Chief Justice Rehnquist had cited cases rejecting the notion that, as the chief justice put it, "a physical item is not 'property' simply because it lacks a positive economic or market value."[128] Justice Breyer contended, however, that such cases in no way revealed "to *whom* the fruits of [such] property belong when [it] bears fruit through the intervention of another."[129] Breyer found the answer to that question in analogies provided by other cases, especially precedents dealing with property evaluation. Such cases made clear, he asserted, that the value of property taken by government is determined by the value "'lost,' not that which the 'taker gained,'"[130] and that the special value of the property to the condemning entity "must be excluded as an element of market value."[131] The principle in such cases indicated that government must pay the current market value of condemned land, not the added value created, for example, by construction of a highway through the property, and that the value of a waterway condemned for construction of a dam would not include the value of electricity the dam later produced. Such analogies convinced Breyer that the respondents had no private property protected by the takings clause at issue in the case, much less viable takings and compensation claims.

The Court in the IOLTA case arguably carried the concept of private property to what could be considered an unreasonable and illogical extreme, as Justices Souter and Breyer made clear in their forceful dissents. But both the prevailing and dissenting opinions in another case from the 1997-98 term demonstrated that all the justices, either under the takings clause or substantive due process, appear committed to according economic interests greater judicial protection than at any other time since 1936, even though the same justices who dissented in the IOLTA case also dissented in the other case.

Eastern Enterprises v. Apfel (1998)[132] involved takings clause and substantive due process challenges to a 1992 federal statute requiring coal operators to provide health benefits for retired miners, as applied to a company that left the coal industry in 1965 after transferring its coal operations to a wholly owned subsidiary and in 1984 selling its interest in the subsidiary to a holding company. Speaking for a plurality, Justice O'Connor concluded that the requirement amounted to an unconstitutional taking of private property. O'Connor conceded that earlier cases had granted Congress considerable discretion in enacting economic legislation, including authority to regulate private contractual agreements and even to impose its requirements retroactively. But those rulings had left open the possibility that such regulations might be unconstitutional if they imposed severe retroactive liability on a limited class of parties who could not have anticipated their liability and if the liability imposed was disproportionate to the parties' experiences. Applying these considerations to Eastern Enterprises, the justice pointed out that the company's liability under the challenged statute was substantial, amounting to between $50 and $100 million. Yet Eastern had ceased its coal mining operations in 1965 and had neither participated in more recent labor-management negotiations and agreements regarding health benefits for workers nor agreed to make contributions under such agreements, even though it was those later agreements that first suggested the coal industry's commitment to fund lifetime benefits for retired miners and their dependents. Benefits during the years Eastern Enterprises employed miners were far less extensive, moreover, than under the later agreements and had been fully subject to alteration and termination. Nor, O'Connor added, did the fact that Eastern was not forced under the law to bear the burden of lifetime benefits for all its former employees mean that its liability did not impose a significant economic burden.

Most disturbing to the plurality was the law's extensive retroactive impact and Eastern's inability to anticipate the liability it imposed. O'Connor noted that the Court had long ago held in *Calder v. Bull* (1798) that the Constitution's prohibition against *ex post facto* laws applied only to penal legislation, but pointed out that the same case had also suggested that the takings clause provided a similar safeguard against retroactive controls over property rights.[133] Asserting that retroactive laws were, in any event, generally disfavored, the justice emphasized that the challenged statute reached back thirty to fifty years to impose liability on Eastern's activities between 1946, when benefits were first created, and 1965, when the company ceased direct coal mining operations. The liability imposed was also not only retroactive, but substantial, and Eastern could not reasonably have anticipated at the time of its operations that the federal government would guarantee retired workers lifetime health benefits several decades later. The challenged law had thus singled out certain employers to bear a substantial burden, based on employer conduct far in the past and unrelated to any commitment the affected employers had made or to any injury they caused. As such, the law had effected an unconstitutional taking of property.

Since Justice O'Connor had rested the plurality's decision on the takings clause, she declined to reach the substantive due process claims raised in the case; in fact, she even quoted from *Ferguson v. Skrupa* (1963)[134] and another post-1937 case[135] that had expressed concerns about use of the "vague contours" of the due process clauses to invalidate economic legislation. But Justice Kennedy, the critical fifth vote for invalidating the statute as applied to Eastern Enterprises, found the plurality's takings clause analysis "incorrect and quite unnecessary for decision of the case," resting his position instead on a conclusion that the law was "arbitrary," "beyond the legitimate authority of government," and thus contrary to substantive due process principles. Like O'Connor, Kennedy conceded that the modern Court had "been hesitant to subject economic legislation to due process scrutiny as a general matter," but also cited cases indicating to him that the justices had "given careful consideration to due process challenges to legislation with retroactive effects."[136]

Justice Thomas filed a brief separate concurrence. Not surprisingly given his avowed opposition to substantive due process, Thomas concurred with O'Connor's takings clause analysis. He also took the occasion, however, to indicate his discomfort with precedent limiting the *ex post facto* clause to criminal cases. "In an appropriate case," he added, "I would be willing to reconsider *Calder* and its progeny to determine whether a retroactive civil law that passes muster under our current Takings Clause jurisprudence is nonetheless unconstitutional under the *Ex Post Facto* Clause."[137]

The four dissenters hardly shared the majority's concern over Eastern's alleged plight. In a brief dissent accusing the plurality and Justice Kennedy of simply substituting "their judgment about what is fair for the better informed judgment" reflected in the challenged statute, Justice Stevens concluded that the "uneasy truce" between companies and miners that had permitted continued coal production in the 1950s and 1960s had "depended more on the value of a handshake than the fine print in written documents." The "implicit understanding on both sides" during that period, Stevens was convinced, was that the companies would provide the miners with lifetime health benefits. "It was this understanding that kept the mines in operation and enabled Eastern Enterprises to earn handsome profits before . . . 1965" and also the understanding accepted by the judges of the courts of appeals.[138]

Justice Breyer joined Justice Stevens's dissent, as did Justices Souter and Ginsburg, and also filed a more extensive dissent of his own, in which the other dissenters concurred. Like Stevens, Breyer flatly rejected the conclusion that it was somehow "fundamentally unfair" for the federal government to require Eastern to pay the health care costs of retired miners employed by the company before 1965, when Eastern had stopped mining coal. After all, declared Breyer, "[f]or many years Eastern benefited from the labor of those miners. Eastern helped to create conditions that led the miners to expect continued health care benefits for themselves and their families after they retired. And Eastern, until 1987, continued to draw sizable profits from the coal industry through a wholly owned subsidiary." Under such circumstances, the justice could see no basis for concluding that Congress had acted "unreasonably or otherwise unjustly in imposing these health care costs upon Eastern."[139]

Breyer also agreed with Justice Kennedy that the takings clause had no application in such a case. That guarantee, he asserted, was not a safeguard against "arbitrary or unfair government action," but an assurance of compensation "for legitimate government action that takes 'private property' to serve the 'public' good." The "private property" the clause had traditionally been construed to protect, moreover, was "physical or intellectual property," while *Eastern Enterprises* involved only "an ordinary liability to pay money, and not to the Government, but to third parties." Citing *Mahon* and more recent cases, he conceded, of course, that government regulation of private property could be so extensive as to amount to a taking, but emphasized that those "precedents concern the taking of interests in *physical* property."[140] He also agreed that, under *Webb's Fabulous Pharmacies*, the takings clause could apply to interest generated from a fund into which government has required an individual to deposit money. But "[h]ere," he pointed out, "there is no specific fund of money; there is only a general liability; and that liability runs, not to the Government, but to third parties." Finally, Breyer noted two recent cases cited by the plurality in which the Court had "arguably acted *as if* the Takings Clause might apply to the creation of a general liability."[141] But both those cases, he reminded the plurality, had *rejected* takings clause claims.

Nor was the justice surprised at the "dearth" of precedential authority for the plurality's approach. Applying the takings clause to a case of the *Eastern Enterprises* variety, he asserted, "bristles with conceptual difficulties." Such a construction might mean, for example, that a takings claim could be raised whenever government assessed taxes or imposed any burden on certain parties to the benefit of others or "when violation means the law's invalidation, rather than simply the payment of 'compensation,'" even though the takings clause was clearly designed merely to secure compensation for government takings of private property, not to prevent the taking per se.[142] Rather than "torture" the takings clause to fit the case, therefore, Breyer, like Kennedy, favored use of its "Fifth Amendment neighbor," the due process guarantee, which "safeguards citizens from arbitrary or irrational legislation," including "unfairly retroactive" statutes.[143] Unlike Kennedy, however, Breyer and the justices joining him saw no violation of due process in the government's treatment of Eastern. He also rejected as "misplaced" the plurality's fear that reliance on due process would risk "resurrecting *Lochner v. New York* . . . and related doctrines of 'substantive due process.'" Invalidating a retroactive law that "upsets settled expectations" of those subject to its requirements merely reflected the due process clause's "basic purpose: the *fair application of law,* which purpose hearkens back to the Magna Carta. It is not to resurrect long-discredited substantive notions of 'freedom of contract.'"[144]

Justice Breyer's assurances to the contrary, the *Eastern Enterprises* and *Washington Legal Foundation* cases made even clearer than previous rulings the willingness of a majority on the Rehnquist Court to use a broad construction of the takings or due process guarantees as vehicles for strict judicial scrutiny of economic regulations. Any predictions about the likely demise of the double standard must be approached, however, with caution. *Lopez* and the Brady Act rulings, it must be remembered, dealt with federal regulations of state and local governments rather than private enterprise, as well as with a type of legislation (gun control) considerably removed from the core of congressional concerns in the commerce field. The context of the Court's decision in *Gore* that grossly excessive jury damage awards violate due process was entirely too discrete to support any firm judgment about the general resurrection of economic due process. And only Justice Kennedy found a substantive due process violation in *Eastern Enterprises.*

Despite the expansive reading currently given the takings clause, moreover, the Court has embraced a very narrow conception of its authority to review state regulations of interstate commerce claimed to interfere with Congress's commercial authority. Not only have the justices limited judicial oversight in such cases largely to state regulations exerting a discriminatory impact on interstate commerce,[145] but three members of the Court—Rehnquist, Scalia, and Thomas—have been among those least willing to invalidate state burdens on commerce. And while Justices Scalia and Thomas have been somewhat more likely than the chief justice to strike down discriminatory state regulations, they have made it clear that they support a very limited role for the courts in burden-on-commerce cases.[146] Scalia, in fact, has assumed the position, remarkably similar to that long advanced by Justice Black,[147] that the Constitution grants the commerce power to Congress, not the courts. Scalia agrees that the Court can forbid "rank" state discrimination against out-of-state businesses, albeit through Article IV's privileges and immunities guarantee rather than the commerce clause. But he rejects any judicial authority to invalidate laws placing an "undue" burden on interstate commerce. In such cases, he has charged, the Court has long "engaged in an enterprise that it has been unable to justify by textual support or even coherent nontextual theory, that it was almost certainly not intended to undertake, and that it has not undertaken very well."[148]

The reluctance of the current Court, and especially Rehnquist, Scalia, and Thomas, to aggressively apply the commerce clause as a restriction on state regulations of interstate trade is more consistent with a high regard for state authority than devotion to laissez-faire. The *Lopez* and Brady Act decisions can also be construed more as states' rights rulings than signs of a rebirth in strict judicial scrutiny of federal regulatory authority. Even so, the dual federalism rhetoric prominent in the latter cases, a majority's application of economic due process in *Gore* and use of such rhetoric in other recent cases, the Court's expansive construction of the takings clause, and its willingness in *Lopez* and the Brady Act cases to second-guess congressional regulatory judgments offer considerable evidence of a fundamental change in the Rehnquist Court's attitude toward the double standard.

5

Unenumerated Rights

The Rehnquist Court, as seen in the previous chapter, has raised serious doubts about the continued viability of the double standard under which issues of economic governmental power and the scope of economic freedoms, including those mentioned nowhere in the Constitution's text, have been left largely to the political process since 1937. In this chapter, we turn to the status of unenumerated noneconomic rights on the Court.

During his nearly thirty-four years on the Supreme Court, Hugo L. Black resisted every effort of his colleagues to include within the Constitution's meaning economic and noneconomic rights neither mentioned in the document's text nor suggested by the history surrounding adoption of its provisions. Early in Black's tenure, Justice Harlan Fiske Stone circulated his draft opinion for the Court in the *Carolene Products* case,[1] which gave substantive due process an exceedingly narrow construction but also indicated that courts could invalidate economic legislation lacking a "rational basis." "As I read the opinion," Black promptly responded, "it approves the submission of proof to a jury or a court under certain circumstances to determine whether the legislature was justified in the policy it adopted. This is contrary to my conception of the extent of judicial power of review."[2] "Would you ever hold any statute unconstitutional on grounds of substantive due process?" Stone replied. "If not, then of course you could not agree with the third [section] in the opinion in the *Carolene* case."[3] When *Carolene Products* was announced, Black declined to join the third section of Stone's opinion.[4]

Despite Stone's reservation of some role for substantive due process on the post-1937 Supreme Court, for the next quarter century the Court, as noted earlier, did not strike down a single law on such grounds, while only two nonracial classifications met their demise via equal protection.[5] Justice Black may have had some cause for optimism, then, when in 1963 he circulated a draft opinion for *Ferguson v. Skrupa*[6] that he hoped would sound the death knell for the substantive due process doctrine, at least in economic cases. Justice Arthur J. Goldberg objected, however, to the "many references" in Black's draft "to the idea that it is no longer this Court's function to pass upon the 'reasonableness' of a State's economic legislation." Goldberg suggested modifications that left the justices "free to think in terms of 'unreasonableness' about the merits of conceivable extremes of state economic regulation when such cases arise."[7] In a notation scrawled on Goldberg's letter suggesting such revisions, Black indicated that he had "agreed to some of these changes with great regret but not to all," adding, "With these changes, we fail to administer the final fatal blow to the idea that this Court can overrule a legislature's belief of reasonableness."[8]

In the field of noneconomic legislation, moreover, substantive due process was not only alive in 1963, but on the verge of a modern flowering. Black's attacks on the natural-law due process formula in earlier cases rejecting incorporation of Bill of Rights safeguards into the Fourteenth Amendment[9] had long made clear that his distaste for flexible conceptions of due process was not confined to the economic sphere. But on that score he was to stand entirely alone. Although principally concerned with property rights, the pre-1937 Court had used substantive due process rhetoric in *Meyer v. Nebraska* (1923)[10] to strike down a statute prohibiting the teaching of a foreign language to school students prior to their completion of the eighth grade, and *Pierce v. Society of Sisters* (1925)[11] employed the same formula to invalidate a state law requiring all children to attend public rather than private schools. The Old Court also resorted to a form of substantive due process in beginning the incorporation of First Amendment guarantees into the Fourteenth Amendment's meaning,[12] and the post-1937 Court completed that process, employing essentially the same approach.[13] Foreshadowing the "fundamental rights" branch of modern equal protection doctrine, *Skinner v. Oklahoma* (1942)[14] invoked the equal protection clause to invalidate a law mandating the selective sterilization of habitual criminals and to suggest that the Constitution guaranteed a "basic civil right" of procreation entitled to close judicial protection.

For more than twenty years after *Skinner*, the Court largely avoided resort to flexible conceptions of due process outside the incorporation context. The concerns that Justice Goldberg's *Skrupa* letter had aroused in Justice Black, however, soon proved prophetic. In 1964, the year following their exchange in *Skrupa*, the Court, per Goldberg, held in *Aptheker v. Secretary of State*[15] that a federal statute denying passports to Communists violated a right of international travel implicit in the Fifth Amendment's due process clause. Viewing the law at issue in *Aptheker* as a clear violation of First Amendment freedoms, Justice Black filed a brief concurrence joining the ruling but rejecting the notion that due process, "standing alone, confers on all our people a constitutional liberty to travel abroad at will."[16]

He was not so restrained the next year when a seven-two majority in *Griswold v. Connecticut* (1965)[17] struck down Connecticut's ban on the use of contraceptives, even in marital relations, Justice William O. Douglas declaring for the Court that the challenged statute violated an unstated "right of privacy older than the Bill of Rights."[18] Perhaps in a futile effort to secure Justice Black's concurrence, Douglas sought to tie the ruling to the Bill of Rights by contending that the privacy concept lay within the penumbra of several specific constitutional guarantees. In concurring opinions, however, Justice Goldberg, joined by Chief Justice Earl Warren and Justice William Brennan, cited the Ninth Amendment as evidence that the Constitution includes protection for other rights than those enumerated in its text,[19] while Justices Harlan and White openly invoked substantive due process, with Harlan finding the Connecticut law in conflict "with basic values 'implicit in the concept of ordered liberty'"[20] and White condemning the statute as an "arbitrary" and "capricious" interference with "the liberty guaranteed by the Fourteenth Amendment."[21]

Although finding the contraceptive ban "every bit as offensive" to him as to the majority, Justice Black rejected both the Court's holding and the rationale of the majority and concurring opinions. Challenging Justice Douglas's reference to a "right of privacy" lying within the penumbra of specific guarantees, Black recommended that his brethren "stick to the [Constitution's] simple language . . . , instead of invoking multitudes of words substituted for those the Framers used."[22] He also dismissed Goldberg's construction of the Ninth Amendment and the Harlan-White resort to substantive due process as nothing more than a return to the Old Court's use of natural-law rhetoric to impose its personal policy and ethical preferences on the people's elected representatives. "That formula," he charged, ". . . is no less dangerous when used to enforce this Court's views about personal rights than those about economic rights."[23] The framers had provided the amendment process as the only appropriate method of constitutional revision. "That method of change," wrote Black, "was good for our Fathers, and being somewhat old-fashioned I must add it is good enough for me."[24]

But only Justice Potter Stewart joined Black's dissent,[25] and during the balance of the Warren Court years, albeit via the developing fundamental rights branch of developing equal protection philosophy rather than through due process, penumbras, or the Ninth Amendment, a majority extended constitutional recognition to other rights not given explicit mention in the document's text, including voting[26] and interstate travel.[27] Laws infringing upon such rights, the justices held, would be struck down unless found necessary to further a compelling governmental interest. The Burger Court limited equal protection's fundamental rights component to guarantees expressed or implied in the Constitution and refused to include the rights to an equal education[28] or welfare benefits[29] within its ambit. But the same Court also invoked equal protection to extend *Griswold*'s reach to unmarried persons in *Eisenstadt v. Baird* (1972)[30] and in *Roe v. Wade* (1973),[31] the most controversial ruling of the post-Warren era, used substantive due process, bolstered with a compelling-interest standard borrowed from recent equal protection doctrine, to uphold a broad right of women to abort unwanted pregnancies.

A number of Burger Court decisions did refuse to extend *Roe* and recognize a right to government-subsidized abortions for poor women;[32] but in *City of Akron v. Akron Center for Reproductive Health* (1983),[33] a majority, speaking through Justice Powell over the dissent of Justice O'Connor, joined by *Roe* dissenters Rehnquist and

White, struck down a number of abortion restrictions and firmly reiterated its commitment to *Roe*. In 1986, the Burger Court again reaffirmed *Roe*.[34] On the eve of William Rehnquist's elevation to the Court's center seat, then, the justices seemed poised for further expansion of sexual privacy rights and judicial recognition of other unenumerated guarantees as well.

The elections of Ronald Reagan and George Bush to the presidency curtailed, of course, such developments. Indeed, had President Reagan's nomination of Robert Bork won Senate approval or Bush been elected to a second term, *Roe* by now would probably have been overruled. But given President Clinton's selection of Ginsburg and Breyer and the moderate voting patterns of Stevens, O'Connor, Kennedy, and Souter, the status of unenumerated noneconomic rights in the Rehnquist Court remains highly complicated and largely determined by the fortunes of shifting coalitions, as the following examination of the Court's decision making in the field will, it is hoped, make clear.

The "Essence" of *Roe*

The Rehnquist Court's first major opportunity for reconsideration and possible reversal of *Roe* came in *Webster v. Reproductive Services* (1989).[35] *Webster* involved a challenge to a Missouri statute that, among other things, (1) declared in its preamble that life begins at conception; (2) required physicians to determine whether the fetus was viable (that is, capable of surviving independent of the womb) before performing an abortion on a woman reasonably believed to have been pregnant twenty or more weeks; (3) forbade use of public employees and facilities in abortions unnecessary to save the mother's life; and (4) prohibited use of public funds, employees, or facilities for counseling abortions in non-life-threatening pregnancies. At that point, it would later become clear, only Chief Justice Rehnquist and Justices White and Scalia favored *Roe*'s outright reversal. Justices O'Connor and Kennedy supported recognition of an abortion right, albeit one subject to more extensive governmental regulation than *Roe* recognized, while *Roe*'s author, Justice Blackmun, and Justices Brennan and Marshall were strongly committed to its retention, and Justice Stevens substantially so. Not surprisingly, perhaps, given that pattern of *Roe* support, Chief Justice Rehnquist indicated at the justices' conference discussion of *Webster*, according to Justice Marshall's notes, that he would not favor overruling *Roe* "as such" in the case. Marshall also recorded the staunchest *Roe* supporters as rejecting its reversal "in toto," while Justice Stevens was listed as "on and off" on the issue.[36] When Rehnquist circulated an opinion substantially weakening *Roe*, however, Stevens wrote the chief justice that he was "not in favor of overruling *Roe v. Wade*, but if the deed is to be done I would rather see the Court give the case a decent burial instead of tossing it out the window of a fast-moving caboose."[37]

Opinions ultimately announced in *Webster* revealed a deeply fragmented Court. Speaking for a majority only with respect to certain provisions of the challenged statute, the chief justice sidestepped a ruling on the law's assertion that "life begins at conception," a proposition clearly at odds with *Roe*, by noting that the state had yet to apply its provisions in a concrete way. Citing the abortion-funding precedents, he also spoke for the Court in upholding the state's prohibition on the use of public employees and facilities for nontherapeutic abortions and dismissed as moot, at the request of the plaintiffs-respondents, the provision forbidding public funding of nontherapeutic abortion counseling.

The chief justice spoke only for himself, White, and Kennedy, however, in upholding the law's requirement that viability tests be conducted before nontherapeutic abortions could be performed on women pregnant for twenty or more weeks, and in urging abandonment of *Roe*'s "rigid" trimester approach to evaluating abortion regulations—a "framework," he declared, "hardly consistent with the notion of a Constitution cast in general terms, as ours is, and usually speaking in general principles, as ours does."[38] Under the trimester approach developed by Justice Blackmun in his opinion for the *Roe* Court, the abortion decision was left to the judgment of the woman and her physician during the first three months of pregnancy; from that point until the fetus became viable, the state's compelling interest in protecting the woman's health justified reasonable regulation of abortion procedures; and during the third trimester of the pregnancy, from the point of viability to term, the state could not only regulate abortion procedures but even forbid nontherapeutic abortions in furthering its compelling interest in potential human life. Since viability tests required under the Missouri statute would sometimes have been performed prior to what turned out to be second-term abortions, Rehnquist conceded that the law was inconsistent with *Roe*'s trimester formula. In his judgment, however, *Roe*'s formula, not the state's viability requirement, should be discarded.

In earlier cases, Justice O'Connor had also been critical of *Roe*'s trimester framework, urging instead a more flexible approach in which government would simply be forbidden to impose an "undue burden" on a woman's decision to abort a pregnancy.[39] In *Webster*, however, she saw no conflict between Missouri's viability testing requirement and abortion precedent. "Where there is no need to decide a constitutional question," she concluded, "it is a venerable principle of this Court's adjudicatory processes not to do so. . . . When the constitutional validity of a State's abortion statute actually turns on the constitutional validity of *Roe v. Wade*, there will be time enough to reexamine *Roe*. And to do so carefully."[40]

In a separate concurrence, Justice Scalia favored *Roe*'s explicit reversal and scorned Justice O'Connor for not seeing *Webster* as an appropriate vehicle for the Court to take that step. Predicting that the case's outcome would be "heralded as a triumph of judicial statesmanship," Scalia declared, "It is not that, unless it is statesmanlike needlessly to prolong this Court's self-awarded sovereignty over a field where it has little proper business since the answers to most of the cruel questions posed are political and not juridical—a sovereignty which therefore quite properly, but to the great damage of the Court, makes it the object of the sort of organized public pressure that political institutions in a democracy ought to receive."[41] As for Justice O'Connor's concern that the Court avoid constitutional rulings if possible, and otherwise make them no broader than required by the facts of an individual case, Scalia emphasized that such a rule included a "frequently applied good-cause exception" and found it "particularly perverse to convert the policy into an absolute in the present case, in order to place beyond reach the inexpressibly 'broader-than-was-required-by-the-precise-facts' structure established by *Roe v. Wade*."[42]

Scalia continued his campaign for *Roe*'s outright reversal in two 1990 parental notification cases. In the first, the Court upheld an Ohio statute that forbade physicians to perform an abortion on an unmarried, unemancipated minor without timely notice to at least one parent or issuance of a court order authorizing the minor to consent to the abortion.[43] To obtain a judicial bypass of the parental notice requirement, the minor was obliged to establish by clear and convincing evidence that she had sufficient maturity and information to make the abortion decision herself; that she was the victim of a pattern of physical, emotional, or sexual abuse by a parent; or that parental notice was not in her best interests. Justice Kennedy, joined by the chief justice and Justices White, Stevens, O'Connor, and Scalia, delivered an opinion of the Court upholding the statute, but also included a section, joined only by Rehnquist, White, and Scalia, in which he held that the Ohio legislature had acted "in a rational manner" in adopting the challenged statute, finding it "both rational and fair for the State to conclude that, in most instances, the family will strive to give a lonely or even terrified minor advice that is both compassionate and mature."[44]

To secure the concurrence of Justices O'Connor and Stevens, Justice Kennedy largely avoided discussion of the doctrinal basis for the ruling, declaring only that the challenged law did "not impose an undue, or otherwise unconstitutional, burden on a minor seeking an abortion."[45] But Justice Scalia was not so diplomatic. Declaring once again that the Constitution contained no abortion right, Scalia asserted that "[i]t is not to be found in the longstanding traditions of our society, nor can it be logically deduced from the text of the Constitution—not, that is, without volunteering a judicial answer to the nonjusticiable question of when human life begins."[46]

The lineup of justices in *Hodgson v. Minnesota* (1990),[47] another parental notification case decided the same day, was even more complex. The statute at issue forbade an abortion on a woman under age eighteen for at least forty-eight hours after both her parents had been notified, but also provided for a judicial bypass. Sitting *en banc*, the Court of Appeals for the Eighth Circuit unanimously held the notification provisions unconstitutional, but by a seven-three vote, it upheld the judicial bypass provision, which provided that if a court enjoined enforcement of the notification requirements the same notice requirement would be effective unless the pregnant woman obtained a court order permitting the abortion. The Supreme Court affirmed both rulings.

In an opinion for the Court, Justice Stevens held that the requirement that both parents, rather than only one, be notified did not reasonably further any legitimate interest that notice to one parent would accomplish and was thus unconstitutional. But in a separate opinion, Justice Kennedy also announced the Court's judgment that a two-parent notification requirement with judicial bypass was constitutional. Justice O'Connor, it seemed, had concluded that two-parent notification was unconstitutional without judicial bypass, but acceptable with the bypass provision. Justice Kennedy, joined by the chief justice, White, and Scalia, agreed that two-parent notification could be required with or without judicial bypass. Although applying somewhat different standards, Justices Stevens and Marshall, the latter joined by Brennan and Blackmun, considered two-parent notification invalid with or without judicial bypass. Thus, six justices considered one-parent notification with bypass constitutional, under two different rationales, while three justices would have held one-parent notification with bypass invalid.

Complaining that such distinctions could not be found in either the Constitution's text or society's traditions, Justice Scalia again urged *Roe*'s total rejection, declaring, "I continue to dissent from this enterprise of devising an Abortion Code, and from the illusion that we have authority to do so."[48] But *Roe*'s defenders were pleased that Justice O'Connor had finally been willing to declare an abortion regulation unconstitutional, at least absent a judicial bypass. In a letter to Chief Justice Rehnquist during deliberations in the *Hodgson* case, Justice Stevens questioned Justice O'Connor's assertion, circulated in a recent memorandum, that a judicial bypass requirement could save an otherwise unconstitutional parental notification requirement. Stevens considered a one-parent requirement entirely reasonable, but only with some sort of state-authorized bypass for the exceptional case, "e.g., a Christian Scientist who will not permit a ruptured appendix to be removed to save a child's life." But he found a two-parent notification requirement unreasonable, even with a bypass provision. "It is counterproductive in broken family cases and is wholly unnecessary in the ideal family in which, as a practical matter, notice to either parent would constitute notice to both. A child who has one parent's consent to any form of surgery should not be compelled to go to court to obtain relief from a statute that is unconstitutional because it is irrational as applied in most cases."[49] On reading Stevens's views, Justice O'Connor decided to change her initial vote to uphold the notice requirements and judicial bypass, voting instead to invalidate the notice provision but affirm the bypass. Later, in letters to Justices Marshall and Blackmun, Justice Brennan emphasized the importance of their joining as much of Justice Stevens's opinon in the case "as possible, now that Sandra has for the first time joined us in holding invalid a law regulating abortion."[50]

Whatever comfort *Hodgson* may have given *Roe* supporters on the Court no doubt disappeared in the face of the five-four ruling the following term in *Rust v. Sullivan* (1991),[51] upholding federal restrictions on abortion counseling against statutory and constitutional challenge. An amendment to the 1970 Public Health Service Act specified that no funds appropriated under Title X of the statute could be used in programs that included abortion as a method of family planning. In 1988, President Reagan's secretary of health and human services, Louis Sullivan, issued regulations prohibiting Title X projects from engaging in counseling, referrals, or other activities advocating abortion as a method of family planning. Speaking for the Court, Chief Justice Rehnquist, joined by White, Scalia, Kennedy, and Souter, held that the regulations were authorized by the statute and rejected claims they violated the First Amendment's guarantees to free speech or the Fifth Amendment abortion right. Rehnquist rested both constitutional rulings largely on the Court's decisions holding that the abortion right did not include a guarantee to funded abortions for poor women, even when government provided prenatal and maternity assistance to the indigent. The regulations did not discriminate on the basis of viewpoint, Rehnquist insisted; they merely reflected government's previously recognized power to make a value judgment favoring childbirth over abortion in the allocation of public funds. Moreover, employees in Title X projects were in no way forced to give up abortion-related speech altogether; they were simply required to keep such activities separate and distinct from Title X projects.

Justice Blackmun's reaction to the challenged regulations was hardly so sanguine. *Roe*'s author vigorously disputed the majority's conclusion that Congress had authorized the ban on abortion counseling in Title X projects. Declaring that the statute on which the regulations allegedly rested were "decidedly ambiguous" and that the general rule against "passing unnecessarily upon important constitutional questions [was] strongest" in such cases, Blackmun found it "both logical and eminently prudent to assume that when Congress intends to press the limits of constitutionality in its enactments, it will express that intent in explicit and unambiguous terms."[52] Nor could he accept the majority's view that the challenged regulations were not viewpoint based. "By refusing to fund these family-planning projects that advocate abortion *because* they advocate abortion, the Government plainly has targeted a particular viewpoint."[53] And, in his view, government had no power to condition receipt of its largesse on the recipient's relinquishment of the "cherished freedom of speech based solely upon the content or viewpoint of that speech."[54]

Blackmun found "most disturbing," however, the impact of the Court's ruling on the exercise of abortion rights. He had dissented in cases refusing to extend *Roe* to require funded abortions for poor women, especially when prenatal and maternal assistance were provided.[55] But those decisions at least had "left intact a woman's ability to decide without coercion whether she will continue her pregnancy to term,"[56] while the abortion-counseling restrictions and the Court's decisions upholding them had gone further, interfering with a woman's right "to be free from affirmative governmental *interference* in her decision"[57] and thereby violating the constitutional guarantee recognized in *Roe*. "Both the purpose and result of the challenged regulations," asserted Blackmun, "are to deny women the ability voluntarily to decide their procreative destiny. For these women, the Government will have obliterated the freedom to choose as surely as if it had banned abortions outright. The denial of this freedom is not a consequence of poverty but of the Government's ill-intentioned distortion of information it has chosen to provide."[58]

By that point, Justice Souter had replaced Justice Brennan on the Court, but Justice Marshall joined Blackmun's dissent. One might have assumed that language in the challenged regulations, indicating that they were designed to "reduce the incidence of abortion," requiring Title X physicians and counselors to provide information and referrals only about childbirth and prenatal care, and stipulating that, if directly asked, they were to respond that abortion was not an "appropriate method" of family planning, might have convinced Justice O'Connor that the regulations imposed an "undue burden" on a woman's decision to abort a pregnancy. While agreeing that one might "well conclude" they were unconstitutional, however, O'Connor chose to rest her vote that the regulations were invalid on statutory grounds. "In these cases," she observed, "we need only tell the Secretary that his regulations are not a reasonable interpretation of the statute; we need not tell Congress that it cannot pass such legislation. If we rule solely on statutory grounds, Congress retains the power to force the constitutional question by legislating more explicitly. It may instead choose to do nothing. . . . It is enough in this litigation to conclude that neither the language nor the history of the [statute] compels the Secretary's interpretation and that the interpretation raises serious First Amendment concerns."[59] While noting that Justice Blackmun had "correctly analyzed" the constitutional issues in the case, Justice Stevens also rested his dissent on statutory grounds. Unlike Blackmun, however, Stevens found nothing ambiguous about the statute on which the regulations purportedly rested. "Not a word in the statute," the justice asserted, "authorizes the Secretary to impose any restrictions on the dissemination of truthful information or professional advice by grant recipients."[60]

Although joining the chief justice's opinion without writing separately, Justice Souter had shared with Rehnquist during deliberations in *Rust* his concern that the Court's opinion make clear that voluntary acceptance of government funds was "not an answer to every First Amendment objection" raised against regulations of the sort at issue in the case. Souter suggested language for Rehnquist's opinion indicating that, under certain circumstances, the doctor-patient relationship would include free speech safeguards, "even when subsidized by the Government."[61] To secure Souter's concurrence, the chief justice incorporated some of his colleague's suggestions, albeit in considerably diluted form.[62]

In the next major abortion case to come before the Court, however, Souter largely parted company with Rehnquist, as did Justice Kennedy, another member of the *Rust* majority. In *Planned Parenthood v. Casey* (1992),[63] the Court upheld provisions of a Pennsylvania statute requiring a woman to give her informed consent to an abortion and to be provided information on which to base that decision at least twenty-four hours before the procedure was performed. The law further mandated one parent's consent, with a judicial bypass option, for minors seeking abortions; exempted medical emergencies from the waiting-period and consent requirements; and imposed reporting and record-keeping obligations on agencies in which abortions were performed. A different lineup of justices, however, struck down a provision requiring married women, except under certain circumstances, to notify their spouses before securing an abortion. Most importantly, a majority of justices either reaffirmed the "essence" of *Roe*, embraced *Roe* entirely, or came close to endorsing *Roe*.

In a joint opinion, Justices O'Connor, Kennedy, and Souter spoke for the Court in certain respects and expressed their own views regarding other issues. Speaking for a majority, they reaffirmed *Roe*'s recognition of a woman's right to choose and obtain an abortion before a fetus becomes viable, without undue interference from the state, as well as *Roe*'s acceptance of state authority to forbid nontherapeutic abortions after viability and legitimate state interests in protecting the woman's health and fetal life from the outset of a pregnancy. Speaking for themselves, they rejected *Roe*'s "rigid" trimester framework and concluded that states merely could not impose any "undue burden" on a woman's decision to obtain an abortion prior to viability.

In deciding that traditional rules of precedent counseled against *Roe*'s reversal, the justices pointed out that, while controversial, *Roe* had proven workable, that millions of women had come to rely on it, that it was by no means a doctrinal anachronism discounted by current society, and that the basic factual premises underlying *Roe* remained essentially unchanged. But they seemed equally determined to avoid any appearance that the Court might cave in to the intense political controversy *Roe* had aroused. "A decision to overrule *Roe*'s essential holding under the existing circumstances," the justices declared, "would address error, if error there was, at the cost of both profound and unnecessary damage to the Court's legitimacy, and to the Nation's commitment to the rule of law. It is therefore imperative to adhere to the essence of *Roe*'s original decision, and we do so today."[64]

Justices Blackmun and Stevens provided the fourth and fifth votes to reaffirm at least *Roe*'s "essence" and to invalidate Pennsylvania's spousal notification provision. Justice Stevens found "unquestionably correct" the Court's application of *stare decisis* in the case, declaring that "[t]he societal costs of overruling *Roe* at this late date would be enormous" and that *Roe* was "an integral part of a correct understanding of both the concept of liberty and the basic equality of men and women." Stevens also took issue with the joint opinion's assumption of an inconsistency between *Roe*'s acceptance of a legitimate state interest in potential human life and its refusal to conclude that such an interest, as opposed to interests in maternal health, could justify regulation of abortions prior to viability. In his view, the critical question, presumably at any stage of a pregnancy, was whether an asserted state interest outweighed the pregnant woman's interest in personal liberty. Applying such an approach to the Pennsylvania regulations, whether under the *Roe* trimester framework or the plurality's "undue burden" standard, convinced Stevens that the twenty-four-hour waiting period and counseling provisions, as well as the spousal notification requirement, were unconstitutional. The justice conceded that a general obligation of physicians to inform patients about abortion risks was appropriate, but considered a "rigid requirement that all patients wait twenty-four hours or (what is true in practice) much longer to evaluate the significance of information that is either common knowledge or irrelevant is an irrational and, therefore, 'undue' burden."[65] The counseling provisions, Stevens asserted, were similarly infirm.

Justice Blackmun praised the joint opinion as "an act of personal courage and constitutional principle," a "flame ... grown bright" "just when so many expected the darkness to fall." In the twilight of his career, however, *Roe*'s author also pointed out the obvious: that while the Court's approach was "worlds apart" from that of the four justices who favored rejecting *Roe*, "the distance between the two approaches is short—the distance [of] but a single vote."[66] Nor, at age eighty-three, was he unmindful, in that June before the 1992 presidential election, when George Bush's reelection seemed assured, that his successor might provide the one vote needed to overturn the decision with which his career would primarily be associated. "I cannot remain on this Court forever," he observed, "and when I do step down, the confirmation process for my successor well may focus on the issue before us today. That, I regret, may be exactly where the choice between the two worlds will be made."[67]

As *Roe* dissenters, Rehnquist and White obviously did not share Justice Blackmun's concerns, nor did Justices Scalia and Thomas. The plurality opinion Rehnquist, White, and Scalia had joined in the *Webster* case had left largely uncertain what standards they favored in abortion cases; all that was truly clear was that few abortion controls would fail to withstand their scrutiny. But whatever those standards were, they and Justice Thomas reaffirmed in *Casey* their commitment to them and agreed that the abortion controls at issue in the case should be upheld "in their entirety." In an opinion joined by the others, the chief justice took obvious comfort in declaring that the new plurality "retains the outer shell of *Roe v. Wade*..., but beats a wholesale retreat from the substance of that case."[68] At the same time, he recognized that the plurality's "unjustified constitutional compromise" had left "the Court in a position to closely scrutinize all types of abortion regulations despite the fact that it lacks the power to do so under the Constitution."[69]

Rehnquist's opinion and a separate effort by Justice Scalia largely tracked arguments that they and other *Roe* opponents had raised for years: that neither the Constitution's text nor society's traditions justified recognition of an abortion right, at least not one of a fundamental character deserving of vigorous judicial protection, and that *Roe* and its progeny unduly encroached upon the domain of elected policymakers. But Rehnquist and Scalia were particularly incensed at the plurality's interpretation of *stare decisis* and concern that complete rejection of *Roe* would be construed as a judicial surrender to political pressure, jeopardizing the Court's legitimacy and the doctrine of judicial review. "Our constitutional watch does not cease merely because we have spoken before on an issue," the chief justice declared; "when it becomes clear that a prior constitutional interpretation is unsound we are obliged to reexamine the question."[70] And Justice Scalia characterized as "frightening" the

notion that we would decide a case differently than the way we otherwise would have in order to show that we can stand firm against public disapproval. ... It is a bad enough idea, even in the head of someone like me, who believes that the text of the Constitution, and our traditions, say what they say and there is no fiddling with them. But when it is in the mind of a Court that believes the Constitution has an evolving meaning...; and that the function of this Court is to "speak before all others for [the people's] constitutional ideals" unrestrained by meaningful text or tradition—then the notion that the Court must adhere to a decision for as long as the decision faces "great opposition" and the Court is "under fire" acquires a character of almost czarist arrogance. We are offended by those marchers who descend upon us, every year on the anniversary of *Roe*, to protest our saying that the Constitution requires what our society has never thought the Constitution requires. These people who refuse to be "tested by following" must be taught a lesson. We have no Cossacks, but at least we can stubbornly refuse to abandon an erroneous opinion that we might otherwise change—to show how little they intimidate us.[71]

Since *Casey*, the Court has continued to uphold abortion regulations, including parental notification provisions permitting a judicial bypass.[72] Both before and after *Casey*, moreover, the justices have rejected substantive due process claims in a variety of fields. In 1989, for example, a majority, speaking through Justice Scalia, rejected a natural father's procedural and substantive due process challenge to a California statute's presumption that a child born to a married woman living with her husband was the offspring of the marriage.[73] The same year, a majority, per Chief Justice Rehnquist, held that a state had no due process obligation to protect a child from his father, despite numerous reports of abuse and the convincing argument of Justice Brennan in dissent that government "inaction can be every bit as abusive of power as action, that oppression can result when a State [through its social services system] undertakes a vital duty and then ignores it."[74] *Collins v. City of Harker Heights* (1992)[75] unanimously rejected the claim of the widow of a city sanitation worker asphyxiated when he entered a manhole to unstop a sewer line that municipalities have a substantive duty to provide minimal levels of safety and security in the workplace, even though state law required such training programs. And in 1993, the Court, over the dissents of Justices Stevens and Blackmun, rebuffed a challenge to Immigration and Naturalization Service (INS) regulations permitting detained juvenile aliens to be released only to the custody of their parents, close relatives, or legal guardians, except under compelling circumstances. Even so, in gay rights, assisted suicide, and related cases—the most controversial fields outside the abortion arena—the Rehnquist Court has arguably assumed the same sort of moderately conservative, pragmatic, and flexible position that prevailed in *Casey*.

The *Bowers* Case

The Burger Court extended the privacy concept not only to nonprocreative heterosexual relations among married and unmarried persons, but even to the abortion decision, despite its obvious impact on prenatal life and the wishes of the pregnant woman's spouse or other sexual partner. A logical next step appeared to be extension of the privacy concept or equal protection doctrine to homosexual relations among consenting adults. But in *Doe v. Commonwealth's Attorney* (1976),[76] the Court summarily affirmed without opinion a three-judge federal district court ruling upholding a Virginia law that made consensual sodomy a criminal offense and in *Bowers v. Hardwick* (1986),[77] decided on the eve of Justice William H. Rehnquist's move to the Court's center seat, a five-four majority, limiting the privacy right to activities relating to the family, marriage, and procreation, upheld Georgia's sodomy law as applied to homosexual conduct. But in *Romer v. Evans* (1996),[78] decided near the end of its 1995-96 term, the Rehnquist Court, over the dissents of the chief justice and Justices Scalia and Thomas, overturned a provision of the Colorado constitution that forbade all state and local legislative, executive, and judicial action designed to protect homosexuals from discrimination.

As late as 1961, all fifty states prohibited sodomy, generally defined as oral or anal intercourse. In 1986, when the Supreme Court decided the *Bowers* case, twenty-four states and the District of Columbia imposed criminal penalties for private acts of sodomy between consenting adults. A policeman charged Michael Hardwick, who described himself as a practicing homosexual, with violating Georgia's sodomy law after he discovered Hardwick and a male companion engaged in oral sex in Hardwick's bedroom. Perhaps because no prosecution for private homosexual sodomy had been initiated in the state since 1939,[79] the local district attorney declined to seek an indictment from a grand jury unless further evidence developed. But fearing future prosecution, Hardwick filed a federal suit seeking to have Georgia's sodomy law declared unconstitutional. Joining him as plaintiffs were a married couple who wished to engage in sodomy in the privacy of their home. Since the couple were in no immediate danger of prosecution under the statute, the district court dismissed their claim for lack of standing. Citing *Doe,* the trial court also dismissed Hardwick's suit, but a divided panel of the Court of Appeals for the Eleventh Circuit reversed, holding that Hardwick possessed a fundamental right under the Ninth Amendment and due process to a private and intimate sexual association—a right that could be infringed only on a showing of a compelling state interest. The circuit panel remanded the case to the district court for trial, but since other federal appeals courts had reached a contrary conclusion in other sodomy cases,[80] the Supreme Court granted certiorari and, following review, reversed the circuit panel.

Justice Byron White delivered the opinion for the five-member majority. White, it will be recalled, had invoked substantive due process in joining the *Griswold* majority's recognition of the right of married persons to use contraceptives. But his conceptions of due process and the reach of the fundamental rights element of modern equal protection doctrine were clearly limited. He joined the Court's 1972 ruling in *Eisenstadt v. Baird,* but not his colleagues' conclusion that the privacy right recognized in *Griswold* extended to unmarried persons. In an *Eisenstadt* concurring opinion, White noted that the record did not indicate the marital status of a woman to whom Baird had given vaginal foam following his lecture on contraception, thereby precipitating his prosecution under a law forbidding the unauthorized distribution of contraceptives. White thus saw "no reason for reaching the novel constitutional question whether a State may restrict or forbid the distribution of contraceptives to the unmarried."[81] The following year, moreover, he joined Justice Rehnquist in dissent in *Roe v. Wade,* declaring, "I find nothing in the language or history of the Constitution to support the Court's judgments. The Court simply fashions and announces a new constitutional right for pregnant women and, with scarcely any reason or authority for its action, invests that right with sufficient substance to override most existing state abortion statutes."[82]

Particularly given his stance in *Eisenstadt* and *Roe,* White's selection as the Court's spokesman in *Bowers* was hardly surprising; nor was the rhetoric of his opinion. The language of the Georgia statute reached heterosexual as well as homosexual sodomy, married as well as unmarried persons. But noting in a footnote that the claim of Michael Hardwick's heterosexual coplaintiffs had been dismissed, White characterized the case as involving only a challenge to the law "as applied to consensual homosexual sodomy" and reserved for another day the statute's constitutional status "as applied to other acts of sodomy."[83] He then rejected the Eleventh Circuit's conclusion that Supreme Court precedents required extension of the privacy right to homosexual sodomy. Construing such earlier cases as *Griswold, Roe,* and *Eisenstadt* as involving only family relations, marriage, and procreation, he concluded "that none of the rights announced in those cases bears any resemblance to the claimed constitutional right of homosexuals to engage in acts of sodomy."[84]

Hardwick had defended the Eleventh Circuit's ruling solely on substantive due process grounds rather than also invoking the Ninth Amendment, equal protection, or the Eighth Amendment guarantee against cruel and unusual punishment, and White confined the Court's review of the statute purely to Hardwick's due process claim. The justice conceded that the Court had utilized due process to extend heightened judicial protection to "fundamental rights" having "little or no textual support in the constitutional language," but had sought "to assure itself and the public that announcing [such] rights . . . involves much more than the imposition of the Justices' own choice of values on the States and the Federal Government."[85] The Court, wrote White, had included within the scope of due process "fundamental liberties that are 'implicit in the concept of ordered liberty,' such that 'neither liberty nor justice would exist if [they] were sacrificed,'"[86] and had also characterized such rights as "deeply rooted in this Nation's history and tradition."[87] It was "obvious" to the majority that "neither of these formulations would extend a fundamental right to homosexuals to engage in acts of consensual sodomy," particularly since "[p]roscriptions against that conduct have ancient roots"[88] and were still in force in nearly half the states and the District of Columbia. Given that history, the notion that a right to engage in homosexual sodomy was "deeply rooted in this Nation's history and tradition" or "implicit in the concept of ordered liberty" struck White and his colleagues as, "at best, facetious."[89] When the Court recognized rights "having little or no cognizable roots in the language or design of the Constitution," its authority was "most vulnerable and [came] nearest to illegitimacy," as had been "painfully demonstrated by the face-off between the Executive and the Court in the 1930's."[90] The justices, declared White, should resist such temptations.

Nor, to the majority, did it make any difference that the conduct at issue occurred in Hardwick's home. *Stanley v. Georgia* (1969)[91] had recognized the right to possess obscenity in the home. But *Stanley*, wrote White, "was firmly grounded in the First Amendment,"[92] while the right Hardwick was asserting had no support in the Constitution's text. *Stanley*, moreover, had carefully distinguished the right recognized there from any asserted guarantee to home possession of drugs, firearms, and stolen goods. Were *Stanley* extended to include sexual conduct between consenting adults, White also found it difficult to determine, "except by fiat," how "to limit the claimed right to homosexual conduct while leaving exposed to prosecution adultery, incest, and other sexual crimes even though they are committed in the home."[93]

Having rejected Hardwick's claim that Georgia's sodomy law interfered with a fundamental right entitled to close judicial protection, White turned to the respondent's contention that the challenged statute lacked even a rational basis. The law, observed White, was based on "the presumed belief of a majority of the electorate in Georgia that homosexual sodomy is immoral and unacceptable,"[94] and that justification satisfied the Court. Laws, wrote White, are "constantly based on notions of morality, and if all laws representing essentially moral choices are to be invalidated under the Due Process Clause, the courts will be very busy indeed."[95]

Two members of the *Bowers* majority filed concurrences. In a brief opinion, Chief Justice Warren Burger cited the long history of legal sanctions against homosexual sodomy and vehemently declared that the classification of such conduct as a fundamental right "would . . . cast aside millennia of moral teaching."[96] Justice Lewis Powell agreed that the due process guarantee included no substantive right to homosexual sodomy, but he had originally voted to affirm the Eleventh Circuit on Eighth Amendment grounds. Because Hardwick had not yet been tried or convicted and had raised no Eighth Amendment claim, the justice later changed his vote.[97] But in his brief *Bowers* concurrence, Powell observed that a prison sentence for homosexual sodomy—"certainly a sentence of long duration—would create a serious Eighth Amendment issue."[98] Asked after a 1990 law school address how he could reconcile his vote in *Bowers* with his support for *Roe v. Wade*, Powell said of *Bowers*, "I think I probably made a mistake in that one."[99]

In one of two dissenting opinions filed in the case, Justice Harry Blackmun, joined by Justices Brennan, Thurgood Marshall, and John Paul Stevens, decried what he considered the majority's "almost obsessive focus on homosexual activity."[100] Under Georgia's sodomy statute, "the sex or status of the persons who engage in the act [at issue] was irrelevant."[101] Consequently, Hardwick's claim that the law unconstitutionally intruded upon his privacy and right to intimate association in no way depended on his sexual orientation.[102] He was simply asserting what Justice Louis D. Brandeis had termed in his *Olmstead* dissent of 1928 "the right to be let alone."[103] This right to be free from governmental intrusion into one's private life included, asserted Blackmun, a "decisional" and a "spatial" component, the former insulating individuals from interference in certain personal decisions, the latter guaranteeing people freedom in certain places. The Georgia statute and the Court's ruling threatened both these elements of the privacy concept. By upholding the statute, the majority had "refused to recognize . . . the fundamental interest all individuals have in controlling the nature of their intimate associations with others."[104] By viewing *Stanley v. Georgia* purely as a First Amendment case and refusing to extend it to the *Bowers* context, despite *Stanley*'s firm grounding in the Fourth Amendment and Justice Brandeis's *Olmstead* dissent, the Court had also failed to give due regard to Hardwick's strong interest in the privacy of his home.

Blackmun was also unimpressed with the majority's conclusion that the Georgia sodomy law possessed a rational basis. Contending that, even under the lenient rationality due process standard, the state is required to show an "actual connection" between a challenged law and the "ill effects it seeks to prevent,"[105] he found the record "barren" of evidence supporting Georgia's contention that the statute served important public health and welfare interests, including prevention of the spread of communicable diseases and the fostering of other illegal activity. He was equally skeptical of the state's "core" defense of the law as an exercise of its power to promote a "decent society." Absent some secular justification for a challenged statute, the state, asserted Blackmun, possessed no power simply to impose the will of religious groups on the entire citizenry. And while government clearly had the authority to protect public sensibilities from "unwilling [public] exposure to sexual activities," that power did not extend to "intimate behavior that occurs in intimate places." There was an important difference, Blackmun concluded, "between laws that protect public sensibilities and those that enforce private morality."[106] Governmental authority extended only to the former; Georgia's sodomy statute was not so limited.

In a dissent joined by Justices Brennan and Marshall, Justice Stevens focused on the statute's prohibition of heterosexual as well as homosexual sodomy. Reiterating

Justice Blackmun's assertion that a society's condemnation of a practice as immoral is an insufficient justification for its prohibition, Stevens cited *Griswold, Eisenstadt,* and other cases upholding the right of married and unmarried persons "to engage in nonreproductive, sexual conduct that others may consider offensive or immoral"[107] and construed those precedents to reach sodomy. Allowing a state selectively to enforce its sodomy law against homosexuals alone required, in Stevens's judgment, the conclusion either that homosexuals "do not have the same interest in 'liberty' that others have" or that states reasonably may apply a general law in a selective fashion. For Stevens, the first possibility was "plainly unacceptable" in a nation based on the proposition that "all men are created equal." The second option appeared to be based on "a habitual dislike for, or ignorance about, the disfavored group."[108] Yet, wrote Stevens, the challenged law "presumably reflect[ed] the belief that *all sodomy* is immoral and unacceptable. . . . For the Georgia statute does not single out homosexuals as a separate class meriting disfavored treatment."[109]

The *Romer* Case

Emboldened by *Bowers,* conservative groups were not content with the mere judicial endorsement of sodomy laws and noncriminal sanctions against homosexual conduct. In certain jurisdictions, they also pressed for repeal of recently enacted state laws and local ordinances forbidding discrimination based on "sexual orientation." The effort culminating in the Supreme Court's decision in *Romer v. Evans* arose in Colorado and involved Amendment Two, a self-executing initiative revision to the state's constitution, adopted in 1992, which provided, "Neither the State of Colorado, through any of its branches or departments, nor any of its agencies, political subdivisions, municipalities or school districts, shall enact, adopt or enforce any statute, regulation, ordinance or policy whereby homosexual, lesbian or bisexual orientation, conduct, practices or relationships shall constitute or otherwise be the basis of or entitle any person or class of persons to have or claim any minority status, quota preferences, protected status or claim of discrimination."[110] Amendment Two's adoption had the immediate effect of repealing Denver, Boulder, and Aspen ordinances that banned discrimination based on sexual orientation in such areas as housing, employment, education, public accommodations, and health and welfare services. Its enactment also meant that passage of any future legislation against such discrimination would require Amendment Two's repeal or modification rather than state or local legislative action alone.

Homosexuals, affected municipalities, and others brought the *Romer* suit in state court claiming the amendment violated equal protection. Following protracted litigation in the Colorado courts, a six-three Supreme Court majority struck down Amendment Two on equal protection grounds toward the end of its 1995–96 term. In a highly unusual move, the Court, speaking through Justice Kennedy, adopted the rationale of a friend of the court brief prepared for the case by Harvard professor Laurence Tribe, who had represented Michael Hardwick in *Bowers,* and joined by a number of other prominent legal scholars. The state's defense of Amendment Two had rested primarily on the claim that the provision did nothing more than repeal existing laws granting homosexuals special protections from various forms of public and private discrimination—safeguards to which they were not constitutionally entitled. Justice Kennedy found the state's construction of the measure "implausible," declaring, "The amendment withdraws from homosexuals, but no others, specific legal protection from the injuries caused by discrimination, and it forbids reinstatement of these laws and policies" except through the cumbersome process of constitutional amendment.[111] Although Colorado's supreme court had declined to hold that Amendment Two would also deny homosexuals "the protection of general laws and policies that prohibit discrimination in governmental and private settings," Kennedy thought that such a construction of the amendment was a "fair, if not necessary, inference from [its] broad language. . . . At some point in the systematic administration of these laws," he observed, "an official must determine whether homosexuality is an arbitrary and thus forbidden basis for decision. Yet a decision to that effect would itself amount to a policy prohibiting discrimination on the basis of homosexuality, and so would appear to be no more valid under Amendment 2 than the specific discrimination the state court held invalid."[112]

Although purporting to subject Amendment Two only to the lenient, rationality standard of review, Kennedy could find no relation between the measure and any legitimate governmental purpose. Under traditional equal protection standards, classifications could not be imposed merely to disadvantage the group against which a law was directed; the discrimination had to relate in some way to some legitimate government objective. But Amendment Two seemed designed solely to make it difficult for a single group to secure specific protection from discrimination—protection other groups could seek through normal political channels. As such, asserted Kennedy, Amendment Two was "unprecedented in our jurisprudence" and "not within our constitutional tradition."[113] Indeed, the "inevitable inference" the amendment created was that it was based purely on "animosity toward the class of persons affected,"[114] but the "bare . . . desire to harm a politically unpopular group [could not] constitute a *legitimate* governmental interest."[115]

Colorado had claimed that Amendment Two reflected respect for freedom of association and assisted the state in conserving resources needed to fight discrimination against suspect and quasi-suspect classes. Kennedy found the amendment's breadth "far removed" from such legitimate purposes. "It is a status-based enactment, divorced from any factual context from which we could discern a relationship to legitimate state interests; it is a classification of persons undertaken for its own sake . . . to make [homosexuals] unequal to everyone else. This Colorado cannot do. A State cannot so deem a class of persons a stranger to its laws."[116]

A particularly acerbic Antonin Scalia, joined by the chief justice and Justice Thomas, vehemently rejected the majority's ruling and rationale. Accusing the Court of confusing a "Kulturkampf" with "a fit of spite," Scalia characterized Amendment Two not as "the manifestation of a 'bare . . . desire to harm homosexuals,'" but as a "modest attempt by seemingly tolerant Coloradans to preserve traditional sexual mores against the efforts of a politically powerful minority to revise those mores through use of the laws."[117] In Scalia's view, his colleagues had distorted equal protection doctrine and in effect repudiated *Bowers*, albeit leaving it formally unchallenged.

The majority, in his judgment, had embraced the novel thesis that a "group is denied equal protection when, to obtain advantage (or, presumably, to avoid disadvantage), it must have recourse to a more general and hence more difficult level of political decisionmaking than others."[118] Scalia doubted, however, whether any "multilevel democracy" could apply such a theory. "For *whenever* a disadvantage is imposed, or conferral of a benefit is prohibited, at one of the higher levels of democratic decision-making," at, for example, the state rather than local level of government, "the affected group has (under this theory) been denied equal protection." Thus, a state law forbidding the awarding of municipal contracts to the relatives of mayors or members of city councils would deny them equal protection since they would be obliged to seek the law's repeal in the state legislature, while others seeking the benefit of city contracts need deal only with municipal officials. "[T]he principle underlying the Court's opinion," observed Scalia, "is that one who is accorded equal treatment under the laws, but cannot as readily as others obtain *preferential* treatment under the laws, has been denied equal protection of the laws. If merely stating this alleged 'equal protection' violation does not suffice to refute it, our constitutional jurisprudence has achieved terminal silliness."[119]

Next, Scalia disputed the majority's conclusion that no rational basis supported Amendment Two. In *Bowers*, which Justice Kennedy had not mentioned in his opinion, the Court had upheld the power of a state to punish homosexual sodomy as a criminal offense. "If it is constitutionally permissible for a State to make homosexual conduct criminal, surely it is constitutionally permissible for a State to enact other laws merely *disfavoring* homosexual conduct. . . . And *a fortiori* it is constitutionally permissible for a State to adopt a provision *not even* disfavoring homosexual conduct, but merely prohibiting all levels of government from bestowing *special protections* upon homosexual conduct."[120] To the argument of the *Romer* plaintiffs that, whatever its status with regard to those who engage in homosexual conduct, Amendment Two could not constitutionally be applied to persons who merely have a homosexual orientation but do not engage in homosexual acts, the justice had three responses. First, he asserted that the plaintiffs were making "a distinction without a difference"[121] since it was virtually impossible to distinguish individuals along such lines. Second, he argued that "[i]f it is rational to criminalize the conduct," as *Bowers* had held, "surely it is rational to deny special favor and protection to those with a self-avowed tendency or desire to engage in the conduct," adding, "where criminal sanctions are not involved, homosexual 'orientation' is an acceptable stand-in for homosexual conduct. A State 'does not violate the Equal Protection Clause merely because the classifications made by its laws are imperfect.'"[122] Finally, the *Romer* plaintiffs were challenging Amendment Two "on its face." It thus would not be sufficient for them to show that the amendment was unconstitutional as applied to persons with only a homosexual "orientation." Instead, they were obliged to show that it could not be validly applied under any "set of circumstances."[123]

To Scalia, Amendment Two was an "eminently reasonable" expression of Colorado's "moral disapproval of homosexual conduct, the same sort of moral disapproval that produced the centuries-old criminal laws that [the Court] held constitutional in *Bowers*. [It] does not . . . prohibit giving favored status to people who are *homosexuals*; they can be favored for many reasons—for example, because they are senior citizens or members of racial minorities. But it prohibits giving them favored status because of *their homosexual conduct*—that is, it prohibits favored status for *homosexuality*."[124] Those opposed to that moral judgment had been sufficiently powerful in certain Colorado communities to secure legislation prohibiting discrimination based on sexual orientation. Scalia had no qualms with such legislative victories: "homosexuals are as entitled to use the legal system for reinforcement of their moral sentiments as are the rest of society." In his judgment, however, homosexuals were also subject to the same sort of "democratic countermeasures," and Amendment Two's supporters had countered "both the geographic concentration and the disproportionate political power of homosexuals [in certain communities] by (1) resolving the controversy at the statewide level, and (2) making the election a single-issue contest for both sides. It put directly, to all the citizens of the State, the question: Should homosexuality be given special protection? They answered no. The Court today asserts that this most democratic of procedures is unconstitutional. Lacking any cases to establish that facially absurd proposition, it simply asserts that it *must* be unconstitutional, because it has never happened before."[125]

Just as Amendment Two had prevented passage of statutes or local ordinances protecting against discrimination based on sexual orientation, statewide laws adversely affecting other groups, such as "drug addicts, smokers, gun owners, or motorcyclists," denied them the opportunity to seek relief in the local arenas of government.

> What the Court says is even demonstrably false at the constitutional level. The Eighteenth Amendment to the Federal Constitution, for example, deprived those who drank alcohol not only of the power to alter the policy of prohibition *locally* or through *state legislation,* but even of the power to alter it through *state constitutional amendment* or *federal legislation.* The Establishment Clause of the First Amendment prevents theocrats from having their way by converting their fellow citizens at the local, state, or federal statutory level; as does the Republican Form of Government Clause prevent monarchists.[126]

For Scalia, however, the historical experience bearing most closely on Amendment Two was the adoption of provisions prohibiting polygamy in the original constitutions of Arizona, Idaho, New Mexico, Oklahoma, and Utah—provisions required by Congress, approved by the Supreme Court in *Davis v. Beason,*[127] and still in effect. "[T]he proposition that polygamy can be criminalized, and those engaging in that crime deprived of the vote," asserted Scalia, "remains good law," and *Romer*'s author, Justice Kennedy, speaking for the Court, had cited *Beason* with approval as recently as 1993. Scalia was at a loss to understand how the provision at issue in *Beason* "was not an 'impermissible targeting' of polygamists, but (the much more mild) Amendment 2 is an 'impermissible targeting' of homosexuals."[128]

The conclusion to Scalia's dissent was every bit as vehement as other sections of his opinion. Terming it "no business of the courts (as opposed to the political branches) to take sides in this cultural war" over the status of homosexuals, Scalia chided the majority for "inventing a novel and extravagant constitutional doctrine to take the victory away from traditional forces" in that struggle, scolded them for "verbally disparaging as bigotry adherence to traditional attitudes," characterized the Court's suggestion that Amendment Two was based purely on a desire to harm homosexuals as "nothing short of insulting," and found it "nothing short of preposterous to call 'politically unpopular' a group which enjoys enormous influence in American media and politics, and which, . . . though composing no more than 4% of the population had the support of 46% of the voters on Amendment 2." When the Court took sides in cultural wars, he caustically added, it tended to side with elites who had decided that homosexuals were entitled to special protection from discrimination rather than "with the more plebian attitudes that apparently still prevail in the United States Congress, which has been unresponsive to repeated attempts to extend to homosexuals the protections of federal civil rights laws" and specifically excluded them from the 1990 Americans with Disabilities Act. Consistent with congressional attitude, asserted Scalia, Amendment Two was "designed to prevent piecemeal deterioration [through local laws] of the sexual morality favored by a majority of Coloradans, and is not only an appropriate means to that legitimate end, but a means that Americans have employed before. Striking it down is an act, not of judicial judgment, but of political will."[129]

Whatever one's sentiments regarding the tone of Justice Scalia's *Romer* dissent or the wisdom of government efforts to regulate the sexual conduct of consenting adults—at least conduct inflicting no serious physical harm—it is difficult logically, as Scalia contended, to reconcile *Romer* with *Bowers*. If a society can criminalize conduct it finds morally unacceptable, surely it can subject those likely to engage in such behavior to milder forms of sanction, absent a finding that members of the group in question constitute a suspect or quasi-suspect class entitled to special judicial protection. Nor can *Romer* and *Bowers* be meaningfully distinguished by the requirement under Amendment Two that homosexuals overcome special procedural hurdles in securing specific legal protection from discrimination. After all, the amendment struck down in *Romer*, unlike the sodomy law upheld in *Bowers*, did not subject homosexuals to criminal prosecution, and, as Scalia convincingly demonstrated in his *Romer* dissent, different groups in a multitiered democracy may reasonably be expected to face varying degrees of difficulty in overcoming burdens to which they are subjected, at least where such groups have not been found to be constitutionally entitled to special judicial protection. *Romer* may thus suggest a readiness on the part of the current majority to overturn *Bowers*.

Such a decision would require the Court to either accept homosexuals as a suspect or quasi-suspect class or reject the rationale underlying *Bowers* and include homosexual behavior within the scope of the right of individual privacy guaranteed via substantive due process. But adding homosexuals to the classes entitled to strict or heightened judicial protection appears problematic at best. Unlike an individual's race or gender, one's sexual orientation is not immediately evident to those charged with enforcement of laws, and homosexuals who conceal their sexual proclivities may entirely escape such burdens. Homosexuals are thus not nearly so vulnerable to systematic discrimination as minorities and women, and criminal prosecutions for homosexual conduct in private settings are probably as rare, if not rarer, in other states as in Georgia. The debate still rages, moreover, whether sexual orientation is an immutable characteristic or a matter of individual choice. And while the political clout of homosexuals as a group varies greatly from area to area, they undoubtedly cannot claim a degree of political powerlessness comparable to that of racial minorities and women at the time discrimination against those groups was first subjected to close judicial scrutiny.

Equally difficult to accept is extension of strict or heightened scrutiny to antigay regulations through the thesis of Andrew Koppelman, endorsed by Cass Sunstein, that such laws are based on an attitude of male supremacy analogous to the notion of white supremacy that underlay the miscegenation law struck down in the *Loving* case.[130] Such a theory does not merely raise serious questions of standing; it would also be extremely hard to convince courts that the dominant, conscious purpose of antigay laws is the perpetuation of male supremacy. As one critic of the Koppelman thesis has observed, "the Georgia legislators responsible for the sodomy statute in *Bowers*, and authors of statutes that forbid same-sex marriages would deny, truthfully and adamantly, that they had any purpose to discriminate against women. They would, in fact, be astonished by such a suggestion."[131] The statute struck down in *Loving* was found "to rest *solely* upon [illegitimate] distinctions drawn according to race,"[132] and courts are generally quite reluctant to strike down laws based on unconscious psychological motivations underlying their adoption.

The Colorado courts in *Romer* had rested strict scrutiny of the regulations at issue there on a fundamental right to equal participation in the political process. That rationale would be limited, however, to suits involving enactments of the Amendment Two variety. Precedents on which that purported fundamental right is said to be based involved, moreover, racial classifications long subject to strict judicial scrutiny, invoked other, established fundamental rights, or were decided on the basis of rationality review rather than strict scrutiny.[133]

Nor, arguably, should *Bowers* be reversed, whatever *Romer*'s implications for the future and however silly government's intrusion into the private sexual lives of consenting adults might be. *Bowers*'s critics see it as inconsistent with the line of decisions from *Griswold*, through *Eisenstadt*, to *Roe*, which, taken together, uphold the right of married and unmarried persons to engage in nonprocreative sexual activity. If nonreproductive heterosexual conduct is constitutionally protected, the argument runs, any law prohibiting homosexual conduct reflects only public animus, an inappropriate basis for legislation.

But *Bowers*'s connection to those earlier cases is more apparent than real. The contraceptive ban struck down in *Griswold* reached sexual intercourse in marriage, a legally recognized relationship. *Eisenstadt* extended *Griswold* to unmarried persons, but did not reject the view that states possess authority to deter fornication. Instead, the Court concluded that the law at issue there was so riddled with exceptions making contraceptives freely available for use in premarital relations that control of fornication could not reasonably be regarded as the statute's purpose. If public disapproval of fornication and, for that matter, such other "victimless" crimes as prostitution and gambling is a legitimate basis for a law interfering with no fundamental right or suspect class, moral disapproval would also appear to be an acceptable basis for sanctions against homosexual behavior.

The *Romer* majority ultimately concluded, of course, that Amendment Two was the product of an impermissible public desire simply to harm persons with a homosexual orientation or status. Admittedly, it is often difficult to distinguish animus against a particular group's status from disapproval of its conduct. But where, as with homosexuality, status is largely defined by proclivity for a particular form of conduct, government arguably should enjoy a large measure of deference, absent interference with a fundamental right or suspect class. As Justice Scalia asserted in his *Romer* dissent, "[i]f it is rational to criminalize the conduct, surely it is rational to deny special favor and protection to those with a self-avowed tendency or desire to engage in the conduct."[134]

The Right to Die

Despite such concerns, the Rehnquist Court's approach to assisted suicide claims was to be equally pragmatic. The Court's assumption in *Cruzan v. Director, Missouri Dept. of Health* (1990)[135] that substantive due process includes a right to refuse unwanted medical treatment rested more heavily on traditional common law principles than on abstract notions of fundamental rights. In *Washington v. Glucksberg* (1997) and *Vacco v. Quill* (1997),[136] the Court unanimously upheld Washington and New York statutes prohibiting physician-assisted suicide. A majority of justices concluded in *Glucksberg* and *Quill*, however, that under certain circumstances, terminally ill patients might be constitutionally entitled to assisted suicide. In a concurring opinion, moreover, Justice Souter drew on the thinking of the second Justice Harlan, his jurisprudential mentor, in developing an elaborate and eloquent defense of "two centuries of American constitutional practice in recognizing unenumerated substantive limits on governmental action."[137]

Chief Justice Rehnquist spoke for the Court in both cases. In rejecting in *Glucksberg* the argument that substantive due process includes a fundamental right to assisted suicide, Rehnquist identified what he termed the Court's "established" approach to substantive due process as embodying two primary features: (1) an effort to limit the concept to rights deeply rooted in the nation's history and tradition, and (2) the requirement that rights so recognized be carefully described. This approach, observed Rehnquist, limits due process's substantive reach to rights that "have at least been carefully refined by concrete examples involving fundamental rights found to be deeply rooted in our legal tradition" and thus "tends to rein in the subjective elements that are necessarily present in due process judicial review."[138] Any governmental action not implicating such a fundamental right, he added, need bear only a "reasonable relation to a legitimate state interest" rather than satisfy a "complex balancing of competing interests."[139]

Given the "consistent and almost universal [national] tradition" rejecting recognition of assisted suicide,[140] Rehnquist obviously disputed any contention that such a right could be considered consistent with the nation's history and long practice. Nor would he agree that *Cruzan* and *Casey* supported recognition of such a right. The right to refuse unwanted medical treatment assumed in *Cruzan,* he asserted, "was not simply deduced from abstract concepts of personal autonomy,"[141] but instead was based on the common law rule and long tradition rejecting forced medical treatment—a legal status obviously never extended assisted suicide. Nor, he added, did the abortion right recognized in *Casey* compel recognition of such a right. "That many of the rights and liberties protected by the Due Process Clause [relate to] personal autonomy does not warrant the sweeping conclusion that any and all important, intimate, and personal decisions are so protected, . . . and *Casey* did not suggest otherwise."[142] Due process did require that laws affecting individual liberty at least be rationally related to legitimate governmental interests. But the challenged statute "unquestionably met" that requirement.[143] Applying the same approach to the equal protection claim at issue in *Quill,* Rehnquist also concluded that the Constitution clearly accepted the line drawn in the law between the refusal of lifesaving medical treatment and assisted suicide.[144] "Throughout the Nation," he observed, "Americans are engaged in an earnest and profound debate about the morality, legality, and practicality of physician assisted suicide. Our holding permits this debate to continue, as it should in a democratic society."[145]

Although the Court was unanimous in upholding the *Glucksberg* and *Quill* statutes, five justices assumed a more complicated and flexible stance than the chief justice's opinions appeared to adopt. Justice O'Connor joined Rehnquist's conclusion that, as she put it, "there is no generalized right to 'commit suicide.'"[146] She reserved judgment, however, on the question whether terminal patients "experiencing great suffering" were entitled to control the circumstances of their imminent deaths. Washington and New York permitted such patients to obtain pain-relieving medication, even to the point of causing unconsciousness and hastening death. There was thus no need, in O'Connor's judgment, to reach the question whether terminal patients in great pain had a right to assistance in ending their lives. She also agreed "that the State's interests in protecting those who are not truly competent or facing imminent death, or those whose decisions to hasten death would not truly be voluntary, are sufficiently weighty to justify a prohibition against physician assisted suicide."[147]

Justices Ginsburg and Breyer substantially agreed with O'Connor's opinion, but Breyer concurred only in the Court's judgment, not the chief justice's opinion. Preferring to cast the constitutional claim raised in the cases as asserting a "right to die with dignity," rather than a right to assisted suicide, Breyer joined the Court's ruling only because terminal patients in Washington and New York were not forced to endure a painful death. Justice Stevens also concurred only in the judgment. Drawing an analogy to the Court's death penalty rulings, Stevens concluded that particular applications of assisted suicide statutes could be found valid or invalid, depending on the circumstances. "A State, like Washington, that has authorized the death penalty and thereby has concluded that the sanctity of human life does not require that it always be preserved," he added, "must acknowledge that there are situations in which an interest in hastening death is legitimate. Indeed, not only is that interest sometimes legitimate, I am also convinced that there are times when it is entitled to constitutional protection."[148]

While the other justices filing or joining separate concurrences in *Glucksberg* and *Quill* registered relatively narrow differences with the chief justice's approach, Justice Souter raised fundamental objections to Rehnquist's formula for analyzing substantive due process claims. Souter conceded that some considered due process "an unduly vague or oxymoronic warrant for judicial review of substantive state law" and that "two centuries of American constitutional practice in recognizing unenumerated, substantive limits on governmental action" had "neither rested on any single textual basis nor expressed a consistent theory."[149] Its "persistence" had convinced Souter, however, of the "legitimacy of the modern justification for such judicial review" that the second Justice Harlan, his jurisprudential mentor, had advanced in his dissent in *Poe v. Ullman*, the 1961 case in which Harlan invoked substantive due process in voting to strike down the Connecticut contraceptive ban later invalidated in the *Griswold* case.[150]

Justice Harlan, according to Souter, had argued in *Poe* for a resolution of substantive due process claims that called for courts to weigh the competing individual and governmental interests at issue in such cases. In assessing the weight to be assigned individual interests, courts were to draw on constitutional text and tradition. But they were also to extend appropriate deference to the legislature; and it was only when a challenged statute's "justifying principle, critically valued, [was] so far from being commensurate with the individual interest as to be arbitrarily or pointlessly applied that the statute must give way. Only if this standard points against the statute can the individual claimant be said to have a constitutional right."[151] Harlan's approach, Souter observed, was fundamentally different from that of the "deviant economic due process cases" of the *Lochner* era,[152] in which the Court had purported to strike down only those regulations found to be "arbitrary," while actually giving economic freedoms an essentially absolute scope and striking down numerous pieces of legislation "that post-New Deal courts have uniformly thought constitutionally sound."[153] Harlan had thus "avoid[ed] the absolutist failing of many older cases without embracing the opposite pole of equating reasonableness with past practice described at a very specific level"[154]—a defect Souter obviously saw in Chief Justice Rehnquist's approach to substantive due process.

Applying Harlan's formula, Souter found the due process interest in assisted suicide "indisputab[ly]" important. He concluded, however, that it was unnecessary to determine whether that interest "might in some circumstances, or at some time, be seen as 'fundamental' to the degree entitled to prevail" over countervailing governmental interests, because the interests asserted in support of the Washington and New York statutes—specifically, the states' interests "in protecting patients from mistakenly and involuntarily deciding to end their lives, and in guarding against both voluntary and involuntary euthanasia"[155]— were to him sufficient "to defeat the . . . claim that . . . [the challenged statutes were] arbitrary or purposeless."[156] Like his mentor, moreover, Souter emphasized a preference for legislative judgment in the field, not only because a legislature is "relatively more competent to deal with an emerging issue as to which facts currently unknown could be dispositive," but also because any right recognized as constitutionally required would, of course, "differ in no essential way from other constitutional rights guaranteed by enumeration or derived from some more definite textual source than 'due process.'" Unenumerated rights should be recognized, therefore, only with the assurance that their recognition "would prove as durable as the recognition of those other rights." To hold otherwise would be to create "a constitutional regime too uncertain to bring with it the expectation of finality that is one of this Court's central obligations in making constitutional decisions." Elected legislators were not "so constrained." Judges thus should avoid intervention, permitting time for "reasonable legislative consideration."[157]

The Scope of Unenumerated Rights

For Justice Souter, the proper approach to application of substantive due process in cases of the *Glucksberg* and *Quill* variety was to determine, as Justice Harlan had recommended, whether the statute at issue "sets up one of those 'arbitrary impositions' or 'purposeless restraints' at odds with" due process.[158] Chief Justice Rehnquist favored, on the other hand, what he termed a more "restrained methodology" in which only those laws affecting a fundamental right would be subjected to meaningful scrutiny, thereby allowing courts to avoid the "complex balancing of competing interests in every case" that the Souter-Harlan formula required.[159]

Although filing no opinions in the assisted suicide cases, two justices presumably would have gone even further—totally or largely rejecting the substantive due process doctrine, whatever its form, as they have in economic cases.[160] Justice Scalia's conception of due process as a procedural guarantee closely resembles Justice Black's "law of the land" approach, under which due process requires government only to follow established laws and procedures, including explicit constitutional guarantees, rather than judicially created standards of procedural "fairness" in depriving a person of life, liberty, or property. Scalia has declared, for example, "that no procedure firmly rooted in the practices of our people can be so 'fundamentally unfair' as to deny due process of law."[161] Language in certain of Scalia's opinions, it will be recalled, suggests that, like Black, he also entirely repudiates substantive due process, dismissing it as an "oxymoron" rather than a constitutional right, declaring that the due process clause "guarantees *no* substantive rights, but only (as it says) due process," and urging the Court to "follow the text of the Constitution, which sets forth certain substantive rights that cannot be taken away, and adds, beyond that, a right to due process when life, liberty, or property is to be taken away."[162] Justice Thomas has regularly concurred in such statements.

Especially in opinions joined by other justices in addition to Justice Thomas, Justice Scalia at times appears to hedge his opposition to substantive due process. In reaffirming his rejection of *Roe*, for example, he asserted in *Casey* that he would also oppose constitutional protection for bigamy, based on "two simple facts: (1) the Constitution says absolutely nothing about it, and (2) the longstanding traditions of American society have permitted it to be legally proscribed."[163] Elsewhere in his opinion, he applied a rational basis standard to uphold the abortion controls at issue in *Casey*. Justice Black, by contrast, would have invariably upheld statutes claimed only to violate due process (rather than some more explicit constitutional guarantee), regardless of whether they conflicted with longstanding traditions or had any rational basis. On the current Court, however, Scalia and Thomas are the justices most likely to reject judicial recognition for unenumerated rights. Chief Justice Rehnquist's approach to substantive due process in *Glucksberg* and *Quill* probably was simply sufficiently narrow that they saw no need to file a separate concurrence.

All other members of the Court, though, appear to embrace a more flexible and potentially expansive conception of substantive due process. Justice O'Connor joined the chief justice's opinions in the assisted suicide cases. But in her *Casey* plurality opinion, she adopted the substantive due process formula that Justice Harlan had advanced in his *Poe* dissent and that Justice Souter, who joined O'Connor's *Casey* opinion, defended in the assisted suicide cases. At one point, for example, she cited Justice Harlan's assertion that "'liberty' is not a series of isolated points picked out in terms of [enumerated rights]. . . . It is a rational continuum which, broadly speaking, includes a freedom from all substantial arbitrary impositions and purposeless restraints, . . . and which also recognizes . . . that certain interests require particularly careful scrutiny of the state needs asserted to justify their abridgment."[164]

Although Justice Kennedy did not concur separately in *Glucksberg* and *Quill*, he also joined O'Connor's *Casey* plurality. Justice Ginsburg joined the Court's decision in the assisted suicide cases, but "for the reasons stated in" O'Connor's concurrence rather than Rehnquist's opinion; and Justice Breyer, who joined O'Connor's opinion "except insofar as it joins the opinions of the Court,"[165] also appeared to embrace Harlan's general approach to defining due process, as did Justice Stevens in his separate concurrence. And although none of the concurring justices specifically joined Justice Souter's opinion, the separate concurrences they filed and joined seemed closer to Souter's reasoning than the chief justice's rationale.

Of the two approaches, moreover, the Harlan-Souter conception of due process as embodying a "continuum" subject to a balancing of competing individual and governmental interests is arguably preferable to one recognizing "isolated points" as "fundamental," and thus largely immune from governmental control, while excluding other unenumerated interests from virtually all judicial protection. Chief Justice Rehnquist dissented in *Roe*, and it is very likely that he personally embraces an extremely narrow conception of substantive due process under which few, and probably no, unenumerated rights would be deemed fundamental. In his *Roe* dissent, for example, he agreed that due process "embraces more than the rights found in the Bill of Rights." But he also indicated support for the idea that laws affecting unenumerated "social and economic" rights need have only a "rational basis" to avoid being declared unconstitutional. "The Court's sweeping invalidation of any restrictions on abortion during the first trimester," he added, "is impossible to justify under that standard, and the conscious weighing of competing factors that the Court's opinion apparently substitutes for the established test is far more appropriate to a legislative judgment than to a judicial one."[166] Since virtually all liberty can be characterized as either "social" or "economic," one would assume that Rehnquist would rarely, if ever, deem a right mentioned nowhere in the Constitution as sufficiently entrenched in American legal tradition to be given meaningful judicial protection.

But in *Glucksberg* and *Quill*, the chief justice was speaking for the Court, not himself alone. Even as weakened by *Casey* and other rulings, moreover, the abortion right remains an important guarantee that government is largely forbidden to deny throughout a pregnancy, and it is difficult to reconcile the Court's continued recognition of abortion rights with Chief Justice Rehnquist's rejection of any right to assisted suicide. In his *Glucksberg* opinion, Rehnquist stressed the virtual unanimity of jurisdictions in proscribing assisted suicides, but abortions were also widely prohibited prior to *Roe*. The *Roe* Court, it should be added, limited the *persons* entitled to constitutional protection to postnatal beings, but in his opinion for the *Roe* majority, Justice Blackmun assigned considerable weight to the state's interest in the *potential* life of a viable fetus, while upholding third-trimester therapeutic abortions. If the health interests supporting third-trimester abortions automatically take precedence over the state's interests in potential life, it is hard to understand how any state interest in the life of a terminally ill patient facing imminent death could invariably outweigh the patient's desire to die. And unlike a fetus, of course, a competent, terminally ill patient makes the choice to secure an assisted suicide. In short, neither the abortion right, prior to *Roe*, nor a right to assisted suicide was firmly grounded in American legal tradition, yet the Court recognizes the former and Rehnquist's *Glucksberg* opinion refuses to recognize the latter, even though state interests justifying abortion restrictions appear weightier than those claimed to support a flat ban on assisted suicide.

As Chief Justice Rehnquist has noted, his approach avoids the *ad hoc* balancing of competing interests that the Harlan-Souter formula requires in every case. But comparison of the Court's disposition of abortion and assisted suicide cases suggests that the selection of rights included and excluded from meaningful judicial recognition under his approach is inherently arbitrary, aggravating rather than "rein[ing] in the subjective elements that are necessarily present in due process judicial review."[167] Essentially the same observation could be made, incidentally, of the Court's broad rejection of homosexual rights in *Bowers* and close scrutiny, via equal protection, of the antigay provision struck down in the *Romer* case.

By candidly weighing competing interests in every case, those who embrace the Harlan-Souter conception of substantive due process avoid the arbitrariness inherent in the Rehnquist approach. As Justice Black long contended, however, judicial lawmaking is endemic to any form of substantive due process. Although most, if not all, constitutional provisions lack self-evident meaning, thereby compelling judicial creativity, the vague, open-ended language of the due process guarantee goes much further, providing unlimited opportunity for such judicial lawmaking—unless, that is, the clause is confined, as Black recommended, to its original law of the land meaning, a construction that entirely excludes substantive due process, whatever its ultimate impact on the reach of due process as a procedural guarantee.

The notion that courts should do *justice* is a compelling, virtually universal force—so overwhelming, in fact, that substantive due process and its relatives are unlikely ever to be completely abandoned. It is thus hardly surprising that Justice Harlan could be one of the most articulate modern defenders of judicial self-restraint, yet argue in his *Poe* dissent that "[w]ere due process merely a procedural safeguard it would fail to reach those situations where the deprivation of life, liberty or property was accomplished by legislation which by operating in the future could, given even the fairest possible procedure in application to individuals, nevertheless destroy the enjoyment of all three."[168]

But however understandable, such thinking is not only based on a tortured reading of the text of the due process guarantee; history also teaches that every such judicial excursion has aroused intense and at times violent turmoil. As Justice Scalia and others have argued, the *Dred Scott* Court's invocation of a variety of substantive due process in defense of slavery is but one example,[169] the *Lochner*-era Court's defense of laissez-faire another, the abortion rulings another, and any future Court recognition of some constitutional right to assisted suicide (or "death with dignity," as Justice Breyer has put it) promises to arouse yet another round of bitter public controversy.

Most critically perhaps, judicial intervention in the political arena via the "vague contours" of due process, whatever its form, is an affront to democratic institutions. In *Casey*, Justice Scalia declared of the Court's abortion pronouncements that "by foreclosing all democratic outlet for the deep passions this issue arouses, by banishing the issue from the political forum that gives all participants, even the losers, the satisfaction of a fair hearing and an honest fight, by continuing the imposition of a rigid national rule instead of allowing for regional differences, the Court merely prolongs and intensifies the anguish."[170] Essentially the same observation could be made of virtually every arena of substantive due process into which the Court has ventured. The ultimate issue is not the wisdom of such judgments, but the legitimacy of the Court's involvement. For those with such concerns, the Court's unanimous rejection of the challenges to the assisted suicide statutes at issue in *Glucksberg* and *Quill* was a promising development. But the concurring opinions filed in those cases indicate that further expansion of substantive due process and the resulting intrusion upon democratic institutions are far from over. It was hardly surprising, therefore, that near the end of the 1998-99 term, a plurality of justices invoked a due process right to loiter in striking down a Chicago ordinance that prohibited "criminal gang members" from remaining in public places "with no apparent purpose" and ignoring police orders to disperse.[171] Or that in the same term, a majority rested the unstated but long-recognized right to interstate travel on the Fourteenth Amendment's privileges or immunities clause—a provision, like due process, with a potentially open-ended meaning that the Court had only invoked once before in the amendment's entire history, in a precedent that was soon overruled. [172]

6

The Religion Clauses

The Rehnquist Court has decided a large number of controversial cases dealing with the scope and limits of the First Amendment's ban on federal laws "respecting an establishment of religion or prohibiting the free exercise thereof," commands long made binding on the states through judicial interpretation of the Fourteenth Amendment's due process clause.[1] In the establishment field, the justices have upheld federal funding of premarital counseling by religious organizations,[2] displays of religious and secular seasonal symbols on public property,[3] provisions of the federal Equal Access Act of 1984 requiring equal facilities for religious and secular student groups in public high schools,[4] state provision of a sign-language interpreter for a deaf student attending a religious high school,[5] and state provision of public school teachers to provide federally funded remedial education to disadvantaged students in religious schools,[6] while also holding that public schools providing access to school facilities after hours to community groups cannot bar religious organizations from such facilities.[7] The Court has struck down, on the other hand, public school commencement prayers[8] and the special New York school district created in Kiryas Joel, an Hasidic Jewish community, to provide remedial classes for handicapped children of that sect attending religious schools.[9]

In rejecting free exercise claims, the justices have upheld the authority of prison officials to forbid Islamic prison inmates to leave work details for religious services,[10] U.S. forest service road construction and timber-harvesting permits in areas of national parks traditionally used by Indian tribes for religious ceremonies,[11] denial of tax deductions for member donations to the Church of Scientology,[12] and the denial of unemployment compensation to employees of a drug counseling agency fired for their ritual use of peyote in ceremonies of the Native American Church.[13] The Court has declared unconstitutional, however, the denial of unemployment compensation to an employee who lost her job with a retail jeweler after her conversion to the Seventh-Day Adventist Church and refusal to engage in further Saturday work,[14] as well as to another employee whose refusal for religious reasons to work on Saturday was based on the doctrine of no particular sect.[15] A Hialeah, Florida, statute prohibiting the ritual slaughter of animals, but permitting their slaughter for virtually all other purposes, met the same fate.[16]

The most significant Rehnquist Court developments with respect to the religion clauses, however, have involved the Court's extensive curtailment, if not abandonment, of the doctrinal standards under which establishment claims have been resolved through most of the modern Court's history, as well as the equally dramatic restrictions a majority has imposed on the reach of the free exercise guarantee. In *Agostini v. Felton* (1997),[17] the case upholding state provision of teachers for religious schools, Justice O'Connor's opinion for a five-four Court gave lip service to traditional establishment clause doctrine—doctrine applied for many years to maintain substantial church-state separation. But she also approved governmental assistance to religious schools of the sort a majority had struck down in two cases decided twelve years earlier, indeed, precisely the same scheme declared unconstitutional in one of those cases.[18]

Earlier, in *Employment Division v. Smith* (1990),[19] upholding the denial of unemployment compensation to employees fired for ritual peyote use, the Court, speaking through Justice Scalia, purported to distinguish *Sherbert v. Verner* (1963)[20] and other precedents subjecting laws affecting religious practices to strict scrutiny, holding instead that religiously neutral laws of general application could be constitutionally enforced against religious practices without the showing of a compelling interest traditionally required in cases of the *Sherbert* variety. And when Congress attempted through the Religious Freedom Restoration Act of 1993 to restore the compelling interest standard in such cases, a majority, per Justice Kennedy, declared that provision an unconstitutional congressional usurpation of ultimate judicial authority to determine the Constitution's meaning.[21] This chapter focuses on these two important doctrinal developments on the Rehnquist Court.

Lemon Under Attack

"Separationists" and "nonpreferentialists" largely define the continuing debate over the meaning of the First Amendment's ban on laws "respecting an establishment of religion." In contending for a construction of the establishment clause permitting only limited, essentially secular contact between church and state, separationists cite the religious persecutions that accounted for much of the nation's colonial settlement, the seemingly sweeping language of the constitutional prohibition on laws "respecting" religion, the grim record of church-state alliances historically, and the negative potential consequences of such ties for modern religions and governments. Nonpreferentialists, by contrast, draw on the tenor of congressional debates over the establishment clause's adoption, church-state connections during both the nation's

formative and modern eras, and considerations of federalism in defending an interpretation of the guarantee that allows government to accommodate religion and forbids only preference for a particular faith or sect.

The ambiguity of the historical record permits strong, historically based arguments supporting both these positions. Strong policy arguments also lend legitimacy
to each. The modern Supreme Court has generally embraced, however, a separationist construction of the establishment clause. In *Lemon v. Kurtzman* (1971),[22] the
most significant establishment ruling of the modern era, the Burger Court continued
that tradition in announcing a three-pronged test for determining whether governmental action affecting religion violates establishment principles. "First," Chief Justice Burger declared for the *Lemon* Court, "the statute must have a secular legislative
purpose; second, its principal or primary effect must be one that neither advances
nor inhibits religion. . . ; finally, the statute must not foster 'an excessive government
entanglement with religion.'"[23]

Lemon was decided in 1971, but the conception of the establishment clause the
Lemon test embraces had its origins in *Everson v. Board of Education*,[24] the 1947 occasion for the Court's first encounter with establishment claims. True, in *Everson* Justice Black drew on Thomas Jefferson's letter to the Danbury Baptist Association[25] in
declaring that "the clause against establishment of religion by law was intended to
erect 'a wall of separation between church and State,'"[26] while in *Lemon* Chief Justice
Burger characterized the language of the establishment clause as "at best opaque" and
declared that "[c]andor compels acknowledgment . . . that we can only dimly perceive the lines of demarcation in this extraordinarily sensitive area of constitutional
law."[27] In *Everson*, however, Justice Black had emphasized the purely secular character
of the school transportation reimbursement scheme at issue there, as well as the limited, incidental effect of such an arrangement on parochial schools,[28] essentially foreshadowing the first two prongs of the *Lemon* standard. The Court first explicitly
embraced these elements of *Lemon*, moreover, in *Abington v. Schempp*,[29] the 1963
case invalidating state-sponsored Bible reading in the public schools. "[T]o withstand the strictures of the Establishment Clause," asserted Justice Tom C. Clark for
the *Schempp* majority, "there must be a secular legislative purpose and a primary
effect that neither advances nor inhibits religion."[30] The "excessive entanglement"
standard was not explicitly adopted by the Court until 1970,[31] the year before *Lemon*
was decided. But it, too, seems entirely consistent with the dominant tone of Justice
Black's *Everson* opinion. After all, while Justice Black wrote of a "wall of separation"
between church and state that "must be kept high and impregnable,"[32] his comparison of transportation to police and fire protection, as well as other exercises of state
police power, made it clear that he meant only that government and the religious
components of religious institutions should be kept completely apart.

Not only does *Lemon* have its roots in the earliest history of the Court's confrontation with establishment issues, but for many years, there was little disagreement
among the justices over the basic principles to be applied in establishment cases.
Where the Court was badly split over the application of such principles in individual
cases, moreover, the dissenters complained that a majority was permitting *too much*
rather than *too little* contact between church and government or took issue with the

majority's perception of the facts. The four *Everson* dissenters contended, for example, that the transportation reimbursement scheme challenged there extended only
to parents of children attending public and Roman Catholic schools, while Justice
Black for the majority found no evidence that there were any children in the township attending, or interested in attending, other schools, adding: "It will be appropriate to consider the exclusion of students of private schools operated for profit when
and if it is proved to have occurred."[33] Had the majority and dissenting justices not
differed over this critical factual issue, the size of the majority vote would undoubtedly have been larger. Justice Jackson, who voted against the reimbursement scheme
"contrary to first impressions,"[34] particularly stressed that issue in his *Everson* dissent; and Justice Felix Frankfurter joined Jackson's opinion.

Nor was *Everson* an isolated exception. When the Court struck down an on-campus released-time religious education program in the public schools the following
year,[35] only Justice Stanley Reed dissented. Yet when a majority in 1952 upheld the
off-campus released-time program at issue in *Zorach v. Clauson*,[36] three justices dissented, challenging a state's "use [of] its compulsory education laws to help religious
sects get attendants presumably too unenthusiastic to go unless moved to do so by
the pressure of . . . state machinery."[37] Three justices also dissented when the Court in
1968 upheld the loan of textbooks to parochial school students.[38] Again, the dissenters' dispute with the majority was not over applicable principles, but over competing perceptions of the facts. They simply contended that parochial schools would
inevitably select and use textbooks for sectarian as well as secular purposes, while the
majority refused to draw such conclusions absent specific evidence.

Contemporary Supreme Court critics of *Lemon*'s progenitors, on the other hand,
were few, indeed. In dissenting from the Court's invalidation of on-campus released-
time programs in 1948, Justice Reed pointed to "the many instances of close association of church and state in American society . . . relations . . . so much a part of our
tradition and culture that they are accepted without more."[39] Reed also suggested
that the "phrase 'an establishment of religion' may have been intended by Congress to
be aimed only at a state church"[40] and warned that "[d]evotion to the great principle
of religious liberty should not lead us into a rigid interpretation of the constitutional
guarantee that conflicts with accepted habits of our people."[41] Justice Stewart, the
lone dissenter from the Court's prayer and Bible-reading rulings in *Engel v. Vitale*
(1962)[42] and *Schempp*, declared voluntary devotional programs in the public schools
a reasonable accommodation of religion, echoed Justice Reed in citing the "countless
[religious] practices of the institutions and officials of our government,"[43] and complained that "the Court's task, in this as in all areas of constitutional adjudication, is
not responsibly aided by the uncritical invocation of metaphors like the 'wall of separation,' a phrase nowhere to be found in the Constitution."[44] But even Stewart joined
Chief Justice Burger's *Lemon* opinion.

In *Lemon* and companion cases,[45] the Court struck down salary supplements and
other forms of secular assistance to parochial schools on the ground that the continuing state surveillance required to assure that the aid at issue was not put to sectarian
uses would create an excessive church-state entanglement. In dissent, Justice White
charged that the Court's approach posed an "insoluble paradox": "The State cannot

finance secular instruction if it permits religion to be taught in the same classroom; but if it exacts a promise that religion not be taught . . . and enforces it, it is then entangled in the 'no entanglement' aspect of the Court's Establishment Clause jurisprudence."[46] White, however, also stood alone. Thus, for the first quarter century of the modern Court's grappling with establishment issues—from 1947 to 1971—consensus remained high regarding basic establishment principles. Where deep division developed over their application in specific contexts, moreover, dissenters accused the majority of failing to maintain sufficient separation of church and state.

What a difference a few appointments can make. A majority on the Rehnquist Court now appears to reject *Lemon*, despite the lip service given it in *Agostini*, and the justices seem bitterly divided over an appropriate alternative approach to establishment issues, whatever the appearance of unanimity in the *Agostini* case. Two years before his 1987 retirement from the Court, Justice Powell filed a brief concurring opinion in *Wallace v. Jaffree*,[47] which overturned an Alabama law authorizing a daily period of silence for meditation or voluntary prayer in the state's public schools. In a separate concurrence, Justice O'Connor had urged a reexamination and refinement of *Lemon*; Justice Rehnquist in dissent advocated discarding the *Lemon* test entirely. In his concurrence, Justice Powell responded to his colleagues:

> *Lemon* . . . identifies standards that have proved useful in analyzing case after case both in our decisions and in those of other courts. It is the only coherent test a majority of the Court has ever adopted. Only once since our decision in *Lemon* . . . have we addressed an Establishment Clause issue without resort to its three-pronged test. See *Marsh v. Chambers* . . . (1983) [upholding state legislative chaplains]. *Lemon* . . . has not been overruled or its test modified. Yet, continued criticism of it could encourage other courts to feel free to decide Establishment Clause cases on an ad hoc basis.[48]

The separate opinion in *Wallace v. Jaffree* that had most aroused Justice Powell's reaction was the dissent Justice Rehnquist filed in the case. Rehnquist, whom President Reagan was to move to the Court's center seat the following year, had used the occasion for a full-scale assault not only on *Lemon*, but on *Everson* and virtually all the other establishment cases in between as well. Rehnquist focused primarily on the historical record, which convinced him that the establishment clause only "forbade establishment of a national religion, and forbade preference among religious sects or denominations. . . . The Establishment Clause did not require government neutrality between religion and irreligion nor did it prohibit the Federal Government from providing nondiscriminatory aid to religion."[49] Rehnquist first dismissed Thomas Jefferson and his "misleading [wall of separation] metaphor," which Justice Black had cited in *Everson* and with which "unfortunately the Establishment Clause [had] been expressly freighted . . . for nearly forty years."[50] Jefferson had been in France at the time the Bill of Rights was adopted; his letter to the Danbury Baptists, "a short note of courtesy," was written fourteen years after the amendments' enactment. "He would [thus] seem to any detached observer," concluded Rehnquist, "as a less than ideal source of contemporary history as to the meaning of the Religion Clauses of the First Amendment."[51]

For Rehnquist, James Madison was a different matter. Madison had "play[ed] as large a part as anyone in the drafting of the Bill of Rights," and his role in the amendments' adoption, as well as that of the First Congress, presented, Rehnquist contended, "a far different picture of [the clause's] purpose than the highly simplified 'wall of separation between church and State.'"[52]

In *Everson*, Justice Black had also relied on Madison's 1785 "Memorial and Remonstrance Against Religious Assessments," in which the future "Father of the Constitution" argued against renewal of tax support for Virginia's established church,[53] as well as on the Virginia Statute for Religious Liberty, in which adoption both Madison and Jefferson had played key roles. A Madison biographer has aptly characterized Madison's "Remonstrance" as a brief for "a complete separation of church and state,"[54] and the Virginia statute carried a similar import. Rehnquist made no effort to dispute such characterizations. Instead, he suggested that Madison the author of the "Remonstrance" and supporter of the statute had acted as a "dedicated advocate"[55] and "zealous believer,"[56] but asserted that Madison's efforts in connection with adoption of the Bill of Rights were "those of the prudent statesman"[57] and "advocate of sensible legislative compromise."[58]

During deliberations on the Bill of Rights in the House of Representatives, Representative Samuel Livermore of New Hampshire proposed that its religion provisions read, "Congress shall make no laws *touching* religion, or infringing the rights of conscience";[59] and the final version, of course, forbids laws "*respecting* an establishment of religion." But the language James Madison originally proposed stipulated only that "[t]he civil rights of none shall be abridged on account of religious belief or worship, nor shall any national religion be established, nor shall the full and equal rights of conscience be in any manner, or on any pretext, infringed."[60] That proposal and certain of Madison's remarks on the House floor convinced Rehnquist that

> [Madison] saw the Amendment as designed to prohibit the establishment of a national religion, and perhaps to prevent discrimination among sects. He did not see it as requiring neutrality on the part of government between religion and irreligion. Thus the Court's opinion in *Everson*—while correct in bracketing Madison and Jefferson together in their exertions in their home State leading to the enactment of the Virginia Statute of Religious Liberty—is totally incorrect in suggesting that Madison carried these views onto the floor of the United States House of Representatives when he proposed the language which would ultimately become the Bill of Rights.[61]

Without speculating why Representative Livermore proposed a ban on laws "touching religion" (a proposal adopted by a vote of thirty-one–twenty) or why the final version replaced a prohibition on "law[s] establishing religion" with the stipulation that Congress "make no law respecting an establishment of religion," Rehnquist further concluded that not only Madison, but "it [presumably Congress] was definitely not concerned about whether the Government might aid all religions evenhandedly."[62]

Other events of the period surrounding adoption of the Bill of Rights convinced Rehnquist that its framers intended only to forbid governmental preference for particular religions. The 1789 reenactment of the Northwest Ordinance had provided that "[r]eligion, morality, and knowledge, being necessary to good government and the happiness of mankind, schools and the means of education shall forever be encouraged."[63] Territorial land grants, observed Rehnquist, were not limited to public schools and were not denied to sectarian schools until 1845. The same Congress that approved the Bill of Rights, he added, also adopted a resolution asking President George Washington to issue a Thanksgiving Day Proclamation. A representative who had opposed the amendments, noted Rehnquist, also voted against the proclamation, asserting that "it is a religious matter, and, as such, is proscribed to us."[64] Two who favored the proclamation, on the other hand, had also supported the amendments. Of early presidents, Rehnquist added, Washington, John Adams, and Madison had all issued Thanksgiving proclamations; only Jefferson declined, observing that religion could "never be safer than in [the people's] own hands, where the Constitution has deposited it."[65] Until 1897, when such aid ceased, Rehnquist continued, the government had regularly appropriated funds for sectarian Indian education by religious groups, and both Justice Joseph Story and Thomas Cooley had endorsed no-preference constructions of the establishment clause.

The *Lemon* test fared no better with Rehnquist than separationist doctrine generally. *Lemon's* "purpose" and "effect" prongs were drawn from *Schempp* and *Everson*, "both of which contain . . . historic errors."[66] The purpose prong had "proven mercurial in application because it has never been fully defined, and we have never fully stated how the test is to operate."[67] If it only required some legislative expression of a secular purpose, it "mean[t] little."[68] If, on the other hand, it "require[d] an absence of *any* intent to aid sectarian institutions, whether or not expressed, few state laws . . . could pass the test" because "one of the purposes behind every statute, whether stated or not, is to aid the target of its largesse."[69] In parochial aid cases, the entanglements prong had proven similarly deficient, creating, as Justice White had long complained, an "insoluble paradox" in which the close state supervision needed to assure that such aid would not be put to sectarian use was itself held to constitute excessive government contact with religion.[70] Such weaknesses, asserted Rehnquist, had led to "unworkable" plurality opinions and "unprincipled," inconsistent rulings.

> For example, a State may lend to parochial school children geography textbooks that contain maps of the United States, but the State may not lend maps of the United States for use in geography class. A State may lend textbooks on American colonial history, but it may not lend a film on George Washington, or a film projector to show it in history class. A State may lend classroom workbooks, but may not lend workbooks in which the parochial school children write, thus rendering them nonreuseable. A State may pay for bus transportation to religious schools but may not pay for bus transportation from the parochial school to the public zoo or natural history museum for a field trip. A State may pay for diagnostic services conducted in the parochial school but therapeutic services must be given in a different building; speech and hearing "services" conducted by the State inside the sectarian school are forbidden, . . . but the State may conduct speech and hearing diagnostic testing inside the sec-

tarian school. . . . Exceptional parochial school students may receive counseling, but it must take place outside of the parochial school. . . . A State may give cash to a parochial school to pay for the administration of state-written tests and state-ordered reporting services, but it may not provide funds for teacher-prepared tests on secular subjects. Religious instruction may not be given in public school, but the public school may release students during the day for religion classes elsewhere, and may enforce attendance at those classes with its truancy laws.[71]

For Rehnquist, the Court's judgment had been "clouded" too long by "the mists of an unnecessary metaphor."[72] His reading of history made it "abundantly" clear that "nothing in the Establishment Clause requires government to be strictly neutral between religion and irreligion, nor does that Clause prohibit Congress or the States from pursuing legitimate secular ends through nondiscriminatory sectarian means."[73] The period of silence for prayer or meditation required by the Alabama law at issue in *Jaffree* served "a secular interest in regulating the manner in which public schools are conducted," and nothing in the establishment clause, in Rehnquist's judgment, "prohibit[ed] any such generalized 'endorsement' of prayer."[74]

No other justice joined Rehnquist's *Jaffree* dissent. But in a separate dissent there, Justice White expressed "appreciat[ion]" for his colleague's explication of the establishment clause's history and, as one long "out of step" with many of the Court's establishment rulings, lent his support to "a basic reconsideration of our precedents."[75] Justice Scalia has been even more vehement than Chief Justice Rehnquist in his assaults on *Lemon* and separationist constructions of the establishment guarantee. Essentially tracking Rehnquist's arguments and emphasizing the Court's increasingly selective use of *Lemon*, Scalia has compared *Lemon* to "some ghoul in a late-night horror movie that repeatedly sits up in its grave and shuffles abroad, after being repeatedly killed and bruised. . . . It is there to scare us (and our audience) when we wish it to do so, but we can command it to return to the tomb at will."[76] Scalia has focused more on defects in *Lemon* and other approaches to establishment issues than on clarifying his own doctrinal stance. But he and Justice Thomas apparently embrace Justice Rehnquist's nonpreferentialist position unreservedly.

A Critique of No Preference

No constitutional provision has posed more difficulty for the modern Court than the First Amendment's establishment and free exercise clauses. Historical and analytical support is available for virtually any construction they might be given, and no approach to their meaning and application is invulnerable to legitimate attack. Arguably, however, the no-preference interpretation that Justice Rehnquist and company have ascribed to the establishment clause is even more vulnerable to criticism than that developed in the *Everson, Engel-Schempp, Lemon* line of cases.

We begin with Chief Justice Rehnquist's reading of the history surrounding the establishment clause's adoption. In attempting to undermine Hugo Black's use of

Madison's Remonstrance and role in adoption of the Virginia Statute of Religious Liberty as a basis for the separationist formula *Everson* embraced, Rehnquist has cited Madison's apparent support for a narrowly worded establishment guarantee at the time Congress was moving toward enactment of the Bill of Rights. In the very course of outlining Madison's stance in his *Jaffree* dissent, however, Rehnquist was obliged to note a House committee's replacement of Madison's version of the establishment clause with one forbidding not merely laws "establishing" religion, but also those "touching" religion, as well as the fact that the final version, of course, prohibits any "law *respecting* an establishment of religion." In a concurrence filed for *Lee v. Weisman* (1993),[77] invalidating commencement prayers, Justice Souter cited such textual developments as "a more powerful argument supporting the Court's jurisprudence following *Everson*" than Rehnquist's nonpreferentialist stance. In *County of Allegheny v. ACLU* (1989),[78] reviewing the constitutionality of religious displays on public property, Justice Stevens had assumed an identical stance.

> Whereas earlier drafts [of the establishment clause] had barred only laws "establishing" or "touching" religion, the final text interdicts all laws "respecting an establishment of religion." This phrase forbids even a partial establishment . . . , not only of a particular sect in favor of others, but also of religion in preference to nonreligion. . . . It is also significant that the final draft contains the word "respecting." Like "touching," "respecting" means concerning, or with reference to. But it also means with respect—that is, "reverence," "good will," regard"—to. Taking into account this richer meaning, the Establishment Clause, in banning laws that concern religion, especially prohibits those that pay homage to religion.[79]

An influential scholarly study has also rejected Rehnquist's reading of congressional records as support for a nonpreferentialist stance, contending that such an argument "requires a premise that the Framers were extraordinarily bad drafters— that they believed one thing but adopted language that said something substantially different, and that they did so after repeatedly attending to the choice of language."[80] Indeed, the very fact that Madison initially introduced a proposal merely banning laws "establishing" religion, and that his recommendation was replaced with stronger language, is itself strong evidence contra to Rehnquist's position.

Chief Justice Rehnquist has based his historical defense of no-preference, of course, on more than the congressional proceedings surrounding adoption of the Bill of Rights. He has also cited other actions by the same Congress that proposed the establishment clause, as well as other early developments in the nation's history— specifically, the 1789 Congress's reenactment of the Northwest Ordinance, with provisions for land grants to private, sectarian schools; the same Congress's adoption of a resolution calling for a presidential Thanksgiving Day Proclamation; and federal financial support for sectarian Indian education. In his *Jaffree* dissent, however, Rehnquist also pointed out that by 1845 congressional land grants were limited to nonsectarian schools and that in 1897 Congress ceased funding Indian education in sectarian schools. Such actions—the first taken over a century before *Everson* was decided, the second over fifty years before—suggest a growing sentiment in Congress that sectarian funding violated the First Amendment, a judgment long predating the modern Court's construction of the establishment clause.

Justice Rehnquist would no doubt respond that what Congress did in 1845 and 1897 should have no bearing on what its 1789 session intended the establishment clause to mean. But the Court has traditionally shown respect for congressional judgments regarding the meaning of constitutional provisions. Moreover, land grants for sectarian schools and government funding of sectarian Indian education stand in marked contrast to both the establishment clause's ban on any law "*respecting* an establishment of religion" and Congress's explicit rejection of a proposal that the First Amendment merely forbid the "establishing" of any religion.

Thanksgiving proclamations, it is true, have not been eliminated, nor have legislative chaplains, military chapels and chaplains, religious inscriptions on money and public buildings, or the religious exhortation opening Supreme Court sessions. In 1954, Congress added "under God" to the pledge of allegiance. But such continuing practices are of doubtful value to a defense of no preference. Certain of these practices, such as inscriptions on public property, long ago lost all religious meaning, while others, including military chapels and chaplains, were designed to avoid governmental interference with religious liberty.[81] They also reflect a fundamental weakness of the political process—the tendency of politicians to play fast and loose with constitutional guarantees to satisfy what they perceive to be majority will.

Justice Brennan underscored such a concern in his dissent for *Marsh v. Chambers* (1983),[82] upholding the constitutionality of a provision for state legislative chaplains. In his opinion for the *Marsh* majority, Chief Justice Burger declined application of *Lemon* and based the decision on "the unambiguous and unbroken history of more than 200 years," a history leaving "no doubt that the practice of opening legislative sessions with prayer has become part of the fabric of our society."[83] In his dissent, Justice Brennan praised Burger's "narrow ... careful opinion," which he construed as "carving out an exception to the Establishment Clause rather than reshaping Establishment Clause doctrine to accommodate legislative prayer."[84] He also conceded that he himself had come "very close" to approving legislative prayers in his *Schempp* concurrence twenty years earlier.[85] But Brennan challenged the Court's assumption that the congressional framers of the establishment clause, who had also provided for congressional chaplains, would not have authorized a practice they considered inconsistent with the First Amendment. "This assumption," declared Brennan, "is questionable. Legislators, influenced by the passions and exigencies of the moment, the pressure of constituents and colleagues, and the press of business, do not always pass sober constitutional judgment on every piece of legislation they enact, and this must be assumed to be as true of the Members of the First Congress as any other."[86]

Brennan further noted that while James Madison had voted for the bill authorizing payment of the first chaplains, he had later concluded that the practice violated the Constitution.[87] To the justice, "Madison's later views may not have represented so much a change of *mind* as a change of *role*, from a Member of Congress engaged in the hurly-burly of legislative activity to a detached observer engaged in unpressured reflection. Since the latter role is precisely the one with which this Court is charged, I am not at all sure that Madison's later writings should be any less influential in our deliberations than his earlier vote."[88] Brennan might also have mentioned, as Justice Souter would subsequently,[89] that Madison had refused during his first three years in office to call for days of prayer and thanksgiving, yielding only during the War of 1812 to announce four such occasions. Brennan might have noted, too, that on his retirement Madison condemned as unconstitutional "[r]eligious proclamations by the Executive recommending thanksgivings & fasts."[90]

James Madison was neither the first nor the last politician to take action contrary to a personal belief that it violated the Constitution or without consideration for its constitutional implications. From the end of Reconstruction to 1957, Congress took no action to enforce the Fifteenth Amendment's clear ban on racial discrimination in voting, despite persistent and blatant violations of that most basic of rights as well as explicit congressional authority to enforce the amendment's provisions through "appropriate legislation." Yet surely no one believes that such inaction reflected a continuing congressional judgment that no such discrimination was taking place or that any occurring was *de minimis*.

The years of congressional inaction in the field of voting rights should not be construed as a judgment on the part of Congress that no constitutional violations were occurring. By the same token, congressional support of certain forms of governmental accommodation to religion should not necessarily be viewed as conferring constitutional legitimacy on such practices. They may have simply reflected political judgments largely divorced from constitutional considerations. From the beginning of the republic, religion has been nearly as politically volatile—and useful to vote-seeking politicians—as race, not simply in recent years, when religious issues have formed a part of the national political agenda. Given that obvious historic fact, as true at the time of the Bill of Rights's adoption as it is today, it is not at all surprising that members of the First Congress could, in the abstract, accept the separationist conception of the establishment clause that its final language embraces (language standing in marked contrast to earlier nonpreferentialist versions the Congress rejected), yet propose an executive proclamation for a day of thanksgiving, extend land grants to sectarian schools, and adopt other nonpreferentialist policies.

Justice Rehnquist and other nonpreferentialists contend in essence that congressional intent regarding the establishment clause's meaning should be determined by reference to related actions of the clause's framers, regardless of its language or the framers' personal views regarding the proper relationship of the church to the state in a constitutional system. Rehnquist, it will be recalled, subjected James Madison to such an analysis in his *Jaffree* dissent. In his Remonstrance and efforts in behalf of Virginia's religious liberty statute, Rehnquist suggested, Madison had been a "zealous believer,"[91] "a dedicated advocate of the wisdom of such measures."[92] In attempting to secure adoption of the Bill of Rights, however, he had acted as a "prudent statesman seeking the enactment of measures sought by a number of his fellow citizens which could surely do no harm and might do a great deal of good"[93]—in short, "an advocate of sensible legislative compromise."[94] For political reasons, Madison had not pushed Congress to adopt the extreme separationist stance he favored elsewhere, reasoned Rehnquist, and his intentions regarding the establishment clause should be measured purely by the role he played in that setting, whatever his underlying motivations.

Such thinking arguably is just as suspect as the assumption that members of Congress or other politicians would never approve a measure that they consider inconsistent with the Constitution, even in as politically sensitive an area as religion. Surely the entire body of a legislator's thoughts, not merely formal proposals and floor remarks, should be considered in a determination of original intent. Especially should this be necessary in an assessment of Madison's understanding of the establishment clause. The amendments he introduced in Congress were not of his own composition, but instead had been "culled largely from the hundreds proposed at the state ratifying conventions."[95] Madison initially had agreed with James Wilson and others that the delegated character of national powers made a Bill of Rights unnecessary,[96] and while he eventually reversed ground, he may well have retained the view that the national government posed a much more attenuated threat to basic liberties than the states—in one of which, Virginia, he had defended a staunch separationist policy. For that reason, he may originally have viewed a ban on establishment of a national religion as a sufficient safeguard against federal abuse of power in the religion field.

The truth is, of course, that the history of church-state relations before and during the period surrounding adoption of the Bill of Rights is entirely too complex and fraught with internal inconsistencies to permit a certain judgment regarding the intentions of the establishment clause's framers. Hugo Black and other chief architects of the conception of the establishment clause which *Lemon* embodies were well aware of that history. In his opinion for the Court in *Engel v. Vitale* (1962),[97] invalidating state-prescribed prayer in the public schools, Justice Black noted, for example, the "unfortunate fact of history that when some of the very groups which had most strenuously opposed the established Church of England found themselves sufficiently in control of colonial governments in this country to write their own prayers into law, they passed laws making their own religion the official religion of their respective colonies."[98] Perhaps for that reason, Black and others focused on the teachings of history in general, rather than purely on the congressional record and remarks of early leaders, in adopting a separationist construction of the establishment clause's basic purpose—a purpose perhaps best captured in Justice Black's assertion "that religion is too personal, too sacred, too holy, to permit its 'unhallowed perversion' by a civil magistrate."[99] Nonpreferentialists respond that it is unfair to compare the horrors of religious persecutions of the distant past with school devotional exercises, government assistance to parochial schools, and other "mild" forms of accommodation. Black regularly countered such complaints with a recitation of Madison's admonition: "[I]t is proper to take alarm at the first experiment on our liberties."[100]

The Endorsement and Coercion Alternatives to No-Preference

The Rehnquist plurality's no-preference stance is the most clear-cut and extreme counterpoint to *Lemon* and the Court's traditional construction of the establishment clause, but it is not the only alternative proposed to date. In a concurrence filed for

Lynch v. Donnelly (1984),[101] upholding a partially religious Christmas display on public property, Justice O'Connor embraced an "endorsement" test for use in establishment cases. Under a "proper" application of *Lemon's* secular purpose and neutral primary effect standards, asserted O'Connor, the establishment clause should only invalidate those actions through which "the government intends to convey a message of endorsement or disapproval of religion."[102] Under *Lemon* and its progenitors, a regulation should not be struck down "merely because it in fact causes, even as a primary effect, advancement or inhibition of religion."[103] Were that the case, the Court could not have upheld tax exemptions for religious, educational, and charitable organizations;[104] Sunday closing laws;[105] or off-campus religious instruction.[106] Instead, according to O'Connor, the clause forbade only those practices "communicating a message of governmental endorsement or disapproval of religion. It is only practices having that effect, whether intentionally or unintentionally, that make religion relevant, in reality or public perception, to status in the political community."[107]

In O'Connor's judgment, the religious display at issue in *Lynch* passed the endorsement test.

> Although the religious and indeed sectarian significance of the creche . . . is not neutralized by the setting, the overall holiday setting changes what viewers may fairly understand to be the purpose of the display—as a typical museum setting, though not neutralizing the religious content of a religious painting, negates any message of endorsement of that content. The display celebrates a public holiday, and no one contends that declaration of that holiday is understood to be an endorsement of religion. The holiday itself has very strong secular components and traditions. Government celebration of the holiday, which is extremely common, generally is not understood to endorse the religious content of the holiday, just as government celebration of Thanksgiving is not so understood. The creche is a traditional symbol of the holiday that is very commonly displayed with purely secular symbols, as it was in Pawtucket.[108]

To O'Connor, such features combined to make the challenged display no more an endorsement of religion than legislative prayers, government recognition of Thanksgiving, religious inscriptions on coins, and appeals to God at the opening of Supreme Court sessions.

In later opinions, O'Connor clarified her position. The true test of endorsement was to be the perception of "an objective observer."[109] Since governmental accommodations of religion were often designed to avoid interference with religious liberty, the objective observer should also be "acquainted with the Free Exercise Clause and the values it promotes."[110] Finally, the touchstone of concern should be whether the particular action at issue makes "a person's religious beliefs relevant to his or her standing in the political community by conveying a message 'that religion or a particular religious belief is favored or preferred,'" thus "sending a clear message to nonadherents that they are outsiders or less than full members of the political community."[111] In sum, O'Connor has observed, "[t]he question under endorsement analysis . . . is whether a reasonable observer would view . . . practices as a disapproval of his or her particular religious choices, in light of the fact that they serve a secular purpose rather than a sectarian one and have largely lost their religious significance over time. . . . Although the endorsement test requires careful and often difficult line-drawing and is highly content specific, no alternative test has been suggested that captures the essential mandate of the Establishment Clause as well as the endorsement test does."[112]

Justice O'Connor's formula has value as an effort to clarify the parameters of the governmental "neutrality" toward religion that traditional establishment doctrine is designed to promote. It has also won scholarly support.[113] But it has also been a target of scholars,[114] and on the Court Anthony Kennedy has been especially critical of O'Connor's "most unwelcome" approach. As a justice very close in philosophy to the Rehnquist no-preference plurality, Kennedy is concerned that a proper application of the endorsement standard would invalidate numerous practices he considers consistent with the establishment guarantee. "[A]s I understand that test," he has asserted, "the touchstone of an Establishment Clause violation is whether nonadherents would be made to feel like 'outsiders' by government recognition or accommodation of religion. Few of our traditional practices recognizing the part religion plays in our society can withstand scrutiny under a faithful application of [the endorsement] formula."[115]

Kennedy's objections to O'Connor's approach appear to be based largely on the results to which faithful application of the endorsement test would lead. But there is a more fundamental weakness to O'Connor's formula as well. Her reliance on the subjective impressions of reasonable or objective observers as to the impact of a challenged action on the psyches of nonadherents seems, with all due respect, decidedly more problematic than any conceptual defects in *Lemon* and its progenitors.

Justice Kennedy's support of a coercion alternative to *Lemon* is even more troublesome. In a concurring and dissenting opinion filed for the Pittsburgh religious display case of 1989, Kennedy expressed willingness "for present purposes to remain within the *Lemon* framework,"[116] at least when the *Lemon* test was "applied with proper sensitivity to our traditions and our case law."[117] But he refused "to be seen as advocating, let along adopting," *Lemon* as the Court's "primary guide" in the establishment field,[118] nor, as noted earlier, would he embrace Justice O'Connor's endorsement approach. Instead, Kennedy read into the Court's establishment precedents "two limiting principles: government may not coerce anyone to support or participate in any religion or its exercise; and it may not, in the guise of avoiding hostility or callous indifference, give direct benefits to religion to such a degree that it in fact 'establishes a [state] religion or religious faith, or tends to do so.'"[119] Under Kennedy's formula, "[n]oncoercive government action within the realm of flexible accommodation or passive acknowledgment of existing symbols does not violate the Establishment Clause unless it benefits religion in a way more direct and more substantial than practices that are accepted in our national heritage."[120]

Justice Kennedy's establishment pronouncements have generally been quite similar in tone to those of the Rehnquist plurality. Indeed, the chief justice and Justices White and Scalia joined Kennedy's opinion in the Pittsburgh religious display litigation. But Kennedy's perception of the establishment clause's reach, unlike that of Rehnquist and company, extends to "more or less subtle coercion,"[121] as well as to more direct and obvious forms of governmental interference with religion. And in *Lee v. Weisman* (1992),[122] Kennedy spoke for the Court in finding the requisite coercive force in a public school's commencement prayer ceremony, even though attendance was not required. Asserted Kennedy:

> The undeniable fact is that the school district's supervision and control of a high school graduation ceremony places public pressure, as well as peer pressure, on attending students to stand as a group or, at least, maintain respectful silence during the Invocation and Benediction. This pressure, though subtle and indirect, can be as real as any overt compulsion. Of course, in our culture standing or remaining silent can signify adherence to a view or simply respect for the views of others. And no doubt some persons who have no desire to join a prayer have little objection to standing as a sign of respect for those who do. But for the dissenter of high school age, who has a reasonable perception that she is being forced by the State to pray in a manner her conscience will not allow, the injury is no less real. . . . It is of little comfort to a dissenter . . . to be told that for her the act of standing or remaining in silence signifies mere respect, rather than participation. What matters is that, given our social conventions, a reasonable dissenter in this milieu could believe that the group exercise signified her own participation or approval of it.[123]

In dissent, Justice Scalia, joined by Chief Justice Rehnquist and Justices White and Thomas, scorned Kennedy's finding of coercion in the case. "The coercion that was a hallmark of historical establishments of religion," Scalia contended, "was coercion of religious orthodoxy and of financial support, *by force of law and threat of penalty.*"[124] Scalia was willing to concede, "for the sake of argument," that establishment had come to mean government financial support of religion and "government-sponsored endorsement of religion—even when no legal coercion is present, and indeed even when no ersatz 'peer-pressure' psycho-coercion is present—where the endorsement is sectarian."[125] But Scalia and company refused to expand "the concept of coercion beyond acts backed by threat of penalty—a brand of coercion that, happily, is readily discernible to those of us who have made a career of reading the disciples of Blackstone rather than of Freud."[126]

Kennedy's approach suffers from more, however, than the invariable disputes its application provokes over the meaning of "coercion." It also flies in the face of the traditional view that establishment clause violations require no showing of coercion. In *Engel v. Vitale*, Justice Black concluded for the Court that "[t]he Establishment Clause, unlike the Free Exercise Clause, does not depend upon any showing of direct governmental compulsion."[127] Justice Kennedy has thus contended that "only . . . *direct* coercion need not always be shown to establish an Establishment Clause violation," adding, "The prayer invalidated in *Engel* was unquestionably coercive in an indirect manner, as the *Engel* Court itself recognized."[128] Justice Black did agree in *Engel*, of course, that officially prescribed prayer "involve[d] coercion." He asserted, in fact, that "[w]hen the power, prestige and financial support of government [are] placed behind a particular religious belief, the indirect coercive pressure upon religious minorities to conform to the prevailing officially approved religion is plain."[129]

But Black also immediately added that "the purposes underlying the Establishment Clause go much further than that,"[130] thereby casting serious doubt on Kennedy's reading of *Engel.*

Kennedy's coercion approach to the establishment clause arguably also renders it a redundancy, given the free exercise clause. As Justice Souter has wisely observed, "laws that coerce nonadherents to 'support or participate in any religion or its exercise,' . . . would virtually by definition violate the right to religious free exercise. . . . Thus, a literal application of the coercion test would render the Establishment Clause a virtual nullity. . . . Without compelling evidence to the contrary, we should presume that the Framers meant the Clause to stand for something more."[131] Kennedy's assertion that direct benefits to religion constitute an establishment only when they rise to a certain degree is equally perplexing. How is the Court to know when the appropriate, or inappropriate, degree has been reached?

Establishment Doctrine on the Rehnquist Court

Not surprisingly, given the variety of approaches reflected in the justices' opinions, the status of establishment clause doctrine on the Rehnquist Court remains complex at best. In the Kiryas Joel school district case,[132] the Court, by a six-three vote, struck down a New York law that had created a village school district consisting entirely of members of the Satmar Hasidic sect, followers of a strict form of Judaism. The statute had given a locally elected school board plenary authority over primary and secondary education in the village, but the board ran only a special education program for handicapped Satmar Hasidic children. Other village children attended private religious schools, and it appeared obvious that the special public school arrangement had been created only because the Satmar Hasidim were financially unable to provide special educational services for their children and opposed their education in religiously and culturally mixed public schools.

Speaking for the Court, Justice Souter, joined by Justices Blackmun, Stevens, O'Connor, and Ginsburg, concluded that the state's creation of a separate school district composed exclusively of members of a particular religious community, combined with the uncertainty that New York would provide such an arrangement for other religious groups, had created an impermissible establishment of religion, especially since alternative methods were available for filling the students' needs. The same justices, minus Justice O'Connor, also reasoned that the state's delegation of discretionary authority over public schools to a group defined by a common religion constituted an impermissible "fusion of government and religion" comparable to that at issue in *Larkin v. Grendel's Den, Inc.* (1982),[133] in which the Court had struck down a statute giving churches power to veto applications for liquor licenses. Justice Kennedy, the sixth justice to join the Court's judgment, concluded that the drawing of political boundaries on the basis of religion was as constitutionally offensive as racial gerrymandering.

In dissent, Justice Scalia, joined by Chief Justice Rehnquist and Justice Thomas, saw the arrangement as an attempt to provide secular educational services for handicapped children while protecting them from the "additional handicap of cultural distinctiveness"[134] that their education with students from other backgrounds would pose. Nor did Scalia see an analogy to *Grendel's Den*. There, he asserted, a government conferred political power on religious institutions, while the Hasidic village case merely involved "a transfer of government power to citizens who share a common religion as opposed to 'the officers of its sectarian organization.'"[135] Scalia considered that difference in the two cases "critical."[136] He also took delight in "the Court's snub of *Lemon* today (it receives only two 'see also' citations . . .)."[137]

Justice Souter's opinion did make little reference to *Lemon*, but probably more for tactical reasons than because of any basic disagreement with its conception of the establishment clause's meaning. For Souter made repeated references to rulings based on *Lemon* and to its progenitors, including *Schempp*, and also stressed the neutrality construction of the establishment clause *Lemon* and earlier precedents embraced. As Justice Scalia had noted in dissent, moreover, all three lower courts in the case had relied on *Lemon*, and the parties had devoted over eighty pages of briefs to its "application and continued vitality."[138] Scalia blamed that emphasis on the fact that lower courts "are not free to ignore Supreme Court precedent at will" and that litigants are "also bound by our case law."[139] But such an assertion merely underscores *Lemon*'s status as the last establishment formula to command majority support and the failure of Scalia and other critics to develop an alternative acceptable to a majority of the Court's membership.

Also noteworthy in the Satmar Hasidic case was the failure of Justice Kennedy to reiterate his establishment philosophy and, especially, Justice O'Connor's abandonment of endorsement or any other "unitary test" in establishment cases. In a concurring opinion again recommending *Lemon*'s rejection, O'Connor proposed that the Court follow the approach it had gradually adopted in free speech and equal protection cases, developing and applying a variety of tests, each suitable for a particular establishment context. Speaking for the nonpreferentialist plurality, Justice Scalia took issue with O'Connor's proposal:

> I would not replace *Lemon* with nothing, and let the case law "evolve" into a series of situation-specific rules . . . unconstrained by any "rigid influence."
> . . . The problem with (and the allure of) *Lemon* has not been that it is "rigid," but rather that in many applications it has been utterly meaningless, validating whatever result the Court would desire. . . . To replace *Lemon* with nothing is simply to announce that we are now so bold that we no longer feel the need even to pretend that our haphazard course of Establishment clause decisions is governed by any principle. The foremost principle I would apply is fidelity to the longstanding traditions of our people.[140]

At the end of the Court's 1994–95 term, Justice O'Connor again embraced the endorsement test and did so without elaborating further on the variable approach to establishment issues she had endorsed in the *Kiryas Joel* case. At issue in *Capitol Square Review and Advisory Bd. v. Pinette*[141] was a local government's decision to deny a Ku Klux Klan petition to erect a cross on a community plaza recognized as a public forum. By a seven-two vote, a majority concluded that no compelling interest justified such a content-based restriction on free speech. Speaking for himself, the chief justice, and Justices Kennedy and Thomas, Justice Scalia preferred confining the endorsement test to situations involving expression by the government itself or government action found to discriminate in favor of private religious expression. Justice O'Connor, joined by Justices Souter and Breyer, found the test applicable, but concluded that less drastic means than a flat ban on the display were available for avoiding the appearance of government sponsorship.

In dissent, Justice Ginsburg emphasized that "[n]o human speaker was present to disassociate the religious symbol from the State" and that "[n]o plainly visible sign informed the public that the cross belonged to the Klan and that Ohio's government did not endorse the display's message."[142] She left open, however, the question whether a clearly visible and prominently displayed disclaimer might insulate such symbols from constitutional challenge. Justice Stevens, the other dissenter, had no such reservations. "I do not think," he asserted, that "*any* disclaimer could dispel the message of endorsement in this case."[143]

The competing positions of the justices in *Capitol Square* turned on the question whether the government could be perceived as endorsing a display otherwise within the ambit of free speech in a public forum. The Court's ruling there thus furnished little evidence as to *Lemon*'s status. Although somewhat more troublesome, another major establishment ruling of the 1994-95 term was susceptible to a similar reading. In *Rosenberger v. Rector and Visitors of the University of Virginia* (1995),[144] a five-four majority drew on *Widmar v. Vincent* (1981)[145] and its progeny[146] in striking down a state university's refusal to fund the printing of a student group's religious newspaper. *Widmar* had held that a state-supported college cannot deny religious groups access to space set aside for student organizations, and the *Rosenberger* Court saw no difference between the provision of space and the funding of printing costs. Speaking through Justice Souter, however, the four dissenters decried what they saw as unprecedented Court approval of a direct government subsidy to religious activity. *Widmar* and company rested, Souter argued, "on the recognition that all speakers are entitled to use the street corner ... and on the analogy between the public street corner and open classroom space .... There is no traditional street corner printing provided by the government on equal terms to all comers, and the forum cases cannot be lifted to a higher plane of generalization without admitting that new economic benefits are being extended directly to religion in clear violation of the principle banning direct aid."[147]

Assuming that *Capitol Square* and *Rosenberger* could be limited to their forum-access contexts, *Kiryas Joel* offered some hope for *Lemon*'s survival. Although Justice Souter's opinion for the Court avoided virtually all mention of *Lemon* by name, it clearly embraced the governmental neutrality approach to establishment issues *Lemon* reflects. The departure of Justice Blackmun, one of *Lemon*'s staunchest defenders, was an obvious setback, but President Clinton's first Supreme Court appointee, Justice Ginsburg, had replaced Justice White, a *Lemon* critic. Ginsburg had joined Souter's *Kiryas Joel* opinion, while she and Clinton's second selection, Justice Breyer, joined Souter's *Rosenberger* dissent, along with Justice Stevens.

Justices Kennedy and especially O'Connor were key to *Lemon*'s real standing, whatever its official status, and in *Agostini v. Felton* (1997),[148] they joined the Rehnquist-Scalia-Thomas nonpreferentialist plurality in overturning two *Lemon*-based precedents and upholding government's authority to send public school teachers into religious school classrooms. Speaking for the Court, Justice O'Connor observed that "the general principles we use to evaluate whether government aid violates the Establishment Clause have not changed," quoting *Lemon's* three-part test with apparent approval. She added, however, that the Court's application of those principles had changed "significantly" since the justices had declared unconstitutional[149] the precise arrangement *Agostini* upheld. No longer would the Court "presume that public employees will inculcate religion simply because they happen to be in a sectarian environment." Nor would their presence in religious institutions any longer be assumed to require the "pervasive monitoring" long held to constitute evidence of an excessive church-state entanglement. "There is no suggestion in the record before us that unannounced monthly visits of public supervisors are insufficient to prevent or to detect inculcation of religion by public employees. Moreover, we have not found excessive entanglement in cases in which States imposed far more onerous burdens on religious institutions than the monitoring system at issue here."[150]

Justice Souter, joined by Stevens, Ginsburg, and Breyer, expressed concern that state-paid teachers "might inadvertently (or intentionally) manifest sympathy" with the religious aims of the sectarian institutions in which they served, as well as the fear that provision of public employees for public schools amounted to a public subsidy of religious instruction that "tended to convey a message to students and to the public that the State supported religion."[151] But the *Agostini* majority clearly favored a more flexible approach to establishment issues than a meaningful application of *Lemon* would have permitted, however divided that majority may have remained on the appropriate doctrinal standard to be applied in such cases. While *Agostini* involved only one field of church-state relations, moreover, *Lemon* may survive in a variety of other establishment areas largely in name alone.

The Dilution of the Free Exercise Guarantee

The weakening, if not outright rejection, of the *Lemon* test is particularly unfortunate at a time when the Court has also significantly narrowed the reach of the First Amendment's guarantee to the free exercise of religion. In *Reynolds v. United States* (1879),[152] one of the earliest cases construing the free exercise clause's meaning, the Supreme Court had drawn a sharp distinction between religious beliefs and religious practices, subjecting the latter to considerable governmental control and upholding the prosecution of a Morman for polygamy, a practice forbidden by Utah territorial law but basic to Reynolds's faith. The modern Court had also occasionally upheld laws imposing what the justices termed an indirect or incidental impact on religious practices. In 1961, for example, a majority approved Sunday closing laws against the free exercise claims of orthodox Jews.[153] But the Court began as well to subject laws burdening religious practices to strict scrutiny, declaring them unconstitutional except where they were found necessary to promote a compelling governmental interest and constituted the means for achieving that goal least restrictive of religious freedom. In *Sherbert v. Verner* (1963),[154] the Court applied that standard to invalidate

South Carolina's denial of unemployment compensation to a Seventh-Day Adventist unable to find employment not requiring Saturday work, despite a convincing argument by Justice Harlan that the majority was forcing the state to carve out a special religious exception to its unemployment compensation law inconsistent with what he considered the Court's unduly expansive establishment clause jurisprudence. And in *Wisconsin v. Yoder* (1972),[155] the Burger Court invoked the same formula in exempting Amish children from compulsory high school education, despite establishment clause concerns that the language of the chief justice's majority opinion appeared to recognize a special status for the Amish that probably would not be extended to others who objected to high school education on religious grounds.

Near the end of Burger's tenure, however, Justice Stevens questioned the propriety of the compelling interest standard in cases involving religiously neutral regulations of general application. In *United States v. Lee* (1982),[156] the chief justice purported to apply a variant of compelling interest doctrine in holding Amish employees and their employers subject to social security taxes. "That formulation of the constitutional standard suggests," Justice Stevens countered in a brief opinion concurring in the judgment, "that the Government always bears a heavy burden of justifying the application of neutral general laws to individual conscientious objectors. In my opinion, it is the objector who must shoulder the burden of demonstrating that there is a unique reason for allowing him a special exemption from a valid law of general applicability."[157] Noting that Congress already exempted self-employed members of religious groups opposed to social security taxes, Stevens thought that extension of the exemption to Amish employed by others would be more than offset by their elimination from the social security rolls. Given the demonstrated Amish capacity for self-sufficiency, on the other hand, the social cost to them would be minimal. Stevens was thus unable to agree with the Court that the government had established an overriding interest in requiring Amish employees to pay social security taxes. What was needed instead, in his judgment, was a different constitutional standard for such cases.

In *Employment Division v. Smith* (1990),[158] upholding the denial of unemployment compensation to drug counselors fired for their ritual use of peyote as Native American Church members, a Rehnquist Court majority went even further, perhaps, than Justice Stevens had intended in his *Lee* concurrence, exempting the enforcement of religiously neutral, generally applicable laws from virtually all review under the free exercise guarantee. Speaking for the Court, Justice Scalia stopped short, whatever his personal preferences, of overruling *Sherbert* and other cases subjecting such regulations to strict scrutiny. Instead, he argued that "[t]he only decisions in which we have held that the First Amendment bars application of a neutral, generally applicable law to religiously motivated action have involved not the Free Exercise Clause alone, but the Free Exercise Clause in conjunction with other constitutional protections, such as freedom of speech and of the press, . . . or the right of parents . . . to direct the education of their children. . . . The present case does not present such a hybrid situation."[159] To the respondents' contention that *Sherbert* and the other unemployment compensation cases in which the compelling interest standard had been applied involved purely free exercise claims, Scalia replied that the *Sherbert* standard had been limited only to the unemployment compensation context, a field characterized by an extensive network of exemptions and thus considerable potential for abuse. "[O]ur decisions in the unemployment cases," he asserted, thus "stand for the proposition that where the State has in place a system of individual exemptions, it may not refuse to extend that system to cases of 'religious hardships' without compelling reasons." Whatever the reach of those decisions, moreover, they had "nothing to do with an across-the-board criminal prohibition on a particular form of conduct."[160] To hold otherwise, making governmental authority dependent on individual religious beliefs, absent a "compelling interest," would make the individual, declared Scalia, quoting *Reynolds*, "a law unto himself."[161]

Concurring only in the Court's judgment, Justice O'Connor favored retention of the compelling interest standard for all cases involving free exercise claims, but concluded that the state's interest in the effective enforcement of its drug laws met that demanding standard. Justice Blackmun, joined by Justices Brennan and Marshall, agreed with O'Connor's assessment of the appropriate standard for such cases, but rejected her application of that standard in the case. Emphasizing that the governmental concern at stake was not "the State's broad interest in fighting the critical 'war on drugs,' . . . but [its] narrow interest in refusing to make an exception for the religious, ceremonial use of peyote," Blackmun characterized the state's claim as "amount[ing] only to the symbolic preservation of an unenforced prohibition" and thus hardly adequate to justify even an indirect infringement on a constitutional right. Convincingly depicting peyote as a distasteful, hardly addictive drug, the religious use of which had "nothing to do with the vast and violent traffic in illegal narcotics that plagues this country,"[162] he also termed "purely speculative" the state's concern that recognition of a drug-law exemption for the ritual use of peyote would lead to a flood of similar religious claims. After all, observed Blackmun, nearly half the states and the federal government had exempted religious peyote use for many years, "and apparently have not found themselves overwhelmed by claims to other religious exemptions."[163]

A majority, however, would hold firm to the Court's new position. When a Texas community relied on its historic preservation ordinance in denying a permit to enlarge a local Roman Catholic church, the area archbishop filed suit under the Religious Freedom Restoration Act (1993), adopted by Congress in the wake of the *Smith* decision. The RFRA prohibited government from "substantially" burdening the free exercise of religion without demonstrating a compelling interest in the regulation at issue and showing that the law embodied means least restrictive of free exercise rights. In *City of Boerne v. Flores* (1997),[164] a six-three majority, per Justice Kennedy, invalidated RFRA and its application in the Texas case. Kennedy agreed that Congress was entitled to broad discretion in choosing the means for enforcing the provisions of the Fourteenth Amendment, through which the free exercise guarantee had been extended to the states.[165] He emphasized, however, that ultimate power to determine the substantive scope of constitutional guarantees lay with the courts, not Congress, and declared RFRA an unconstitutional attempt to usurp judicial authority. In separate dissents, Justices O'Connor, Souter, and Breyer recommended use of the case as a vehicle for a full reexamination of *Smith.* But the majority obviously was not so inclined.

Smith is clearly a source of concern for all religious groups. It is likely to impinge more heavily, however, on unorthodox religious groups and their practices than on members of mainstream sects. The latter's rituals, after all, are part of "our traditions" and thus either infringe no criminal law or enjoy special legislative exemption from such "neutral" regulations (as in the case of sacramental wine consumption). At the same time, the sorts of governmental accommodations of religion that the non-preferentialists favor (devotional exercises in the public schools, assistance to religious schools, religious symbols on public property) principally benefit—and realistically are designed primarily for—the dominant faiths. Read together, then, the *Smith* rationale and a severely weakened *Lemon* test arguably create an inherently discriminatory way of reacting to religious issues. On the one hand, *Smith* offers little or no protection to the religious liberty claims of unorthodox groups, except in those rare situations in which a sect's practices are singled out for special restrictions—as, for example, when Hialeah, Florida, forbade ritual sacrifice of animals while permitting virtually every other form of animal slaughter.[166] On the other hand, the Rehnquist Court's flexible establishment formula enables government increasingly to accommodate public policy to mainstream religious traditions.

Whatever *Lemon's* chances for survival, moreover, it remains, as Justice Powell long ago observed, the only coherent standard yet devised for evaluating establishment claims. Its requirements are obviously inconsistent with a number of religious trappings in our national life, but it is far better simply to accept such anomalies than to rewrite establishment doctrine in the extreme fashion the Rehnquist plurality has proposed. As the chief justice and Justice Scalia have demonstrated, a respectable historical defense of nonpreferentialism is entirely possible to erect. But the no-preference position also flies in the face of the establishment clause's final language and the First Congress's explicit rejection of versions compatible with a nonpreferentialist construction of the guarantee. Its acceptance would require rejection of the entire modern history of the establishment clause's construction in the Court; realistically, it would be impossible to achieve in a society that obviously is religiously diverse but dominated by Judaeo-Christian faiths—faiths regularly preferred in the rituals of civic religion.

Most importantly, perhaps, the triumph of nonpreferentialism, or some other doctrine indulgent of increased church-state ties, would aggravate the very problem the First Amendment's religion clauses were partly designed to avoid. Speaking for the Court in a 1973 case invalidating various forms of governmental assistance to religion,[167] Justice Powell issued a wise warning regarding the consequences growing from governmental accommodation of religion:

> [W]e know from long experience with both Federal and State Governments that aid programs of any kind tend to become entrenched, to escalate in cost, and to generate their own aggressive constituencies. And the larger the class of

recipients, the greater the pressures for accelerated increases. Moreover, the State itself, concededly anxious to avoid assuming the burden of educating children now in private and parochial schools, has a strong motivation for increasing this aid as public school costs rise and population increases. In this situation, where the underlying issue is the deeply emotional one of Church-State relationships, the potential for seriously divisive political consequences needs no elaboration. And while the prospect of such divisiveness may not alone warrant the invalidation of state laws that otherwise survive the careful scrutiny required by the decisions of this Court, it is certainly a "warning signal" not to be ignored.[168]

Such pressures are not limited to the parochial aid arena, and the impact that the Court's adoption of nonpreferentialism would have on such pressures in every area of establishment clause concern also "needs no elaboration."

7

Freedom of Expression and Association

Cases involving the First Amendment's religion clauses, as we saw in the previous chapter, have embroiled the Rehnquist Court in fundamental doctrinal battles. In litigation involving the Constitution's guarantees to freedom of expression and association, however, the justices have largely applied and elaborated on existing doctrine sculpted essentially during the Warren and Burger eras. Given the close divisions in certain issue areas and the pragmatic, flexible jurisprudence of the Court's center, moreover, the doctrinal elaborations the Rehnquist Court justices have contributed to the expression and association elements of First Amendment law have been subtle and complex.

The Reach of Protected Expression

Like their modern predecessors, members of the Rehnquist Court have assumed a flexible stance with respect to the substance of the First Amendment's guarantees to free expression and association. In fact, they have even been willing to recognize forms of protected expression their counterparts avoided embracing. In *Street v. New York* (1969),[1] for example, the Warren Court reversed the conviction of a man who had burned an American flag on a city street after learning of the shooting of civil rights marcher James Meredith in Mississippi. In his opinion for the majority, however, Justice Harlan rested the Court's decision on a finding that the jury could have convicted Street for words he uttered during the incident rather than for the flag burning, thereby dodging a ruling on the constitutional status of flag burning as a form of symbolic speech. Justice Black, who believed that Street's conviction clearly rested on his conduct rather than his speech, dissented, moreover, finding it beyond "belief that any thing in the Federal Constitution bars a State from making the deliberate burning of the American flag an offense," and adding, "It is immaterial to me that words are spoken in connection with the burning. It is the *burning* of the flag that the State has set its face against."[2] And while no other justice accepted Justice Black's well-known contention that the First Amendment protected only speech, not "symbolic" speech, Chief Justice Warren and Justice Abe Fortas, two of the most liberal-activist jurists ever to occupy the high bench, as well as Justice White, also registered *Street* dissents supporting the power of government to protect the flag from desecration. Yet, when the flag-burning issue came before the Rehnquist Court, a narrow majority concluded on two occasions that such conduct fell within the First Amendment's reach.[3]

In the first case, a five-four majority overturned the conviction of Gregory Lee Johnson, who had burned a flag during a political demonstration near the site of the 1984 Republican national convention in Dallas, Texas. Johnson was convicted under a state statute prohibiting the "desecration" of certain venerated objects, including a state or national flag. Citing the context in which Johnson's offense occurred, Justice Brennan concluded for the majority that the flag burning at issue constituted expressive conduct subject to First Amendment protection. In *United States v. O'Brien* (1968),[4] the Warren Court had upheld a federal statute prohibiting the destruction of draft cards, as applied to an antiwar demonstrator who burned his card as a symbol of political protest. The *O'Brien* majority had concluded that an important governmental interest unrelated to the suppression of expression could be used to justify incidental restrictions on First Amendment freedoms in cases in which speech and nonspeech activities were combined in the same course of conduct. Justice Brennan rejected the state's contention in the flag-burning case, however, that prosecution of Johnson served the important governmental interest in preventing breaches of the peace. Government, Brennan concluded, could not simply assume that a particular form of expression would inevitably incite a riot, but instead was obliged to examine the surrounding circumstances in each case to determine whether the speech at issue had actually incited imminent lawless action. Yet, the justice declared, "no disturbance of the peace [had] actually occurred or threatened to occur because of Johnson's burning of the flag."[5] Nor would Brennan accept the state's claim that Johnson's conduct amounted to "fighting words," long held to be excluded from constitutional protection. That exception to protected expression, after all, had consistently been limited to face-to-face verbal assaults likely by their very nature to provoke violent retaliation, and "[n]o reasonable onlooker would have regarded Johnson's generalized expression of dissatisfaction with the policies of the Federal Government as a direct personal insult or an invitation to exchange fisticuffs."[6]

In a final effort to justify Johnson's prosecution, the state had claimed a legitimate and substantial interest in preserving the flag as a symbol of nationhood and national unity. Since such a contention clearly related to the suppression of expression rather than to interests unrelated to its control, Brennan found the state's interest in preservation of the flag as a national symbol "outside of *O'Brien*'s test altogether" and thus subject to strict judicial scrutiny.[7] For Brennan, application of such a statute led to an inevitable conclusion. "If there is a bedrock principle underlying the First Amendment," he asserted, "it is that the government may not prohibit the expression of an idea simply because society finds the idea offensive or disagreeable."[8] And neither the Constitution's text nor the Court's prior cases provided any basis for concluding that "a separate judicial category exists for the American flag alone."

> Indeed, we would not be surprised to learn that the persons who framed our Constitution and wrote the Amendment that we now construe were not known for their reverence for the Union Jack. The First Amendment does not guarantee that other concepts virtually sacred to our Nation as a whole—such as the principle that discrimination on the basis of race is odious and destructive—will go unquestioned in the marketplace of ideas. We decline, therefore, to create for the flag an exception to the joust of principles protected by the First Amendment.[9] . . . [This Court's decision is] a reaffirmation of the principles of freedom and inclusiveness that the flag best reflects, and of the conviction that our toleration of criticism such as Johnson's is a sign and source of our strength. . . . The way to preserve the flag's special role is not to punish those who feel differently about these matters. It is to persuade them that they are wrong.[10]

Not all members of the majority seemed as enthusiastic about the Court's decision. Justice Blackmun joined Brennan's opinion, but not without informing his colleague that he had "struggled with this difficult and distasteful little (big?) case."[11] Justice Kennedy joined the Court's opinion "without reservation," but observed that "sometimes we must make decisions we do not like." Kennedy made it clear that this was, for him, one of those occasions, finding it "poignant but fundamental that the flag protects those who hold it in contempt"—even someone who "was not a philosopher and perhaps did not even possess the ability to comprehend how repellent his statements must be to the Republic itself."[12]

The four dissenters found Johnson's conduct not only personally offensive, but subject to government control as well. In challenging the Court's decision, Chief Justice Rehnquist, joined by Justices White and O'Connor, emphasized the uniqueness of the flag as the ultimate national symbol, the widespread national and state policy against flag desecration, and the availability of numerous alternative avenues through which Johnson could have expressed his political views.

More than eighty years earlier, the Court had upheld a statute forbidding use of the American flag for advertising purposes.[13] More recent cases dealing with flag-desecration claims had specifically left open the question of governmental power to prohibit destruction of a flag.[14] Only two years before its decision in the Texas flag-burning case, the Court had upheld congressional authority to grant exclusive use of the word "Olympic" to the U.S. Olympic Committee, declaring that "when a word [or symbol] acquires value 'as the result of organization and the expenditure of labor, skill, and money' by an entity, that entity constitutionally may obtain a limited property right in the word [or symbol]."[15] Rehnquist asserted that Congress and the states, as representatives of the people, surely had a "similar interest in the flag." He also considered Johnson's conduct clearly within the reach of the fighting-words exception to free speech, first recognized in *Chaplinsky v. New Hampshire* (1942).[16] Here, as in *Chaplinsky*, he declared, "it may equally well be said that the public burning of the American flag by Johnson was no essential part of any exposition of ideas, and at the same time it had a tendency to incite a breach of the peace. . . . [H]is act, like Chaplinsky's provocative words, conveyed nothing that could not have been conveyed and was not conveyed just as forcefully in a dozen different [other] ways."[17]

In a separate dissent, Justice Stevens termed flag burning "disagreeable conduct that, in my opinion, diminishes the value of an important national asset." In his judgment, government had a "significant and legitimate" interest in preserving the flag as a unique national symbol, and he dismissed as "trivial" any burden on expression that a statute forbidding flag burning imposed "by requiring that an available, alternative mode of expression—including uttering words critical of the flag— . . . be employed."[18] Stevens also took issue with the Court's assumption that the Texas statute permitted content-based suppressions of expression. "The concept of 'desecration,'" reasoned Stevens, "does not turn on the substance of the message the actor intends to convey, but rather on whether those who view the *act* will take serious offense." Thus, even a person intending to convey a message of respect for the flag through its public burning would be guilty of its desecration "if he knows that others—perhaps simply because they misperceive the intended message—will be seriously offended."[19] The case, in short, dealt not, Stevens contended, with "disagreeable ideas," but with "disagreeable conduct." Johnson was prosecuted because of the method he chose to express his views, just as he clearly would have been subject to prosecution had he chosen to spray-paint his message on the Lincoln Memorial. The only difference was that the public asset in that situation would have been tangible, while the asset at stake in *Johnson* was intangible.

Stevens's assertion that the Texas flag-desecration statute was not content based is difficult to embrace, as is the chief justice's attempt to extend *Chaplinsky* beyond its historic context of face-to-face verbal assaults directed at particular persons. There is considerable power in the argument, however, that the unique character of the American flag as a national symbol lends legitimacy to federal and state attempts to protect it from "desecration," much in the way that Congress is empowered to confer special safeguards through its authority over copyrights, patents, and trademarks. Given the virtually limitless alternative means of expression available to political protesters, moreover, the burden a statute of the sort at issue in *Texas v. Johnson* imposes on First Amendment freedoms would appear marginal at best. Ultimately, however, the dissenters' effort to exempt a unique national symbol from the First Amendment's reach suffers from essentially the same difficulty Justice Harlan discerned in the California attempt to cleanse the public vocabulary of offensive epithets, at issue in *Cohen v. California* (1971):[20] exclusion of one national symbol from First Amendment coverage, like exclusion of one offensive word, would inevitably lead to pressures to extend that principle to potentially limitless additional symbols.

Whatever the substantive merits of the majority's position, the Rehnquist Court's flag-burning decision quickly became a convenient target for political gamesmanship. President Bush, who had even visited a flag factory in a successful effort to distance his politics from those of his "card-carrying ACLU member" 1988 Democratic opponent, promptly announced his support of a constitutional amendment protecting the flag from desecration. While declining so extreme a move, Congress enacted the Flag Protection Act of 1989, providing criminal penalties for anyone who "knowingly mutilates, defaces, physically defiles, burns, maintains on the floor or ground, or tramples upon" a U.S. flag, except in disposing of a "worn or soiled" flag. The following year, a five-four majority, again speaking through Justice Brennan, declared the federal statute unconstitutional; the four dissenters in *Texas v. Johnson*, speaking on this occasion through Justice Stevens alone, registered a dissent essentially tracking the arguments he and Rehnquist had advanced in the Texas case.[21] In conference, the chief justice had argued that "*Johnson* was wrong." Initially he circulated a brief dissent noting government attempts to distinguish the federal case from *Johnson*, then adding, "But, persuaded as I was last term, and as I am now, that the Texas statute at issue in *Johnson* was constitutional, the correct decision of the present case is for me an *a fortiori* proposition,"[22] although when Stevens filed his opinion, Rehnquist withdrew his dissent.[23]

A 1992 decision including cross burning among the forms of symbolic speech ignited an intense debate among the justices over related issues regarding the First Amendment's reach. In *R.A.V. v. City of St. Paul* (1992),[24] a white youth was charged under Minnesota's Bias-Motivated Crime Ordinance for burning a cross on a black family's lawn. The statute prohibited the display of any symbol that one knew or reasonably should have known "arouses anger, alarm or resentment in others on the basis of race, color, creed, religion, or gender." Terming the ordinance substantially overbroad and impermissibly content-based, the trial court dismissed the charge; but the Minnesota supreme court reversed, citing earlier cases limiting the law's reach to fighting words and also concluding that it was narrowly tailored to serve the city's compelling interest in protecting the community against bias-motivated threats to public safety and order, thereby overcoming the claim that the ordinance was impermissibly content based. Speaking through Justice Scalia, the Supreme Court reversed the state supreme court, declaring the antibias ordinance facially invalid under the First Amendment.

Joined by the chief justice and Justices Kennedy, Souter, and Thomas, Justice Scalia refused to rest their decision on *R.A.V.*'s claim that the law was substantially overbroad, holding the ordinance invalid instead on the ground that it unconstitutionally prohibited speech on the basis of its subject matter. Scalia conceded that fighting words and certain other recognized categories of expression could be regulated because of their content, but rejected the traditional view that those forms of speech were completely excluded from constitutional protection. He concluded, moreover, that such expression could not be regulated on the basis of government hostility or favoritism toward the messages they contained. Under that standard, St. Paul's ordinance was facially unconstitutional because it imposed special burdens on speech relating to the disfavored subjects of "race, color, creed, religion, or gender," while permitting other forms of abusive invective.

In practical operation the ordinance goes even beyond mere content discrimination, to actual viewpoint discrimination. Displays containing some words—odious racial epithets, for example—would be prohibited to proponents of all views. But "fighting words" that do not themselves invoke race, color, creed, religion, or gender—aspersions upon a person's mother, for example—would seemingly be usable *ad libitum* in the placards of those arguing *in favor* of racial, color, etc. tolerance and equality, but could not be used by that speaker's opponents. One could hold up a sign saying, for example, that all "anti-Catholic bigots" are misbegotten; but not that all "papists" are, for that would insult and provoke violence "on the basis of religion." St. Paul has no such authority to license one side of a debate to fight freestyle, while requiring the other to follow Marquis of Queensbury Rules.[25]

Concurring in the judgment, Justice White, joined by Justices Blackmun and O'Connor, and in part by Justice Stevens, favored invalidating the St. Paul ordinance as overboard on its face and scored Scalia for concluding that, under certain circumstances, fighting words were entitled to constitutional protection. Drawing on *Chaplinsky* and other cases excluding fighting words and certain other categories of expression from the First Amendment's reach, White contended that "[a]lthough the [challenged] ordinance as construed reaches categories of speech that are constitutionally unprotected, it also criminalizes a substantial amount of expression that—however repugnant—is shielded by the First Amendment." In purporting to limit the ordinance's coverage to fighting words, Minnesota's high court had concluded that under its antibias measure St. Paul could prohibit expression that "by its utterance" caused "anger, alarm or resentment." But the Court's fighting words cases had made clear, White contended, "that such generalized reactions are not sufficient to strip expression of its constitutional protection. The mere fact that expressive activity causes hurt feelings, offense, or resentment does not render the expression unprotected."[26] Since the St. Paul ordinance, even as construed by the state's highest court, reached much protected as well as unprotected expression, declared White, it was fatally overbroad.

In a brief concurrence, Justice Blackmun agreed with Justice White's conclusion that the St. Paul ordinance was void for overbreadth. But Blackmun also expressed concern about the possible impact on First Amendment law of Justice Scalia's suggestion that "a State cannot regulate speech that causes great harm unless it also regulates speech that does not (setting law and logic on their heads)." If governments were forbidden to categorize speech, excluding some forms from virtually all protection, Blackmun feared that protection for expression would be reduced "across the board." If, on the other hand, the Court's decision were simply an "aberration—a case where the Court manipulated doctrine to strike down an ordinance whose premise it opposed, namely, that racial threats and verbal assaults are of greater harm than fighting words," Blackmun worried that the Court had "been distracted from its proper mission by the temptation to decide the issue over 'politically correct speech' and 'cultural diversity.'" The justice saw no compromise of First Amendment values in a law "that prohibits hoodlums from driving minorities out of their homes by burning crosses on their lawns," but saw "great harm in preventing the people of Saint Paul from specifically punishing the race-based fighting words that so prejudice their community."[27]

While also concurring in the Court's judgment, Justice Stevens criticized both the majority and concurring opinions for yielding to "the allure of absolute principles."[28] Speaking for the Court, Justice Scalia had rejected the traditional approach under which fighting words and certain other categories of expression were denied virtually all constitutional protection, but at the same time, in Stevens's judgment, had established a "near-absolute ban on content-based regulations of" such expression, thereby embracing an absolutism of his own. "[W]ithin a particular 'proscribable' category of expression, the Court holds," observed Stevens, "a government must either proscribe *all* speech or no speech at all."[29] By reaffirming the categorical approach to free speech exceptions, on the other hand, Justice White in his concurrence had embraced another absolute. Stevens rejected both approaches. "Unlike the Court, I do not believe that all content-based regulations are equally infirm and presumptively invalid. Unlike Justice White, I do not believe that fighting words are wholly unprotected by the First Amendment. To the contrary, I believe our decisions establish a more complex and subtle analysis, one that considers the content and context of the regulated speech, and the nature and scope of the restriction on speech." Applying that more flexible approach to the St. Paul ordinance, Stevens concluded that, were the measure not overbroad, "such a selective, subject-matter regulation on proscribable speech [would be] constitutional."[30] For Stevens, in short, "[c]onduct that create[d] special risks or special harms [could] be prohibited by special rules," and there were "legitimate, reasonable, and neutral justifications" for permitting government to treat cross burning by such special rules,[31] albeit under more narrowly drawn regulations than St. Paul had adopted.

The previous year, the Court had also extended constitutional protection to another form of symbolic speech, but only barely so. Instead, a majority found nude dancing, unlike cross burning, merely within the First Amendment's outer perimeters, thereby calling to mind the Court's historic discomfort with erotic expression— as well as a radio announcer's long-ago pitch for a movie about a southern sheriff who resorted to vigilante tactics in ridding his county of vice elements: "And remember, 'Walking Tall' is rated 'R' for violence, not sex. So bring the kids. Good family fun!" In *Barnes v. Glen Theatre* (1991),[32] two Indiana establishments brought suit in federal district court, seeking an injunction against enforcement of a provision of the state public decency statute requiring exotic dancers to wear pasties and g-strings in their performances. The trial court rejected the claim that totally nude dancing constituted protected expression, but the court of appeals reversed, including non-obscene nude dancing within the First Amendment's reach and invalidating the Indiana statute as an infringement on the message of eroticism and sexuality nude dancers conveyed to their audiences. The Supreme Court, by a five-four vote, overturned the court of appeals.

Chief Justice Rehnquist, joined by Justices O'Connor and Kennedy, applied the *O'Brien* standard in concluding that the public decency law had only an incidental impact on protected expression and furthered important governmental interests unrelated to the suppression of ideas—specifically, the state's interests in protecting societal order and morality. The evil the state was seeking to prevent, Rehnquist reasoned, was public nudity, whether or not combined with expressive activity and regardless of any erotic messages the proscribed performances might convey. Extending the rationale of his opinion for the Court in the Oregon peyote case, Justice Scalia concluded in a concurring opinion that general laws regulating conduct and not specifically directed at expression were subject to challenge only under a lenient, rationality standard of review. Indiana's ban on nude dancing, in Scalia's judgment, was rationally related to the state's legitimate opposition to public nudity. Justice Souter, the final member of the majority, agreed that the *O'Brien* test was appropriate and concluded that the state's interest in protecting against the secondary effects of adult entertainment establishments, including prostitution and sexual assaults, was sufficient to justify the Indiana statute's application to nude dancing. Such an interest was in no way related, Souter added, to the expression inherent in nude dancing, but merely to the pernicious criminal activities typically associated with such establishments. Since the requirement of pasties and g-string would have only a minor impact on any message dancers might wish to convey, moreover, it was no more extensive than necessary to further the state's interest in controlling criminal activities.

In a thoughtful dissent, Justice White, joined by Justices Marshall, Blackmun, and Stevens, took sharp issue with the conclusion of the majority justices that the Indiana regulation was directed at public nudity rather than erotic expression.

> It is only because nude dancing performances may generate emotions and feelings of eroticism and sensuality among the spectators that the State seeks to regulate such expressive activity, apparently on the assumption that creating or emphasizing such thoughts and ideas in the minds of the spectators may lead to increased prostitution and the degradation of women. But generating thoughts, ideas, and emotions is the essence of communication. The nudity element of nude dancing performances cannot be neatly pigeonholed as mere "conduct" independent of any expressive component of the dance. . . . That the performances in the Kitty Kat Lounge [one of the two businesses challenging the statute] may not be high art, to say the least, and may not appeal to the Court, is hardly an excuse for distorting and ignoring settled doctrine.[33]

Under that doctrine, contended White, the ban on nude dancing was to be overturned absent a compelling interest, and neither the state nor the plurality had suggested that the challenged statute could withstand such scrutiny.

Since the law, in the dissenters' judgment, was not a truly general regulation of conduct unrelated to the suppression of speech, they also rejected Justice Scalia's argument that the ban on nude dancing, like general drug laws applied to the ritual use of peyote, was subject only to lenient, rational basis review.

> We agree with Justice Scalia that the Indiana statute would not permit 60,000 consenting Hoosiers to expose themselves to each other in the Hoosier Dome.

No one can doubt, however, that those same 60,000 Hoosiers would be perfectly free to drive to their respective homes all across Indiana and, once there, to parade around, cavort, and revel in the nude for hours in front of family and friends. It is difficult to see why the State's interest in morality is any less in that situation, especially if, as Justice Scalia seems to suggest, nudity is inherently evil, but clearly the statute does not reach such activity. . . . [T]he State's failure to enact a truly general proscription requires closer scrutiny of the reasons for the distinctions the State has drawn.[34]

In his concurrence, Justice Scalia had accused the dissenters of misreading his conception of a "general law" subject only to rationality scrutiny as a consequence of its impact on constitutional rights. Such a law would not necessarily restrict targeted conduct in all places at all times. Instead, Scalia asserted, it should be considered general if it regulated conduct "without regard to whether that conduct is expressive. . . . One may not go nude in public, whether or not one intends thereby to convey a message, and similarly one *may* go nude in private, again whether or not that nudity is expressive."[35] It is difficult, however, to challenge Justice White's assertion that "the purpose of applying the law to the nude dancing performances in respondents' establishments is to prevent their customers from being exposed to the distinctive communicative aspects of nude dancing."[36] White noted, for example, that, according to Indiana's attorney general, the state's supreme court had held that the challenged statute, in the justice's words, "cannot and does not prohibit nudity as a part of some larger form of expression meriting protection when the communication of ideas is involved."[37] Counsel for the state had also assured the Court that the statute would be inapplicable to nudity in theatrical productions; nor was any evidence presented of any state attempt to apply the law to nudity in performances for plays, ballets, or operas.

Even so, one can well appreciate the concern motivating Justice Scalia's efforts to deny meaningful constitutional protection to conduct generally subject to governmental control, yet in some way connected to the exercise of individual rights. Calling to mind the earlier efforts of Justice Black to distinguish speech and other constitutionally protected freedoms from conduct nowhere mentioned in the Constitution's text, Scalia emphasized in his concurrence that

[t]he First Amendment explicitly protects "the freedom of speech [and] of the press"—oral and written speech—not "expressive conduct." When any law restricts speech, even for a purpose that has nothing to do with the suppression of communication . . . , we insist that it meet the high, First-Amendment standard of justification. But virtually *every* law restricts conduct, and virtually *any* prohibited conduct can be performed for an expressive purpose—if only expressive of the fact that the actor disagrees with the prohibition. . . . It cannot reasonably be demanded, therefore, that every restriction of expression incidentally produced by a general law regulating conduct pass normal First Amendment scrutiny, or even . . . that it be justified by an "important or substantial" governmental interest.[38]

Such concerns had prompted Scalia to lead the Court in immunizing sanctions against ritual use of peyote from meaningful free exercise challenge. But he saw "even greater reason to apply [that] approach to the regulation of expressive conduct [since] [r]elatively few can plausibly assert their illegal conduct is being engaged in for religious reasons; but almost anyone can violate almost any law as a means of expression. In the one case, as in the other, if the law is not directed against the protected value (religion or expression) the law must be obeyed."[39]

Justice Scalia's reasoning is sound, but reaches only certain of the problems inherent in the Court's willingness to extend significant constitutional protection to certain forms of expressive conduct. Even Scalia is willing to strike down censorial laws directed at symbolic speech, such as the desecration statutes at issue in the flag-burning cases. His and the Court's extension of the First Amendment beyond "speech" and "press" to any activities a majority of justices deem "symbolic" of those express freedoms, whatever the context, confers on the amendment, moreover, a potentially limitless meaning and on the courts broad authority to rule on the reasonableness of otherwise valid laws, especially since, as Justice Scalia contends, virtually every regulation of conduct can somehow be claimed to interfere with expression. Justice Black's futile campaign long ago for a First Amendment jurisprudence tied closely to its language, and thus excluding conduct symbolic of speech from its scope, may thus have possessed more wisdom than his critics were willing to concede.[40] Given the increasingly flexible, pragmatic approach of the current Court to most constitutional issues, however, the First Amendment dichotomies Black embraced carry even less weight now than in the justice's own era.

Exceptions to Protected Expression

The majority's indication in *R.A.V.*, the cross-burning case, that laws discriminating among types of fighting words were subject to strict judicial scrutiny could ultimately be the basis for a significant change in the Court's response to claims involving that long-recognized exception to protected expression. In the main, however, the Rehnquist Court to date has largely adapted existing precedent regarding free speech exceptions to newly emerging issues rather than attempted fundamental changes in established doctrine.

Evangelist Jerry Falwell's suit against *Hustler Magazine* and its publisher, Larry C. Flynt, posed for the justices the issue whether a state's interest in protecting public figures from emotional distress was sufficient to deny First Amendment protection to speech that was patently offensive and intended to inflict emotional injury, yet could not reasonably have been interpreted as stating actual facts about the public figure in question. The inside front cover of *Hustler's* November 1983 issue carried a parody of a Campari Liqueur advertisement series that featured interviews with various celebrities about their "first time" to sample Campari, but clearly played on the sexual double entendre of the general subject of "first times." In the *Hustler* parody "interview," Jerry Falwell was reported to have stated that his "first time" occurred during a drunken orgy with his mother in an outhouse. A disclaimer in small print at the bottom of the page read, "ad parody—not to be taken seriously." And *Hustler's* table of contents listed the ad as "Fiction; Ad and Personality Parody." But Falwell promptly filed a diversity suit for libel, invasion of privacy, and intentional infliction of emotional distress in a federal district court. The district court directed a verdict for *Hustler* on the privacy claim, and the jury found against Falwell on the libel claim on the ground that the magazine's parody could not have reasonably been understood as describing actual facts or events. But the jury ruled for the evangelist on the emotional distress claim, recommending that he be awarded $100,000 in compensatory damages and $50,000 each in punitive damages from the magazine and its publisher. The Court of Appeals for the Fourth Circuit affirmed the emotional distress judgment and rejected the petitioners' argument that the "actual malice" libel standard of *New York Times v. Sullivan* (1964),[41] under which public officials and public figures could recover libel damages only for knowing or reckless falsehoods, also had to be met before Falwell could recover damages for emotional distress. Instead, the appeals court concluded that *Hustler* could be sanctioned for inflicting emotional distress if it acted intentionally or recklessly, regardless of whether its ad parody purported to describe actual events.

Speaking through Chief Justice Rehnquist, the Supreme Court reversed the court of appeals' decision and rationale. To assure adequate protection for the free flow of ideas and opinions on matters of public interest and concern, Rehnquist held, a caricature parody could be the basis for the recovery of damages for the intentional infliction of emotional distress only if it also included a false statement of fact made with "actual malice," that is, as required by *New York Times* and later cases, with knowledge the statement was false or reckless disregard for its truth or falsity. "Were we to hold otherwise," observed the chief justice, "there can be little double that political cartoonists and satirists would be subjected to damages awards without any showing that their work falsely defamed its subject."[42] Yet history had made "clear that our political discourse would have been considerably poorer without them."[43] To Falwell's contention that the *Hustler* parody had been so "outrageous" that it should have been distinguished from traditional political cartoons, Rehnquist conceded that the ad was "at best a distant cousin" of the work of Thomas Nast and other prominent political cartoonists of the past and present, "and a rather poor relation at that." But the Court doubted that a principled standard could be established for separating the two, and Rehnquist was "quite sure that the pejorative description 'outrageous' does not supply one. 'Outrageousness' in the area of political and social discourse has an inherent subjectiveness about it which would allow a jury to impose liability on the basis of the jurors' tastes or views, or perhaps on the basis of their dislike of a particular expression. An 'outrageousness' standard thus runs afoul of our longstanding refusal to allow damages to be awarded because the speech in question may have an adverse emotional impact on the audience."[44]

In a 1991 case, a majority also refused to equate deliberate misquotations with knowing or reckless falsehoods, unless the alterations resulted in a material change in the meaning of the statement at issue. The Sigmund Freud Archives fired its projects director, Jeffrey M. Masson, after Masson became disillusioned with Freudian psychology and began advancing his own psychological theories. Following several taped interviews with Masson, *New Yorker* author Janet Malcolm wrote a lengthy article on Masson's relationship with the archives. Included in the piece were six quoted passages purportedly from the Malcolm interviews that did not appear on interview tapes. Before the article's publication, Masson allegedly expressed concern about several errors in those passages. After its publication and with knowledge of Masson's allegations, Alfred A. Knopf published Malcolm's work as a book, portraying Masson in a very unflattering light. Masson then brought a libel action under California law in a federal district court against the *New Yorker,* Malcolm, and Knopf. With the parties in dispute over whether Malcolm had conducted additional untaped interviews from which the passages at issue might have been drawn, the district court granted the defendants' motion for summary judgment, concluding that the alleged inaccuracies were either substantially true or were rational interpretations of ambiguous conversations and thus did not raise a jury question of actual malice required in libel actions involving public figures under the *New York Times* decision. The court of appeals affirmed, but the Supreme Court reversed and remanded.[45]

Speaking for the Court, Justice Kennedy agreed with the court of appeals that only substantial truth is required in libel cases, but rejected the lower court's conclusion that an altered quotation cannot be the basis for libel damages if it is a "rational interpretation" of a public figure's actual statements. Instead, where a writer used a quotation a reasonable reader would consider a verbatim repetition of a speaker's statement, the quotation must be construed as purporting to convey what the speaker actually said. Since five of the six published passages Masson claimed to be erroneous differed materially in meaning from his tape-recorded statements, Kennedy added, he was entitled to a jury decision whether those statements were knowingly or recklessly false.

In an opinion concurring and dissenting in part, Justice White, joined by Justice Scalia, took issue with the Court's conclusion that a deliberate misquotation could not constitute a knowing falsity unless the alteration resulted in a material change in the meaning the quotation conveyed. "The issue," asserted White, was "whether Masson spoke the words attributed to him, not whether the fact, if any, asserted by the attributed words is true or false."[46] The justice found the Court's justifications for its position equally dubious. He questioned first Kennedy's observation that an interviewer attempting to rely on notes rather than verbatim transcripts would often "knowingly attribute" to the subject words not used by the speaker, dismissing such a suggestion as "nothing more than an assertion that authors may misrepresent because they cannot remember what the speaker actually said." To the Court's assumption that authors may find it necessary to reconstruct even with the benefit of a recording, White wondered why authors should be free to put their "reconstruction[s] in quotation marks rather than report without them." And while White conceded, as Kennedy had suggested, that misquotations that did not materially alter a statement's meaning inflicted no injury to reputation compensable as defamatory, he contended that the ultimate issue of defamation was irrelevant to "whether [an] author deliberately put within quotation marks and attributed to the speaker words that the author knew the speaker did not utter." In White's judgment, "malice" in the context of the *New York Times* standard meant a "deliberate falsehood or reckless disregard for whether the fact asserted [was] true or false." A deliberate misquotation, he contended, met that standard, whether or not it "materially" changed the substance of a public figure's actual words.[47]

Although granting constitutional protection to parody and to immaterial alterations of damaging quotations, the Court has been unwilling to recognize a separate constitutional privilege for assertions of "opinion" rather than "fact." In a lawsuit spanning nearly fifteen years, which came before the Court on three occasions, a high school wrestling coach in Ohio sought damages for a newspaper article that implied he had lied under oath in a court proceeding growing out of an altercation during a wrestling match with a rival school. The trial court ultimately granted summary judgment for the newspaper, and the Ohio appeals court affirmed, considering itself bound by the conclusion of the state supreme court in a separate action growing out of the same incident that the article at issue was constitutionally protected opinion rather than an assertion of fact. The Supreme Court, speaking through Chief Justice Rehnquist, reversed, concluding that statements that could not reasonably be interpreted as stating actual facts about an individual were constitutionally protected, but refusing to create a wholesale libel exception for "opinion." If statements at issue in a case could be reasonably construed as assertions of fact, even if couched in terms of opinion, they were potentially libelous; the assertions contained in the disputed article, the chief justice maintained, were "not the sort of loose, figurative, or hyperbolic language which would negate the impression that the writer was seriously maintaining that petitioner committed the crime of perjury. Nor does the general tenor of the article negate this impression."[48]

Justice Brennan, joined by Justice Marshall, agreed in dissent with the Court's summary of principles applicable in such cases—that statements of "pure opinion" were fully protected under the First Amendment, as were statements that could not reasonably be interpreted as stating actual facts, and that the indicia for distinguishing factual assertions from opinion were "the type of language used, the meaning of the statement in context, whether the statement is verifiable, and the broader social circumstances in which the statement was made."[49] But the dissenters parted company with the majority on the application of those standards, concluding instead that the disputed statements could not be reasonably construed as stating or implying defamatory facts and asserting that the reporter responsible for the article had made "it clear at which point he runs out of facts and is simply guessing."[50] Brennan readily agreed that the reporter "*is* guilty. He is guilty of jumping to conclusions, of benightedly assuming that court discussions are always based on the merits, and of looking foolish to lawyers." The justice insisted, however, that the journalist was not "liable for defamation," adding, "Ignorance, without more, has never served to defeat freedom of speech. The constitutional protection does not turn upon 'the truth, popularity, or social utility of the ideas and beliefs which are offered.'"[51]

By immunizing all but knowing or reckless falsehoods from damage judgments and criminal prosecution in cases involving comment about the public activities of government officials and public figures, the Supreme Court's rulings in the *New York Times* case and its progeny have significantly curtailed the availability of libel laws to inhibit wide-open debate on issues of public concern. The actual malice rule those cases embraced does not assure, however, the absolute freedom of the press Justice

Black favored in opposing all libel proceedings. The rule's acceptance of liability for "reckless" falsehoods, moreover, ultimately clothes judges, as Black charged, with limitless discretion to determine what defamatory falsehoods will, and will not, be subject to sanction.[52]

If the recklessness of a falsehood is to be the standard for determining liability, however, a newspaper article at issue in a 1989 case before the Rehnquist Court seemed a prime candidate for a finding of malice. During a 1983 municipal judge-ship election campaign in Hamilton, Ohio, a local newspaper, the *Journal News*, endorsed the incumbent. A month before the election, the incumbent's director of court services resigned his position and was arrested on bribery charges, which a grand jury was investigating as election day approached. A week before the election, the *Journal News* ran a front-page story quoting a grand jury witness as stating that Daniel Connaughton, the incumbent's opponent for the judgeship, had used "dirty tricks" and offered her and her sister jobs and a trip to Florida "in appreciation" for their assistance with the grand jury inquiry. Connaughton then filed a libel action in federal district court. Following a trial, a jury found by the preponderance of the evi-dence that the article at issue was defamatory and false, and by clear and convincing proof that it was published with actual malice, awarding Connaughton compen-satory and punitive damages. The court of appeals and the Supreme Court, speaking through Justice Stevens, affirmed.

Initially, Justice Stevens had concluded that the article at issue was subject to First Amendment protection. After further study of the record, however, he had changed his mind, asserting in a memorandum to his colleagues that he was "now persuaded that the defamatory story was not only false, but that the people responsible for printing it either knew or should have known that it was false and that they surely acted recklessly in not interviewing the key witness in the case and also in not even listening to the tapes describing the corruption in the municipal court before they decided to support the incumbent judge for re-election and to publish the story that gave rise to the lawsuit."[53] Stevens then wrote an opinion for the Court finding the *Journal News* liable for actual malice, and while several concurring justices attempted to clarify or take issue with elements of Stevens's analysis, none took issue with the finding of malice.[54]

In the obscenity field as in libel cases, the Rehnquist Court has pursued an essen-tially cautious approach, albeit one perhaps somewhat more deferential to govern-mental power than that reflected in Burger Court decisions. Under the Burger Court obscenity standards announced in *Miller v. California* (1973),[55] material can be con-sidered obscene if (1) its dominant theme, taken as a whole, appeals to the prurient interest of the average person, applying contemporary local community standards; (2) it depicts or describes sexual conduct in a patently offensive manner; and (3) it lacks serious literary, artistic, political, or scientific value. The Rehnquist Court has reaffirmed the *Miller* standards and clarified their meaning. In *Pope v. Illinois* (1987),[56] for example, a majority rejected trial court instructions to a jury to judge the value of an allegedly obscene work by determining how the state's "ordinary citi-zens" would view it. Emphasizing that community standards were relevant only to an inquiry into a work's prurient appeal and offensiveness, Justice White concluded for the Court that the proper question in such cases was whether a "reasonable person" would find that the material at issue possessed serious value.

A minority of justices, moreover, has continued to question the *Miller* formula. In *Pope*, for example, Justice Brennan, who authored the principal dissent in *Miller* and its companion case,[57] filed a brief dissenting opinion reiterating his "view that *any* regulation of such material with respect to consenting adults suffers from the defect that 'the concept of "obscenity" cannot be defined with sufficient specificity and clarity to provide fair notice to persons who create and distribute sexually oriented materials, to prevent substantial erosion of protected speech as a byproduct of the attempt to suppress unprotected speech, and to avoid very costly institutional harms'" to the judiciary.[58] In a bench memorandum prepared before oral argument in the case, one of Justice Marshall's clerks agreed that "*Miller* is terrible" and reminded the justice that "it's been a while since we wrote to say so."[59] But Marshall filed no opinion in *Pope*. Instead, he and Brennan joined a dissent by Justice Stevens, who had not yet been appointed to the Court when *Miller* was decided, but shared the Brennan-Marshall distaste for the *Miller* formula. Taking issue with the reasonable person standard under which, according to the *Pope* majority, the value of alleged obscenity was to be measured, Stevens contended that a juror asked to apply such a test "might well believe that the majority of the population who find no value in such a book are more reasonable than the minority who do find value."[60] The safeguards of the First Amendment, Stevens contended, "surely must not be contingent on this type of subjective determination."[61] In his judgment, "communicative material of this sort [was] entitled to the protection of the First Amendment if *some reasonable persons* could consider it as having serious literary, artistic, political, or scientific value."[62]

In another separate opinion, Justice Blackmun disagreed with Justice Stevens's suggestion that the majority's reasonable person approach to the value prong of the *Miller* formula could promote jury deference to majority will. To Blackmun, White's opinion stood only "for the clear proposition that the First Amendment does not permit a majority to dictate to discrete segments of the population—be they composed of art critics, literary scholars, or scientists—the value that may be found in various pieces of work. That only a minority may find value in a work does not mean that a jury would not conclude that 'a reasonable person would find such value in the material, taken as a whole.'"[63]

For his part, Justice Scalia agreed that the majority's reasonable person formula was faithful to *Miller*, but stressed the need for *Miller*'s reexamination. Highly skeptical of any effort at "objective assessment of (at least) literary or artistic value, there being many accomplished people who have found literature in Dada, and art in the replication of a soup can," Scalia considered the Court "better advised to adopt as a legal maxim what has long been the wisdom of mankind. . . . Just as there is no use arguing about taste, there is no use litigating about it. For the law courts to decide 'What is Beauty' is a novelty even by today's standards."[64] Even though such concerns motivated *Miller*'s critics, however, Scalia neither joined Brennan, Stevens, and company, nor hinted at his own preferred approach to the obscenity issue.

Even *Miller*'s critics on the Court have long recognized broad governmental power to protect juveniles from exposure to pornography, whether or not obscene for adults, and from their exploitation in sexual performances. In 1982, for example, a unanimous Court upheld New York's ban on the production, sale, and distribution of child pornography, whether or not obscene under the *Miller* standards.[65] Years before, the Court had also upheld restrictions on the sale of erotic magazines to minors.[66] The justices on the Rehnquist Court split, however, on the question whether the right to possess obscenity in the privacy of the home, first recognized in the *Stanley* case,[67] should be extended to child pornography.

In *Osborne v. Ohio* (1990),[68] a six-three majority reversed the conviction of a man sentenced to six months in prison for possession of four photographs, each of which depicted a nude adolescent male posed in a sexually explicit position, but only because of the Court's uncertainty that Osborne's conviction was based on a finding that the state had proved each element of the offense. On the First Amendment question, the Court, per Justice White, distinguished *Stanley* and upheld a statute prohibiting the possession or viewing of child pornography even in the privacy of one's home, as construed by the Ohio supreme court to reach only nudity that constituted a lewd exhibition or focused on the subject's genitals. Unlike the general statute at issue in *Stanley*, Justice White reasoned, the challenged law furthered Ohio's compelling interests in protecting the physical and psychological well-being of minors and in destroying the market for the exploitive use of children. The ban, the justice added, would also encourage the destruction of such materials, which otherwise might be used by pedophiles in the seduction of other children and would become for the child victim a haunting permanent record of sexual abuse. Given exemptions contained in the statute, White doubted its provisions, even on their face, suffered from the substantial overbreadth required to find them unconstitutional. As narrowed in meaning by the state supreme court, however, the statute clearly survived the overbreadth scrutiny that would doom restrictions reaching innocuous photographs of naked children and other constitutionally protected material.

Justice Brennan, joined by Justices Marshall and Stevens, challenged the majority's overbreadth analysis and reading of *Stanley*. In rejecting Osborne's overbreadth claim, Justice White's majority opinion had cited *New York v. Ferber* (1982),[69] the case upholding a state ban on child pornography. In his *Osborne* dissent, Justice Brennan emphasized that the law at issue in *Ferber* made it a crime to use children in sexual performances and that Ferber had been convicted for selling films depicting young boys masturbating. Even as narrowed by Ohio's supreme court, the statute at issue in *Osborne* went much further, Brennan contended, penalizing "lewd exhibitions of nudity" and "graphic focus" on the genitals, whether or not in the context of sexual conduct. The state court's construction, he added, had hardly eliminated the statute's vague, broad sweep. "Michelangelo's 'David,'" he asserted, for example, "might be said to have a 'graphic focus' on the genitals, for it plainly portrays them in a manner unavoidable to even a casual observer."[70] In objecting to the majority's refusal to extend *Stanley* to the possession of child pornography, Brennan pointed out that *Ferber* had dealt with the production and distribution of child pornography, not its mere possession, thus placing child pornography on "the same level of First Amendment protection as *obscene* adult pornography, meaning that its production and distribution could be proscribed."[71] Brennan obviously agreed with the Court that the sexual exploitation of children was a serious problem, but insisted that Ohio possessed adequate means for pursuing that concern without distinguishing *Stanley*, adding, "Indeed the State already has enacted a panoply of laws prohibiting the creation, sale, and distribution of child pornography and obscenity involving minors ... [and] has not demonstrated why these laws are inadequate and why the State must forbid mere possession as well."[72]

A child pornography case decided the year before the *Osborne* ruling provoked an interesting debate among the justices regarding the ways available to government for curing the overbreadth of a statute claimed to interfere with First Amendment rights. After Douglas Oakes took photographs of his partially nude and physically mature fourteen-year-old stepdaughter, he was convicted of violating a Massachusetts statute that prohibited adults from posing or exhibiting nude minors for reproduction in books, magazines, or other formats. The state supreme court reversed the conviction on grounds of substantial overbreadth without reaching the question whether the law at issue could have been constitutionally applied to Oakes's conduct. When the statute was later amended to require a finding of "lascivious intent," however, the Supreme Court remanded the case to the state courts for a determination whether Oakes's conduct was subject to criminal prosecution. Speaking for herself, the chief justice, and Justice White, Justice O'Connor concluded that the statute's revision had mooted Oakes's overbreadth claim. Justice Scalia, joined by Justice Blackmun, agreed with the O'Connor plurality that the case should be remanded for review of Oakes's as-applied challenge to the statute, and Blackmun also concluded that the law was not substantially overbroad. But Scalia, joined by Justices Brennan, Marshall, and Stevens, as well as Justice Blackmun, took sharp issue with O'Connor's assertion that a legislature's post-conviction revision of a statute could eliminate any overbreadth defense against its enforcement.

> If the promulgation of overbroad laws affecting speech was cost free, as Justice O'Connor's new doctrine would make it—that is, if *no* conviction of constitutionally proscribable conduct would be lost, so long as the offending statute was narrowed before the final appeal—then legislatures would have significantly reduced incentive to stay within constitutional bounds in the first place. When one takes account of those overbroad statutes that are never challenged, and of the time that elapses before the ones that are challenged are amended to come within constitutional bounds, a substantial amount of legitimate speech would be "chilled" as a consequence of the rule Justice O'Connor would adopt.[73]

Nor would Scalia accept the interpretation of the precedent on which Justice O'Connor largely rested the plurality's approach to the overbreadth issue raised in the case. The plurality had relied heavily on *Bigelow v. Virginia*,[74] a 1975 case involving the conviction of the editor of a weekly newspaper under a statute making it a misdemeanor to sell or circulate any publication that encouraged or prompted women to procure abortions. Following Bigelow's conviction, the statute was amended to eliminate the possibility that it could again be applied to the defendant or would chill the rights of others in a similar position. Speaking for the *Bigelow*

Court, Justice Blackmun concluded, "As a practical matter, the issue of [the challenged statute's] overbreadth has become moot for the future. We therefore decline to rest our decision on overbreadth and we pass on to the further inquiry . . . whether the statute as applied to appellant infringed constitutionally protected speech."[75] Justice O'Connor concluded in *Oakes* that *Bigelow* stood for the proposition that overbreadth analysis was inappropriate once the statute at issue had been amended or repealed. But in his opinion, an opinion *Bigelow* author Justice Blackmun joined, Justice Scalia convincingly challenged O'Connor's reading of the earlier case, arguing that the *Bigelow* Court had simply declined to reach the overbreadth claim there because, given the state's revision of the challenged statute, that claim "was no longer of general interest ('ha[d] become moot for the future'), whereas the issues involved in the as-applied challenge were of continuing importance."[76] In a dissenting opinion finding the statute substantially overbroad, moreover, Justice Brennan, joined by Justices Marshall and Stevens, emphasized that five members of the Court—a majority—had rejected the plurality's overbreadth analysis.

A number of obscenity cases before the Rehnquist Court have involved relatively narrow procedural questions or aroused little dispute among the justices. One 1994 case dealt with the federal Protection of Children Against Sexual Exploitation Act of 1977, which prohibits one from "knowingly" transporting, shipping, receiving, distributing, or reproducing visual depictions of minors engaged in sexually explicit conduct. Applying a literal interpretation to the law, the Court of Appeals for the Ninth Circuit had declared it facially unconstitutional on the ground that it required no showing that a defendant knew a performer was a minor. Rejecting that "most grammatical reading of the statute," Chief Justice Rehnquist held for the majority that the term "knowingly" in the law applied to the minority of performers as well as the sexually explicit nature of the performance—prompting Justice Scalia, joined by Justice Thomas, to declare in dissent that for Rehnquist to term the Ninth Circuit's reading of the statute its "most natural grammatical reading" was "understatement to the point of distortion—rather like saying that the ordinarily preferred total for 2 plus 2 is 4."[77] Scalia insisted that he had no concern "that holding the purveyors and receivers of this material absolutely liable for supporting the exploitation of minors [would] deter any activity the United States Constitution was designed to protect." He had no doubt, however, that the challenged law imposed "criminal liability upon those not knowingly dealing in pornography" and thus "establishe[d] a severe deterrent, not narrowly tailored to its purposes, upon fully protected First Amendment activities."[78] In another case, the Court struck down a city licensing scheme for sexually oriented businesses on the ground that the challenged regulation lacked appropriate procedural safeguards to assure adequate protection for erotic expression. But the justices disagreed over the number and type of procedural devices required in such cases,[79] with only Justice Brennan, joined by Justices Marshall and Blackmun, favoring application of all the procedural standards initially established by the Warren Court in 1965,[80] whatever the nature of the licensing provision under challenge.

Even provisions of the Communications Decency Act (CDA) provoked little debate among the justices when they came up for decision during the 1996 term. The CDA made criminal the "knowing" transmission of "obscene or indecent" Internet

messages to any recipient under eighteen years of age, as well as the "knowing" sending or displaying to such persons of any message that, in context, depicted or
described sexual or excretory activities or organs in a patently offensive manner. In
declaring the "indecent transmission" and "patently offensive display" provisions
unconstitutional for a seven-two majority, Justice Stevens emphasized the breadth
and indefinite character of the "indecency" standard and the challenged statute's failure to require that offensive material also lack socially redeeming value. Justice
O'Connor, joined by the chief justice, filed a partial dissent in which she characterized the CDA as largely simply an attempt to establish "adult zones" on the Internet.
But even O'Connor agreed that the challenged provisions violated the First Amendment to the extent they unduly restricted adult access to the material at issue. Under
the current cyberspace technology, she explained, "a speaker cannot be reasonably
assured that the speech he displays will reach only adults because it is impossible to
confine speech to an 'adult zone.' Thus, the only way for a speaker to avoid liability
under the CDA is to refrain completely from using indecent speech. But this forced
silence impinges on the First Amendment right of adults to make and obtain this
speech and, for all intents and purposes, 'reduce[s] the adult population [on the
Internet] to reading only what is fit for children.'"[81] The challenged provisions, in
O'Connor's view, were therefore valid as applied to an Internet conversation involving "only an adult and one or more minors," but the CDA, she added, was "akin to a
law that makes it a crime for a book-store owner to sell pornographic magazines to
anyone once a minor enters his store. Even assuming such a law might be constitutional in the physical world as a reasonable alternative to excluding minors completely
from the store, the absence of any means of excluding minors from chat rooms in
cyberspace restricts the rights of adults to engage in indecent speech in those rooms.
The 'indecency transmission' and 'specific person' provisions share this defect."[82]

Earlier, federal "dial-a-porn" regulations had met a similar fate. Amendments to
the federal communications law imposed a blanket prohibition on "indecent" as well
as "obscene" interstate commercial telephone messages. Terming the statute's ban on
indecent messages an undue restriction on adult access to erotic expression, far
exceeding controls necessary to promote government's compelling interest in protecting minors from exposure to such messages, the Court, per Justice White,
declared that portion of the law unconstitutional. Reiterating their view that the First
Amendment protects the distribution of obscene materials to adults, Justice Brennan, joined by Justices Marshall and Stevens, favored invalidating the obscenity provisions on overbreadth grounds as well, observing that both the Federal Communications Commission and the Court of Appeals for the Second Circuit had found that
"a scheme involving access codes, scrambling, and credit card payment [was] a feasible and effective way to serve [the] compelling state interest" in protecting children.[83]
In an opinion concurring in the Court's judgment, Justice Scalia asserted that "[t]he
more narrow the understanding of what is 'obscene,' and hence the more pornographic what is embraced within the residual category of 'indecency,' the more reasonable it becomes to insist upon greater assurance of insulation from minors." But
Scalia also agreed that "a wholesale prohibition upon adult access to indecent speech
cannot be adopted merely because the FCC's alternate proposal could be circum-

vented by as few children as the evidence suggests." Where the government acts as patron rather than regulator, however, the Court has invoked more lenient standards of review. A 1998 majority upheld a congressional statute that required review of National Endowment for the Arts (NEA) grant applications to take into consideration general standards of "decency and respect" for the diverse beliefs and values of the American public. In dissent, Justice Souter scored the regulation as a forbidden form of viewpoint discrimination. But the majority upheld the scheme against overbreadth and vagueness challenges, while Justice Scalia emphasized in a concurrence what he viewed as fundamental distinctions between the "abridging" and "funding" of expression.[84]

Both before and after the retirements of Justices Brennan and Marshall, however, the Court's willingness to extend federal and state racketeering regulations and their forfeiture provisions to distributors of obscenity sparked sharp debate among the justices. In Indiana, a local prosecutor filed a civil action against the operator of an adult bookstore under that state's Racketeer Influenced and Corrupt Organizations (RICO) statute, alleging a pattern of racketeering activity in the distribution of obscene books and films and seeking forfeiture of all property used in that enterprise. In a separate action against the same bookstore operator under Indiana's Civil Remedies for Racketeering Activity (CRRA) law, the state also petitioned for a court order authorizing the pretrial seizure of all property subject to forfeiture. After an *ex parte* hearing on the prosecutor's motion, the trial court ordered the immediate seizure of the defendant's bookstore and contents, but certified constitutional claims to the state court of appeals for resolution. The court of appeals declared the RICO and CRRA provisions unconstitutional, but the Indiana supreme court reversed, upholding both the statutes' validity and the seizure order. In another Indiana case, an adult bookstore owner charged with a misdemeanor under the state obscenity statute was also charged with felony offenses under the RICO law based on the predicate obscenity offense. The trial court in that case declared the RICO statute unconstitutionally vague as applied to predicate obscenity offenses, but the Indiana court of appeals reversed and reinstated the charges, and the state supreme court declined review. Reviewing both cases, the Supreme Court, speaking through Justice White, overturned the pretrial seizure of property in the civil proceeding, but upheld the RICO and CRRA regulations.

The bookstore operators had claimed that the statutes were unconstitutionally vague as applied to the obscenity offenses, which provided the predicate on which the RICO and CRRA actions were based. Rejecting that contention, Justice White reasoned that the RICO and CRRA statutes simply encompassed Indiana's obscenity law and termed the petitioners' attack on the "inherent vagueness" of obscenity standards "nothing less than an invitation to overturn *Miller*—an invitation we reject."[85] Nor did the majority see any constitutional significance in the more severe punishment imposed by the RICO violations than for obscenity convictions. The stiffer RICO punishments might serve as an additional deterrent to those who otherwise might sell obscene materials and might result in certain cautious booksellers removing constitutionally protected materials from their shelves. But White saw deterrence as a legitimate objective of obscenity laws and considered the mere assertion that the statute might lead to some degree of self-censorship an insufficient basis for declaring it invalid. The Court found equally unpersuasive the petitioners' contention that RICO actions were constitutionally permissible only for persons previously convicted of the proper number of predicate offenses. The Court, observed White, had never before required a "warning shot" in such cases.[86]

In a separate opinion joined by Justices Brennan and Marshall, Justice Stevens concurred in the majority's rejection of the pretrial seizure at issue in the litigation, but challenged other portions of the Court's decision and rationale. Under Indiana's statutes, a person convicted of two misdemeanor counts for sale of an obscene magazine was considered to be engaged in a "pattern of racketeering activity," a felony punishable not only by up to eight years in prison, but also subject to a variety of civil sanctions, including a court order dissolving the enterprise, forfeiting its property to the state, and enjoining the defendant from engaging in the same type of business in the future. In upholding the law's constitutionality, Stevens added, Indiana's highest court had "categorically stated that if the elements of a pattern of racketeering activity have been proved, all of a bookstore's expressive material, obscene or not, are subject to forfeiture."[87] Thus, both as written and as authoritatively construed, the law clearly reflected the state's desire to extend its reach beyond obscene materials to constitutionally protected expression, under the guise of regulating racketeering. For Stevens, "[f]ulfillment of that intent surely would overflow the boundaries imposed by the Constitution."[88] In his view, moreover, there was a significant difference between enterprises selling books, magazines, and videotapes and those engaged in other lawful or unlawful commercial activities. "Seldom will First Amendment protections have any relevance to the sanctions that might be invoked against an ordinary commercial establishment. Nor will use of RICO/CRRA sanctions to rid that type of enterprise of illegal influence, even by closing it, engender suspicion of censorial motive." Stevens considered such sexually explicit material "noxious," but found it "nevertheless true that a host of citizens desires them, that at best remote and indirect injury to third parties flows from them, and that purchasers have a constitutional right to possess them."[89]

In *Alexander v. United States* (1993), Justice Kennedy invoked similar reasoning, as well as the traditional judicial distaste for prior restraints, in challenging the constitutionality of the federal RICO statute. Based on a finding that seven items sold at several of a major pornography dealer's stores were obscene, a federal court convicted him of both obscenity and RICO charges, imposed a prison term and fine, and required the defendant to forfeit to the federal government his businesses and almost $9 million in funds acquired through such activities. In affirming the forfeiture order, the court of appeals rejected Ferris Alexander's claims that RICO's forfeiture provisions were void for overbreadth and constituted a prior restraint on expression. That court also declined to reach Alexander's claim that the forfeiture order violated his Eighth Amendment right against excessive fines and rejected his claim that the forfeiture order was grossly disproportionate to the offense, holding that proportionality review under the constitutional guarantee against cruel and unusual punishments was inapplicable to sentences of less than life imprisonment without possibility of parole. Although vacating the lower court's judgment and remanding the case for review of Alexander's excessive fines claim, Chief Justice Rehnquist concluded for the Supreme Court that forfeiture was a permissible criminal punishment rather than a prior restraint and rejected the petitioner's overbreadth and related First Amendment contentions, concluding that the threat of forfeiture had no more of a "chilling effect" on protected expression than the threat of prison terms or large fines for person convicted of distributing unprotected obscenity.

In a brief separate opinion, Justice Souter agreed with the majority that the forfeiture did not constitute a prior restraint and that a remand was required on the excessive fines issue. But Souter also contended that Alexander's expressive materials could be forfeited only after a judicial finding that they were obscene or otherwise unprotected. In a forceful opinion joined by Justices Blackmun and Stevens, and in part by Justice Souter, Justice Kennedy not only opposed forfeiture of nonobscene material, but also declared that the RICO scheme's application to expression constituted a forbidden prior restraint.

After tracing the history of the Court's confrontations with prior restraints, including its invalidation of the gag law at issue in *Near v. Minnesota* (1931),[90] Kennedy contended,

> The government's stated purpose under RICO, to destroy or incapacitate the offending enterprise, bears a striking resemblance to the motivation for the state nuisance statute struck down as an impermissible prior restraint in *Near*. . . . What is happening here is simple: Books and films are condemned and destroyed not for their own content but for the content of their owner's prior speech. Our law does not permit the government to burden future speech for this sort of taint. . . . What is at work in this case is not the power to punish an individual for his past transgressions but the authority to suppress a particular class of disfavored speech. The forfeiture provisions accomplish this in a direct way by seizing speech presumed to be protected along with the instruments of its dissemination, and in an indirect way by threatening all who engage in the business of distributing adult or sexually explicit materials with the same disabling measures. . . . Though perhaps not in the form of a classic prior restraint, the application of the forfeiture statute here bears its censorial cast.[91]

Like Justice Souter, and apart from the prior restraint issue, Justice Kennedy also rejected any governmental power to impound and destroy books and films not previously adjudged to be obscene. In upholding authority under the RICO statute to seize a convicted defendant's entire inventory, obscene or not, Chief Justice Rehnquist had cited *Arcara v. Cloud Books, Inc.* (1986),[92] in which the Court had upheld an injunction issued under a general nuisance statute to close an adult bookstore that was being used as a place of prostitution and lewdness. Kennedy agreed that *Arcara* had found unconvincing the argument that the closure at issue there would burden constitutionally protected bookselling activities, but only because the owners were free to sell, and their customers to buy, materials at a new location. "Alexander and the public do not have those choices here," asserted Justice Kennedy, "for a simple reason. The Government has destroyed the inventory. Further, the sanction in *Arcara* did not involve a complete confiscation or destruction of protected expression as did the forfeiture in this case. Here the inventory forfeited consisted of hundreds of original titles and thousands of copies, all of which are presumed to be protected speech."[93] In distinguishing earlier cases invalidating pretrial seizures of allegedly obscene publications from the forfeiture of such materials under RICO,[94] the chief justice had argued that in those cases materials had been seized without a prior judicial determination they were obscene. Kennedy declared, however, that "the same constitutional defect [was] present in the case before us today. . . . Thus, while in the past we invalidated seizures which resulted in a temporary removal of presumptively protected materials from circulation, today the Court approves of government measures having the same *permanent* effect."[95] Kennedy considered the Court's condoning of such action a "deplorable abandonment of fundamental First Amendment principles."[96]

While recognizing, and even expanding, governmental authority over obscenity as an exception to the categories of protected expression, the Rehnquist Court has also continued to extend constitutional protection to commercial speech, another form of expression long excluded from the First Amendment's reach. Commercial speech first began to receive constitutional protection during Chief Justice Burger's tenure,[97] and in the 1980 *Central Hudson* case, the Burger Court adopted a three-pronged test under which commercial expression could be regulated if the control at issue promoted a substantial governmental interest, directly advanced that interest, and did so through means narrowly tailored to achieve its objective.[98] Applying those standards, the Rehnquist Court has struck down regulations forbidding lawyers to send truthful, nondeceptive solicitation letters to prospective clients[99] and a state's complete statutory ban on the advertising of liquor prices,[100] but upheld federal statutes prohibiting the broadcasting of lottery advertising by broadcasters licensed in a state that did not allow lotteries, while allowing such broadcasts by stations licensed in a prolottery state, even as applied to a broadcaster located in a nonlottery state but near the border of a lottery state.[101]

As in other First Amendment fields, the Rehnquist Court's commercial speech pronouncements have not always enjoyed unanimous approval among the justices. Justice Thomas concurred, for example, with the Court's 1996 decision striking down the state ban on the advertisement of liquor prices, but rejected application of the *Central Hudson* balancing approach in such litigation. "In cases . . . in which the government's asserted interest is to keep legal users of a product or service ignorant in order to manipulate their choices in the marketplace," declared Thomas, "the balancing test . . . should not be applied, in my view. Rather, such an 'interest' is *per se* illegitimate and can no more justify regulation of 'commercial' speech than it can justify regulation of 'non-commercial' speech."[102] Justice Scalia shared Thomas's "discomfort with the *Central Hudson* test, which seems to me to have nothing more than policy intuition to support it."[103] But when Scalia concluded for a majority in an earlier case that governmental restrictions on commercial speech need not employ means to accomplish the interests underlying such regulations that were least restrictive of expression, Justice Blackmun, joined by Justices Brennan and Marshall, filed a dissent, noting that in reaching such a decision the majority had found it necessary to concede "that it must repudiate the Court's repeated assertion[s]" to the contrary.[104]

Time, Place, and Manner Regulations

Like its predecessors, the Rehnquist Court has extended First Amendment and related safeguards to expression on public property, while also recognizing various degrees of governmental power to impose reasonable, nondiscriminatory regulations of time, place, and manner on such activities. In 1987, for example, the Court unanimously overturned a resolution of the board of airport commissioners at Los Angeles International Airport banning all First Amendment activities from the airport's central terminal area, with Justice O'Connor concluding for the justices that no conceivable government interest could justify such an absolute prohibition of speech.[105] And in a 1992 case, the chief justice concluded for a majority that an airport terminal operated by the public is a nonpublic forum and upheld restrictions on the distribution of literature and solicitation of contributions in terminals operated by the Port Authority of New York and New Jersey.[106] Other regulations have been subjected to a similar, case-by-case analysis. In 1987, Justice Brennan spoke for the Court in declaring unconstitutionally overbroad a Houston, Texas, ordinance making it illegal in any manner to oppose, molest, abuse, or interrupt police officers in the performance of their duties. And only Chief Justice Rehnquist disagreed with the Court's conclusion that the ordinance, absent an authoritative state court construction, was unconstitutional.[107]

The next year, a majority declared invalid a District of Columbia regulation prohibiting the display, within 500 feet of an embassy, of signs bringing the foreign government in question into disrepute, with Justice O'Connor declaring such a control a content-based restriction on political speech in a public forum that was not narrowly tailored to serve a compelling governmental interest. But the justices upheld a companion provision prohibiting people from congregating within 500 feet of an embassy and failing to heed an order to disperse. As interpreted by the court of appeals, the congregation provision permitted dispersal only of gatherings directed at an embassy and then only when police reasonably believed the embassy's "security or peace" was threatened. So construed, O'Connor held, the regulation was neither overbroad nor unduly vague.[108] In other cases, majorities have rejected the contention that a postal sidewalk is a traditional public forum subject to broad constitutional obligations and upheld as reasonable postal regulations prohibiting solicitation on postal premises;[109] intervened in a clash between civil rights activists and the Ku Klux Klan in Forsyth County, Georgia, by declaring facially unconstitutional a parade permit and fee system held to grant unduly broad discretion to the county administrator;[110] upheld a municipal noise regulation requiring music performers in a city band shell to use a sound system and technicians provided by the city;[111] struck down a city ban on news racks containing "commercial handbills" that did not apply to newspaper racks;[112] invalidated an ordinance that banned residential signs but included numerous exemptions from its coverage, challenged by a resident wishing to display a political sign from her home;[113] upheld a federal regulation denying food stamps to the families of striking workers;[114] and struck down application of a state public accommodations law to private organizers of Boston's St. Patrick's Day parade who had excluded homosexuals from participation.[115]

Of several contentious issues raised in such litigation, probably the most significant has involved what sorts of public property constitute "public forums," subject to broad First Amendment protection. The Supreme Court has long characterized streets, parks, and certain other forms of public property as traditional public forums immemorially held in trust for the use of the public as sites for communication and assembly.[116] Regulations limiting speech in such areas must further a compelling governmental interest and be narrowly drawn to achieve that end, while content-neutral time, place, and manner regulations in traditional public forums must be narrowly tailored to serve a significant governmental interest, leaving open ample alternative means of communication.[117] Property the government chooses to designate a public forum for particular purposes is subject to essentially the same standards. All other types of property are considered by the Court nonpublic forums subject to reasonable, viewpoint-neutral government restrictions of speech in such areas.

Certain members of the Court have challenged what they see as the majority's effort to limit the public forum concept only to sites traditionally dedicated to expression and assembly, thereby converting a doctrine originally intended to expand the reach of free speech into a device for restricting its scope. When a majority concluded in 1992 that an airport terminal is a nonpublic forum for First Amendment purposes, Justice Kennedy, joined on the issue by Justices Blackmun, Stevens, and Souter, declared that "[o]ur public forum doctrine ought not to be a jurisprudence of categories rather than ideas or convert what was once an analysis protective of expression into one which grants the government authority to restrict speech by fiat."[118] Rejecting the Court's categorical approach as "flawed at its very beginning," Kennedy favored an "objective [inquiry], based on the actual, physical characteristics and uses of the property."[119] He also took issue with his colleagues' "notion that traditional public forums are property which have public discourse as their principal purpose." Streets and sidewalks, he reasoned, were principally designed for transportation, not expression, and public parks as much for beauty and open spaces as discourse. "Thus under the Court's analysis, even the quintessential public forums would appear to lack the necessary elements of what the Court defines as a public forum."[120] Kennedy found equally troublesome the Court's further requirement that property could be considered a "designated" public forum only on the basis of clear evidence of the government's intent.

In Kennedy's judgment, the public forum concept should not be limited to traditional forums, but should also extend to "open, public spaces and thoroughfares which are suitable for discourse..., whatever their historical pedigree and without concern for a precise classification of the property." The need for such an approach, he observed, was obvious: "Without this recognition our forum doctrine retains no relevance in times of fast-changing technology and increasing insularity. In a country where most citizens travel by automobile, and parks all too often become locales for crime rather than social intercourse, our failure to recognize the possibility that new types of government property may be appropriate forums for speech will lead to a serious curtailment of our expressive activity."[121] Especially since the Court had held that private property of a similar nature, such as the premises of a shopping center, was not subject to First Amendment requirements,[122] Kennedy thought it important to include such public areas within the ambit of the forum concept. The Court had been willing to adapt the Constitution to changing technologies in other fields, and Kennedy considered such flexibility equally appropriate for the First Amendment. Where (1) property shared the physical similarities of more traditional forums, (2) government had permitted or acquiesced in broad public access, and (3) expressive activity would not significantly interfere with the uses to which the property had been primarily dedicated, Kennedy favored extending the First Amendment's reach. Metropolitan airports, he concluded, clearly met those conditions.

In a society in which public interactions increasingly occur in shopping malls and on related forms of private property, Kennedy's analysis has special force, despite the considerable subjectivity inherent in the factors he would apply in determining whether a particular type of property should be designated a public forum. Even Kennedy's formula, however, varies the level of judicial scrutiny to be extended government regulations of expression on public property according to the type of forum a particular piece of property is found to constitute. Rather than engage in the type of analysis Kennedy has recommended, or narrowly restrict the public forum concept in the manner the Court has adopted, the justices might be better advised to drop the categorical approach, of whatever variety, and return to the general balancing of interests analysis that the Court arguably applied to content-neutral regulations of expression on public property until recent years. Such an approach would include consideration of the sorts of factors Kennedy and others have invoked in attempting to distinguish varying types of forums and the constitutional standards applicable to each, yet without burdening First Amendment law with further rhetorical baggage.

Abortion Protests

Undoubtedly, the most closely watched Rehnquist Court forum cases have involved anti-abortion protests at abortion clinics and the residences of clinic staffs—phenomena with which the justices are directly familiar as a result of annual demonstrations at the Court on each anniversary of *Roe v. Wade* and other days when the justices hear oral argument or announce decisions in abortion cases.[123] Shortly after Justice Rehnquist's move to the Court's center seat, a majority upheld a Brookfield, Wisconsin, ordinance prohibiting residential picketing. Rejecting the constitutional claims of abortion protesters, the Court read the law at issue to reach only offensive and disturbing picketing focused on particular "captive" residences, while allowing demonstrators to enter residential neighborhoods, proselytize or distribute literature door-to-door, and contact residents through the mail or by telephone. Although questioning whether the ordinance could be limited on its face to single-residence picketing, Justice White thought it constitutional as applied to such activities. But

Justice Brennan, joined by Justice Marshall, dissented, concluding that the challenged law reached well beyond "intrusive or coercive" interferences with residential privacy. And in a separate dissent, Justice Stevens concluded that the ordinance gave town officials far too much enforcement discretion and that the law could easily be amended to reach only conduct that unreasonably interfered with the privacy of the home.[124]

In a 1993 victory for the anti-abortion movement, the Court, speaking through Justice Scalia, rejected use of Reconstruction-era civil rights legislation as a basis for an injunction against abortion clinic protests in the Washington, D.C., metropolitan area. Provisions of the Civil Rights Act of 1871 (now 42 U.S.C. sec. 1985 [3]) authorized civil actions against those conspiring to deprive people or classes of people "of the equal protection of the laws, or of equal privileges and immunities under the laws," as well as conspiracies "for the purpose of preventing or hindering the constituted authorities of any State or Territory from giving or securing to all persons within such State or Territory the equal protection of the laws." In a concurring and dissenting opinion, Justice Souter concluded that the second clause could reach anti-abortion protests that substantially interfered with the ability of local police to secure all persons equal protection and favored remanding the case to the federal trial court for such a determination. Justice Stevens, joined by Justice Blackmun, filed a dissent declaring the suit to be a valid action against a sex-based conspiracy to interfere with interstate travel, a right long held subject to protection from private as well as governmental interference.[125] And Justice O'Connor, joined by Justice Blackmun, also dissented, finding the anti-abortion protests at issue a class-based conspiracy preventing government officials from guaranteeing equal protection. But Justice Scalia concluded for the majority that the goals of anti-abortion protesters did not reflect animus against women, that the right of abortion was not subject to federal judicial protection from private interference, that any incidental burdens the protests might impose on interstate travel were insufficient to establish a violation of that right, and that the contention that the protests had hindered state authorities was not properly before the Court.[126]

Other attempts to curb anti-abortion protests have enjoyed somewhat greater success on the Court. In a 1994 suit by women's rights organizations and abortion clinic operators against a coalition of anti-abortion groups, the justices, per Chief Justice Rehnquist, unanimously rejected the contention that actions under the federal RICO statute required proof of an economic purpose behind the racketeering activities at issue in a case.[127] That same year, in *Madsen v. Women's Health Center* (1994),[128] the Court upheld certain provisions of a state court injunction against anti-abortion demonstrations in Melbourne, Florida, while striking down other provisions as unconstitutional. Protests directed at a Melbourne clinic and its staff followed a familiar pattern. Demonstrators congregated on the paved portion of the street leading to the clinic and marched in front of driveways. As vehicles approaching the clinic slowed to allow protesters to move out of the way, "sidewalk counselors" approached and attempted to give vehicle occupants anti-abortion literature. The number of protesters varied from a few to four hundred, and the noise included singing, chanting, and the use of loudspeakers and bullhorns. Demonstrators also picketed the residences of clinic employees, shouted at passersby, rang the doorbells of neighbors, provided them with literature identifying particular clinic staff members as "baby killers," and at times confronted the minor children of clinic employees alone in their homes. The noise of the protesters could be heard in the clinic, aggravating the stress of patients and requiring higher levels of sedation, thereby increasing the risks associated with such procedures. As enlarged after an initial order proved inadequate, the injunction issued against the protesters, among other things, excluded them from a 36-foot buffer zone around the clinic entrances and driveway, as well as certain other portions of its property; restricted excessive noisemaking within earshot of patients in the clinic and "images observable" to the patients; prohibited demonstrators within a 300-foot area around the clinic from approaching patients without their consent; and created a 300-foot buffer zone around the residences of clinic staff. The Supreme Court upheld the 36-foot buffer zone around the clinic's entrances and driveway and the antinoise provisions, but invalidated other portions of the injunction, including extension of the 36-foot buffer to other areas than the clinic entrances and driveway.[129]

In his opinion for the Court, the chief justice first rejected the anti-abortion petitioners' claim that the challenged injunction should be subjected to strict judicial scrutiny because it was directed only at their speech and thus, in their view, was content or viewpoint based. Rehnquist conceded that the court order was directed at anti-abortion speech alone, but insisted that the fact "petitioners all share the same view regarding abortion [did] not in itself demonstrate that some invidious content- or viewpoint-based purpose motivated the issuance of the order. It suggests only that those in the group *whose conduct* violated the court's order happen to share the same opinion regarding abortions being performed at the clinic. In short, the fact that the injunction covered people with a particular viewpoint does not itself render the injunction content or viewpoint based."[130]

Although considering the injunction content neutral, Rehnquist was unwilling to subject it to the standard applied to content-neutral statutes regulating expression in public forums—the requirement that the regulation at issue be narrowly tailored to serve a significant governmental interest. Instead, citing differences between injunctions and statutes, including what the Court saw as the "greater risks of censorship and discriminatory application" flowing from the former, he applied a somewhat more rigorous standard, under which such injunctions could "burden no more speech than necessary to serve a significant governmental interest."[131] Applying that standard, he concluded that the injunction at issue furthered a number of significant governmental interests—among them, the state's strong interests in protecting a woman's freedom to seek abortion services, in ensuring public safety and order, in promoting the free flow of vehicular and pedestrian traffic, in protecting property rights, and in residential privacy.[132] But he also held that only a portion of the 36-foot buffer zone and the antinoise requirement burdened no more speech than necessary to accomplish such goals. He noted, for example, that the ban on observable images was not limited to those continuing threats against patients and staff and that the clinic could easily simply pull its curtains to avoid exposure to the protesters' placards.

In his concurring and dissenting opinion, Justice Stevens took issue with the standard of scrutiny applied in the case. In his judgment, injunctions were entitled to a more lenient standard of review than statutes.

As the Court notes legislation is imposed on an entire community, . . . regardless of individual culpability. By contrast, injunctions apply solely to an individual or a limited group of individuals who, by engaging in illegal conduct, have been judicially deprived of some liberty—the normal consequence of illegal activity. Given this distinction, a statute prohibiting demonstrations within 36 feet of an abortion clinic would probably violate the First Amendment, but an injunction directed at a limited group of persons who have engaged in unlawful conduct in a similar zone might well be constitutional.[133]

Justice Scalia, on the other hand, joined by Justices Kennedy and Thomas, contended in another separate opinion that injunctions on expression were "*at least* as deserving of strict scrutiny as a statutory, content-based restriction." Not only could injunctions, like statutes, be designed to suppress ideas rather than achieve any proper governmental end, but even more obviously, asserted Scalia, "they are the product of individual judges rather than of legislatures—and often of judges who have been chagrined by prior disobedience of their orders. The right to free speech should not lightly be placed within the control of a single man or woman." Injunctions were also more potent weapons than statutes, Scalia added, since those subject to a statute can disobey its provisions, claiming its unconstitutionality as an adequate defense, while an injunction could only be challenged in the courts. "Thus, persons subject to a speech-restricting injunction who have not the money or not the time to lodge an immediate appeal face a Hobson's Choice: they must remain silent, since if they speak their First Amendment rights are no defense in subsequent contempt proceedings. This is good reason to require the strictest standard for issuance of such orders."[134]

But Justice Scalia had even more fundamental objections to Chief Justice Rehnquist's opinion for the Court. In declining strictest judicial scrutiny for the injunction at issue in the case, Rehnquist had conceded that it applied only to persons of one persuasion regarding abortion rights. Even so, he rejected the contention that the injunction was content based and thus subject to strict review, emphasizing that only anti-abortion protesters, after all, were interfering with the important governmental interests the injunction was issued to protect. Justice Scalia countered such reasoning, arguing that the injunction had the same vice of "*lend[ing] itself* to use" for "invidious, thought-control purposes" as content-based statutes "having the invidious purpose of suppressing particular ideas." Moreover, while he favored strict scrutiny for injunctions that were "not technically content based," Scalia considered the injunction before the Court "content based (indeed, viewpoint based) to boot." Citing excerpts from the trial record in the case indicating that pro-choice demonstrators had not been arrested for engaging in conduct forbidden anti-abortion protesters by the injunction, Scalia argued that the court order was "tailored to restrain persons distinguished not by proscribable *conduct*," based on their violation of the original injunction, "but by proscribable *views*."[135] Drawing extensively on a videotape of the protests, he also discounted the degree to which they interfered with vehicular or pedestrian traffic and access to the clinic. Later, contrasting the Court's disposition of the case with its decision in a 1982 case involving a black boycott of racially discriminatory businesses in Mississippi,[136] he suggested the outcome might well have been different had the case then before the Court "not involve[d] the disfavored class of abortion protesters."[137] In conclusion, Scalia emphasized that the case was a free speech case, not an abortion suit, and delivered a dire—and, given his views on certain First Amendment issues, somewhat uncharacteristic—warning of the threat the Court's decision posed for free speech rights.

> The proposition that injunctions against speech are subject to a standard indistinguishable from (unless perhaps more lenient in its application than) the "intermediate scrutiny" standard we have used for "time, place, and manner" legislative restrictions; the notion that injunctions against speech need not be closely tied to any violation of the law, but may simply implement sound social policy; and the practice of accepting trial-court conclusions permitting injunctions without considering whether those conclusions are supported by any finding of fact—these latest by-products of our abortion jurisprudence ought to give all friends of liberty great concern.[138]

When in 1997 the Court upheld certain provisions of another injunction directed at anti-abortion protests and struck down other provisions, Scalia again objected to the majority's approach. Speaking through the chief justice, the Court upheld fixed buffer zones requiring protesters to remain fifteen feet away from the doorways, driveways, and driveway entrances of several upstate New York abortion clinics, but concluded that a 15-foot floating buffer zone around people and vehicles entering and leaving the clinics imposed an undue burden on First Amendment rights. The justices also rejected a challenge to a provision permitting two anti-abortion counselors at each site to approach people within the fixed buffer zone, but requiring them to "cease and desist" their counseling if requested by those approached. Both Rehnquist and Scalia resorted to essentially the same reasoning they had applied in earlier litigation, but on this occasion Scalia took particular exception to the cease and desist provision. The trial judge's willingness to allow two abortion counselors to move within the fixed buffer zone was proof to Scalia that the buffer was not designed to assure unfettered access to the clinics, but was really intended to guarantee patients and staff a "right to be left alone" by the protesters. The justice obviously considered that "supposed right" a wholly inadequate justification for the restrictions the injunction had imposed on the protesters' free speech rights.[139]

Expression in Special Environments

The Supreme Court has long adjusted the scope of freedom of expression to the special characteristics of particular settings or environments beyond the public forum context. To a somewhat greater degree than the Court of earlier periods, the Rehnquist Court has extended considerable deference to government in such cases, including those involving students, inmates, and government employees. In Chief

Justice Warren's last year on the bench, a seven-two majority, over Justice Black's particularly vehement dissent, held in *Tinker v. Des Moines School District* (1969)[140] that public school students and teachers retain their First Amendment rights on school property, subject only to regulations prohibiting substantial interferences with the educational process or school discipline. In the last year of Chief Justice Burger's tenure, the Court distinguished *Tinker* in upholding sanctions against a student who delivered a sexually offensive speech during a school assembly.[141] And two years later, in *Hazelwood School District v. Kuhlmeier* (1988),[142] a Rehnquist Court majority substantially undermined *Tinker* in upholding a high school principal's decision to excise articles on student pregnancy and the impact of divorce from the school newspaper. Characterizing the newspaper and its production as a part of the school's educational curriculum rather than a student public forum, the majority, per Justice White, found the principal's decision reasonably related to legitimate interests in protecting the privacy of students and safeguarding younger students from exposure to inappropriate material.

But in dissent, Justice Brennan, joined by Justices Marshall and Blackmun, scored the Court's distinction between curriculum-related and incidental student expression, contending that neither *Tinker* nor subsequent cases drew such lines. Nor would he accept what he dismissed as the "obscure tangle of three excuses" the majority had used to justify greater control over student-sponsored speech than *Tinker* would permit: the school prerogative to control curriculum, the supposed pedagogical interest in shielding high school students "from objectionable viewpoints and sensitive topics," and the school's need to dissociate itself from student expression. Under *Tinker*, asserted Brennan, schools could forbid only that student expression that materially interfered with their curriculum goals, and the censorship in which the principal engaged "in no way further[ed] the curricular purposes of a student *newspaper*, unless one believes that the purpose of the student newspaper is to teach students that the press ought never report bad news, express unpopular views, or print a thought that might upset its sponsors."[143] The notion that a high school audience could be shielded from objectionable viewpoints and sensitive topics struck the justice as an impermissible form of "thought control." And while he agreed that school officials had a legitimate interest in dissociating themselves from student speech, he also contended that means "short of censorship" were clearly available to accomplish that purpose. "The young men and women of Hazelwood East expected a civics lesson" from their work with its student newspaper, Brennan concluded, "but not the one the Court teaches them today."[144]

Decisions dealing with the expression rights of prisoners have followed a similar pattern. In *Procunier v. Martinez* (1974),[145] the Burger Court overturned as unduly broad California regulations providing for the censorship of inmate mail, but Justice Powell, in his opinion for the Court, declined to cast the First Amendment issue in the case in terms of prisoner rights, focusing instead on the rights of persons wishing to correspond with inmates. Later that year, the Court upheld another California regulation prohibiting news media interviews with specific individual inmates against the First Amendment claims of both newspersons and prisoners. But in his opinion for the Court, Justice Potter Stewart concluded that "a prison inmates retains [only] those First Amendment rights that are not inconsistent with his status as a prisoner or with the legitimate penological objectives of the corrections system."[146] The outcome of such cases would depend, added Stewart, on a balancing of the free speech interests of inmates against those of the state in the deterrence of crime, rehabilitation, and security.

Those precedents still stand but, according to Rehnquist Court dissenters, have been construed in a manner unduly deferential to the authority of prison officials. In *Turner v. Safley* (1987),[147] a majority invalidated a penal regulation forbidding inmates to marry other inmates or civilians except for compelling reasons, as determined by the prison superintendent, with a pregnancy or birth of an illegitimate child generally the only circumstances considered sufficiently "compelling" to justify an exemption from the marriage ban. In the same case, however, the Court upheld a regulation that permitted correspondence between immediate family members who were inmates of different institutions within the prison system and between inmates "concerning legal matters," but allowed other inmate correspondence only if prison officials deemed it in the best interests of the parties. Two years later, moreover, a majority in *Thornburgh v. Abbott* (1989)[148] upheld federal Bureau of Prison regulations that generally allowed inmates to receive publications from the "outside," but authorized a warden, applying specific criteria, to reject a publication found "to be detrimental to the security, good order, or discipline of the institution or if it might facilitate criminal activity," so long as no publication was rejected solely because its content was "religious, philosophical, political, social, sexual, or . . . unpopular or repugnant"; no list of excluded publications was established; and each issue of a publication was separately reviewed.

In reviewing the regulations relating to correspondence between inmates and noninmates at issue in *Martinez*, the Burger Court had required that such restrictions must further a substantial interest unrelated to the suppression of expression, such as interests in security, good order, and rehabilitation; the regulation was to be no more restrictive of speech than necessary to further such interests. In *Turner* and *Thornburgh*, however, the Rehnquist Court concluded that post-*Martinez* rulings[149] had laid down a different, more lenient standard of scrutiny to which regulations of inmate rights were to be subjected. Under that standard, such controls need only be "reasonably related to legitimate penological interests."[150] The Court's decision to apply such a standard "rather than *Martinez'* less deferential approach," Justice Blackmun explained for the *Thornburgh* Court, was based on its concern that strict review "simply was not appropriate for consideration of regulations that are centrally concerned with the maintenance of order and security within prisons."[151] The *Martinez* standard was thus to be limited to regulations concerning outgoing personal correspondence from prisoners—controls not centrally concerned with the maintenance of prison order and security.

In a *Thornburgh* dissent joined by Justices Brennan and Marshall, Justice Stevens accused the majority of misreading *Martinez's* fundamental premise. In *Martinez*, wrote Stevens, Justice Powell, "with characteristic wisdom," had rejected application of the strictest, compelling interest standard of scrutiny for censorship of inmate mail, but had also realized that an "'undemanding standard of review' could not be squared with the fact 'that the First Amendment liberties of free citizens are implicated in censorship of prisoner mail.'"[152] Powell thus opted for an intermediate, substantial-interests standard that protected the rights of nonprisoners to correspond with inmates while assuring prison officials adequate authority to further important penological objectives. The *Thornburgh* Court had converted Powell's distinction between the constitutional rights of prisoners and nonprisoners, Stevens argued, into a distinction between the rights of "nonprisoners who are senders and those who are receivers," relegating little constitutional protection to the former.[153] Stevens rejected the Court's reconstruction of *Martinez* and assertion that post-*Martinez* cases had somehow embraced such an approach. Even under the Court's "manipulable 'reasonableness' standard,"[154] moreover, the justice considered the challenged regulations "an impermissibly exaggerated response to security concerns,"[155] based primarily on nothing more than administrative convenience.

Rehnquist Court decisions relating to free speech in another special setting have also provoked debate among the justices. Under the Warren Court's decision in *Pickering v. Board of Education* (1968)[156] and its progeny,[157] government employees enjoy a right of free speech on matters of public concern, but the scope of that right is to be determined in individual cases by balancing the interests of the employee, as a citizen, in commenting against the government's interests in an efficient public service. The Rehnquist Court has followed the *Pickering* approach, but in *Waters v. Churchill* (1994),[158] a four-justice plurality, speaking through Justice O'Connor, concluded that the speech at issue in cases involving public employees discharged for their expression should be what the employer reasonably thought the employee said, not what a judge or jury ultimately concluded was said. Thus, if the employer reasonably concluded that the speech at issue was not a matter of public concern or interfered unduly with agency operations, the firing would be upheld. At the same time, the employer was obliged to conduct an investigation to assure that his conclusions about what the employee had said were reasonable. Justice Scalia, joined by Justices Kennedy and Thomas, read *Pickering*, however, to mean that a public employer's disciplining of an employee violated the First Amendment only if in retaliation for speech on a matter of public concern. Since, in Scalia's judgment, the discharge at issue had not been retaliatory, he found no First Amendment violation. He also objected to the plurality's conclusion that an agency must establish procedural standards to assure that an employer's judgment in a case was reasonable. Earlier cases, he asserted, had held "that public employees who, like Churchill, lack a protected property interest in their jobs, are not entitled to any sort of a hearing before dismissal."[159] In his dissent, on the other hand, Justice Stevens, joined by Justice Blackmun, was just as insistent that a public employee's expression on a matter of public importance could be the basis for discharge only if it was "unduly disruptive,"[160] as determined by a judge or jury, and not because the employer reasonably (but erroneously) reached such a conclusion. "The risk that a jury may ultimately view the facts differently from even a conscientious employer," observed Stevens, was "not, as the plurality would have it, a needless fetter on public employers' ability to discharge their duties. It is the normal means by which our legal system protects legal rights and encourages those in authority to act with care."[161]

Equally vigorous debates have arisen over the proper place of patronage in the hiring and firing of government employees. Expanding upon Burger Court decisions,[162] a majority held in 1990 that personnel decisions based on political affiliation or support were an impermissible infringement on First Amendment rights. While earlier decisions had been limited to discharges and their "substantial equivalent," the Court, speaking through Justice Brennan, held that hirings, promotions, transfers, and recalls based on patronage considerations were equally impermissible, except for positions in which party affiliation was relevant to job performance.[163] In dissent, Justice Scalia, joined by the chief justice and Justice Kennedy, and in part by Justice O'Connor, emphasized the long tradition of patronage in the nation's history and contended "that the desirability of patronage [was] a policy question to be decided by the people's representatives,"[164] rather than a constitutional question for resolution in the courts. Scalia viewed the majority's decision, in fact, as amounting to nothing less than a judicial requirement that a state maintain a civil service system based on merit selection. Even under the sort of balancing test the Court had applied, moreover, the justice considered the advantages of patronage in stabilizing political parties and preventing fragmentation sufficient to outweigh any First Amendment claims raised against its use. In an opinion concurring in the Court's decision, however, Justice Stevens chided Scalia for confusing the judicial obligation to invalidate unconstitutional conditions on public employment with an inappropriate judicial command that a state create a civil service system, and termed "startling" his colleague's contention "that a long history of open and widespread use of patronage practices immunizes them from constitutional scrutiny."[165]

Justice Scalia's generally restrictive view of the expression rights of public employees can also be seen in his dissent from a 1987 decision overturning the discharge of county employee Ardith McPherson for a remark against President Reagan. After hearing of the 1981 attempt on the president's life, McPherson, a data-entry employee in the Harris County, Texas, constable's office, remarked to a coworker, "if they go for him again, I hope they get him." Justice Marshall ruled for a majority that the comment at issue dealt with a matter of public concern; that there was no evidence that the remark interfered with the effective functioning of the office; that the discharge was based on no assessment that her comment reflected a character trait making her unfit to perform her duties, which involved no confidential or policy-making role; and that there was no danger her statement would have a detrimental impact on her relationship with the constable, with whom she apparently had only negligible contact. Noting that McPherson had been summarily discharged for "a single, off-hand comment directed to only one other worker," Justice Powell asserted in a concurrence that it "border[ed] on the fanciful" to suggest that her conduct had lowered office morale, disrupted the workforce, or otherwise undermined the office mission. "The undisputed evidence," observed Powell, "shows that [the respondent] made an ill-considered—but protected—comment during a private conversation, and the Constable made an instinctive, but intemperate, employment decision on the basis of this speech. I agree that on these facts, McPherson's private speech is protected by the First Amendment."[166]

Justice Scalia, joined in dissent by the chief justice and Justices White and O'Connor, accused the majority, however, of "significantly and irrationally" expanding the definition of expression about matters of "public concern" and also argued that a police official's interest in preventing employee statements that approved of violence surely outweighed any First Amendment interests in making such comments. Quoting the constable's counsel, Scalia argued that no law enforcement agency should be obliged to permit its employees to "ride with the cops and cheer for the robbers."[167]

When a majority struck down federal ethics legislation prohibiting lower-level government employees from accepting honoraria for unofficial speeches or writings on matters of public concern, Justice Scalia was again among the dissenters. Applying the *Pickering* balancing test, the majority, per Justice Stevens, found considerable force in the government's asserted concern that federal officers not misuse or give the appearance of misusing their power through the acceptance of compensation for their unofficial and nonpolitical speeches and publications. Stevens concluded, however, that no evidence had been presented that the payment of honoraria had actually led to misconduct on the part of lower-echelon personnel. Several features of the ban also cast doubt, Stevens asserted, on the government's contention that honoraria posed a serious threat to the efficiency of the civil service. Speaking for himself, Scalia, and Justice Thomas, however, Chief Justice Rehnquist complained that the majority had understated the weight to be accorded the government's justifications for the honoraria ban by focusing on atypical situations in which the government's interests were "at their lowest ebb: a mail handler employed by the Postal Service who lectured on the Quaker religion; an areospace engineer who lectured on black history; a microbiologist who reviewed dance performances; and a tax examiner who wrote articles about the environment. . . . Undoubtedly these are members of the class, but they by no means represent the breadth of the class" covered by the ban.[168] At least, contended the chief justice, the Court should have upheld application of the regulation to expression related to an employee's work.

Rehnquist Court decisions in the field of freedom of expression have hardly been confined to the areas that have been the focus of this chapter. Over the years of the chief justice's tenure, shifting majorities have struck down various election regulations raising First Amendment claims, including a federal ban on direct corporation expenditures of funds for elections,[169] a state requirement that political parties conduct closed primaries,[170] Colorado legislation regulating circulation of ballot initiatives,[171] a prohibition on party endorsement of primary candidates,[172] and an Ohio ban on the distribution of anonymous campaign literature.[173] The Court has upheld, though, restrictions on minor party access to the ballot,[174] a ban on write-in votes,[175] laws forbidding vote solicitations and the display of campaign literature near polling places,[176] and antifusion laws prohibiting candidates from appearing on the ballot as the candidate of more than one political party.[177]

In other First Amendment fields, the Court has upheld enhanced sentences for crimes based on racial bias against victims;[178] a federal regulation designating certain foreign films as "political propaganda";[179] a special assessment imposed on agricultural growers, handlers, and processors of fruit trees to pay for generic product advertising;[180] and a news source's recovery of damages for a newspaper's breach of its promise of confidentiality in exchange for the source's information.[181] Struck down, on the other hand, have been a scheme that imposed a sales tax on general interest magazines, while exempting newspapers and religious, professional, trade, and sports journals;[182] damages awarded against a newspaper that published a rape victim's name;[183] New York's "Son of Sam" statute expropriating the income that convicted criminals derived from descriptions of their crimes;[184] a lower court's conclusion that the commercial character of a song parodying a copyrighted title created a presumption against its protection as fair use;[185] and various restrictions on the solicitation of charitable contributions.[186] Just as the Burger Court refused to read special media confidentiality privileges into the First Amendment,[187] moreover, a unanimous Rehnquist Court declined to insulate confidential peer review materials from disclosure in court challenges to university tenure decisions.[188]

Such cases have often provoked considerable debate among the justices. When a majority upheld government designation of certain foreign expressive materials as "political propaganda," for example, Justice Stevens reasoned for the Court that the term was "neutral" and emphasized the lack of evidence that the designation had actually interfered with exhibition of a significant number of foreign-made films. But in a vigorous dissent, Justice Blackmun, joined by Justices Brennan and Marshall, accused the majority of "ignoring the realities of public reaction to [such a] designation" and read the challenged statute's legislative history as demonstrating "that Congress fully intended to discourage communications by foreign agents."[189] Even so, the justices' decisions and opinions in these cases, like those given greater attention in this chapter, have largely simply elaborated on doctrine established in an earlier era, albeit with differences in nuance and doctrinal detail, as well as a shifting of the weights assigned competing governmental and individual interests.

8

Criminal Justice

The Supreme Court's docket of criminal justice cases given full review, like its docket of cases accepted for review in general, has declined considerably since Chief Justice Rehnquist's move to the Court's center seat. Even so, the Court has produced a remarkably wide-ranging array of decisions dealing with the rights of suspects and defendants in criminal cases. In one of several rare cases construing the Constitution's ban on *ex post facto* laws, a unanimous Court in 1987 struck down application of a state's revised sentencing guidelines to a defendant whose crimes occurred before their effective date.[1] In one of its more controversial rulings, however, a majority rejected *ex post facto* and other challenges to the indefinite civil commitment of an habitual child molester scheduled for release from prison. Speaking for a five-four majority in *Kansas v. Hendricks* (1997),[2] Justice Thomas concluded that the civil commitment of a dangerous pedophile comported with substantive due process, did not constitute double jeopardy, and was beyond the reach of the *ex post facto* clause, which applied only to penal statutes. But Justice Breyer, joined by Justices Stevens and Souter, and in part by Justice Ginsburg, dissented. Since the law under which Hendricks was committed did not provide treatment for Hendricks and other inmates until after their release from prison, and only inadequate treatment thereafter, Breyer was convinced that Hendricks's commitment was actually an attempt to subject him to further punishment in violation of the *ex post facto* guarantee.

Among decisions challenging police and prosecutorial misconduct was a 1995 ruling overturning a capital murder conviction on a finding that the state had failed to disclose evidence favorable to the accused, including a computer printout of license numbers of automobiles parked at the crime scene the night of the murder, which did not list the defendant's license, and various statements of a police informant who was never called to testify.[3] But in 1999, the Court narrowly applied *Brady v. Maryland* (1963), the principal precedent governing prosecutorial failure to disclose exculpatory evidence, and upheld a murder conviction and death sentence based on the testimony of an exceptionally confident trial witness who had appeared confused and uncertain in police interviews not shared with the defendant or his counsel. Given other evidence presented in the case, Justice Stevens asserted for the majority, the petitioner had not shown the required "reasonable probability" that his conviction or sentence would have been different had transcripts of the witness's interviews been disclosed. In an earlier case, a majority, speaking through the chief justice over the dissents of Justices Blackmun, Brennan, and Marshall, required a showing of bad faith on the part of police before their failure to preserve semen samples in a child rape case could be the basis for reversal of the defendant's conviction.[4] In other cases involving general due process challenges to criminal proceedings, the justices have upheld a federal bail statute permitting pretrial detention of potentially dangerous suspects;[5] refused to presume that a defendant who received a harsher sentence after retrial than following his original guilty plea and sentence had been the victim of judicial vindictiveness;[6] struck down a trial judge's instructions to a jury as inadequate to satisfy the due process requirement that guilt be established beyond a reasonable doubt,[7] while upholding another judge's instructions against such a claim in a later case;[8] and rejected the due process claim that a general guilty verdict in a multiple-object conspiracy be overturned if the evidence presented by the prosecution was inadequate to support conviction as to one object of the conspiracy.[9]

Numerous decisions, of course, have involved specific procedural guarantees of the Bill of Rights and their Fourteenth Amendment counterparts. In a 1992 case, the justices concluded that an eight-and-a-half-year delay between a federal defendant's arrest and arraignment violated his Sixth Amendment right to a speedy trial.[10] Among the Court's rulings construing the Fifth Amendment's guarantee against double jeopardy have been a 1995 decision permitting a defendant's prosecution on cocaine charges, even though his involvement with the drug had been a basis for increasing his earlier sentence on a marijuana conviction;[11] extension of the double jeopardy guarantee to nonsummary criminal contempt convictions connected with another criminal prosecution;[12] rejection of a challenge to prosecutions for both conspiracy and a substantive offense growing out of the same incident, on the ground that the two crimes were not the "same offense" for double jeopardy purposes;[13] and a ruling upholding a defendant's murder prosecution following his breach of a guilty plea agreement involving the offense.[14] In a 1994 Sixth-Fourteenth Amendment right to counsel case, the justices held that an uncounseled misdemeanor conviction could be used to increase the defendant's sentence in a subsequent case, so long as no prison sentence, for which counsel would have been required,[15] had been imposed in the misdemeanor case. In other counsel cases, the Court upheld a state trial judge's order forbidding a defendant to consult with his attorney during a brief court recess;[16] held void for vagueness a state court rule forbidding lawyers to make statements to the press which they knew, or reasonably should have known, would have a prejudicial impact on a court proceeding;[17] and refused to construe a federal statute as requiring court-appointed lawyers to represent indigent clients in civil cases.[18]

Of several cases involving the Sixth-Fourteenth Amendment right of defendants to confront their accusers, the most controversial have dealt with judicial efforts to shield child sex abuse victims from direct courtroom exposure to alleged offenders. Justice Scalia has led those favoring a broad, literal interpretation of the confrontation right in such cases. When a majority in *Coy v. Iowa* (1988)[19] voted to overturn the conviction of a man charged with sexually assaulting two thirteen-year-old girls, Justice Brennan was originally assigned to write the Court's opinion invalidating the trial court's decision granting a state motion to place a screen between Coy and the girls during his trial. But when Brennan rested his draft essentially on fundamental fairness grounds rather than on the language of the confrontation clause, Justice Scalia circulated an opinion concurring in the judgment on confrontation grounds, and ultimately Scalia, not Brennan, authored an opinion of the Court holding "that the Confrontation Clause guarantees the defendant a face-to-face meeting with witnesses appearing before the trier of fact."[20] Even so, Scalia hardly mustered a majority for the absolutist construction of the confrontation right his *Coy* opinion came close to embracing. Justice Kennedy did not participate in the case, and Justice O'Connor, joined by Justice White, noted in a concurrence that, in her view, an accused's confrontation rights were "not absolute but rather may give way in an appropriate case to other competing interests so as to permit the use of certain procedural devices designed to shield a child witness from the trauma of courtroom testimony."[21] Justice Blackmun, joined by the chief justice in dissent, assumed a similar stance and also pointed to exceptions to the general rule against admission of hearsay evidence and to the obvious acceptance of testimony by blind witnesses as proof an accused's ability to see opposing witnesses was not essential to enjoyment of the right to confrontation.

In *Maryland v. Craig* (1990),[22] the Court's next major child sex abuse case involving confrontation claims, Justice Scalia found himself in dissent. Speaking for the majority, Justice O'Connor held that the confrontation clause did not categorically prohibit a witness's testimony outside the defendant's physical presence and upheld use of closed-circuit television where necessary to protect a child witness from the trauma of a face-to-face meeting. Decrying the Court's failure to safeguard a "categorical" constitutional guarantee of "unmistakable clarity" from the "tide of prevailing current opinion," Justice Scalia, joined by Justices Brennan, Marshall, and Stevens, declared, on the other hand, that the confrontation clause's central purpose "was to assure that none of the many policy interests from time to time pursued by statutory law could overcome a defendant's right to face his or her accusers in court."[23] The majority's conclusion to the contrary was, to Scalia, "rather like saying 'we cannot say that being tried before a jury is an indispensable element of the Sixth Amendment's guarantee of the right to jury trial.'"[24] Nor would Scalia accept the majority's use of exceptions to the rule against hearsay evidence as support for its position. The language of the confrontation clause, he insisted, obviously referred only "to those who give testimony against the defendant at trial" and acknowledged no exceptions to its "irreducible literal meaning," while the Constitution made no explicit reference to the status of hearsay evidence.[25] Concluded Scalia,

> The Court today has applied "interest-balancing" analysis where the text of the Constitution simply does not permit it. We are not free to conduct a cost-benefit analysis of clear and explicit constitutional guarantees, and then to adjust their meaning to comport with our findings. The Court has convincingly proved that the Maryland procedure serves a valid interest, and gives the defendant virtually everything the Constitution guarantees (everything, that is, except confrontation). I am persuaded, therefore, that the Maryland procedure is virtually constitutional. Since it is not, however, actually constitutional I would affirm the [lower court] judgment . . . reversing [the defendant's] conviction.[26]

Justice Scalia also joined Justice Thomas in dissent from one of the Rehnquist Court's more notable decisions involving the treatment of prison inmates. When Louisiana prisoner Keith Hudson suffered minor bruises, facial swelling, loosened teeth, and a cracked denture in an altercation with prison guards, whose supervisor merely told them "not to have too much fun," the inmate filed suit; and a district court awarded damages, concluding that the officers had used excessive force constituting cruel and unusual punishment. The court of appeals reversed, holding that inmates must prove "significant" injury in such cases and that Hudson's injuries were "minor," requiring no medical treatment. The Supreme Court, speaking through Justice O'Connor, overturned the appeals court, declaring that use of excessive physical force against an inmate could constitute cruel and unusual punishment whether or not the prisoner suffered serious injury. Justice Thomas contended in dissent, however, that "a use of force that causes only insignificant harm to a prisoner may be immoral, it may be tortious, it may be criminal, and it may even be remediable under other provisions of the Constitution, but it is not 'cruel and unusual punishment.'"[27]

Based on the majority's reading of precedent,[28] Justice O'Connor concluded that the key question in determining whether prison misconduct constituted cruel and unusual punishment was "whether force was applied in a good-faith effort to maintain or restore discipline, or maliciously and sadistically to cause harm."[29] The extent of injury suffered by an inmate, she added, was simply one factor to be considered in making such a determination. O'Connor also distinguished excessive force cases from earlier rulings holding that uncomfortable prison living conditions and deliberate indifference to inmate health needs amounted to constitutional violations only if the deprivations incurred were "serious."[30] Routine discomfort, she explained, was part of the penalty inmates pay for their crimes, and "society does not expect that prisoners will have unqualified access to health care."[31] The intentional infliction of injury, however, was quite another matter.

Justice Thomas took sharp issue with O'Connor's rationale, arguing convincingly that under prior holdings only the deliberate infliction of *serious* injuries had been held to constitute cruel and unusual punishment. He found equally unconvincing the majority's attempt to distinguish excessive force cases from those involving housing and medical deprivations. Thomas was puzzled that "the seriousness of injury [should] matter when doctors maliciously decide not to treat an inmate, but not when guards maliciously decide to strike him."[32] Thomas readily agreed that the treatment to which Hudson was subjected was not "acceptable conduct." He contended, however, that relief properly lay with the states, not the federal courts, adding, "The Eighth Amendment is not, and should not be turned into, a National Code of Prison Regulation."[33]

However narrow his construction of the Eighth Amendment's guarantee against cruel and unusual punishments, Justice Thomas spoke for a majority in 1998 when, for the first time in its history, the Court invoked the amendment's provision against excessive fines.[34] Customs agents discovered Hosep Kukor Bajakajian attempting to board an international flight carrying $357,144 without complying with a regulation requiring passengers to file a report when transporting more than $10,000 in currency out of the country. Following a bench trial, a district judge found that the entire $357,144 was subject to forfeiture, but concluded that full forfeiture would be grossly disproportionate to the offense and ordered Bajakajian instead to forfeit only $15,000, in addition to serving three years' probation and paying a $5,000 fine. The court of appeals affirmed, and the Supreme Court held that full forfeiture was a grossly disproportionate punishment constituting an excessive fine. The crime, reasoned Justice Thomas, was solely a reporting offense; Bajakajian had a right to transport the currency at issue out of the country so long as he reported his action. His offense was also unrelated to other criminal activity. The maximum possible penalties for violation of the reporting regulation—six months and a $5,000 fine—confirmed, moreover, the minimal culpability attached to the conduct at issue and were dwarfed, of course, by the huge forfeiture the government had sought. Had the offense not been discovered, added Thomas, the government would have been deprived only of the information that the money had left the country. Nor, concluded Thomas, did customs forfeiture statutes enacted around the time of the Eighth Amendment's adoption alter the situation. Those laws had involved full forfeiture but were not considered punishment for a criminal offense, serving instead the remedial purpose of reimbursing the government for losses accruing from evasion of customs duties.

In a dissent joined by Chief Justice Rehnquist and Justices O'Connor and Scalia, Justice Kennedy took issue with virtually every element of the majority's rationale. In disputing Thomas's contention that full forfeiture was grossly disproportionate to Bajakajian's offense, Kennedy argued that the "crime of smuggling or failing to report cash is more serious than the Court is willing to acknowledge," especially given the dependence of drug dealers, money launderers, and tax evaders on smuggled and unreported cash. Characterizing Bajakajian as "far from an innocent victim," Kennedy emphasized, moreover, the highly suspicious nature of the respondent's conduct: his repeated lies to government agents, attempts to persuade others to lie in his behalf, and effort to conceal a large sum of money in a case with a false bottom, even though transporting such an amount from the country was not itself a crime. Bajakajian was an immigrant reared as a member of the Armenian minority in Syria, and the trial judge had attributed his deceit to a distrust of government stemming from "cultural differences." But Kennedy charged that such a "patronizing excuse demean[ed] millions of law-abiding Armenian immigrants by suggesting they cannot be expected to be as truthful as every other citizen."[35] His most fundamental concern, however, was that the Court's abandonment of the deference traditionally accorded legislatures in the imposition of punishments for crimes might lead to greater reliance on mandatory prison sentences in lieu of fines. "Drug lords will be heartened by this," predicted the justice, "knowing the prison terms [unlike forfeitures] will fall upon their couriers while leaving their own wallets untouched."[36]

Albeit perhaps risking snickers from those familiar with his own apparent penchant for adult pornography, Justice Thomas also joined the Court in a rare ruling overturning on entrapment grounds the conviction of a Nebraska farmer for receiving child pornography through the mail. Although reaffirming its requirement that defendants raising an entrapment defense prove that the government placed the seed of the crime in the accused's mind, a five-four Court concluded that the federal sting operation leading to Keith Jacobson's arrest met that demanding standard. Justice Thomas's most frequent voting allies dissented, with Justice O'Connor, joined by Rehnquist and Kennedy, and in part by Scalia, rejecting the majority's finding that Jacobson had no predisposition to commit the crime. But Thomas joined the majority in condemning the government's tactics.[37]

The Rehnquist Court has also decided a number of cases dealing with the harmless error rule, under which criminal convictions infected with a constitutional error are permitted to stand if the prosecution establishes beyond a reasonable doubt that the error did not affect the verdict against the defendant.[38] In a 1988 case, for example, the Court concluded that psychiatric testimony presented in violation of the accused's right to counsel could not be disregarded as harmless error; but a 1999 decision extended the rule to a judge's instructions to jurors that omitted an element of an offense.[39] As in the Warren and Burger eras, however, a substantial number of Rehnquist Court criminal procedure cases have involved search and seizure, interrogation, and capital punishment questions. This chapter focuses on those issue areas and on recent judicial restrictions on the use of peremptory challenges in jury selection.

Search and Seizure

During Chief Justice Burger's tenure, the Supreme Court recognized a number of exceptions to the rule excluding illegally seized evidence from judicial proceedings. A staunch opponent himself of the exclusionary rule except in the most egregious cases, Burger contended that it had no constitutional basis, barred reliable evidence from the truth-determining process, exacted tremendous social costs through the freeing of guilty defendants, and exerted a limited deterrent effect on police misconduct.[40] Although refusing to abandon the exclusionary rule entirely, a Burger Court majority rejected the constitutional underpinnings on which Justice Tom Clark's opinion for the Court in *Mapp v. Ohio* (1961),[41] extending the rule to state cases, had clearly rested. Instead, a majority has characterized the rule as merely a judicially created prophylactic designed primarily to deter police misconduct, future extension of which would depend on the degree to which it served that deterrent function. Applying such an approach, the Court refused to extend the exclusionary rule to grand jury hearings,[42] civil proceedings,[43] and the use of evidence seized by police in a "good faith" reliance on an invalid search warrant,[44] among other contexts.

Every bit as strong a critic of the exclusionary rule as his predecessor, Chief Justice Rehnquist and a majority of his colleagues have continued the process of diminishing the rule's reach. During their years on the Rehnquist Court, Justices Brennan and Marshall remained aggressive defenders of the rule as an integral, if implicit, part of the Fourth Amendment guarantee against unreasonable searches and seizures—a guarantee binding as much on judges who determine the admissibility of evidence as on police who seize it for use in court.[45] In 1990, Justice Brennan spoke for a narrow majority in refusing to extend to questioning of all defense witnesses the prosecutor's authority under earlier cases to introduce illegally obtained evidence in an effort to impeach a defendant's trial testimony. Disputing as "suspect" the assumption that defendants could easily find witnesses willing to engage in "perjury by proxy," Brennan contended that "the mere threat of a subsequent criminal prosecution for perjury [was] far more likely to deter witnesses from intentionally lying on a defendant's behalf than to deter a defendant, already facing conviction for the underlying offense, from lying on his own behalf."[46]

Generally, however, exclusionary rule claims have succumbed to an analysis in which, according to Brennan and Marshall, "the 'costs' of excluding illegally obtained evidence loom to exaggerated heights and . . . the 'benefits' of . . . exclusion are made to disappear with a mere wave of the hand."[47] In 1987, for example, a majority extended the good-faith exception to evidence obtained by police who had relied upon a statute authorizing warrantless administrative searches, and a 1995 ruling further extended the exception to evidence seized illegally as a result of the clerical errors of court employees.[48] Following the departures of Brennan and Marshall, moreover, Justice Stevens appeared to be the only member of the Court opposed to a narrow, flexible conception of the rule.[49]

Usually, though not invariably, the Rehnquist Court has narrowly construed the Fourth Amendment in other issue areas as well. A 1986 Burger Court decision had upheld warrantless airplane surveillance of a marijuana crop from an altitude of 1,000 feet, concluding that a suspect had no reasonable expectation of privacy from such observations.[50] In 1989, the Rehnquist Court extended that decision in approving aerial observations by police in a helicopter 400 feet above a suspect's greenhouse. Speaking for a plurality, Justice White, joined by the chief justice and Justices Scalia and Kennedy, stressed that the helicopter was flying at a legally acceptable altitude from which any member of the public or police could have legally observed the greenhouse. But Justice O'Connor joined the decision only because she found it reasonable to conclude that there was considerable public use of airspace at altitudes of 400 feet and above. Four justices dissented: Justice Brennan, joined by Marshall and Stevens, on the ground that people reasonably expect privacy from such low-flying aircraft, and Justice Blackmun, because he believed the prosecution had the burden of establishing that private helicopters routinely fly over residential property at low altitudes.[51] In other cases, however, the Court also concluded that defendants had no constitutionally protected privacy interest in garbage placed in opaque bags outside their house for trash collectors[52] or in external police observations of the inside of a barn located sixty yards from a house;[53] that the Fourth Amendment was inapplicable to a search by U.S. agents of the Mexican residence of a Mexican citizen with no ties to the United States;[54] that a high-speed police chase resulting in a suspect's death constituted neither a search nor a seizure;[55] that the Fourth Amendment imposed no absolute ban on no-knock entries into dwellings, only a judicial balancing of competing law enforcement and privacy interests to determine the reasonableness of such searches;[56] and that no higher standard was applicable to no-knock entries that resulted in the destruction of property.[57]

The Court has significantly expanded, too, the reach of permissible searches without a warrant. In a 1993 case, the justices agreed that *Terry v. Ohio* (1968),[58] the Warren Court decision permitting warrantless weapons frisks of suspects reasonably believed to be armed and dangerous, could be extended to police seizure of non-threatening contraband detected by touch during a pat-down search. But they refused to uphold seizure of a lump a policeman determined to be crack cocaine only after squeezing, sliding, and otherwise manipulating the contents of the defendant's pocket, which the officer already knew contained no weapon.[59] And a 1991 decision refused to approve the warrantless search of a closed container in an automobile based purely on a suspect's consent to search the vehicle.[60] In a 1987 case, however, a majority extended the warrant exception long allowed administrative inspections of closely regulated businesses to a vehicle dismantling establishment, despite the protests of Brennan, Marshall, and O'Connor that the business in question was hardly a type subject to pervasive governmental control.[61] A later case upheld the detention at an international airport and luggage inspection by Donker, a narcotics detector dog, of a suspect who matched a police drug-courier profile, even though Justice Marshall, joined by Justice Brennan in dissent, convincingly argued that many innocent travelers also met the profile's characteristics.[62] While refusing to uphold as a permissible warrantless search incident to a lawful arrest the search of a suspect's bag when the arrest was based on drug paraphernalia found in the bag,[63] the Court in another cases has approved inspection of passengers' belongings based on probable cause to search a car and a limited protective sweep of a house in connection with an arrest there, on the ground that police had a reasonable basis for believing that a dangerous individual was hiding on the premises.[64] During the 1998-99 term, the Court unanimously rejected a full search of an automobile based solely on issuance of a speeding ticket, but in one of its more controversial rulings, a six-three majority in 1991 upheld random bus searches based on the passengers' consent.[65]

At issue in *Florida v. Bostick* (1991), the bus sweep case, was the Broward County sheriff department's version of an increasingly common police approach to drug interdiction. When the bus on which Bostick was riding made a scheduled stop, two officers boarded, questioned him without any articulable suspicion that he was engaged in illegal activity, then requested his consent to search his luggage for drugs, but advising him that he had a right to refuse their request. After lower courts denied Bostick's motion to suppress cocaine found in his luggage, the Florida supreme court reversed, concluding that a reasonable passenger would not have felt free to leave the bus to avoid questioning and adopting a per se rule invalidating the sheriff department practice of "working the buses." The Supreme Court majority, speaking through Justice O'Connor, rejected the state supreme court's per se approach, adopting instead a more flexible formula, under which the determination of whether Bostick's consent to the search at issue had been coerced would be based on the "totality of the circumstances," and remanding the case to the Florida courts for application of that standard. The state high court had erred, concluded O'Connor, in assuming that a search by armed police of a passenger in the confined quarters of a bus, at a temporary stop, was inherently coercive. Nor would the majority accept Bostick's contention that no reasonable person would freely consent to a search of luggage containing illegal drugs; the reasonable person test, O'Connor asserted, "presupposes an *innocent* person."[66] O'Connor emphasized, moreover, that the police had specifically informed Bostick of his right not to consent to be searched and at no time had threatened him with a gun.

Initially, Justice Souter had filed a partial dissent, objecting to O'Connor's conclusion in a draft of her opinion that no seizure of Bostick had occurred in the case. But when his colleague made appropriate revisions, Souter withdrew his opinion.[67] In a dissent joined by Justices Blackmun and Stevens, however, Justice Marshall insisted that the real issue in the case was "not whether a passenger in respondent's position would have felt free to deny consent to the search of his bag, but whether such a passenger—without being apprised of his rights—would have felt free to terminate the antecedent encounter with the police."[68] Since Bostick was confronted by armed police in the cramped confines of a bus likely to depart the terminal at any moment, Marshall considered the encounter's "coercive quality" undeniable[69] and contended that "a passenger unadvised of his rights and otherwise unversed in constitutional law *has no reason to know* that the police cannot use his refusal to cooperate against him."[70] Marshall would have limited police to questioning only those passengers reasonably believed to be involved in criminal wrongdoing or advising all passengers of their right to refuse questioning "to dispel the aura of coercion and intimidation that pervades such encounters. There is no reason to expect," he asserted, "that such requirements would render the Nation's buses law-enforcement-free zones."[71]

Another decision extended precedents[72] permitting limited warrantless stops of suspects based on the tip of a reliable informer. The anonymous tip at issue in *Alabama v. White* (1990) was completely lacking in indicia of reliability that earlier decisions had required. But since independent police work corroborated a number of details in the tip—that the suspect would leave her apartment at a certain time in a particular vehicle—a majority upheld an investigatory stop of her vehicle. Justice Stevens, joined by Justices Brennan and Marshall, dissented nonetheless, contending that an "anonymous neighbor's prediction about somebody's time of departure and probable destination is anything but a reliable basis for assuming that the commuter is in possession of an illegal substance."[73]

Other rulings involving warrantless vehicle searches have also extended considerable deference to police. A unanimous Court found a Fourth Amendment seizure when trailer park personnel and deputy sheriffs dispossessed owners of a mobile home by tearing it from its foundation and moving it to another lot.[74] But *Michigan Department of State Police v. Sitz* (1990)[75] upheld variable police highway sobriety checkpoints of all motorists as a permissible means of promoting the important societal interest in highway safety, distinguishing such checkpoints from random stops invalidated in an earlier case.[76] Dissenters, on the other hand, emphasized the relatively few arrests (143 of 41,000 motorists) resulting from the system over a period of several years, finding it "inconceivable that a higher arrest rate could not have been achieved by more conventional means."[77] In a 1996 case, a unanimous Court, per Justice Scalia, held that police who stopped a vehicle for possible traffic violations could seize drug evidence, even if the traffic stop was merely a pretext for searching suspected drug dealers.[78] The next year, a seven-two majority, per the chief justice, held that police making a traffic stop could order a passenger as well as the driver from the car and seize cocaine that fell to the ground as the passenger exited the vehicle. That ruling prompted Justices Stevens and Kennedy to object in dissent to the Court's condoning of police seizures of persons "who are not even suspected of having violated the law."[79] In 1989, the justices agreed that police use of a roadblock into which a suspect fatally crashed a stolen car constituted a seizure.[80] But in 1998, as noted earlier, the Court concluded that a high-speed police car chase that resulted in the death of a fleeing suspect constituted neither a search nor a seizure,[81] while a 1991 decision upheld a police search, based on probable cause, of a container in an automobile, even though they lacked probable cause to search the vehicle itself.[82]

Relying heavily in the latter case on *Carroll v. United States*,[83] the 1925 ruling upholding warrantless probable cause searches of vehicles that might otherwise leave a searching officer's jurisdiction, the majority, per Justice Blackmun, overruled a 1979 decision forbidding searches of closed containers in movable vehicles when there was probable cause only to search the container. Under the Court's decision in *United States v. Ross* (1982),[84] a warrantless probable cause search of a vehicle could include search of closed containers found inside. Blackmun could "see no principled distinction . . . between the paper bag found by the police in *Ross* and the paper bag found by the police here. Furthermore, by attempting to distinguish between a container for which the police are specifically searching and a container which they come across in a car, we have impeded law enforcement."[85] By contrast, Justice Stevens, joined by Justice Marshall, declared in dissent that "[n]either evidence uncovered in the course of a search nor the scope of the search conducted can be used to provide *post hoc* justification for a search unsupported by probable cause at its inception."[86]

Rehnquist Court rulings have also expanded the reach of precedents permitting warrantless inventory searches.[87] In one case, the justices struck down an inventory of a locked suitcase in which marijuana was discovered, citing the absence of any police policy governing such searches.[88] But in another case, a seven-two majority upheld seizure of drug evidence during an inventory over the protests of dissenters that the inventory procedures at issue gave undue discretion to the police. Speaking for the Court, Chief Justice Rehnquist relied heavily on police use of established procedures and the absence of a showing that the inventory was merely a pretext for an otherwise impermissible evidence search. Justice Marshall, joined by Justice Brennan, emphasized in dissent, on the other hand, that an officer's determination whether to impound and inventory a vehicle was entirely discretionary, while decisions "as to which areas to search and what sorts of items to inventory" were subject to "little guidance." Noting one policeman's testimony that an officer inventoried "whatever arouses his suspicio[ns]," Marshall charged that "these so-called procedures left the breadth of the 'inventory' to the whim of the individual officer."[89]

Decisions relating to the "plain view" exception to the warrant requirement have followed a similar pattern. During Rehnquist's first term as chief justice, a six-three majority, speaking through Justice Scalia, emphasized that police lawfully in a particular area can seize items (such as stereo equipment) that come within their view only if they have probable cause to believe the items seized are evidence of a crime.[90] In 1990, however, a majority rejected the conclusion of a plurality in an earlier case[91] and upheld the warrantless plain view seizure of evidence, even though its discovery was not inadvertent, despite the forceful contention of Justice Brennan, joined by Justice Marshall in dissent, that "[t]he rationale behind the inadvertent discovery requirement [was] simply that we will not excuse officers from the general requirement of a warrant to seize if the officers know the location of evidence, have probable cause to seize it, intend to seize it, and yet do not bother to obtain a warrant particularly describing that evidence."[92] In another ruling, a divided Court concluded that police who discover evidence in plain view during an initial illegal search can later seize that evidence pursuant to a valid warrant, so long as the basis for issuance of the warrant was wholly independent of the initial illegal entry.[93] Again dissenting, Justice Marshall, joined by Justices Stevens and O'Connor, complained that the majority had failed to provide "sufficient guarantees that the subsequent search was, in fact, independent of the illegal search."[94] But in a separate opinion, Justice Stevens went further, reaffirming his dissent from the Court's 1984 decision in *Segura v. United States*[95]—a dissent Justices Brennan, Marshall, and Blackmun had joined. *Segura* had upheld such searches where the evidence seized was not discovered in the initial, illegal search, but only during the later, valid search. But Stevens "remain[ed] convinced that the *Segura* decision itself was unacceptable because, even then, it was obvious that it would 'provide government agents with an affirmative incentive to engage in unconstitutional violations of the privacy of the home.'"[96] The Court's approval of such searches where the evidence ultimately seized had first been observed during the initial illegal entry was, for Stevens, an even greater cause for alarm.

Challenges to compulsory drug-testing programs have produced mixed reactions in the Rehnquist Court. In two important 1989 cases, *Skinner v. Railway Labor Executives' Association*[97] and *National Treasury Employees Union v. Von Raab*,[98] shifting majorities upheld drug testing of certain railroad employees following major train accidents and incidents or the violation of safety rules, as well as tests for federal customs employees seeking promotion to positions involving drug interdiction, the carrying of firearms, or handling of classified materials. Speaking for the majority in the railway case, Justice Kennedy conceded that the drug and alcohol testing at issue constituted a search and seizure. Balancing, however, the important interests in railway safety against what the Court considered to be the relatively limited threats to employees' legitimate privacy expectations in a heavily regulated industry, Kennedy concluded that the Fourth Amendment required neither a warrant nor even individualized suspicion of those tested. Citing the national crisis in law enforcement created by narcotics smuggling and the corresponding need for physically fit enforcement personnel of unimpeachable integrity and judgment, Kennedy reached the same conclusion in upholding application of the customs regulations to drug inter-diction agents and employees carrying firearms. But the Court remanded for further proceedings the testing requirement for personnel who would handle classified materials since it was unclear whether certain of those employees were likely to have access to sensitive information.

Dissenting in both cases, Justice Marshall, joined by Justice Brennan, scored the majority for "tak[ing] its longest step yet toward reading the probable-cause require-ment out of the Fourth Amendment."[99] For even minimal intrusions on personal privacy, asserted Marshall, prior cases had required some showing of "individualized suspicion to justify the search," and in his judgment, probable cause was "an indis-pensable prerequisite for [the sort of] full-scale search" that mandatory drug testing constituted.[100] Marshall and Brennan were not the only dissenters, moreover. Justice Scalia joined Kennedy's opinion upholding the railway regulations because, as he put it in the customs case, "the demonstrated frequency of drug and alcohol use by the targeted class of employees, and the demonstrated connection between such use and grave harm, rendered the search a reasonable means of protecting society." Joined by Justice Stevens in the customs case, by contrast, Scalia dissented, "because neither fre-quency of use nor connection to harm [was] demonstrated or even likely" there. Instead, for Scalia the customs rules were simply "a kind of immolation of privacy and human dignity in symbolic opposition to drug use."[101] Out of 3,600 employees tested, no more than five had tested positive for drugs. In fact, there had not been "*even a single instance* in which any of the speculated horribles" against which the program was designed to protect "actually occurred: an instance, that is, in which the cause of bribe-taking, or of poor aim, or of unsympathetic law enforcement, or of compromise of classified information, was drug use."[102] And in Scalia's judgment, "symbolism, even symbolism for so worthy a cause as the abolition of unlawful drugs, [could not] invalidate an otherwise unreasonable search."[103]

In 1995, however, Justice Scalia spoke for a majority in upholding drug testing of high school athletes. Finding no clear practice approving or disapproving such searches at the time of the Fourth Amendment's adoption, Scalia balanced compet-ing constitutional and governmental interests. Weighing the important social inter-est in deterring student drug use against the attenuated privacy expectations of stu-dent athletes accustomed to communal undressing and what the justice viewed as the limited intrusion upon personal privacy involved in the collection of urine sam-ples under conditions virtually identical to those typically encountered in public restrooms, Scalia found no Fourth Amendment violation. Justice Ginsburg con-curred with the Court, but only on the assumption that its ruling did not extend to all students rather than student athletes alone. Justice O'Connor objected in dissent, on the other hand, to this further extension of permissible suspicionless searches without a warrant.[104]

Mandatory drug testing of Georgia political candidates prompted a different response from the Court. Speaking for an eight-one majority in 1997, Justice Gins-burg conceded that *Skinner* and other cases had recognized exceptions to the general constitutional requirement that searches be based on individualized suspicion of wrongdoing—exceptions justified by "special" governmental needs apart from the general interest in effective law enforcement. She also agreed that the urinalysis required of political candidates under the system at issue constituted a relatively limited intrusion on personal privacy. She concluded, however, that the state had failed to show any substantial interest the regulation effectively served, especially since candidates selected their own test date and thus could easily avoid detection. In his lone dissent, however, Chief Justice Rehnquist declared, "[S]urely the State need not wait for a drug addict, or one inclined to use drugs illegally, to run for or actually become Governor before it installs a prophylactic mechanism."[105]

Interrogations and Confessions

Under the Warren Court's decision in *Miranda v. Arizona* (1966),[106] custodial police questioning of suspects could take place only after they were informed that they had a right to remain silent and not submit to questioning, that they had a right to counsel during any interrogation they permitted, that they were entitled to court-appointed counsel if indigent, and that their statements would be recorded for possible use as evidence. Statements secured in violation of *Miranda* were held to have been inherently coerced and excluded from use in court. The five-four *Miranda* decision, like the Fourth Amendment exclusionary rule, proved extremely controversial, with members of the Supreme Court among its most caustic critics. As with the Fourth Amendment rule, too, the Burger Court relegated *Miranda* to the status of a judicially created, nonconstitutional set of standards designed primarily to deter police misconduct and approved numerous exceptions to its application. The justices held, among other things, that confessions secured in violation of *Miranda* or related requirements could be used to impeach a defendant's trial testimony,[107] to secure other prosecution evidence,[108] and to locate evidence that would have been "inevitably discovered" anyway.[109] The Court further held that the *Miranda* warnings did not apply to grand jury proceedings, which lacked, in the Court's view, the inherently coercive atmosphere of custodial police interrogations.[110]

The Rehnquist Court has generally followed a similar pattern in resolving *Miranda* and related interrogation issues. In a 1995 decision, a majority, per Justice Ginsburg, refused to presume the validity of a state court determination that a defendant convicted of murdering his former wife had not been "in custody" at the time he confessed to the crime, leaving that issue for independent review by a federal court in a habeas corpus proceeding. Justice Thomas, joined by the chief justice, emphasized in dissent, on the other hand, gruesome details of the brutal stabbing death and asserted that "the Alaska trial judge—who first decided [the] question almost a decade ago—was in a far better position . . . to determine whether [the petitioner] was 'in custody' for purposes of *Miranda*."[111] Earlier, a divided Court had overturned on traditional coerced confession grounds the statements a suspected child murderer, in prison on an unrelated charge, had given an inmate undercover informant who promised him protection from other inmates in exchange for the truth about his crime.[112] Building on a 1981 ruling,[113] a majority in 1990 invalidated the conviction of a defendant questioned by a deputy sheriff in an interview he was compelled to attend without his lawyer, even though his earlier interrogation by federal officers had ended when he invoked his right to counsel.[114] Previously, moreover, the Court had concluded that a suspect who invoked his right to counsel could not be subjected to further questioning without counsel, even in the context of a separate interrogation by police unaware of the suspect's request.[115]

In the main, however, Rehnquist Court interrogation rulings have sided with police and prosecutors. Distinguishing *Payton v. New York* (1980),[116] a Burger Court decision overturning warrantless home arrests except under exigent circumstances, a 1990 majority upheld a statement secured from a suspect at a police station following his illegal arrest in his home. Justice White emphasized for the Court that *Payton* was designed to protect the physical integrity of the home, while Justice Marshall, joined by Justices Brennan, Blackmun, and Stevens, declared in dissent that the incriminating statements were "the fruits of [the] illegal entry" and scored the majority's assumption that the "physical exit [of police] from the suspect's home *necessarily* breaks the causal chain between the illegality [of the arrest] and any subsequent statement by the suspect."[117] In other cases, majorities have held that a police officer's statement that a suspect would be appointed an attorney "if and when he went to court" was sufficient to satisfy *Miranda*;[118] that a distraught wife's conversation with her husband, a suspect in the killing of their son, did not amount to interrogation even though recorded by police and conducted in their presence;[119] that a suspect need not be aware of all the crimes about which he was to be questioned before waiving his right to silence;[120] that a suspect's refusal to make written statements to police without his attorney present did not preclude further discussion with police, during which the suspect agreed to oral statements;[121] that a prosecutor's single question to a defendant about his postarrest silence, to which the trial judge sustained a defense objection, did not violate a Burger Court ruling[122] forbidding a prosecutor's use of such silence to impeach the defendant's credibility;[123] that a statement secured in violation of a defendant's right to counsel could be used to impeach his trial testimony;[124] that an accused's request for counsel at a bail hearing for a crime with which he had been charged did not constitute an invocation of his *Miranda* counsel right precluding police interrogation on unrelated, uncharged offenses;[125] and that an undercover agent posing as a fellow inmate was not required to give *Miranda* warnings to another prisoner before asking him incriminating questions.[126] In a related field, moreover, the Court held that a per se rule against admission of polygraph evidence in court-martial proceedings did not violate the Fifth or Sixth Amendment rights of the accused to present a defense.[127]

While joining the decision in the polygraph case, Justice Kennedy, joined by Justices O'Connor, Ginsburg, and Breyer, filed a concurrence questioning the wisdom of a per se rule against admission of such evidence, thought that a later case "might present a more compelling [basis] for introduction of [polygraph] testimony,"[128] and expressed agreement with various elements of Justice Stevens's dissent in the case. But Stevens dissented alone, attacking, among other things, both the majority's arguable break with precedent condemning as unconstitutional rules excluding entire categories of testimony on the basis of presumed unreliability[129] and inconsistencies between the military's per se rejection of polygraph evidence and its heavy reliance on such tests as an investigatory tool.

Until their departures from the Court, however, Justices Brennan and Marshall were the most frequent critics of rulings recognizing exceptions to the *Miranda* doctrine and related limits on interrogation rights. On a rare occasion when Justice Brennan authored the Court's opinion in such a case, moreover, he did so for strategic purposes, and with apologies to his colleagues. In *Pennsylvania v. Muniz* (1990),[130] the Court reviewed claims growing out of a drunk-driving conviction. Speaking for a majority, with Justice Marshall alone in dissent, Justice Brennan concluded that Muniz's slurred responses to police questions before he was given the *Miranda* warnings had not been testimonial and thus were not subject to the right against compulsory self-incrimination. But he also held that Muniz's inaccurate answer to a question regarding his sixth birthday constituted incriminating testimonial evidence since the content of his response supported evidence of his confused mental state. Speaking for himself and three other members of the Court, Brennan further concluded that a number of questions police asked Muniz were "routine booking questions" exempted from *Miranda*'s reach, while Chief Justice Rehnquist, joined by three other justices, argued that *Miranda* was inapplicable to such questions because they were not intended to elicit testimonial responses.

In an early draft of his opinion, Brennan had expressed "substantial doubt" that many of the questions the police had asked Muniz fell within the booking exception to *Miranda* and had proposed remanding the case for further proceedings on that question.[131] Brennan had also indicated that police must demonstrate an "administrative need" to ask such questions before they could be included within *Miranda*'s booking exception. When Justice O'Connor objected and noted that she was "concerned that an 'administrative need' test for booking questions [would] burden the States' routine law enforcement procedures,"[132] Brennan revised the opinion. And when one of Brennan's clerks informed him that Justice Marshall might circulate a dissent challenging the booking exception altogether, Brennan wrote his frequent ally, emphasizing that he, too, of course, had "great difficulty acknowledging . . . any exceptions to *Miranda*," but that *Muniz* had "posed a troubling strategic choice." Every other justice recognized the booking exception, and at least five wanted it "to be defined broadly." Had he drafted an opinion suggesting that no such exception to *Miranda* should be recognized, five or more of their colleagues would have written separately, and Brennan would have lost control over the breadth of the exception the Court was willing to embrace. "I made the strategic judgment, therefore," he explained to Marshall, "to concede the existence of an exception to use my control over the opinion to define the exception as narrowly as possible, suggesting that the exception may not apply here and remanding on [that] issue. As you will recall, Sandra forced my hand by threatening to lead the revolution, and therefore I felt it necessary to amend the draft so as to avoid the remand." But his opinion, Brennan insisted, still described the booking exception "in narrow terms, and in my view it leaves the law no worse off than it already was before, since every circuit has already found such an exception to exist." Brennan would understand should Marshall choose to file a dissent and was "quite prepared to take [his] lumps." He was concerned, however, that Marshall's criticisms of the booking exception might prompt lower courts to give it a broader reading than Brennan intended. "This would defeat the strategic judgment to concede only what is absolutely necessary to prevent Sandra and the others from taking over this point."[133]

When Justice Marshall circulated a dissent, Justice Brennan asked him to make several modifications, but with limited success.[134] In his final opinion, Marshall favored suppressing all Muniz's responses.[135]

Decline of the Peremptory Challenge

In another field of criminal justice, the Supreme Court has long invoked the equal protection guarantee to overturn criminal convictions based on systematic discrimination against members of the defendant's racial group in jury selection.[136] During Chief Justice Burger's tenure, moreover, the justices construed the due process guarantee to confer upon defendants of whatever race or gender the right to a jury potentially composed of a random cross-section of the community, applying such an approach to overturn the conviction of a white defendant based on discrimination against blacks in jury selection,[137] as well as a male defendant's conviction under a jury selection scheme that discriminated against women.[138] On the eve of Chief Justice Rehnquist's elevation to the Court's center seat, the justices went further, rejecting portions of the Warren Court's decision in Swain v. Alabama (1965)[139] by holding in Batson v. Kentucky (1986)[140] that prosecutors must provide racially neutral explanations for their peremptory challenges to prospective jurors of the defendant's race.

Traditionally, peremptory strikes, unlike for-cause challenges of prospective jurors, had been by definition subject to no limits, permitting lawyers to eliminate jurors they found unacceptable, whatever the motivation. Consistent with that approach, the Swain Court held that a prosecutor's use of the peremptory challenge could be invalidated as discriminatory only if that prosecutor, "in case after case, whatever the circumstances, whatever the crime and whoever the defendant or the victim may be, is responsible for the removal of Negroes who have been selected as qualified jurors by the jury commissioners and who have survived challenges for cause, with the result that no Negroes ever serve on petit juries."[141] Not surprisingly, a number of lower courts read Swain to require proof of the repeated striking of blacks over a number of cases to establish an equal protection violation.[142] Justice Powell concluded for the Batson majority, however, that the Swain standard had placed a "crippling burden of proof" on defendants, a burden inconsistent with the approach embraced in later cases for assessing a prima facie case of discrimination under the equal protection guarantee.[143] Under principles embraced in those rulings, wrote Powell, a defendant could establish a prima facie case of discriminatory use of peremptory challenges based solely on evidence drawn from the defendant's trial. To establish such a case, defendants were obliged to show only that they were members of a cognizable racial group, that the prosecutor had exercised peremptory challenges to remove jurors of the defendant's race, and that such facts as well as any other relevant circumstances raised an inference that the prosecutor had used peremptories to exclude prospective jurors on racial grounds. Once that prima facie showing had been made, the burden of proof would shift to the prosecutor to present a racially neutral explanation for the challenges.

In separate dissents, Chief Justice Burger and Justice Rehnquist emphasized the peremptory challenge's long history and rejected the contention that its use reflected the sort of racial bias against which the equal protection clause was directed. Observed Rehnquist,

> In my view, there is simply nothing "unequal" about the State's using its peremptory challenges to strike blacks from the jury in cases involving black defendants, so long as such challenges are also used to exclude whites in cases involving white defendants, . . . and so on. This case-specific use of peremptory challenges by the State does not single out blacks, or members of any other race for that matter, for discriminatory treatment. Such use of peremptories is at best based upon seat-of-the-pants instincts, which are undoubtedly crudely stereotypical and may in many cases be hopelessly mistaken. But as long as they are applied across-the-board to jurors of all races and nationalities, I do not see . . . how their use violates the Equal Protection Clause.[144]

Justice Marshall was hardly persuaded. In a concurrence supporting total elimination of the peremptory challenge as the only effective way to eliminate the racial bias inherent in its use, Marshall charged that "'seat-of-the-pants instincts' as to how particular jurors will vote . . . may often be just another term for racial prejudice," adding, "Even if all parties approach the Court's mandate with the best of conscious intentions, that mandate requires them to confront and overcome their own racism on all levels—a challenge I doubt all of them can meet."[145]

A number of Rehnquist Court decisions have elaborated on *Batson*'s restriction of the peremptory challenge. A 1987 majority, over the chief justice's lone dissent, applied *Batson* to all cases then pending on appeal,[146] while a 1991 ruling extended *Batson* to civil cases[147] and a ruling the next year applied it to an accused's use of peremptories.[148] In 1995, on the other hand, the justices concluded that a race-neutral explanation required to offset the presumption of bias in a *Batson* hearing need not be persuasive, or even plausible, and accepted a prosecutor's explanation that a black male had been challenged not on the basis of race, but because he had long, unkempt hair, a moustache, and a beard.[149] And in a 1990 decision, a five-four majority, per Justice Scalia, rejected a white defendant's claim that a prosecutor's use of peremptories to exclude black jurors violated the Sixth-Fourteenth Amendment representative cross-section requirement recognized in earlier cases, while Justice Marshall argued in dissent that "what is denominated a 'jury' is not a 'jury' in the eyes of the Constitution unless it is drawn from a fair cross section of the community," and that racial use of the peremptory challenge violated that principle, whatever the race of the defendant and the excluded jurors.[150]

When a majority later invoked the equal protection guarantee in permitting white defendants to raise *Batson* challenges, it was Scalia's turn to dissent. Citing precedent permitting parties in a case to assert the constitutional rights of other persons,[151] the Court, speaking through Justice Kennedy, granted a white defendant standing to apply *Batson* in asserting the third-party equal protection claims of prospective black jurors struck by the prosecution because of their race. But Justice Scalia, joined by Chief Justice Rehnquist, contended in dissent that peremptory challenges to black jurors, unlike systematic racial discrimination in jury selection, "implie[d] nothing more than the undeniable reality (upon which the peremptory strike system is largely based) that all groups tend to have particular sympathies and hostilities—most notably, sympathies towards their own group members. Since that reality is acknowledged as to *all* groups, and forms the basis for peremptory strikes as to *all* of them, there is no implied criticism or dishonor to a strike."[152] Race-based peremptory challenges, in Scalia's view, thus did not reflect racial animus against black jurors, and the justice was at a loss to understand what third-party rights a white defendant could assert to invoke *Batson*.

Given precedent prohibiting gender discrimination in the selection of the jury venire, or jury pool, efforts to extend *Batson* to sex-based peremptories were inevitable. In *J. E. B. v. Alabama ex rel. T. B.* (1994),[153] the Court obliged. During the petitioner's paternity and child support trial, the state had used nine of its ten peremptory challenges to remove male jurors, and the trial court empaneled an all-female jury, rejecting application of *Batson* in such proceedings. Speaking for a six-three majority, Justice Blackmun reversed, dismissing the state's claim that male jurors might be more sympathetic and receptive to the arguments of a man in a paternity suit with the blunt assertion, "We shall not accept as a defense to gender-based peremptory challenges 'the very stereotype the law condemns.'"[154] Although forbidding peremptories based "solely" on gender, however, Blackmun approved their use to remove members of any group or class subject only to "rational basis" protection under the equal protection guarantee,[155] as well as strikes based on characteristics disproportionately associated with one gender (such as military experience), so long as such challenges were not mere pretexts for gender-based strikes.

In a brief opinion concurring in the judgment, Justice Kennedy emphasized that the equal protection guarantee was intended to protect individual rather than group rights and declared that "[n]othing would be more pernicious to the jury system than for society to presume that persons of different backgrounds go to the jury room to voice prejudice. . . . The jury pool must be representative of the community, but that is a structural mechanism for preventing bias, not enfranchising it."[156] While also concurring, Justice O'Connor itemized the costs of extending *Batson* to gender-based peremptories, including lengthier trials, an increase in the number and complexity of appeals based on jury selection challenges, and the inability of litigants to act even on accurate gender-based assumptions about juror attitudes.

Not surprisingly, Chief Justice Rehnquist, who had dissented in *Batson*, opposed its extension to gender-based peremptory challenges. Emphasizing that racial classifications were considered "inherently suspect" and subject to strict judicial scrutiny, while classifications based on sex were "judged under a heightened, but less searching standard of review,"[157] Rehnquist contended that such differences also meant "the balance should tilt in favor of peremptory challenges when sex, not race, is the issue," adding, "The two sexes differ, both biologically and, to a diminishing extent, in experience. It is not merely 'stereotyping' to say that these differences may produce a difference in outlook which is brought to the jury room. Accordingly, use of peremptory challenges on the basis of sex is generally not the sort of derogatory and invidious act which peremptory challenges directed at black jurors may be."[158]

Justice Scalia's dissent, joined by the chief justice and Justice Thomas, was characteristically biting. Since the case involved a male's challenge to an all-female jury, Scalia dismissed as "quite irrelevant" passages in the majority opinion "demonstrat[ing] . . . how thoroughly up-to-date and right-thinking we Justices are in matters pertaining to the sexes (or as the Court would have it, the genders), and how sternly we disapprove the male chauvinist attitudes of our predecessors."[159] He challenged as "patently false," moreover, Blackmun's equation of gender-based peremptories and the exclusion of women from jury venires, declaring, "Women were categorically excluded from juries because of doubt that they were competent; women are stricken from juries by peremptory challenges because of doubt that they are well disposed to the striking party's case. . . . There is discrimination and dishonor in the former, and not in the latter."[160] Since any strike bottomed on group characteristics could be considered based on a "stereotype," the justice questioned whether any peremptory could logically escape *Batson*'s reach; but even assuming the "theoretically boundless" *Batson* principle would be limited to classifications traditionally subjected to heightened scrutiny, he considered the Court's "quest for 'reasoned peremptories'" a contradiction in terms. The peremptory challenge, asserted Scalia, "loses its whole character when (in order to defend against 'impermissible stereotyping' claims) 'reasons' for strikes must be given. The right of peremptory challenge "'is, as Blackstone says, an arbitrary and capricious right; and it must be exercised with full freedom, or it fails of its full purpose.'" . . . The loss of the real peremptory will be felt most keenly by the criminal defendant . . . , whom we have until recently thought 'should not be held to accept a juror, apparently indifferent, whom he distrusted for any reason or for no reason.'"[161]

Batson's critics make a convincing case. It is interesting, however, that they are also among the justices most vehement in their opposition to affirmative action programs, to be considered in the next chapter. Affirmative action policies, after all, are obviously not based on any negative stereotypes about the white males they are alleged to victimize, just as racial, gender, and other peremptory challenges reflect no personal animus toward those they strike, only crude hunches about how persons with common characteristics may behave as jurors. Yet *Batson*'s critics on the Court have helped to form majorities subjecting affirmative action programs to strict judicial scrutiny, while rejecting such review, or indeed any review, of peremptories. *Batson*'s critics no doubt would cite the peremptory challenge's long history of unfettered use to justify the distinction. Even so, the contrast in their positions is not without irony.

Capital Punishment

The Burger Court resolved a number of major issues in the continuing constitutional debates over the death penalty. Over the objections primarily of Justices Brennan and Marshall, the Court refused to conclude that a death sentence is per se unconstitutional for first-degree murder under the Eighth-Fourteenth Amendment ban on cruel and unusual punishments, resting its position on what it considered legitimate and important governmental interests in retribution and deterrence.[162] At the same time, a somewhat different majority held that capital punishment is unconstitutional if arbitrarily or capriciously imposed; rejected as invalid under that standard both mandatory death sentences[163] and those left to the unbridled discretion of the judge and jury;[164] and upheld provisions limiting their discretion through such devices as separate penalty hearings, automatic appeals, and requirements conditioning imposition of a death sentence on a finding of one or more statutorily specified aggravating circumstances. By rejecting the death penalty in rape cases, at least those involving adult victims, the justices also appeared to limit its use largely, if not entirely, to murder cases.[165] And another ruling struck down state limitations on the types of mitigating factors that could be considered in determining a capital defendant's fate, despite the concern of some that such a requirement would leave sentencing once again to the judge's or jury's whim.[166]

Rehnquist Court decisions, like those of the Burger Court, have both accepted and declined death penalty claims. In certain cases, the justices have found unconstitutional vagueness in a state's specification of aggravating circumstances,[167] while rejecting such challenges in other cases.[168] Reaffirming the Burger Court's opposition to restrictions on the sorts of mitigating factors that can be considered in the penalty phase of capital cases, the Court has struck down such limits,[169] as well as a scheme precluding juror consideration of any mitigating circumstances unless the jury unanimously agreed on its presence in a particular case.[170] But a majority, over the dissents of Justices Brennan and Marshall, and partial dissents by Justices Blackmun and Stevens, upheld the death sentence in murder cases for defendants other than the triggerman where they were major participants in a felony resulting in murder and had acted with reckless disregard for the victim's life.[171] And in another case, the Court rejected a defendant's claim to an Eighth Amendment right to an instruction to jurors that they could consider their residual doubts about the defendant's guilt a mitigating circumstance during penalty deliberations.[172]

In arguably the most significant cases, however, a majority has largely rejected the claims of death row inmates. First, while opposing execution of defendants less than sixteen at the time of their crimes, the Court has approved death sentences for those sixteen or older. In 1988, the Court overturned the death sentence of a defendant who was fifteen at the time of his offense. A plurality, speaking through Justice Stevens, found a national consensus against capital punishment in such cases, with Stevens defending his position by citing the modern rarity of death sentences for such defendants, the decision of the eighteen states that had legislated on the issue to establish sixteen as the minimum age, the reduced culpability of juveniles relative to adult offenders, and the doubtful deterrent effect of the death penalty on younger defendants.[173] But Justice O'Connor, who provided the fifth vote in the case, favored stronger evidence of a national consensus condemning such executions, noting, among other things, that the federal government and nineteen states had authorized capital punishment without setting a minimum age, while also providing for some fifteen-year-olds to be prosecuted as adults. Because the available evidence suggested the consensus on which the plurality rested its decision, however, O'Connor concluded that defendants committing capital crimes before age sixteen should be subjected to death sentences only under statutes specifying a minimum age for execution. In dissent, on the other hand, Justice Scalia, joined by the chief justice and Justice White, disputed the existence of any national consensus holding "that no criminal so much as one day under 16, after individualized consideration of his circumstances, including the overcoming of a presumption that he should not be tried as an adult, can possibly be deemed mature and responsible enough to be punished with death for any crime," and found no "plausible basis" for making such an assumption.[174] The risk of construing the constitutional guarantee against cruel and unusual punishments through an assessment of evolving societal standards of decency, asserted Scalia, was "that it is all too easy to believe that evolution has culminated in one's own views." To avoid such risks, he added, the Court looked to "objective signs of how today's society views a particular punishment."[175] Viewing legislative enactments as the "most reliable objective signs" of societal opinion, Scalia rejected the plurality's consensus thesis. Nor did the extreme rarity of executions for offenders below sixteen weaken his resolve. After all, he noted, in 1927, when the rate of total executions was almost five times that of the post-1950 period, no juvenile under sixteen at the time of his offense had been executed in nearly seventeen years. To the plurality's use of statistics demonstrating a decline in juvenile executions in other nations, moreover, Scalia responded that "[w]e must never forget that it is a Constitution for the United States of America that we are expounding."[176]

When the Court the next year confronted a statute permitting execution of defendants sixteen or older, a five-four majority upheld the death sentence for an accused who was seventeen at the time he robbed, raped, sodomized, and murdered a gas station attendant.[177] Again, Justice O'Connor cast the controlling vote, agreeing that no national consensus forbade imposition of the death penalty on sixteen- or seventeen-year-old murderers, but also insisting that courts must determine whether the death sentence was proportional to the extent of the defendant's blameworthiness in individual cases. Speaking for a plurality that also included the chief justice and Justices White and Kennedy, Justice Scalia countered that judicial determinations of societal standards should be based solely on state and federal statutes and the behavior of prosecutors and juries, rather than on public opinion polls, interest groups, and professional associations. He further argued that the sort of proportionality analysis O'Connor had embraced was appropriate only when there was also objective evidence, in law or jury decisions, establishing a social consensus against the penalty at issue.

Justice Brennan, joined in dissent by Justices Marshall, Blackmun, and Stevens, took sharp issue with the plurality's approach to resolving the constitutionality of juvenile executions. In Brennan's judgment,

the rejection of the death penalty for juveniles by a majority of the States, the rarity of the sentence for juveniles, both as an absolute and a comparative matter, the decisions of respected organizations in relevant fields that this punishment is unacceptable, and its rejection generally throughout the world, offer[ed] . . . a strong grounding for the view that [juvenile executions] are not constitutionally tolerable.[178]

He also condemned juvenile executions as clearly disproportionate to their level of culpability. In many laws distinguishing juveniles and adults, legislatures had surely recognized differences in their levels of responsibility, and Brennan seriously doubted that individualized consideration of juvenile culpability could "ensure that only exceptionally mature juveniles, as blameworthy for their crimes as an adult, are sentenced to death."[179] Nor could he and other dissenters agree that juvenile executions would serve the governmental interests in deterrence and retribution that a majority had invoked in upholding capital punishment for adults. Clearly, he asserted, a punishment "disproportionate to the offender's blameworthiness by definition [was] not justly deserved."[180] Nor, given their profound convictions about their own omnipotence and immortality, was a death sentence likely to exert a significant deterrent effect on juvenile offenders. Juvenile executions thus not only violated contemporary standards of decency and were disproportionate to the diminished culpability of minors; they also served no legitimate function of criminal punishment.

On the same day the Court ruled on juvenile executions, a majority, in *Penry v. Lynaugh* (1989),[181] upheld imposition of the death sentence on a mentally retarded defendant who had been abused as a child and was considered by a psychologist to have the mental age of a six-and-a-half-year-old, but remanded the case for further proceedings based on the trial judge's failure to instruct jurors they could consider mitigating evidence of the defendant's mental retardation and history of abuse as a child in deciding whether to impose the death sentence. Relying on legislative enactments and the conduct of sentencing juries rather than opinion surveys and related measures, Justice O'Connor concluded for the majority that there was insufficient evidence of a national consensus forbidding execution of mentally retarded murderers capable of appreciating the wrongfulness of their actions. Writing for herself, moreover, O'Connor agreed that retardation was a factor that might diminish a defendant's culpability and, in its most severe form, might even completely absolve a person of criminal liability. She refused to embrace the proposition, however, that execution of the mentally retarded was inherently contrary to the constitutional guarantee against cruel and unusual punishments.

At the penalty phase of the defendant's trial, the judge instructed jurors to consider all evidence introduced at trial in determining whether the accused had acted deliberately and with a reasonable expectation of causing the victim's death, whether there was a probability he would be a continuing threat to society, and whether the killing was an unreasonable reaction to any provocation by the victim. But the judge had denied the defendant's request for instructions defining the terms of these issues and authorizing a grant of mercy based upon mitigating circumstances. In requiring a remand, Justice O'Connor, like the Texas court of criminal appeals, had found these instructions inadequate to have assured jury consideration of Penry's retardation and history of abuse as mitigating circumstances. Justice Scalia, joined by Rehnquist, White, and Kennedy, pointed out, however, that the Court had upheld the Texas

instructions in a 1976 case[182] and argued that they allowed juries to consider all mitigating factors in a case, including those relating to the defendant's mental handicap
and child abuse. By replacing that approach "with a scheme that simply dumps
before the jury all sympathetic factors bearing upon the defendant's background and
character, and the circumstances of the offense, so that the jury [could] decide without further guidance whether he 'lacked the moral culpability to be sentenced to
death,'" the Court, declared Scalia, was mandating the sort of unbridled jury discretion earlier cases had rejected as arbitrary and capricious. "In holding that the jury
had to be free to deem Penry's mental retardation and sad childhood relevant for
whatever purpose it wished, the Court," the justice added, "has come full circle, not
only permitting but requiring what [it] once condemned."[183] As in the juvenile execution field, moreover, Scalia attacked any proportionality review of sentences not
widely forbidden by current societal standards.

Justice Brennan, joined by Justice Marshall, concluded, on the other hand, that
execution of the mentally retarded was grossly disproportionate to the culpability of
such defendants and served no legitimate interest of criminal punishment. "Even if
mental retardation alone were not invariably associated with a lack of the degree of
culpability upon which death as a proportionate punishment is predicated," he
added, "[jury] consideration of retardation as a mitigating factor [was] inadequate to
guarantee, as the Constitution requires, that an individual who is not fully blameworthy for his or her crime because of a mental disability does not receive the death
penalty."[184] While terming Justice O'Connor's treatment of the competing arguments
"adequate" and "fair," Justice Stevens, joined by Justice Blackmun, concluded in a
brief separate opinion that O'Connor's "explication . . . compel[led] the conclusion
that such executions are unconstitutional."[185]

Ultimately, the Court also condoned the growing use of victim-impact statements
in capital sentencing hearings. In *Booth v. Maryland* (1987),[186] a five-four majority,
per Justice Powell, struck down a statute requiring introduction of such evidence
during the penalty phase of capital cases. Two years later, *South Carolina v. Gathers*[187]
reaffirmed *Booth*. During the penalty phase of Gathers's murder trial, a prosecutor
read from a religious tract his victim was carrying and commented on personal qualities inferred from the victim's possession of the tract and a voter registration card.
Speaking for another five-four majority, Justice Brennan reversed Gathers's death
sentence based on the prosecutor's comments. But Justice White joined *Gathers* only
on *Booth*'s authority, and in *Payne v. Tennessee* (1991),[188] decided after Justice Brennan's retirement, a six-three majority overruled *Booth* and *Gathers*.

In his opinion for the *Booth* Court, Justice Powell had concluded that the presen-
tation of victim-impact evidence shifted the focus of sentencing hearings away from
the defendant's blameworthiness and toward such irrelevant factors as the relative
worth of the victim's character and the ability of the victim's family to articulate its
grief. At the same time, defendants would also have difficulty rebutting such evidence
without shifting the focus of the hearing away from their culpability, the only relevant issue, according to the Court, in such proceedings. The admission of such "emo-
tionally charged" evidence, asserted Powell, "create[d] a constitutionally unaccept-

able risk that the jury may impose the death penalty in an arbitrary and capricious manner."[189] Justice Brennan's opinion for the *Gathers* majority essentially tracked Powell's *Booth* rationale.

Chief Justice Rehnquist held for the *Payne* Court, by contrast, that a jury or judge could properly consider the harm a defendant's crime had caused in determining whether to impose the death sentence, and victim-impact statements were an appropriate source of such evidence. Describing in graphic and extensive detail Payne's gruesome stabbing murder of his girlfriend and her two-year-old daughter and the savage attempted murder of her three-year-old son, the chief justice argued that an assessment of the harm caused by such crimes had long been "an important concern of the criminal law, both in determining the elements of the offense and in determining the appropriate punishment." It was for that reason, he asserted, that "two equally blameworthy criminal defendants may be guilty of different offenses [such as murder and attempted murder] solely because their acts cause differing amounts of harm."[190] Rehnquist also challenged the *Booth* and *Gathers* majorities' concern that the admission of victim-impact evidence would permit a jury to conclude, for example, "that the killer of a hardworking, devoted parent deserves the death penalty, but that the murderer of a reprobate does not," with Rehnquist declaring that such evidence was "designed to show instead *each* victim's 'uniqueness as an individual human being,' whatever the jury might think the loss to the community resulting from his death might be." The victim in *Gathers*, for example, had been "an out of work, mentally handicapped individual, perhaps not, in the eyes of most, a significant contributor to society, but nonetheless a murdered human being,"[191] observed Rehnquist, unmindful perhaps of the extraordinary sympathy—and scorn for his killer—such a pitiful victim would be likely to arouse in a jury.

Nor was the chief justice moved by arguments that the Court should decline to overturn precedents of such recent vintage as *Booth* and *Gathers*. Rehnquist conceded that *stare decisis* was "the preferred course because it promotes the even-handed, predictable, and consistent development of legal principles, fosters reliance on judicial decisions, and contributes to the actual and perceived integrity of the judicial process."[192] In a remarkably broad and highly questionable reading of the Court's decisions in a number of economic cases,[193] however, he contended that the force of precedent was at its "acme in cases involving property and contract rights, where reliance interests are involved," while "the opposite [was] true," he added, without citation to precedent, "in cases such as the present one involving procedural and evidentiary rules."[194] *Booth* and *Gathers* had been decided "by the narrowest of margins, over spirited dissents"; in the majority's view, they had "defied consistent application in the lower courts"; the Court of the post-Warren era had overturned thirty-three of its previous constitutional rulings since 1971; and, concluded Rehnquist, *Booth* and *Gathers* should also fall.

In separate concurrences, Justices O'Connor, Scalia, and Souter amplified themes in Rehnquist's opinion, albeit with variations in emphasis and nuance. Justice Scalia seemed particularly scornful of *stare decisis*, asserting that "[t]o the extent it rests upon anything more than administrative convenience, [it] is merely the application to judicial precedents of a more general principle that the settled practices and expectations of a democratic society should generally not be disturbed by the courts." Not surprisingly, Scalia thought *Booth* and *Gathers*, not *Payne*, were in conflict with those "fundamental values underlying the doctrine of *stare decisis*."[195] Justice Marshall, joined by Justice Blackmun, devoted most of his dissent, on the other hand, to excoriating the majority for its "astonishing" disregard of precedent. For Marshall, adherence to *stare decisis* was "in many respects even *more* critical in [such cases than in] adjudication involving commercial entitlements," particularly since their enforcement "frequently require[d the] Court to rein in the forces of democratic politics."[196] The Court could legitimately expect compliance with its directives only if the public was convinced that its decisions reflected legal principle rather than the proclivities of individual justices. "By signaling its willingness to give fresh consideration to any constitutional liberty recognized by a 5-4 vote 'over spirited dissen[t],'" declared Marshall, "the majority invites state actors to renew the very policies deemed unconstitutional in the hope that this Court may now reverse course, even if it has only recently reaffirmed the constitutional liberty in question."[197] The majority's response to the Tennessee supreme court's acceptance of victim impact evidence despite *Booth* and *Gathers* had confirmed Marshall's fears: "Far from condemning this blatant disregard for the rule of law, the majority applauds it. . . . It is hard to imagine a more complete abdication of this Court's historic commitment to defending the supremacy of its own pronouncements on issues of constitutional liberty."[198] In a separate dissent joined by Justice Blackmun, Justice Stevens echoed Marshall's attack on the majority's "trivialization" of *stare decisis*, while condemning the use of victim-impact evidence as "serv[ing] no purpose other than to encourage jurors to decide in favor of death rather than life on the basis of their emotions rather than their reason."[199] Given the "current popularity" of capital punishment and "the political strength of the 'victims' rights' movement," Stevens had no doubt the decision would be "greeted with enthusiasm by a large number of concerned and thoughtful citizens." Equally convinced, however, that public opinion had played a role in the Court's decision, he declared that "[t]oday is a sad day for a great institution."[200]

Gross racial disparities in imposition of the death penalty have also escaped effective challenge, absent direct evidence that a particular death sentence was based on the defendant's race or color. Counsel for Georgia inmate Warren McCleskey argued that his death sentence for murder of a white policeman during an armed robbery should be overturned based on the Baldus study, a statistical survey of over 2,000 Georgia murder cases. The study had concluded, among other things, that defendants charged with killing whites were 4.3 times as likely to receive the death penalty as defendants charged with killing other victims, while black defendants were slightly more likely to receive a death sentence than others. Citing precedent requiring a showing of "purposeful discrimination" to establish an equal protection claim, however, Justice Powell held for a five-four Court that under that standard McCleskey was obliged to "prove that the decisionmakers in *his* case acted with discriminatory purpose."[201] Since McCleskey had not made such a showing, his equal protection claim failed. His claim under the cruel and unusual punishment clause met the same fate. The Court's previous rulings, Powell reasoned, had eliminated only unbridled discretion in the imposition of death sentences. Georgia's death penalty statute met that requirement, and McCleskey's statistics had not proved that the remaining jury discretion was exercised arbitrarily or capriciously in his case. A sentencing system, Powell added, need not be perfect, but only "as fair as possible," and the Baldus study had not demonstrated to the Court's satisfaction a "constitutionally significant risk of racial bias affecting the Georgia capital sentencing process."[202]

The majority may have been most concerned, however, with the potential implications that it saw in acceptance of McCleskey's claim. Were the Court to declare racial disparities in death sentences as prima facie evidence of a constitutional violation, contended Powell, "we could soon be faced with similar claims as to other types of penalty."[203] Nor would they necessarily be limited to racial bias. "If arbitrary and capricious punishment is the touchstone," he observed, "such a claim could—at least in theory—be based upon any arbitrary variable."[204] In the majority's judgment, moreover, arguments of the sort McCleskey had raised were inappropriate for judicial decision. Were the level of discretion permitted under earlier decisions in death penalty cases to be further restricted, legislatures, not courts, should make that judgment. "It is not the responsibility—or indeed even the right—of this Court to determine the appropriate punishment for particular crimes," declared Powell. "It is the legislatures, the elected representatives of the people, that are 'constituted to respond to the will and consequently the moral values of the people.'"[205]

Three of the four *McCleskey* dissenters also filed opinions. Justice Brennan began his dissent with a reaffirmation of his long-held opposition to all death sentences, however administered. Only Justice Marshall joined that portion of Brennan's dissent, but Justices Blackmun and Stevens joined the rest of the Brennan opinion, while also filing dissents of their own. Brennan first argued that the Court had never before focused on individual sentences in reviewing constitutional challenges to capital punishment schemes. Instead, the justices had required defendants to establish only that the system under which they were sentenced posed a "significant risk" that "impermissible considerations . . . infected sentencing decisions." McCleskey, Brennan argued, had more than met that requirement, basing his "challenge not on speculation about how a system *might* operate, but on empirical documentation of how it *does* operate." For Brennan, the Baldus study had revealed "that the risk that race influenced McCleskey's sentence [was] intolerable by any imaginable standard."[206] Georgia's long history of racial discrimination in its criminal justice system buttressed the Baldus statistics, and the unique, irrevocable character of executions demanded the closest judicial scrutiny to assure a sentencing scheme free of such impermissible influences.

Emphasizing the equal protection concerns inherent in McCleskey's claim, Justice Blackmun, joined wholly or in part by the other dissenters, also scored the lenient standard of scrutiny the majority had applied in the case, as well as the heavy burden of proof placed on McCleskey—a burden standing in marked contrast to that embraced in *Batson* the previous year. Blackmun attached considerable weight, moreover, to the broad discretion of Georgia prosecutors in deciding whether to seek the death penalty in individual cases, drawing on the Baldus study to point out that prosecutors were five times more likely to seek the death penalty in cases involving black defendants and white victims as in black-defendant/black-victim cases, and three times as likely as in white-defendant/black-victim cases. The justice found most disturbing, however, the Court's concern that a ruling in McCleskey's favor might generate further constitutional challenges. "If a grant of relief to him were to lead to a closer examination of the effects of racial considerations throughout the criminal justice system," wrote Blackmun, "the system, and hence society, might benefit."[207]

In a brief separate dissent that Blackmun joined, Justice Stevens also took issue with the Court's concerns, disputing the notion that acceptance of McCleskey's claim would doom the death penalty in Georgia and perhaps elsewhere. "One of the lessons of the Baldus study," observed Stevens, "is that there exist certain categories of extremely serious crimes for which prosecutors consistently seek, and juries consistently impose, the death penalty without regard to the race of the victim or the race of the offender. If Georgia were to narrow the class of death-eligible defendants to those categories, the danger of arbitrary and discriminatory imposition of the death penalty would be significantly decreased, if not eradicated."[208]

For a time after the departure of Justices Brennan and Marshall, no member of the Court embraced their insistence that no death penalty statute could pass constitutional muster. Justice Blackmun had made clear in the dissent he filed for *Furman v. Georgia* (1972),[209] however, that while he opposed the abrupt judicial invalidation of a death penalty statute only a year after the Court had upheld its use,[210] he found capital punishment personally abhorrent. In *McCleskey* and other post-*Furman* cases, Blackmun's discomfort with the prevailing approach to the issue had become increasingly apparent. It was hardly surprising, then, that during his last term on the bench, he ultimately decided "that the decision whether a human being should live or die is so inherently subjective—rife with all of life's understandings, experiences, prejudices, and passions—that it inevitably defies the rationality and consistency required by the Constitution."[211]

Justice Blackmun had "faith" that the Court would eventually come to the same conclusion. But Justice Scalia's concurrence in the Court's denial of certiorari in the same case would hardly have given Scalia's elderly colleague cause for optimism. Death penalty opponents, wrote Scalia, give weight to "'intellectual, moral and personal' perceptions, but never to the text and tradition of the Constitution." But "the latter rather than the former . . . ought to control," he added, and those indicia of constitutional meaning clearly supported the death penalty.[212] Justice Blackmun had begun his dissent by describing "with poignancy," as Scalia put it, the death-by-injection to which the petitioner was to be subjected. Blackmun had chosen, Scalia observed,

one of the less brutal of the murders that regularly come before us—the murder of a man ripped by a bullet suddenly and unexpectedly, with no opportunity to prepare himself and his affairs, and left to bleed to death on the floor of a tavern. The death-by-injection which Justice Blackmun describes looks pretty desirable next to that. It looks even better next to some of the other cases currently before us which Justice Blackmun did not select as the vehicle for his announcement that the death penalty is always unconstitutional—for example, the case of the 11-year-old girl raped by four men and then killed by stuffing her panties down her throat. . . . How enviable a quiet death by lethal injection compared with that![213]

Justice Blackmun might have replied that government should be held to higher standards than its most despicable citizens. But lacking Justice Scalia's certitude and gift for invective, Blackmun did not respond.

9

Equal Protection

Unprecedented expansion in the reach of the Constitution's guarantee to equal protection of the laws was clearly among the most significant and controversial developments of the Warren Court era. The Court's decisions in *Brown v. Board of Education* (1954, 1955)[1] and related cases outlawing racial segregation in the public schools and other fields of national life are only the most obvious examples. Drawing on dicta in pre-Warren cases,[2] the Court concluded that discriminatory action that was based on "suspect" classifications or interfered with "fundamental rights" was to be subjected to "strict scrutiny" and upheld only if found necessary to further a compelling governmental interest. Under the suspect categories branch of modern equal protection doctrine, the Warren Court not only subjected racial discrimination to strict review, but suggested that classifications based on poverty[3] and status of birth[4] might qualify as suspects as well. Discriminatory legislation found to interfere with voting,[5] representational,[6] associational,[7] interstate travel, and welfare rights,[8] whether stated in the Constitution or not, succumbed, on the other hand, to the "new" equal protection doctrine's fundamental rights branch.

Pulling back somewhat from such Warren Court trends, the Burger Court, in *San Antonio Independent School District v. Rodriguez* (1973),[9] limited fundamental rights doctrine to guarantees expressed or implied in the Constitution's text, declining, among other things, to recognize fundamental rights to an equal education[10] or welfare benefits.[11] Moreover, while adding alienage to the list of constitutional suspects,[12] albeit with a governmental function exception[13] and considerable deference extended to congressional restrictions on aliens,[14] the justices refused to grant suspect status to age[15] or wealth.[16] At the same time, however, the Court refused to relegate all discrimination not accorded strict scrutiny to the lenient, rational-basis equal protection review to which economic and related controls had traditionally been subjected.[17] Instead, shifting standards of "intermediate" scrutiny, requiring a close relationship between a challenged regulation and a substantial governmental interest, were applied to "quasi-suspect" classifications based on gender[18] and status of birth,[19] leaving the reach of equal protection potentially more open-ended than in the Warren era.

Rehnquist Court rulings relating to equal protection doctrine have followed a somewhat similar pattern. The justices have been reluctant, for example, to use equal protection as a vessel for rights not mentioned elsewhere in the Constitution. In 1999, a majority invoked the right to interstate travel in striking down a California statute limiting needy new residents, for their first year in the golden state, to the welfare benefits they would have received in their prior state of residence. Justice Stevens rested the interstate travel guarantee the statute was found to inhibit on what the Court apparently considered the more concrete foundation of the Fourteenth Amendment's long-neglected privileges or immunities clause rather than on the equal protection standard traditionally invoked in travel cases.[20] The Court has continued to subject gender classifications to intermediate scrutiny. Indeed, in striking down the Virginia Military Institute's all-male admissions policy, Justice Ginsburg asserted for the Court that a state's justifications for gender classifications must be "exceedingly persuasive" and further noted that prior cases had not "equat[ed] gender classifications, for all purposes, to classifications based on race or national origin," for which the Court "thus far" had "reserved [its] most stringent judicial scrutiny."[21] Such language prompted Justice Scalia in a lone dissent (Justice Thomas did not participate in the case) to contend that the Court was actually subjecting to strict scrutiny a policy that, in his judgment, survived intermediate review by promoting a substantial interest in educational diversity. In a brief opinion concurring in the Court's judgment, moreover, Justice Rehnquist cautioned that earlier opinions indicating that gender classifications required an "exceedingly persuasive justification" were intended to emphasize "the difficulty of meeting the applicable [intermediate scrutiny] test, not as a formulation of the test itself."[22]

Clarifying Burger Court precedent, a unanimous Rehnquist Court also agreed in 1988 that intermediate scrutiny was appropriate for laws burdening children on the basis of their status of birth and struck down a state's six-year statute of limitations on child support suits filed in behalf of children born outside marriage.[23] In 1998, however, a badly fragmented Court upheld Immigration and Nationality Act provisions stipulating that the citizenship of a child of an alien father and citizen mother is established at birth, while the citizenship of a child of an alien mother and citizen father could be established only by the father acknowledging his paternity or through paternity proceedings conducted while the child remained a minor.[24] Announcing the Court's judgment in a suit brought by a young woman born to a Philippine mother and an American father, Justice Stevens, joined by the chief justice, invoked the intermediate scrutiny standard normally applied to gender discrimination and found the challenged provision substantially related to several important governmental objectives. Five justices would have found the regulation invalid under that standard. But two of that number, Justice O'Connor, joined by Justice Kennedy, concluded that the child did not have standing to raise the gender discrimination claims of her father, absent evidence he was unable to assert his own rights, and found the regulation valid under rationality analysis.

A 1988 ruling, however, distinguished *Plyler v. Doe*,[25] a 1982 Burger Court decision overturning a Texas policy that denied undocumented school-age children the free public education provided children who were U.S. citizens or legally admitted aliens. Speaking for a five-four majority and reading *Plyler* as standing in effect for the proposition that children should not be punished for the sins of their parents, Justice O'Connor relied on the *Rodriguez* decision in upholding a North Dakota provision permitting local school boards to assess a user fee for transportation of students to and from public schools.[26] In dissent, on the other hand, Justice Marshall, joined by Justice Brennan, reaffirmed his contention in a *Rodriguez* dissent that wealth classifications are suspect and education is an important interest entitled to meaningful protection under the equal protection clause, while in a separate dissent joined by Justice Blackmun, Justice Stevens found no rational basis for the user fee.

Another case rejected an unduly broad reading of Burger Court decisions restricting the reach of reapportionment law. In *Salyer Land Co. v. Tulare Water Storage District* (1973)[27] and *Ball v. James* (1981),[28] the Burger Court, applying a rationality standard, had exempted selection of water storage district governing boards from the "one person, one vote" principle. But in *Quinn v. Millsap* (1989),[29] a unanimous Court made clear that *Salyer* and *Ball* did not mean that governmental units lacking general governmental powers were wholly beyond the equal protection guarantee's reach.

The Court has also handed down a number of decisions regarding the reach of federal civil rights statutes in sexual harassment cases. At the end of Chief Justice Burger's tenure, the Court, in *Meritor Savings Bank, FSB v. Vinson*,[30] held, per Justice Rehnquist, that the creation of a "hostile work environment" through sexual harassment constituted sexual discrimination forbidden by Title VII of the 1964 Civil Rights Act and that unwelcome advances were actionable even if the employee's participation was voluntary. Speaking through Justice O'Connor, moreover, the Rehnquist Court held in 1993 that sexual harassment under Title VII need not seriously affect an employee's psychological well-being or lead the employee to suffer injury.[31]

The Court decided several of its potentially most significant harassment cases, however, in its 1997-98 and 1998-99 terms. In *Gebser v. Lago Vista Independent School District*,[32] a Texas high school student and her parents sought damages from the school system for the sexual misconduct of one of its teachers, Frank Waldrop. At a meeting with his principal and the parents of two other students, Waldrop had apologized for sexually suggestive comments he had made to students in his class. When a police officer later discovered Waldrop and Miss Gebser engaging in sexual intercourse, moreover, the school district fired him and the state revoked his teaching license. But his principal had not reported the complaints about his classroom remarks to Lago Vista's superintendent, the school district's coordinator of compliance with Title IX of the Education Act amendments of 1972, forbidding discrimination in federally funded programs. Nor had the district promulgated or distributed an official grievance procedure for lodging sexual harassment complaints or issued a formal antiharassment policy.

Compliance with Title IX is normally pursued administratively, with the withdrawal of federal funds the ultimate sanction for noncompliance, and when Miss Gebser and her parents sought damages from the school system under Title IX and a state negligence law, a federal district court granted Lago Vista summary judgment. The Court of Appeals for the Fifth Circuit affirmed, concluding that school districts are not liable under Title IX for a teacher's sexual harassment of a student unless the teacher's supervisor actually knew of the abuse, had power to end it, yet failed to do so.

A five-four Supreme Court majority, speaking through Justice O'Connor, agreed. Earlier cases had held that Title IX implicitly authorized damage suits as a supplement to the administrative enforcement explicitly provided for in the statute,[33] and the plaintiffs had contended that damages were appropriate in such cases based on principles of *respondeat superior*, holding employers responsible for the conduct of employees without school officials actually being aware of the discrimination in question. Justice O'Connor refused to read Title IX so broadly. Title IX's express administrative enforcement provisions required actual notice to officials of a federally funded institution and an opportunity for voluntary compliance before administrative enforcement could proceed. In that way, federal funds would not be diverted from their beneficial purposes at an institution where officials were unaware of discrimination in their programs and would have been willing to institute prompt corrective measures. Allowing recovery of damages without actual notice, O'Connor reasoned, would be at odds with Title IX's express provisions conditioning administrative enforcement on notice and an opportunity for voluntary compliance.

> It would be unsound . . . for a statute's *express* system of enforcement to require notice to the recipient and an opportunity to come into voluntary compliance while a judicially *implied* system of enforcement permits substantial liability without regard to the recipient's knowledge of its corrective actions upon receiving notice. . . . Moreover, an award of damages in a particular case might well exceed a recipient's level of federal funding. . . . Where a statute's express enforcement scheme hinges its most severe sanction on notice and unsuccessful efforts to obtain compliance, we cannot attribute to Congress the intention to have implied an enforcement scheme that allows imposition of greater liability without comparable conditions.[34]

Justice Stevens, joined in dissent by Justices Souter, Ginsburg, and Breyer, attacked the Court's holding as clearly inconsistent with basic principles of agency law, as well as "questionable as a factual matter."[35] Under agency principles, as Stevens construed them, an institution was responsible for any employee misconduct aided by the employee's relationship with that institution. In fact, the U.S. Office of Civil Rights had recently issued a guidance statement indicating that school districts were liable for the misconduct of teachers who were "aided by their positions of authority with the institution in carrying out their harassment of their students."[36] Asserted the justice:

This case presents a paradigmatic example of [just such] a tort that was made possible, that was effected, and that was repeated over a prolonged period because of the powerful influence that Waldrop had over Gebser by reason of the authority that his employer, the school district, had delegated to him. As a secondary school teacher, Waldrop exercised even greater authority and control over his students than employers and supervisors exercise over their employees. His gross misuse of that authority allowed him to abuse his young student's trust.[37]

Since Waldrop clearly had power to maintain order in his class, including the "ample authority" to protect students from sexual harassment by other students, Stevens also considered the teacher's failure to prevent his own harassment of Miss Gebser "the consequence of his lack of will, not his lack of authority."[38] Nor could Stevens see how Congress's specification of a notice requirement and an opportunity for voluntary compliance as prerequisites for administrative enforcement "illuminate[d] the question of what the victim of discrimination on the basis of sex must prove in order to recover damages in an implied right of action." In an earlier case, after all, the Office of Civil Rights had declined to terminate federal funding despite its finding of a Title IX violation because the school district in question had come into compliance. "That fact," Stevens reminded the majority, "did not affect the Court's analysis, much less persuade the Court that a damages remedy was unavailable."[39]

But Stevens appeared most concerned, perhaps, about what he thought might be the ultimate consequences of the Court's ruling. Title IX's prohibition against discrimination based on sex was designed, he contended, to induce school boards to establish policies minimizing the dangers of harassment for students. "The rule that the Court has crafted," warned Stevens, "creates the opposite incentive. As long as school boards can insulate themselves from knowledge about this sort of conduct, they can claim immunity from damages liability."[40]

Justice Stevens reserved the question whether a school district could escape damages liability under Title IX with an effective harassment policy. In a separate dissent joined by Justices Souter and Breyer, however, Justice Ginsburg indicated that she would recognize such a policy as an affirmative defense against a school's liability. "The burden would be the school district's to show that its internal remedies were adequately publicized and likely would have provided redress without exposing the complainant to undue risk, effort, or expense. . . . [T]o the extent that a plaintiff unreasonably failed to avail herself of [such] . . . measures, and consequently suffered avoidable harm, she would not qualify for Title IX relief."[41]

While *Gebser* limited use of Title IX for damage suits against school districts for the misconduct of their teachers, *Burlington Industries v. Ellerth* (1998),[42] decided several days later, found employers vicariously liable, under certain circumstances, for their supervisors' harassment of employees in violation of Title VII of the 1964 Civil Rights Act, forbidding sexual discrimination in employment. In her suit against Burlington, Kimberly Ellerth claimed that she was forced to quit her job after only fifteen months as a result of constant sexual harassment by one of her supervisors,

Ted Slowik, a midlevel manager who had authority to hire and promote employees, subject to higher approval, but was not considered a company policymaker. Ellerth refused all Slowik's advances, yet suffered no tangible forms of retaliation and was even promoted once during her tenure with Burlington. Despite knowledge of the company's policy against sexual harassment, she also never informed anyone in authority of Slowik's conduct.

The Supreme Court, per Justice Kennedy, construed Title VII, however, to permit damages against an employer in such cases even though the employee suffered no adverse, tangible job consequence and without a showing that the employer was negligent or otherwise at fault for a supervisor's misconduct. The Court further held that an employer could raise an affirmative defense against such vicarious liability by establishing that it took reasonable care to prevent and promptly correct any sexual harassment and that the employee unreasonably failed to take advantage of such opportunities or to otherwise avoid harm. Such a defense was to be available, however, only in hostile work environment cases involving no tangible retaliation against the employee; on the other hand, in so-called quid pro quo situations, in which refusal of a supervisor's advances resulted in adverse consequences to an employee, the employer could raise no affirmative defense against liability. Under the circumstances of Ellerth's case, noted Kennedy, Burlington Industries was subject to vicarious liability, but would have the opportunity on remand to establish the affirmative defense.

Justice Thomas, joined by Justice Scalia, dissented. Drawing on lower court cases involving racial discrimination claims, Thomas concluded that an employer should be liable for hostile work environments created by a supervisor's sexual harassment of workers only if the employer was negligent, that is, "only if the employer either knew, or in the exercise of reasonable care should have known, about the hostile work environment and failed to take remedial action."[43] Ellerth had never contended that Burlington Industries had been negligent in permitting her harassment, and Thomas had no doubt Burlington had acted reasonably. "The company had a policy against sexual harassment," he observed, "and respondent admitted that she was aware of the policy but nonetheless failed to tell anyone with authority over Slowik about his behavior. . . . Burlington therefore cannot be charged with knowledge of Slowik's alleged harassment or with a failure to exercise reasonable care in not knowing about it."[44] Terming the majority's affirmative defense against vicarious liability "vague," Thomas also complained that the Court's failure to explain how employers might rely on it would "ensur[e] a continuing reign of confusion in this important area of the law."[45]

Thomas, again joined by Scalia, dissented on the same ground in *Faragher v. City of Boca Raton* (1998), another Title VII sexual harassment case decided along with *Ellerth*. Beth Ann Faragher brought her suit against the city after she and other Boca Raton lifeguards were repeatedly subjected by their male supervisors to "uninvited and offensive touching," lewd remarks, and degrading comments about women. Applying a standard similar to that announced in *Burlington Industries*, Justice Souter not only remanded the case for a possible finding of vicarious liability, but also concluded for the Court that Boca Raton had not exercised reasonable care in seeking to prevent the supervisors' harassing conduct. The district court in the case had found that the city entirely failed to disseminate its sexual harassment policy among beach employees, keep track of the conduct of supervisors, or assure employees that they could bypass harassing supervisors in registering complaints. The city, concluded Souter, thus had no basis for asserting the affirmative defense recognized in *Burlington Industries.* "Unlike the employer of a small workforce, who might expect that sufficient care to prevent tortious behavior could be exercised informally," added the justice, "those responsible for city operations could not reasonably have thought that precautions against hostile environments in any one of many departments in far-flung locations could be effective without communicating some formal policy against harassment, with a sensible complaint procedure."[46]

Debates among the justices over the reach of federal sexual harassment regulations continued in the 1998-99 term when a five-four majority extended Title IX to particularly egregious student harassment of other students. Speaking for the Court in a case brought by the mother of a child who had been subjected to repeated harassment for many months by one of her fifth-grade classmates, with virtually no remedial response by school officials, Justice O'Connor held that Title IX damages were appropriate when a school receiving federal funds acted with deliberate indifference to known acts of student-on-student harassment. Justice Kennedy, joined in dissent by the chief justice and Justices Scalia and Thomas, accused the majority, on the other hand, of converting Title IX "into a Federal Student Civility Code," warned of likely difficulties in defining peer harassment and assessing school responsibility for such incidents, and declared, "I can conceive of few interventions more intrusive upon the delicate and vital relations between teacher and student, between student and student, and between the State and its citizens than the one the Court creates today by its own hand. Trusted principles of federalism are superseded by a more contemporary imperative."[47]

At the end of the same term, the Court decided a number of discrimination claims arising under the 1990 Americans with Disabilities Act (ADA). In one case, severely myopic twin sisters challenged United Air Lines' refusal to hire them as pilots on global flights. With eyeglasses the sisters had 20/20 vision, but they could not satisfy United's requirements with respect to uncorrected eyesight. Obviously taking into account the quadruple increase in lawsuits extension of the ADA to correctable disabilities was likely to generate, a seven-two Court, speaking through Justice O'Connor, limited the law's coverage to serious disabling conditions that could not be corrected and thus, in the words of the law, to persons who were "[un]able to perform a major life activity that the average person in the general population can perform." Justice Stevens, joined by Justice Breyer, declared in dissent, on the other hand, that a "generous, rather than a miserly, construction" would be more faithful to the ADA's broad intended purposes. By the same seven-two margin, the Court upheld the discharge of a UPS mechanic who was required to drive commercial vehicles as part of his duties and was fired when it was learned that his high blood pressure exceeded U.S. Department of Transportation requirements. Emphasizing that the petitioner had failed to show that he could not, with appropriate medication, perform a number of mechanic jobs, Justice O'Connor concluded for the majority that his complaint also fell outside the ADA's scope. In a third case, a unanimous Court ruled that employers who set job qualifications based on a federal agency's safety standards are not obliged to dispense with such requirements merely because one of their workers—in this case, a truck driver blind in one eye—obtains a waiver from the agency. Monocularity, Justice Souter observed for the Court, did not invariably impose a substantial limitation on a person's ability to acquire employment, and the waiver program at issue in the case was simply an experiment used to obtain data, not a regulation on an equal footing with the federal vision standard to which the worker's employer adhered.

In contrast with these narrow constructions of the ADA, however, a six-three majority the same day gave a relatively broad reading to a Justice Department regulation requiring that government programs or services provided under the statute be offered "in the most integrated setting appropriate to the needs" of people with disabilities covered by the law. Speaking for the Court in a case involving two mentally handicapped women seeking a transfer from a regional state mental hospital in Atlanta to a group home or other community-based facility, Justice Ginsburg construed the "most integrated setting" requirement to mean that such a transfer was "in order when the State's treatment professionals have determined that community placement is appropriate, the transfer from institutional care to a less restrictive setting is not opposed by the affected individual, and the placement can be reasonably accommodated" in light of state resources and the needs of other patients. In dissent, however, Justice Thomas, joined by the chief justice and Justice Scalia, scorned the majority's conclusion that the women were the victims of discrimination, declaring that assertion "equivalent to finding discrimination under Title VII where a black employee with deficient management skills is denied in-house training by his employer (allegedly because of lack of funding) because other similarly situated employees are given the in-house training. Such a claim would fly in the face of our prior case law, which requires more than the assertion that a person belongs to a protected group and did not receive some benefit." The majority's reading of the ADA, warned Thomas, "imposes significant federalism costs, directing States how to make decisions about their delivery of public services," contrary to earlier decisions invoking federalism principles to "erect limits on the Federal Government's ability to direct state officers or to interfere with the functions of state governments."[48]

The most controversial Rehnquist Court equal protection decisions, however, have involved race. Some have narrowly construed federal civil rights statutes. In *Patterson v. McLean Credit Union* (1989),[49] for example, a narrow majority, speaking through Justice Kennedy, construed a remnant of federal Reconstruction legislation to forbid only racial discrimination in the making of private employment contracts and the enforcement of contractual obligations through legal process, not racial harassment in the course of employment. But the Court's most significant racial rulings have involved challenges to the use of color-conscious remedies in the elimination of the nation's legacy of racial discrimination. In *Brown v. Board of Education*, the Supreme Court held that public schools segregated racially by law stigmatize minority children, adversely affecting their ability to learn. Such education, the justices unanimously declared, is "inherently" unequal and thus violative of the Constitution's guarantee to equal protection of the laws. The following year, in *Brown* II, the Court remanded *Brown* and its companion cases to the trial courts in which they were originally filed with instructions that those tribunals and defendant school officials were to proceed "with all deliberate speed" to implement the principles announced in *Brown* I.

The difficulty, of course, was that the principles established in *Brown* II were far from clear. Those interested in minimizing the ruling's impact, including a number of federal jurists, concluded that the Court had intended only to eliminate laws and related governmental action requiring segregated education, not to mandate actual racial integration. Judge John J. Parker of the Court of Appeals for the Fourth Circuit was typical. Although the concerns of civil rights groups had contributed to the defeat of Parker's 1930 nomination to the Supreme Court, the North Carolinian had forged a commendable civil liberties record on the Fourth Circuit. Like most racial moderates, however, Judge Parker believed that the economic and social conditions of southern African Americans must be substantially improved before segregation could be eliminated. In *Briggs v. Elliott* (1951), South Carolina's *Brown* counterpart, Judge Parker spoke for two members of a three-judge panel in upholding separate but equal education over the vehement dissent of District Judge J. Waties Waring, Charleston aristocrat turned racial liberal, who accused the majority of perpetuating the South's "slavocracy." Earlier, in conference, Judge Parker had urged deference to states' rights, claimed that South Carolina officials would "equalize" the schools if given time, and warned of the calamities racial mixing would provoke.[50]

Following *Brown* II, Parker was part of a unanimous three-judge panel—by this point, Judge Waring had retired—that enjoined South Carolina from maintaining official segregation, but refused to impose a time limit for compliance. The court's brief, unsigned opinion included rhetoric that was to become a staple of the massive resistance movement:

> It is important that we point out exactly what the Supreme Court has decided and what it has not decided in this case. It has not decided that the federal courts are to take over or regulate the public schools of the states. It has not decided that the states must mix persons of different races in the schools or must require them to attend schools or must deprive them of the right of choosing the schools they attend. What it has decided, and all that it has decided, is that a state may not deny to any person on account of race the right to attend any school that it maintains. This, under the decision of the Supreme Court, the state may not do directly or indirectly; but if the schools which it maintains are open to children of all races, no violation of the Constitution is involved even though the children of different races voluntarily attend different schools, as they attend different churches. Nothing in the Constitution or in the decision of the Supreme Court takes away from the people freedom to choose the schools they attend. The Constitution, in other words, does not require integration. It merely forbids discrimination. It does not forbid such segregation as occurs as the result of voluntary action. It merely forbids the use of governmental power to enforce segregation. The Fourteenth Amendment is

a limitation upon the exercise of power by the state or state agencies, not a limitation upon the freedom of individuals."[51]

Whether or not so intended, this passage—penned not by a writer for the *Fiery Cross* but by a respected federal judge—provided a virtual blueprint for the legal perpetuation of racial segregation in the public schools and many other fields as well. States could remove from the statute books all vestiges of state-mandated segregation. If segregation continued to exist through private, "voluntary" choice, so be it. The state was no longer at fault; the Constitution was preserved.

Southern states readily adopted such a legal strategy, along with a variety of quasi-legal and outright illegal weapons of massive resistance. Under Alabama's 1955 pupil placement law, for example, students were no longer to be formally assigned to schools on the basis of race. But school officials were authorized to consider such factors as a student's "psychological" qualifications; the "physical effect" upon pupils; possibilities of threat, disorder, or economic retaliation; and "established social and psychological relationships" in determining student assignments to particular schools. Other states opted for "freedom of choice" and related devices. It hardly mattered. Whatever the form, the result was invariably the same—the persistence of complete or virtually complete segregation of the public schools.

To laypersons reading such regulations in the context of those turbulent times, their intent was clear. But courts are generally blind to legislative motive. A three-judge federal district court concluded that Alabama's new pupil placement law was susceptible to constitutional application, and thus was not invalid on its face.[52] The Supreme Court declined to disturb that judgment.

After well over a decade of such devices, however, the high Court's patience wore thin. In *Green v. New Kent County* (1968),[53] arguably the most significant post-*Brown* school case, the justices unanimously struck down a freedom of choice plan that had left a school district almost completely segregated. To pass constitutional muster, Justice Brennan declared for the Court, any student assignment scheme must "promise realistically to convert promptly to a system without a 'white' school and a 'Negro' school, but just schools."[54] In short, meaningful integration was necessary in converting the dual school systems *Brown* had condemned into unitary systems consistent with equal protection.

The premises underlying the shift in approach that *Green* announced are familiar. *Brown* I and II had termed state-mandated segregation in the public schools inherently unequal, citing its deleterious effects on minority children. Eliminating those effects would require more than mere revisions in the law. Instead, ostensibly nonracial modes of pupil placement shown to have little or no impact on traditional segregated patterns were to be presumed part and parcel of campaigns to preserve segregation, whatever their form.

Arguably, such thinking also has been at the bottom of modern affirmative action programs and other color-conscious remedies for past discriminations. A simple ban on racial and related discrimination in employment or the admission practices of colleges and universities, followed by little or no change in patterns of hiring and admissions, may lead one to suspect that the discrimination has not ended, merely become more covert. Given the nation's unfortunate history of racial and related forms of discrimination and the obvious persistence of racial and gender stereotypes, such suspicions—and the result-based affirmative action programs they generate—seem entirely logical. Viewed in this light, the varieties of affirmative action and the aggressive approach to desegregation *Green* mandated may well reflect hard-nosed judgments about human nature more than the goals of radical social reformers.

This chapter focuses on the Rehnquist Court's racial equal protection record, particularly the Court's responses to the motivations underlying *Green* and modern affirmative action programs. Its underlying thesis is that an unduly wooden commitment to a "color-blind" (or "gender-blind") Constitution in the near term, combined with a naive faith in the adequacy of negative rather than affirmative remedies for racial and related forms of discrimination, may obstruct that worthy principle's ultimate triumph.

School Desegregation

Not surprisingly perhaps, the Rehnquist Court has been most willing in the school desegregation field to accept the notion that the persistence of racial imbalance requires the continuation of affirmative, race-conscious remedies. Even here, however, the justices have supported a gradual relaxation of judicial oversight—most significantly in *Freeman v. Pitts* (1992),[55] the DeKalb County, Georgia, school case.[56] In response to a court order, the DeKalb system had first begun to desegregate student assignments in 1969, but with decidedly modest results. The system's first action was to create attendance zones establishing two schools that were more than 50 percent black, even though the districtwide student population was less than 6 percent black. Within three years, five other schools in the system had also become majority black. Between 1969 and 1975, the number of students attending racially identifiable schools actually increased and grew more quickly than the increase in black students. By 1975, in fact, 73 percent of DeKalb's black elementary pupils and 56 percent of black high school students were attending black schools, although only 12 and 13 percent, respectively, of those student populations were black. The system opened thirteen new elementary schools from 1969 to 1975; six had a total of four black students in 1975. In 1972, a majority-to-minority pupil transfer program was adopted. But as a result of limitations imposed by school officials, including a failure to provide transportation and restrictions on the availability of transfer schools, only one-tenth of one percent of the students were participating in the program as of the 1975–76 school year.

In 1976, a district court concluded that limitations on the transfer program and modifications in attendance zones had perpetuated the vestiges of DeKalb's dual school system. Yet the system took little remedial action in the succeeding decade. The majority-to-minority transfer program had expanded to comprise 6 percent of the student population, and the system had also adopted magnet school programs. But the latter encompassed less than 1 percent of DeKalb students. Even so, when school officials sought dismissal of the litigation in 1986, claiming that they had achieved unitary status, the district court largely obliged, finding the system unitary in terms of four of six factors identified in *Green* as critical to the conversion of dual into unitary systems: student assignments, transportation, physical facilities, and extracurricular activities. Since the DeKalb system was not yet unitary with respect to faculty assignments and resource allocation, the remaining two *Green* factors, the district court refused to dismiss the suit. Finding that continuing racial imbalance was the product of demographic changes rather than a vestige of *de jure* segregation, however, the court declined further relief in student assignments and other areas in which it had concluded that compliance had been achieved—even though compliance in the area of pupil placement had been only fleetingly achieved.

The Court of Appeals for the Eleventh Circuit reversed, holding that a district court should retain full remedial authority until unitary status had been achieved in all the *Green* categories at the same time for several years. But the Supreme Court disagreed. Speaking through Justice Kennedy, the Court held that a judge could relinquish supervision and control over a school district in incremental stages before total compliance had been achieved. The district court's finding that growing resegregation was attributable to demographic forces, concluded Kennedy, was "credible."

In a concurring opinion, Justice Souter agreed with the majority that a trial court need not maintain complete control over all elements of a school system until total compliance had been achieved. Souter also warned, however, that district judges should make certain before relinquishing control that unremedied *Green*-type factors were not themselves likely to generate further shifts in housing patterns, aggravating racial imbalance in student assignments.

In a separate concurrence, Justice Blackmun, joined by Justices Stevens and O'Connor, would have placed a burden on the school system to establish that its limited remedial efforts had not contributed to demographic shifts in housing patterns. A majority of the justices, however, assumed with the district court that growing racial imbalance in the system was the result of demographic shifts unconnected with past discriminatory practices. Justice Scalia charged in a concurring opinion, moreover, that "prior, government-enforced discrimination" could no longer "realistically be assumed to be a significant factor" accounting for racial imbalance in the public schools. "At some time," contended Scalia, "we must acknowledge that it has become absurd to assume, without any further proof, that violations of the Constitution dating from the days when Lyndon Johnson was President, or earlier, continue to have an appreciable effect upon current operation of schools."[57]

A majority has been unwilling to date to embrace entirely Justice Scalia's apparent assumption that racial discrimination in the operation of the nation's schools is such a relic of the past that judicial oversight must soon be eliminated. In *United States v. Fordice* (1992),[58] moreover, the Court held that a state's mere adoption of racially neutral policies for its colleges and universities did not necessarily fulfill its obligations to eliminate *de jure* segregation in such institutions. Justice Scalia contended, on the other hand, that the affirmative desegregation obligations *Green* had imposed on primary and secondary schools had "no proper application in the context of higher education."[59] Scalia favored extending to colleges and universities the approach the Court had adopted for 4-H and Homemaker Clubs supported by a state university's agricultural extension service, requiring only that any racial imbalance in such organizations be wholly the result of private choice.[60] The *Fordice* majority refused to extend that stance to the segregation of public colleges and universities. Even so, the Court has relaxed judicial control over local school systems, including those, like DeKalb, with an unimpressive record of meeting their obligations to eliminate all vestiges of *de jure* segregation. It thus seems inclined to join Scalia in giving insufficient weight to the obvious persistence of racial tensions and traditional racial attitudes in the nation when assessing the continued need for judicial oversight.

Affirmative Action

The Rehnquist Court's response to affirmative action issues even more clearly reflects the majority's relatively sanguine attitude about the current state of race relations in the United States. In *Metro Broadcasting, Inc. v. FCC* (1990),[61] a narrow five-four majority, reaffirming principles established in the *Fullilove* decision of 1980,[62] upheld FCC regulations permitting the transfer of a limited category of radio and television stations only to minority-controlled companies. Speaking for the majority, Justice Brennan emphasized the broad authority of Congress under its explicit authority to enforce the Fourteenth Amendment's equal protection guarantee. Benign race-conscious congressional measures, even if not designed merely to compensate specific victims of past governmental or societal discrimination, were constitutional, asserted Brennan, if substantially related to important governmental objectives within the reach of congressional power. The challenged FCC regulations, he concluded, promoted the important First Amendment interest in broadcast diversity and thus the widest possible dissemination of information from diverse and antagonistic sources.

When state rather than federal affirmative action regulations were challenged, the Court initially held that state controls must be narrowly tailored to remedy the effects of past discrimination. A six-three majority, in *City of Richmond v. J.A. Croson Co.* (1989),[63] struck down Richmond's requirement that city contractors award at least 30 percent of the dollar amount of each contract to minority subcontractors. Distinguishing *Croson* from a federal set-aside program upheld in the *Fullilove* case, Justice O'Connor cited Congress's explicit enforcement powers under the Fourteenth Amendment, as well as national evidence of societal discrimination in a variety of fields. Asserted O'Connor, "While the states and their subdivisions may take remedial action when they possess evidence that their own spending practices are exacerbating a pattern of prior discrimination, they must identify that discrimination, public or private, with some specificity, before they may use race-conscious relief."[64]

Justice Marshall, joined by Justices Brennan and Blackmun, registered a forceful dissent. Marshall challenged the majority's refusal to accept national findings and evidence regarding conditions in Richmond as an adequate basis for endorsing the city's assertion that the set-aside program was needed to correct the effects of past discrimination. "The essence of the majority's position," observed Marshall, "is that Richmond has failed to catalog adequate findings to prove that past discrimination has impeded minorities from joining or participating fully in Richmond's construction contracting industry." Marshall found "deep irony" in that position. "As much as any municipality in the United States, Richmond knows what racial discrimination is; a century of decisions by this and other federal courts has richly documented the city's disgraceful history of public and private racial discrimination."

The city had shown that "minority-owned businesses [had] received virtually no city contracting dollars and rarely if ever belonged to area trade associations." Municipal officials had testified to widespread discrimination in Richmond's construction industry, and national findings on which the Court had relied in the *Fullilove* case had established "that pervasive discrimination in the Nation's tight-knit construction industry had operated to exclude minorities from public contracting."[65] Given such evidence and Richmond's racial history, Justice Marshall could not understand how the Court could insist on more conclusive evidence of past discrimination. "The members of the Richmond City Council have spent long years witnessing multifarious acts of discrimination, including, but not limited to, the deliberate diminution of black residents' voting rights, resistance to school desegregation, and publicly sanctioned housing discrimination. Numerous decisions of federal courts chronicle this disgraceful recent history."[66] How, Marshall asked, could a court "second-guess" such a council's judgment regarding remedies needed to correct the evils of the past?

The Court's first African American justice also took issue with Justice O'Connor's conclusion that the racial composition of the Richmond city council required exceptionally close judicial scrutiny of its affirmative action regulations. O'Connor had cited the five-four majority of blacks to whites on the council in justifying strict review of the challenged set-aside program. Marshall retorted that "such insulting judgments have no place in constitutional jurisprudence." Such an assumption, he charged, "implies a lack of political maturity on the part of this Nation's elected minority officials that is totally unwarranted."[67] Certainly, he added, the ratio of whites to blacks on the council was hardly an adequate reason to establish that white subcontractors were a suspect class deserving of special judicial protection traditionally extended to despised minorities or that the set-aside in any way was intended to stigmatize whites because of their race. For Marshall, therefore, the challenged set-aside should not be subjected to the sort of strict review the Court had established for segregation laws, but by a more lenient intermediate standard requiring only that racial classifications promote important governmental interests. The set-aside, he argued, served not only the city's interest in eradicating the effects of past discrimination, but also "the prospective one of preventing the city's own spending decisions from reinforcing and perpetuating the exclusionary effects of past discrimination."[68] "The more government bestows its rewards on those persons or businesses that were positioned to thrive during a period of private racial discrimination," contended Marshall, "the tighter the deadhand grip of prior discrimination becomes on the present and future."[69]

Marshall's specific criticisms of the Court's stance in *Croson* were difficult to answer. So, too, was the underlying theme of his dissent—a theme succinctly captured by Justice Blackmun in a brief separate opinion joining Marshall's "perceptive and incisive" dissent. "I never thought that I would live to see the day," wrote Blackmun, "when the city of Richmond, Virginia, the cradle of the Old Confederacy, sought on its own, within a narrow confine, to lessen the stark impact of persistent discrimination. But Richmond, to its great credit, acted. Yet this Court, the supposed bastion of equality, strikes down Richmond's efforts as though discrimination had never existed or was not demonstrated in this particular litigation. Justice Marshall convincingly discloses the fallacy and the shallowness of that approach."[70]

It was possible to read *Croson* as concluding that the city had simply failed to surmount an evidentiary hurdle. But it appeared to have said more. *Croson* seemed to hold that racial and related forms of discrimination were largely confined to the past and that modern remedies for past discrimination were thus themselves inherently suspect unless racially neutral. Equally troubling was the majority's assumption that federal officials enjoy a wider latitude than states and their local units in combating discrimination, even where state laws did not conflict with federal regulations. The power given Congress under the Reconstruction amendments flowed largely from the belief that state and local governments would be unwilling to guarantee equal treatment to the newly freed slaves. To construe those basic safeguards as somehow limiting state authority to promote equal protection, as Justice Marshall eloquently asserted in *Croson*, threatened to turn the amendments "on their heads."[71]

Ultimately, of course, the Court agreed that federal and state affirmative action arrangements should not be measured by different standards, deferential for the former and strict for the latter. Instead of subjecting both to deferential review, as Marshall preferred, however, a majority concluded that affirmative action programs at whatever level of government must survive strict judicial scrutiny. Under attack in *Adarand Constructors, Inc. v. Pena* (1995)[72] was the federal government's practice of giving general contractors on government projects a financial incentive to hire subcontractors controlled by "socially and economically disadvantaged individuals," especially government use of race-based presumptions in identifying such subcontractors. Applying the deferential standard of review of federal regulations announced in *Metro Broadcasting*, a court of appeals rejected Adarand's claim that the provision violated the equal protection component of the Fifth Amendment due process clause. The Supreme Court disagreed, requiring strict review for federal as well as state affirmative action programs and remanding the case for further proceedings consistent with that position.

In rejecting *Metro Broadcasting*'s conclusion to the contrary, the *Adarand* Court, per Justice O'Connor, cited three general propositions purportedly established by *Croson* and other earlier cases: "First, skepticism: '"[a]ny preference based on racial and ethnic criteria must necessarily receive a most searching examination."' . . . Second, consistency: 'the standard of review under the Equal Protection Clause is not dependent on the race of those burdened or benefited by a particular classification'; . . . all racial classifications reviewable under the Equal Protection Clause must be strictly scrutinized. And third, congruence: '[e]qual protection analysis in the Fifth Amendment [federal] area is the same as that [for states] under the Fourteenth Amendment.'"[73] *Metro Broadcasting* had "squarely rejected" the congruence standard and undermined the other two propositions. To that extent, declared O'Connor, *Metro Broadcasting* was overruled and both federal and state/local racial classifications subjected to strict judicial scrutiny.

The justice also took pains "to dispel the notion that strict scrutiny is 'strict in theory, but fatal in fact.'" Agreeing that "[t]he unhappy persistence of both the practice and the lingering effects of racial discrimination against minority groups in this country is an unfortunate reality, and government is not disqualified from acting in response to it," O'Connor asserted that "race-based action" would be upheld where narrowly tailored to promote a compelling governmental interest.[74]

For that last assertion, however, Justice O'Connor did not necessarily secure a Court. Justice Scalia observed in a separate opinion that "government can never have a 'compelling interest' in discriminating on the basis of race in order to 'make up' for past racial discrimination in the opposite direction," adding, "Individuals who have been wronged by unlawful racial discrimination should be made whole; but under our Constitution there can be no such thing as either a creditor or a debtor race. That concept is alien to the Constitution's focus upon the individual. . . . To pursue the concept of racial entitlement—even for the most admirable and benign of purposes—is to reinforce and preserve for future mischief the way of thinking that produced race slavery, race privilege and race hatred. In the eyes of government, we are just one race here. It is American."[75] Justice Thomas's condemnation of the sort of affirmative action programs from which he had once benefited was even more vehement. Accusing *Adarand* dissenters of assuming that there was "a racial paternalism exception to the principle of equal protection," Thomas termed "government-sponsored racial discrimination based on benign prejudice . . . just as noxious as discrimination inspired by malicious prejudice."[76] Borrowing from Chief Justice Warren's reasoning in the *Brown* case, Thomas charged that "[s]o-called 'benign' discrimination teaches many that because of chronic and apparently immutable handicaps, minorities cannot compete with them without their patronizing indulgence. These programs stamp minorities with a badge of inferiority and may cause them to develop dependencies or to adopt an attitude that they are 'entitled' to preferences."[77]

In dissent, Justice Stevens, joined by Justice Ginsburg, took sharp issue with Justice O'Connor's opinion and, indirectly, with the Scalia and Thomas concurrences. Stevens obviously agreed with O'Connor's assertion that any government action relying on a racial classification deserves a "skeptical" reception in the courts. Observing that "uniform standards are often anything but uniform," however, the justice subjected O'Connor's "comments on 'consistency,' 'congruence,' and *stare decisis* [to] the same type of skepticism."[78] Stevens first found "no moral or constitutional equivalence between a policy that is designed to perpetuate a caste system and one that seeks to eradicate racial subordination. Invidious discrimination is an engine of oppression, subjugating a disfavored group to enhance or maintain the power of the majority. Remedial race-based preferences reflect the opposite impulse: a desire to foster equality in society. The consistency that the Court espouses would disregard the difference between a 'No Trespassing' sign and a welcome mat."[79] Stevens was equally dubious of the majority's "supposed inability" to distinguish between "invidious" and "benign" discrimination, asserting that "[i]ts presence in everyday parlance" demonstrated people understood the difference "between good intentions and bad." And the Court itself had long recognized the distinction between "intentional" discrimination and that having only a discriminatory "effect."[80] Noting that gender discrimination is subjected only to intermediate scrutiny rather than the strict review that racial classifications are accorded, he also warned that "today's lecture about 'consistency' [could] produce the anomalous result that the Government can more easily enact affirmative-action programs to remedy discrimination against women than it can enact affirmative-action programs to remedy discrimination against African Americans—even though the primary purpose of the Equal Protection Clause was to end discrimination against the former slaves. . . . When a court becomes preoccupied with abstract standards, it risks sacrificing common sense at the altar of formal consistency."[81]

Nor could Stevens join the Court's insistence that *stare decisis* required equal standards of scrutiny for federal, state, and local affirmative action policies. Emphasizing the deference traditionally extended Congress in the exercise of its lawmaking authority, the Fourteenth Amendment's express grant of civil rights enforcement powers to Congress along with its imposition of restrictions on state power, and federal affirmative action programs as a reflection of "the will of our entire Nation's elected representatives," Stevens read precedent as clearly recognizing and endorsing broader latitude for Congress than for state and local governments in such cases. To bolster his position, he quoted extensively from Justice Scalia's separate opinion in *Croson*, in which his colleague had asserted, among other things, that "it is one thing to permit racially based conduct by the Federal Government—whose legislative powers concerning matters of race were explicitly enhanced by the Fourteenth Amendment . . . —and quite another to permit it by the precise [state and local] entities against whose conduct in matters of race that Amendment was specifically directed."[82] In a separate dissent joined by Justice Breyer, Justice Ginsburg substantially echoed Stevens's concerns and, like Justice Souter in another dissent, bemoaned the unnecessarily broad reach of the Court's opinion.

The Rehnquist Court may also be moving toward repudiation of Justice Powell's conclusion in the *Bakke* case[83] that a university's desire to secure a diverse student body constituted a compelling interest justifying nonquota affirmative action admission policies. In *Bakke*, Justice Powell had provided the critical fifth vote for a majority invalidating the quota at issue there and for a different majority upholding some consideration of race in university admissions. But only Powell had concluded both that all racial classifications are subject to strict judicial scrutiny and that a university's interest in a diverse student body is sufficiently compelling to justify race-conscious admission policies. Concluding that Powell's opinion in the *Bakke* case did not constitute precedent on the diversity issue, the Court of Appeals for the Fifth Circuit, in *Hopwood v. Texas* (1995),[84] invalidated an affirmative action plan at the University of Texas and rejected diversity considerations as an adequate justification for such policies. The Supreme Court denied certiorari,[85] and Justice Ginsburg, joined by Justice Souter, rested her decision to deny review on the fact that the challenged program had long been discontinued and that a final judgment on the questions raised in the case "must await . . . a program genuinely in controversy."[86] The Court's review of a later challenge to a school board's diversity-based decision to discharge a white teacher rather than a black teacher with equal seniority was cut short, moreover, when the white teacher's suit was settled out of court.[87] The future of diversity-based affirmative action decisions, however, appears dubious at best on the Rehnquist Court.

Racial Gerrymandering

The current Court's approach to equality issues reflects more, of course, than an assumption that racial bias is largely a relic of the past. Also prominent is the view that race-conscious remedies for discrimination are themselves inherently inconsistent with principles captured in the notion of the color-blind Constitution. This theme is especially evident in the Court's recent grappling with the constitutional status of majority-black congressional districts created under prodding from the U.S. Justice Department to insure compliance with federal voting rights legislation. Part of North Carolina is subject to the provisions of Section 5 of the 1965 Voting Rights Act requiring the U.S. attorney general or district court in Washington to "pre-clear" any new voting regulation adopted by a state or county with a history of suffrage discrimination. When the state sought approval for a new congressional districting scheme that created a single majority-black district, the attorney general objected, contending that a second majority-black district could have been created to enhance minority voting strength. The state's revised plan, which the attorney general approved, contained two majority-black districts. One stretched approximately 160 miles along Interstate 85 and, for much of its length, was no wider than the interstate corridor. Five North Carolina white residents claimed that the district amounted to an unconstitutional racial gerrymander. A three-judge district court dismissed their complaint, holding that the favoring of minority voters was not unconstitutionally discriminatory and that the challenged plan had not led to proportional underrepresentation of white voters.

In *Shaw v. Reno* (1993),[88] the Supreme Court reversed. A congressional reapportionment scheme, asserted Justice O'Connor for a five-four majority, could be so irrational in shape that it was understandable only as an attempt to segregate voters into separate districts on the basis of race. Such racial gerrymanders, like other racial classifications, were inherently suspect and subject to the most exacting scrutiny, regardless of the race affected. The Court had never held, observed O'Connor, "that race-conscious state decisionmaking is impermissible in *all* circumstances. What appellants object to is redistricting legislation that is so extremely irregular on its face that it rationally can be viewed only as an effort to segregate the races for purposes of voting, without regard for traditional districting principles and without sufficiently compelling justification."[89] Certainly, such classifications bore a heavier burden of justification than the typical partisan gerrymander.

Citing *United Jewish Organizations v. Carey*,[90] a 1977 case, Justice White, joined by Justices Blackmun and Stevens, dismissed as "both a fiction and a departure from settled equal protection principles"[91] the majority's notion that North Carolina's plan was an unconstitutional deprivation of the appellants' rights, even though it left whites with a voting majority in a disproportionate number of districts. In the past, the Court had subjected to probing constitutional review only direct denials of the right to vote and devices that had the "intent and effect of unduly diminishing"[92] the electoral influence of a particular political or racial group. The North Carolina case met neither condition. White doubted that a state's efforts to enhance minority voting strength constituted a discriminatory purpose within the reach of the equal protection guarantee. "But even assuming that it does," he added, "there is no question that appellants have not alleged the requisite discriminatory effects."[93] After all, whites (with 70 percent of the state's voting population) still enjoyed a voting majority in ten, or 83 percent, of North Carolina's twelve districts.

Nor was White impressed with the significance the Court seemed to attach to the bizarre shape of the state's second majority-black district. In previous gerrymandering cases, plaintiffs had the burden of demonstrating that the scheme at issue had a discriminatory purpose and effect. Shape alone had not shifted the burden to the state and had "no bearing on whether the [challenged] plan ultimately [was] found to violate the Constitution."[94] Finally, White saw no connection between a state's efforts to remedy minority vote dilution and affirmative action programs; with the former unlike the latter, contended White, there was no injury to one racial group, no preferential treatment for another.

The other dissents essentially tracked White's reasoning. The *Shaw* majority saw little distinction, however, between the North Carolina scheme and "the most egregious racial gerrymanders of the past."[95] They accepted the appellants' contention, moreover, "that redistricting legislation that is so bizarre on its face that it is 'unexplainable on grounds other than race,' . . . demands the same close scrutiny that we give other state laws that classify citizens by race."[96]

Shaw v. Reno left open the question whether a bizarrely shaped district was a necessary prerequisite for finding a majority-black congressional districting scheme unconstitutional. In *Miller v. Johnson* (1995),[97] a Georgia redistricting case, the Court, speaking through Justice Kennedy, concluded that such a finding was unnecessary.

[T]he essence of the equal protection claim recognized in *Shaw* is that the State has used race as a basis for separating voters into districts. Just as the State may not, absent extraordinary justification, segregate citizens on the basis of race in its public parks . . . and schools, . . . so did we recognize in *Shaw* that it may not separate its citizens into different voting districts on the basis of race. . . . [*Shaw*] was not meant to suggest that a district must be bizarre on its face before there is a constitutional violation. Nor was our conclusion in *Shaw* that in certain instances a district's appearance (or, to be more precise, its appearance in combination with certain demographic evidence) can give rise to an equal protection claim, . . . a holding that bizarreness was a threshold showing, as appellants believe it to be. . . . Shape is relevant not because bizarreness is a necessary element of the constitutional wrong or a threshold requirement of proof, but because it may be persuasive circumstantial evidence that race for its own sake, and not other districting principles, was the legislature's dominant and controlling rationale in drawing its district lines.[98]

The next year, the Court issued its second decision in *Shaw*. On remand, the federal trial court had agreed that North Carolina's redistricting plan was based significantly on race, but found sufficiently compelling justifications underlying the arrangement to satisfy strict scrutiny. In *Shaw v. Hunt* (1996),[99] or *Shaw* II, the Court, per Chief Justice Rehnquist, disagreed, holding that there was no compelling interest to support the predominant role of race in the challenged plan. Finding that provisions of the 1965 Voting Rights Act, as amended, required neither race-based districting nor the particular shape of the district under review, the Court also declined to reach the question whether, under appropriate circumstances, a state's desire to comply with the Voting Rights Act could itself constitute a compelling state interest.

Joined in dissent by Justices Ginsburg and Breyer, Justice Stevens scorned as "seriously misguided" the majority's "aggressive supervision of state action designed to accommodate the political concerns of historically disadvantaged minority groups."[100] Reiterating themes of earlier opinions he had written or joined in cases involving challenges to race-conscious governmental policies, the justice objected to the Court's subjection of North Carolina's districting plan to strict scrutiny. Even under that standard, however, he considered the plan valid. "[S]ome legislators," he declared, "felt that the sorry history of race relations in North Carolina in past decades was a sufficient reason for making it easier for more black leaders to participate in the legislative process and to represent the State in the Congress of the United States. Even if that history does not provide the kind of precise guidance that will justify certain specific affirmative action programs in particular industries, . . . it surely provides an adequate basis for a decision to facilitate the election of representatives of the previously disadvantaged minority."[101] He found equally substantial the state's interest in avoiding the litigation that would have been necessary to overcome Justice Department objections to its initial plan or the suit that would have inevitably resulted from a plan "ensur[ing] the election of white legislators in 11 of [North Carolina's] 12 congressional districts."[102]

Although without the support of Ginsburg and Breyer, Justice Stevens also attacked the majority's failure "to supply a coherent theory of standing to justify its emerging and misguided race-based district jurisprudence," just as he had raised such concerns in *Miller v. Johnson*, and Justice White had in *Shaw* I.

> Here it appears that no individual has been burdened more than any other. The supposedly invidious messages that *Shaw I* contends will follow from extremely irregular race-based districting will presumably be received in equal measure by *all* State residents. For that reason, the claimed violation of a shared right to a color-blind districting process would not seem to implicate the Equal Protection Clause at all precisely because it rests neither on a challenge to the State's decision to distribute burdens and benefits unequally, nor on a claim that the State's formally equal treatment of its citizens in fact stamps persons of one race with a badge of inferiority.[103]

Decided along with *Shaw* II was *Bush v. Vera*,[104] a challenge to majority-black congressional districting in Texas. A five-four Court overturned the districts at issue there; but Justice O'Connor mustered only the support of the chief justice and Justice Kennedy for her conclusion that while not all race-conscious districting was unconstitutional, race had been the "predominant" factor underlying the Texas scheme. Justice Thomas, joined by Justice Scalia, contended, on the other hand, that race necessarily "predominated" in the creation of any majority-black district based on "racial demographics."

In a highly unusual move, however, Justice O'Connor also filed a separate concurrence indicating her view that a state's desire to comply with requirements of the Voting Rights Act would qualify as a compelling interest justifying a predominantly race-based districting arrangement. The four dissenters clearly shared her view. Justice Stevens, joined in dissent by Justices Ginsburg and Breyer, also found the challenged districts valid under any equal protection standard, urged deference to legislative bodies in such matters, and warned that "our equal protection jurisprudence can sometimes mislead us with its rigid characterization of suspect classes and levels of scrutiny."[105]

In a separate dissent for both *Bush* and *Shaw* II, Justice Souter, joined by Justices Ginsburg and Breyer, argued convincingly that pre-*Shaw* reapportionment and vote dilution cases had "required evidence of substantial harm to an identifiable group of voters," yet "[i]f what *Shaw* I [and its progeny] call[ed] harm [was] identifiable at all in a practical sense, it ... seem[ed] to play no favorites, but to fall on every citizen and every representative alike."[106] He recalled that under *Shaw*, the injury said to result from majority-black districting was reinforcement of "the perception that members of the same racial group ... think alike, share the same political instincts, and will prefer the same candidates at the polls," leading officials elected under such a system "to believe that their primary obligation is to represent only the members of that group, rather than their constituency as a whole."[107] If the consideration of race in districting decisions embodied "such notions," declared Souter, "their shadows fall on majorities as well as minorities, whites as well as blacks, the politically dominant as well as the politically impotent." Such injuries thus bore "virtually no resemblance to the only types of claims for gerrymandering" the Court had recognized in the past. Emphasizing the complexities of districting and the complex mix of factors inherent in such considerations, Souter further complained that the "Court's failure to devise a concept of *Shaw* harm that distinguishes those who are injured from those who are not, or to differentiate violation from remedy, [was] matched by its inability to provide any manageable standard to distinguish forbidden districting conduct from the application of traditional state districting principles and the plans that they produce."[108] Souter's recommendation: the Court should "admit *Shaw*'s failure in providing a manageable constitutional standard and to allow for some faith in the political process."[109]

Shaw II had assumed, without holding, that a state's interest in avoiding a violation of the Voting Rights Act might qualify as a compelling interest justifying race-based districting under certain circumstances. In her *Bush* concurrence, Justice O'Connor embraced that position. In the future, such a rationale might be used to support the *Shaw* and *Bush* dissenters' preference for greater deference to the political process. The Court's decisions to date, however, have appeared to reflect more the reasoning of Justices Thomas and Scalia than the more cautious approach ostensibly embraced in the majority and plurality opinions in such cases.

The Color-Blind Constitution

Acceptance of the Court's growing assumption that racial prejudice is a relic of the past, largely irrelevant to an assessment of modern governmental policies, depends, of course, on one's perception of reality. The conclusion that all race-conscious policies are inherently suspect and subject to strict judicial scrutiny, whatever their nature, is vulnerable to criticism, however, on a variety of fronts.[110] The bare language of the equal protection clause obviously is too nebulous to support such a contention. Nor can a defense based on original intent pass muster. As has often been noted, the very Congress that drafted the Fourteenth Amendment enacted race-conscious legislation designed for the sole benefit of the former slaves. Indeed, it is ironic that Justice Scalia and like-minded colleagues so easily ignore this important key to the Fourteenth Amendment's meaning, yet defend a jurisprudence of original intent.[111]

In attempting to decide whether a particular type of governmental classification is inherently suspect, the Court in the 1970s created a formula that took into account whether the factor at issue was an accident of birth irrelevant to the burdens to which the state could legitimately subject a person, whether the class affected was politically powerless, and whether it had long suffered systematic government abuse.[112] The *Bakke* case and subsequent rulings have established that such factors have no relevance to racial classifications and that all racial discrimination, whatever its nature, is inherently suspect and subject to strict judicial review purely in light of the Fourteenth Amendment's historic purposes. Arguably, however, that reading of history, as noted above, is seriously flawed, and whites hardly meet the requirements of suspectness developed in the earlier cases.

Arguably, too, not even the author of the concept of a color-blind Constitution intended to reject all race-conscious legislation. The first Justice John Marshall Harlan fought for the Union during the Civil War. But he was from a Kentucky slaveholding family and, for a time after the war, a vehement opponent of abolition. Even after his transformation into an outspoken proponent of the goals of Reconstruction, moreover, Harlan I continued to defend the necessity of segregated public schools.[113] And when the issue of segregated education arose in 1899,[114] just three years after his eloquent plea for a color-blind Constitution in his dissent from the Court's *Plessy* decision, he spoke for the brethren in dodging the issue.

A close reading of Harlan I's *Plessy* dissent suggests, moreover, that he was hardly challenging a political majority's power to use race-conscious remedies in redressing the effects of the nation's racist past. All are familiar with his moving assertion that "[o]ur constitution is color-blind, and neither knows nor tolerates classes among citizens. In respect of civil rights, all citizens are equal before the law. The humblest is the peer of the most powerful. The law regards man as man, and takes no account of his surroundings or of his color when his civil rights as guarantied by the supreme law of the land are involved."[115] But this very language demonstrates, conclusively in my judgment, that Justice Harlan's focus was purely on the context in which *Plessy* had arisen: the decision of the politically and socially superior race to subject a minority, widely viewed as inferior, to the indignities of second-class citizenship.

The text immediately preceding Harlan I's appeal to a color-blind Constitution makes this abundantly clear. "The white race," he declared, "deems itself to be the dominant race in this country. And so it is, in prestige, in achievements, in education, in wealth, and in power. So, I doubt not, it will continue to be for all time, if it remains true to its great heritage, and holds fast to the principles of constitutional liberty. But in view of the Constitution, in the eye of the law, there is in this country no superior, dominant, ruling class of citizens. There is no caste here."[116]

Justice Harlan's scornful rejoinder to the majority's conclusion that segregation laws treat both races equally also bears remembering. "Every one knows that the statute in question had its origin in the purpose, not so much to exclude white persons from railroad cars occupied by blacks, as to exclude colored people from coaches occupied by or assigned to white persons. . . . The thing to accomplish was, under the guise of giving equal accommodations for whites and blacks, to compel the latter to keep to themselves while traveling in railroad passenger coaches. No one [except his colleagues, he might have added] would be so wanting in candor as to assert the contrary."[117]

Not only was Justice Harlan's concern directed at legislation imposed by a dominant race on a subservient race; the purpose behind segregation laws also had a significant influence on his thinking. Such regulations, he declared, had been "cunningly devised to defeat legitimate results of the war" and perpetuate the substance if not the form of slavery, albeit "under the pretense of recognizing equality of rights."[118] The result of such "cunning," he warned, would be "to render permanent peace impossible, and to keep alive a conflict of races, the continuance of which must do harm to all concerned."[119] Opponents of affirmative action and other race-conscious policies complain that such schemes aggravate racial tensions. They are hardly designed, however, to maintain the racial dominance of one race and the legal and social inferiority of another. Indeed, the first Harlan would probably be amazed to learn that his stirring brief against the perpetuation of the racial status quo has now become the principal rallying cry against efforts by the dominant race in our society to eliminate the effects of the nation's racist past. There is more than a little irony, in fact, in the use to which *Plessy* is currently being put.

It is ironic, too, that Justice Scalia and others who exhort Harlan I's color-blind Constitution see racial prejudice as largely a problem of the past. By 1883, the first Reconstruction was largely dead. The Republican Party had come to view racial reform as a liability, and party leaders, embarking on their own "southern strategy," were attempting to make peace with the states of the former Confederacy. In the *Civil Rights Cases* of that year, the nation's highest Court arrogantly and unfeelingly suggested that special protections for the former slaves were no longer necessary. "When a man has emerged from slavery, and by the aid of beneficent legislation has shaken off the inseparable concomitants of that state," declared Justice Bradley for the majority, "there must be some stage in the progress of his elevation when he takes the rank of a mere citizen, and ceases to be the special favorite of the laws."[120] Harlan I dismissed his brethren's assumption as "scarcely just,"[121] and with good reason. Justice Scalia and company could do worse than to subject certain of their own premises to similar scrutiny.

Epilogue

President Reagan envisioned a Rehnquist Court willing to repudiate the Warren era's human rights legacy, as well as *Roe v. Wade* and other Burger Court decisions expanding the reach of individual liberty. Whether out of personal conviction or considerations of political expediency, George Bush attempted to pursue essentially the same goal. To date, their efforts have achieved only partial success, largely because Justices O'Connor, Kennedy, and Souter have proved much less predictable than their appointing presidents no doubt would have preferred, while President Clinton's selections of Justices Ginsburg and Breyer brought two additional moderate legal pragmatists to the Court, and Justice Stevens has maintained a moderately liberal civil liberties record throughout his tenure. Even the chief justice and Justices Scalia and Thomas have sided, moreover, with civil liberties claims in certain contexts, of which Justice Scalia's broad, literalist approach to the right of confrontation in child sex abuse cases is the most notable example.

The result to date has been a Court with a generally conservative, yet essentially mixed, civil liberties record. Race- and gender-conscious policies, especially affirmative action programs and racial gerrymandering, have faced a heavy burden of justification. A majority of the justices has also continued the campaign of retrenchment in criminal justice cases begun in the Burger era, extending broad deference to government in death penalty cases, recognizing additional exceptions to the *Miranda* doctrine and Fourth Amendment exclusionary rule, and further expanding the opportunities for police to conduct searches without a valid warrant. But while individual justices have vigorously condemned the *Lemon* decision as an unduly expansive reading of the First Amendment's establishment clause, and a majority has increasingly condoned government assistance to religious schools, the *Lemon* test has not yet been formally abandoned and the Court remains vigilant against officially sponsored devotional exercises in the public schools. By the same token, although *Roe's* trimester framework has been abandoned, a majority continues to forbid undue burdens on a woman's decision to choose an abortion over childbirth. And while the Court has refused to extend the right of privacy generally to homosexual privacy and physician-assisted suicide, a majority has arguably subjected discrimination based on sexual preference to heightened scrutiny and refused to rule out a right of terminally ill patients to assisted suicide under all circumstances. The Rehnquist Court's civil liberties record has thus by no means been a uniform repudiation of the Warren era and expansive Burger Court rulings.

In economic cases, however, a majority could be moving, albeit very cautiously at this point, toward a rejection or substantial modification of the constitutional double standard under which the post-1936 Court has extended varying degrees of meaningful judicial protection to noneconomic personal freedom, while relegating the safeguarding of property rights largely to the political process. Not only has the Court expanded state immunity from lawsuits initiated to enforce federal rights and resurrected long-discredited and vaguely defined principles of dual federalism to invalidate otherwise valid congressional statutes said to interfere unduly with state sovereignty; the equally discredited Old Court's use of substantive due process to measure the reasonableness of government economic decisions is experiencing a rebirth on the Rehnquist Court as well. And while Justices Scalia and Thomas have roundly condemned substantive due process as an illegitimate instrument of judicial power, they have also led the Court in its growing and arguably unprecedented use for essentially the same purposes of the Fifth-Fourteenth Amendment's takings clause—a guarantee that, unlike substantive due process, is available by its terms solely for the protection of economic interests and thus is a particularly more convenient tool for jurists antagonistic to further judicial expansion in the scope of privacy and related noneconomic freedoms. Whether such rulings will be largely limited to their somewhat specialized contexts to date or significantly expanded in reach, only time will tell. If extended to a broad field of litigation, however, they could become the most important element of the Reagan-Bush judicial legacy—and one entirely consistent with the conservative Republican economic philosophy, as well as much more central to the party's traditional core than its modern social agenda.

The Rehnquist Court's economic and federalism pronouncements are certainly defensible, as are the concerns of most of its current members about race- and gender-conscious government policies and support for narrow constructions of the rights of suspects and defendants in criminal cases. The impact of such trends on the Court's image as a national symbol is, however, more troubling. Through most of its history, the Court has hardly been a vigorous exponent of equal justice under law. Indeed, its first sustained defense of individual freedom was in the service of laissez-faire, when a late-nineteenth- and early-twentieth-century majority, in defiance of numerous precedents leaving the resolution of economic questions to the political process, extolled the rights of commercial interests against the attempts of democratic institutions to redress the more odious social and economic consequences of the

Industrial Revolution. The post-1936 Court, particularly during the Warren era, rejected that past, returning ultimate responsibility for economic matters to the voters and their elected representatives, while converting the Constitution into a powerful weapon in behalf of racial minorities, the politically unorthodox and dispossessed, religious dissidents, broad expressive freedom, and criminal defendants.

Such developments made the Warren Court, especially, an object of intense national controversy—and a convenient political target, particularly on the part of Republican presidents bent on breaking the Democratic Party's post–Civil War hold on the South and the GOP's status as the minority party of the post-Depression era. President Nixon's selection of William Rehnquist, an extreme conservative with at best a checkered civil rights and civil liberties past, was clearly part of that strategy, as were President Reagan's elevation of the justice to the Court's center seat and, in varying degrees, other Reagan-Bush appointments to the Court.

For segments of the population weary of civil rights battles; convinced, as Justice Scalia apparently is, that racial discrimination is largely a relic of the past; dubious of "criminal-coddling" judges; and vehemently resentful of *Roe v. Wade* and a host of other civil liberties decisions, Republican promises to revolutionize the Supreme Court had tremendous appeal. But for many Americans, particularly the most vulnerable among us, the generally conservative direction of the Court's decisions, whatever their legal merits, has raised serious questions about its continued commitment to the principle of equal justice for all—concerns aggravated by the departures of Justices Brennan, Marshall, and Blackmun, and only partially relieved by the current domination of moderate pragmatists on the Court. At a time of deep polarization of the nation and growing incivility in the political arena, such doubts may represent the most significant challenge to the Rehnquist Court's legacy.

Bibiliographical Note

This book is based primarily on the decisions and opinions of the Rehnquist Court. The first chapter draws heavily on Senate confirmation proceedings relating to the appointments of Chief Justice Rehnquist and other justices selected to the Court during his tenure. Secondary sources cited in the notes contributed especially to an understanding of the confirmation process, the inner workings of the Court, and individual justices, as did other studies not cited in the text, such as David Savage's *Turning Right: The Making of the Rehnquist Supreme Court* (New York: John Wiley, 1993). The Thurgood Marshall Papers at the Library of Congress, open to researchers on a largely unrestricted basis since the justice's death, were of tremendous value; and the Lewis F. Powell, Jr., Papers at Washington and Lee University were also consulted for the one term Justice Powell served on the Rehnquist Court.

As indicated in this study and elsewhere, however, Justice Marshall's papers were released only over the vigorous protests of family members and the justice's former colleagues; the papers of other justices who have left the bench during Chief Justice Rehnquist's tenure in the Court's center seat remain generally unavailable, at least for the Rehnquist Court portion of their careers. Under pressure from other justices, Justice Brennan limited access to his Rehnquist Court files largely to his official biographer, at least pending completion of that study. Justice White's papers are not available, as Dennis Hutchinson makes clear in his commendable recent biography of the justice, *The Man Who Once Was Whizzer White* (New York: Free Press, 1998); Justice Blackmun's papers are currently being organized for submission to the Library of Congress.

My efforts to interview the justices were equally unavailing. Over the years, I have conducted interviews with a number of federal and state jurists. Even as a graduate student, in fact, I had a fruitful conversation with Justice Tom C. Clark in connection with his opinions in prejudicial publicity cases, including *Sheppard v. Maxwell* (1966), decided only the previous year. Early in my academic career, Justice Black spoke frankly with me on two memorable occasions regarding his judicial and constitutional philosophy, with only pending cases, for obvious reasons, an inappropriate subject for inquiry. Black had his notes of the Court's conferences destroyed before his death, but only because he thought such cryptic and often illegible notations in his files and those of other justices could be misleading to readers, and not because of a concern for preserving the secrecy of the Court's proceedings, as his voluminous Library of Congress papers make clear.

Certain members of the current Court occasionally undertake television interviews in tightly controlled settings, as well as speaking engagements and stints as university lecturers, especially during their summer recesses. In fact, shortly after Justice Scalia graciously declined my request for an interview, I learned from one of my more conservative Republican friends that he had recently given an unpublicized talk to area lawyers in my eastern North Carolina community, the guest of a federal judge who once played a minor role on President Nixon's Watergate defense team. Although generally skeptical about the prospects of a broad-ranging interview, Chief Justice Rehnquist did suggest that I might submit written questions for his review and possible response. After recalling a previous experience with the chief justice during his tenure as associate justice I decided against that effort. Several years before his elevation to the Court's center seat, I had interviewed Justice Rehnquist in connection with research for a possible article comparing and contrasting legal positivist elements in his thinking with those of Justice Black. His comments were very revealing, not only about my specific subject, but also with respect to his concerns about the directions of Supreme Court decision making and American politics generally in the post-1936 era. When I shared a copy of the manuscript with him, however, he asked that I delete all reference to our interview, prompting me to drop my publication plans.

The Rehnquist Court's efforts to limit scholarly and media access to its work, discussed in the second chapter of this book, has extended, of course, to its law clerks. By signed agreement, clerks are obliged to refrain from discussing the work of the Court and the chamber they serve, even after the clerkship concludes. Some clerks have been willing to share their experiences and impressions with students of the Court, but without attribution. While such information is probably accurate in most instances, I have avoided such sources in my previous studies for obvious reasons, except in extremely rare circumstances where necessary to spare a source needless embarrassment. My research for this study included no interviews with clerks.

Since the major purpose of my study was to examine major trends in constitutional doctrine on the Rehnquist Court, such research restrictions were only mildly frustrating rather than a serious obstacle to the successful completion of my project. For those who believe, however, that broad scholarly and media access to the Court is important to a full understanding and appreciation of its work, as well as vital to the openness of governmental institutions so essential to a democratic society, the current Court's fetish for secrecy is a genuine cause for concern.

Notes

Preface

1. Lou Cannon, *Reagan* (New York: G. P. Putnam's, 1982), p. 270.

2. South Carolina v. Katzenbach, 383 U.S. 301 (1966).

3. Bob Jones University v. United States, 461 U.S. 574 (1983).

4. The controversy that campaign aroused is the focus of Lincoln Caplan, *The Tenth Justice: The Solicitor General and the Rule of Law* (New York: Knopf, 1987).

5. See especially Sheldon Goldman, *Picking Federal Judges: Lower Court Selection from Roosevelt through Reagan* (New Haven: Yale University Press, 1997).

6. See, for example, James F. Simon, *The Center Holds: Power Struggle Inside the Rehnquist Court* (New York: Simon & Schuster, 1995).

7. See, for example, *The Burger Court: Political and Judicial Profiles*, ed. Charles M. Lamb and Stephen C. Halpern (Urbana and Chicago: University of Illinois Press, 1991); Richard Funston, *Constitutional Counter-Revolution?* (Cambridge, Mass.: Schenkman Publishing, 1977).

8. The double standard was first suggested, of course, in footnote four of Justice Stone's opinion for the Court in United States v. Carolene Products Co., 304 U.S. 144 (1938).

9. 116 S. Ct. 1620 (1996).

10. 478 U.S. 186 (1986).

11. Washington v. Glucksberg, 117 S. Ct. 2258 (1997); Vacco v. Quill, 117 S. Ct. 2293 (1997).

Chapter One

1. *New York Times*, September 27, 1986.

2. U.S. Congress, Senate, Committee on the Judiciary, Hearings, *Nomination of Justice William Hubbs Rehnquist to be Chief Justice of the United States*, 99th Cong., 2d sess., 1986 (hereinafter 1986 Rehnquist Hearings). The hearings were conducted July 29–31 and August 1, 1986.

3. The memorandum is reprinted in ibid., pp. 314–15.

4. 163 U.S. 537 (1896).

5. Rehnquist's reference, of course, was to Swedish sociologist Gunnar Myrdal's *An American Dilemma: The Negro Problem and Modern Democracy* (New York: Harper, 1944), which was among the controversial social science studies of the effects of segregated education on minority children that Chief Justice Warren would cite in footnote eleven of Brown v. Board of Education, 347 U.S. 483 (1954).

6. 345 U.S. 461 (1953).

7. The memoranda are reprinted in 1986 Rehnquist Hearings, pp. 312–13.

8. Ibid., pp. 137–38.

9. *Washington Post,* July 22, 1986.

10. 1986 Rehnquist Hearings, p. 277.

11. Ibid., pp. 310–11.

12. The first memorandum, which Cronson thought he had typed, was entitled "A Few Expressed Prejudices on the Segregation Cases" and carried Cronson's initials. The *Brown* and *Terry* memoranda are in the Robert H. Jackson Papers, Library of Congress.

13. 1986 Rehnquist Hearings, pp. 300–301.

14. Richard Kluger, *Simple Justice: The History of Brown v. Board of Education and Black Americans' Struggle for Equality* (New York: Knopf, 1976), pp. 603–10, reprinted in ibid., pp. 326–33.

15. Kluger, *Simple Justice,* p. 332.

16. 319 U.S. 624 (1943).

17. "Who Writes Decisions of the Supreme Court," *U.S. News & World Report,* December 13, 1957, pp. 74–75.

18. 408 U.S. 1 (1972).

19. Laird v. Tatum, 409 U.S. 824 (1972).

20. *New York Times,* October 11, 1972.

21. Quoted in 1986 Rehnquist Hearings, pp. 233–34.

22. Ibid., p. 231.

23. John P. MacKenzie, *The Appearance of Justice* (New York: Scribner's, 1974).

24. 1986 Rehnquist Hearings, p. 232.

25. The letter, dated November 29, 1971, is reprinted in U.S. Congress, Senate, Committee on the Judiciary, *Nominations of William H. Rehnquist of Arizona, and Lewis F. Powell, Jr., of Virginia to be Associate Justices of the Supreme Court of the United States,* 92d Cong., 1st sess., 1971, pp. 486–92.

26. See 1986 Rehnquist Hearings, pp. 984–1077, for such testimony.

27. Ibid., p. 1036.

28. Ibid., p. 158.

29. 334 U.S. 1 (1948).

30. 1986 Rehnquist Hearings, p. 262.

31. Ibid., p. 266.

32. *New York Times,* August 6, 1986.

33. *New York Times,* August 1, 1986.

34. *New York Times,* August 8, 1986.

35. *New York Times,* August 12–14, 1986.

36. *New York Times,* August 15, 1986.

37. Ibid.

38. *New York Times,* August 28, 1986.

39. *New York Times,* September 4, 1986.

40. *New York Times,* September 10, 1986.

41. *New York Times,* September 11, 1986.

42. *New York Times,* September 12, 1986.

43. *New York Times,* September 17, 1986.

44. *New York Times,* September 19, 1986.

45. Nixon v. Administrator of General Services, 433 U.S. 425 (1977).

46. 410 U.S. 113 (1973).

47. 438 U.S. 265 (1978).

48. *New York Times,* July 23, 1986.

49. For critical analyses of Justice Scalia's judicial philosophy and record, see Richard A. Brisbin, Jr., *Justice Antonin Scalia and the Conservative Revival* (Baltimore: Johns Hopkins University Press, 1997); David A. Schultz and Christopher E. Smith, *The Jurisprudential Vision of Justice Antonin Scalia* (Lanham, Md.: Rowman & Littlefield Publishers, 1996).

50. *New York Times,* June 20, 1986.

51. *New York Times,* June 22, 1986.

52. *New York Times,* June 26, 1986.

53. *New York Times,* July 3, 1986.

54. *New York Times,* August 10, 1986.

55. U.S. Congress, Senate, Committee on the Judiciary, *Nomination of Judge Antonin Scalia to be Associate Justice of the Supreme Court of the United States,* 99th Cong., 2d sess., 1986, pp. 17–19 (hereinafter Scalia Hearings).

56. *New York Times,* August 8, 1986.

57. Scalia Hearings, p. 121.

58. Ibid., p. 23.

59. Ibid., p. 5.

60. Ibid., p. 13.

61. Ibid., p. 89.

62. Ibid., pp. 48–49.

63. Quoted in ibid., p. 88.

64. Ibid., pp. 88–89.

65. Ibid., p. 91.

66. Ibid., p. 94, quoting from Antonin Scalia, "The Disease as Cure," *Washington University Law Quarterly* 1 (1979): 147–60.

67. Scalia Hearings, p. 94.

68. Dred Scott v. Sandford, 19 How. 393 (1857).

69. U.S. Congress, Senate, Committee on the Judiciary, *Nomination of Judge Sandra Day O'Connor of Arizona to serve as an Associate Justice of the Supreme Court of the United States,* 97th Cong., 1st sess., 1981, pp. 282–83.

70. Ibid., p. 283.

71. Ibid., pp. 287–88.

72. Ibid., p. 61.

73. Henry J. Abraham, *Justices and Presidents: A Political History of Appointments to the Supreme Court,* 3d ed. (New York: Oxford University Press, 1992), pp. 340–42.

74. *New York Times,* June 18, 1986.

75. Of many studies of the Bork confirmation battle, see, for example, Ethan Bronner, *Battle for Justice: How the Bork Nomination Shook America* (New York: Norton, 1989).

76. U.S. Congress, Senate, Committee on the Judiciary, *Nomination of Anthony M. Kennedy to be Associate Justice of the Supreme Court of the United States*, 100th Cong., 1st sess., 1987, p. 5 (hereinafter Kennedy Hearings).

77. Ibid., p. 201.

78. See, for example, Black's dissent in Griswold v. Connecticut, 381 U.S. 479 (1965).

79. Kennedy Hearings, pp. 87–88.

80. Ibid., p. 48.

81. Quoted in ibid., p. 90.

82. Ibid., pp. 90–91.

83. Beller v. Middendorf, 632 F. 2d 788 (9th Cir., 1988).

84. Gerdom v. Continental Airlines, Inc., 692 F. 2d 602 (9th Cir., 1982).

85. Spangler v. Pasadena Bd. of Education, 611 F. 2d 1239 (9th Cir., 1979).

86. Kennedy Hearings, p. 388.

87. Ibid., pp. 267–68.

88. Ibid., pp. 333–34.

89. Abraham, *Justices and Presidents*, pp. 360–61.

90. Quoted in "Insider Baseball: How Sununu Sold Souter," *Harper's Magazine*, November, 1990, p. 24.

91. A copy of President Bush's announcement of the Souter nomination is reprinted in *Congressional Quarterly Almanac* 46 (1990): 509.

92. Quoted in U.S. Congress, Senate, *Nomination of David H. Souter to be Associate Justice of the Supreme Court of the United States*, 101st Cong., 2d sess., 1990, p. 119 (hereinafter Souter Hearings).

93. Ibid., p. 120.

94. Griswold v. Connecticut, 381 U.S. 479 (1965).

95. See, for example, Duncan v. Louisana, 393 U.S. 145 (1968).

96. Souter Hearings, p. 56.

97. 384 U.S. 436 (1966).

98. Conservative columnist William F. Buckley, Jr., used Souter's praise of Brennan in comparing what he termed Souter's "cowardly" efforts to appease Senate liberals with Brennan's attempt to cultivate Wisconsin senator Joseph McCarthy and other "Commie-hunters" during his confirmation hearings. "The Valor of Judge Souter," *National Review*, October 15, 1990.

99. Souter Hearings, p. 17.

100. Ibid.

101. See, for example, Craig v. Boren, 429 U.S. 190 (1976).

102. Souter Hearings, pp. 75–76.

103. Ibid., p. 71.

104. Andrew Hacker, *Two Nations* (New York: Scribner's, 1992), p. 201.

105. This profile is drawn from a number of periodical accounts, including "The Crowning Thomas Affair," *U.S. News & World Report*, September 16, 1991, pp. 25–30, and my chapter on "Bush and the Courts," in Dilys M. Hill and Phil Williams (eds.), *The Bush Presidency: Triumphs and Adversities* (London: Macmillan, 1994), pp. 84–108.

106. A. Leon Higginbotham, Jr., "An Open Letter to Justice Clarence Thomas from a Federal Judicial Colleague," *University of Pennsylvania Law Review* 140 (1992): 1005–28.

107. Quoted in *Washington Post*, July 2, 1991.

108. Quoted in Higginbotham, "An Open Letter," p. 1012.

109. Quoted in *Washington Post*, July 2, 1991.

110. Quoted in "The Crowning Thomas Affair," p. 26.

111. For a summary of Thomas's EEOC tenure, see *Washington Post*, September 10, 1991.

112. For a profile of Thomas's second wife, Virginia Lamp Thomas, see *Washington Post*, September 10, 1991.

113. Lewis Lehrman, "The Declaration of Independence and the Right to Life," *American Spectator*, April 1987, pp. 21–23.

114. For an early analysis of Thomas's constitutional philosophy, see Scott D. Gerber, "The Jurisprudence of Clarence Thomas," *Journal of Law and Politics* 8 (1991): 107–41. For Thomas's own brief summaries of his thinking, see "The Higher Law Background of the Privileges and Immunities Clause of the Fourteenth Amendment," *Harvard Journal of Law & Public Policy* 12 (1989): 63–70; "Toward a 'Plain Reading' of the Constitution—The Declaration of Independence in Constitutional Interpretation," *Howard Law Journal* 30 (1987): 983–95.

115. Quoted in *Washington Post*, September 10, 1991.

116. *Washington Post*, September 10, 1991.

117. See, for example, BMW of North America, Inc. v. Gore, 116 S. Ct. 1589, 1610 (1996) (Scalia, J., joined by Thomas, J., dissenting).

118. Compare, for example, Roe v. Wade, 410 U.S. 113 (1973), with Lochner v. New York, 198 U.S. 45 (1905).

119. U.S. Congress, Senate, Committee on the Judiciary, *Nomination of Judge Clarence Thomas to be Associate Justice of the Supreme Court of the United States*, 102d Cong., 1st sess., 1991, part 1, p. 109 (hereinafter Thomas Hearings).

120. Michael Kinsley, "Liar or Boob?" *New Republic*, October 21, 1991, p. 4.

121. Thomas Hearings, part 1, p. 222.
122. Ibid.
123. Ibid., p. 147.
124. *Washington Post*, September 11, 1991.
125. Ibid., October 8, 1991.
126. Thomas Hearings, part 4, pp. 157–58.
127. Ibid., p. 195.
128. "The Crowning Thomas Affair," p. 29.
129. See, for example, Jane Mayer and Jill Abramson, *Strange Justice: The Selling of Clarence Thomas* (New York: Houghton Mifflin, 1994), pp. 106–9, and passim.
130. Thomas Hearings, part 4, p. 200.
131. Carter v. Sedgwick County, Kansas, 705 F. Supp. 1474 (D. Kan., 1988).
132. Thomas Hearings, part 4, p. 253.
133. "Hearings Turn Off Judges," *National Law Journal*, October 28, 1991, p. 1.
134. *Washington Post*, October 5, 1992.
135. Ibid.
136. See, for example, Mayer and Abramson, *Strange Justice*, and Timothy M. Phelps and Helen Winternitz, *Capitol Games* (New York: Hyperion, 1992).
137. *New York Times*, April 9, 1993.
138. *New York Times*, June 8, 1993.
139. *New York Times*, June 13, 1993.
140. *New York Times*, June 9, 1993.
141. *New York Times*, June 13, 1993.
142. Frontiero v. Richardson, 411 U.S. 677 (1973); Craig v. Boren, 429 U.S. 190 (1976).
143. *New York Times*, June 15, 1993.
144. U.S. Congress, Senate, *Nomination of Ruth Bader Ginsburg, to be Associate Justice of the Supreme Court of the United States*, 103d Cong., 1st sess., 1993, p. 148 (hereinafter Ginsburg Hearings).
145. Ibid., p. 149.
146. Lemon v. Kurtzman, 403 U.S. 602 (1971).
147. Everson v. Bd. of Education, 330 U.S. 1 (1947).
148. Ginsburg Hearings, p. 154.
149. Lamb's Chapel v. Center Moriches School Dist., 508 U.S. 394, 398 (1993) (Scalia, J., joined by Thomas, J., concurring in judgment).
150. Ginsburg Hearings, p. 155.
151. Ibid., p. 269.
152. 19 How. at 393.
153. Ginsburg Hearings, pp. 272–73.
154. Ibid., p. 274.
155. Ibid., p. 411.
156. Ibid., pp. 531–32.
157. *New York Times*, April 7, 1994.
158. In Regent of the University of California v. Bakke, 438 U.S. 265 (1978), for example, he dissented from the Court's decision invalidating a minority admissions program at a state medical college.
159. See his dissent from the Court's denial of review in Callins v. Collins, 114 S. Ct. 1127 (1994).
160. *New York Times*, March 12, 1993.
161. *New York Times*, April 11, 1994.
162. Roberts v. United States Jaycees, 468 U.S. 609 (1984).
163. Hodgson v. Minnesota, 497 U.S. 417 (1990).
164. *New York Times*, April 11, 1994.
165. U.S. Congress, Senate, *Nomination of Stephen G. Breyer to be an Associate Justice of the Supreme Court of the United States*, 103d Cong., 2d sess., 1994, p. 356 (hereinafter Breyer Hearings).
166. 381 U.S. 479.
167. Breyer Hearings, p. 425.
168. Daniel A. Farber, "Legal Pragmatism and the Constitution," *Minnesota Law Review* 72 (1988): 1331.
169. Breyer Hearings, p. 431.
170. Ibid.
171. Ibid., pp. 434–35.
172. Ibid., p. 439.
173. New Life Baptist Academy v. East Longmeadow School Dist., 885 F. 2d 940 (1st Cir., 1989).
174. Breyer Hearings, p. 444.
175. 494 U.S. 872 (1990).
176. Sherbert v. Verner, 374 U.S. 398 (1963).
177. City of Boerne v. Flores, 117 S. Ct. 2157 (1997).
178. Breyer Hearings, p. 451; for Hatch's questioning of Judge Breyer regarding *Smith*, see Breyer Hearings, pp. 120–22.
179. See, for example, Lucas v. South Carolina Coastal Council, 112 S. Ct. 2886 (1992); Dolan v. City of Tigard, 114 S. Ct. 2309 (1994).
180. Pennsylvania Coal Co. v. Mahon, 260 U. S. 393 (1923).
181. Penn Central Transp. Co. v. New York City, 438 U.S. 104 (1978).
182. Breyer Hearings, p. 113.
183. Monroe H. Freedman to Joseph R. Biden, Jr., July 13, 1994, quoted in ibid., pp. 325–35.
184. Stephen Gillers to Lloyd Cutler, July 8, 1994, and Geoffrey C. Hazard, Jr., to Lloyd Cutler, July 11, 1994, quoted in ibid., pp. 318–22.
185. U.S. v. Ottati & Goss, Inc., 900 F. 2d 429 (1st Cir., 1990).
186. Breyer Hearings, p. 316.
187. See Mark Silverstein, *Judicious Choices: The New Politics of Supreme Court Confirmations* (New York: W.W. Norton, 1994).

Chapter Two

1. Warren Burger, Memorandum to the Conference, November 5, 1986, Thurgood Marshall Papers, Library of Congress, Box 407. A press account of the Philadelphia committee's announcement had appeared in the *New York Times*, October 25, 1986.

2. William H. Rehnquist to Thurgood Marshall, July 26, 1991, Marshall Papers, Box 525.

3. Ibid. Regarding 1986 legislation restricting the Court's authority to transport associate justices to and from their residences, see the confidential memorandum from Richard Schickele, staff counsel, to Supreme Court Marshal Alfred Wong, November 20, 1986, Marshall Papers, Box 407.

4. *Washington Post*, January 1, 1998. Excerpts from the chief justice's report are reprinted in *Washington Post*, January 2, 1998.

5. *Washington Post*, January 1, 1998.

6. See, for example, Ronald Stidham et al., "The Voting Behavior of President Clinton's Judicial Appointees," *Judicature* 80 (1996): 16–20.

7. *Washington Post*, January 3, 1998.

8. *Washington Post*, January 11, 1998.

9. Tinsley E. Yarbrough, "Reagan and the Courts," in *The Reagan Presidency: An Incomplete Revolution*, ed. Dilys M. Hill, Raymond A. Moore, and Phil Williams (London: Macmillan, 1990), p. 88.

10. *New York Times*, July 18, 1988.

11. *New York Times*, July 19, 1988.

12. *St. Louis Post-Dispatch*, July 16, 1988.

13. Harry M. Blackmun to John Paul Stevens, July 19, 1988, Marshall Papers, Box 436.

14. Wannett Smith to John Paul Stevens, undated, Marshall Papers, Box 436.

15. *New York Times*, September 29, 1988.

16. *New York Times*, June 22, 1986.

17. See, for example, *New York Times*, July 26, 1986.

18. See, for example, Jeffrey D. Hockett, *New Deal Justice: The Constitutional Jurisprudence of Hugo L. Black, Felix Frankfurter, and Robert H. Jackson* (Lanham, Md.: Rowman & Littlefield, 1996).

19. "Rude Robes," *Newsweek*, October 19, 1992, p. 5.

20. For summaries, see, for example, David A. Schultz and Christopher E. Smith, *The Jurisprudential Vision of Justice Antonin Scalia* (Lanham, Md.: Rowman & Littlefield, 1996); David M. O'Brien, *Storm Center: The Supreme Court in American Politics*, 4th ed. (New York: Norton, 1996), p. 282.

21. This discussion is drawn from a profile by Joan Biskupic in the *Washington Post*, February 18, 1997.

22. Printz v. United States, 117 S. Ct. 2365 (1997).

23. Washington v. Glucksberg, 117 S. Ct. 2258 (1997); Vacco v. Quill, 117 S. Ct. 2293 (1997).

24. Maryland v. Wilson, 117 S. Ct. 882 (1997).

25. Quoted in O'Brien, *Storm Center*, p. 282.

26. See David J. Garrow, "The Rehnquist Reins," *New York Times Magazine*, October 6, 1996, pp. 65ff.

27. Quoted in ibid., p. 68.

28. 492 U.S. 490 (1989).

29. Ibid., p. 532.

30. Garrow, "The Rehnquist Reins," p. 69.

31. Edward Lazarus, *Closed Chambers: The First Eyewitness Account of the Epic Struggles Inside the Supreme Court* (New York: Random House, 1998), p. 457.

32. Ibid., p. 458.

33. See, for example, Albert P. Melone, "Revisiting the Freshman Effect Hypothesis: The First Two Terms of Justice Anthony Kennedy," *Judicature* 74 (1990): 6–13; Thea F. Rubin and Albert P. Melone, "Justice Antonin Scalia: A First Year Freshman Effect?" *Judicature* 72 (1988): 98–102.

34. Robert H. Bork, *Slouching Towards Gomorrah: Modern Liberalism and American Decline* (New York: Harper-Collins, 1996).

35. Texas v. Johnson, 491 U.S. 397 (1989); United States v. Eichman, 496 U.S. 310 (1990).

36. Justice Scalia's speech is summarized in the *Washington Post*, May 23, 1997.

37. Harry A. Blackmun, Memorandum to the Conference, February 9, 1990, Marshall Papers, Box 493.

38. Sandra Day O'Connor to Harry A. Blackmun, February 9, 1990, Marshall Papers, Box 493.

39. *Washington Post*, June 9, 1997.

40. *New York Times*, October 24, 1995.

41. Carol S. Steiker, memorandum to Thurgood Marshall, April 22, 1988, Marshall Papers, Box 427.

42. Byron R. White to Harry A. Blackmun, October 1, 1986, Marshall Papers, Box 407.

43. William H. Rehnquist, "Who Writes Decisions of the Supreme Court," *U.S. News & World Report*, December 13, 1957, pp. 74–75.

44. *New York Times*, April 27, 1958.

45. Lazarus, *Closed Chambers*, p. 263.

46. Robert H. Bork, *The Tempting of America: The Political Seduction of the Law* (New York: Simon & Schuster, 1990).

47. Lazarus, *Closed Chambers*, p. 264.

48. Ibid., p. 265.

49. Letter to William H. Rehnquist, November 21, 1988, Marshall Papers, Box 462.

50. Thurgood Marshall to William H. Rehnquist, November 14, 1988, Marshall Papers, Box 462.

51. Thurgood Marshall to William H. Rehnquist, November 1, 1990, Marshall Papers, Box 524.

52. Lazarus, *Closed Chambers*, p. 265.

53. Tinsley E. Yarbrough, *John Marshall Harlan: Great Dissenter of the Warren Court* (New York: Oxford University Press, 1992), pp. 143–44.

54. Frank M. Johnson, Jr., to Thurgood Marshall, June 7, 1985, Marshall Papers, Box 570.

55. 488 U.S. 469 (1989).

56. Derrick Bell to Thurgood Marshall, February 15, 1989, Marshall Papers, Box 570.

57. Derrick Bell to Thurgood Marshall, March 18, 1990, Marshall Papers, Box 572.

58. Max Frankel to Thurgood Marshall, March 16, 1990, Marshall Papers, Box 572; *Washington Post*, October 6, 1998.

59. Anthony M. Kennedy to William H. Rehnquist, August 1, 1991, Marshall Papers, Box 525.

60. Harry A. Blackmun to William H. Rehnquist, August 6, 1991, Marshall Papers, Box 525.

61. Harry A. Blackmun to William H. Rehnquist, August 9, 1991, Marshall Papers, Box 525.

62. Antonin Scalia to William H. Rehnquist, August 9, 1991, Marshall Papers, Box 525.

63. John Paul Stevens, "Some Thoughts on Judicial Restraint," *Judicature* 66 (1982): 177–83.

64. Tinsley E. Yarbrough, *Mr. Justice Black and His Critics* (Durham, N.C.: Duke University Press, 1988).

65. 403 U.S. 15 (1971).

66. Yarbrough, *John Marshall Harlan*, pp. 143, 322.

67. See the tables and statistics in Robert A. Carp and Ronald Stidham, *Judicial Process in America*, 4th ed. (Washington, D.C.: Congressional Quarterly Press, 1998), pp. 58–59. For an interesting and diverse, though generally critical, collection of essays on the roles of law clerks, see the issue on "Law Clerks: The Transformation of the Judiciary," in *The Long Term View: A Journal of Informed Opinion* 3 (1995): 1–110.

68. Richard A. Posner, *The Federal Courts: Crisis and Reform* (Cambridge, Mass.: Harvard University Press, 1985), p. 107.

69. Ibid.

70. Ibid., p. 108.

71. Ibid., pp. 108–9.

72. Ibid., p. 110.

73. Ibid., p. 117.

74. Harry T. Edwards, "The Rising Workload and Perceived 'Bureaucracy' of the Federal Courts: A Causation-Based Approach to the Search for Appropriate Remedies," *Iowa Law Review* 68 (1983): 888. See also Harry T. Edwards, "A Judge's View on Justice, Bureaucracy, and Legal Method," *Michigan Law Review* 80 (1981): 259.

75. Posner, *The Federal Courts*, p. 117.

76. William H. Rehnquist, Memorandum to the Conference, November 24, 1989, Marshall Papers, Box 492.

77. John Paul Stevens to William H. Rehnquist, December 19, 1989, Marshall Papers, Box 492.

78. 487 U.S. 654 (1988).

79. William H. Rehnquist, Memoranda to the Conference, May 8, 1990, May 7, 1991, Marshall Papers, Boxes 493, 525.

80. William H. Rehnquist to Harry A. Blackmun, June 21, 1991, Marshall Papers, Box 525.

81. Harry A. Blackmun to William H. Rehnquist, June 20, 1991, Marshall Papers, Box 525.

82. For general discussions of the Court's conferences, see Henry J. Abraham, *The Judicial Process*, 7th ed. (New York: Oxford University Press, 1998), pp. 213–15, and O'Brien, *Storm Center*, pp. 283–96.

83. For a discussion of statistics on the time devoted to cases in conference, see O'Brien, *Storm Center*, pp. 284–85.

84. John Paul Stevens to William H. Rehnquist, October 28, 1988, Marshall Papers, Box 462.

85. Brutsche v. Cleveland-Perdue, 498 U.S. 949 (1990).

86. Ronald E. Elberger to William H. Rehnquist, January 22, 1990, Marshall Papers, Box 493.

87. William H. Rehnquist, Memoranda to the Conference, January 26, 31, 1990, Marshall Papers, Box 493.

88. Sandra Day O'Connor, Memorandum to the Conference, October 15, 1990, Marshall Papers, Box 537. The case was Perry v. Louisiana, 498 U.S. 38 (1990), which was reversed and remanded for reconsideration in light of the Court's decision in Washington v. Harper, 494 U.S. 210 (1990), rejecting substantive and procedural due process challenges to the involuntary treatment of mentally ill prisoners with antipsychotic drugs.

89. *New York Times*, March 5, 6, 7, 1985.

90. Alfred Wong, Memorandum to the Con-

ference, March 17, 1988, Marshall Papers, Box 435.

91. Alfred Wong, Memorandum to the Conference, December 18, 1989, Marshall Papers, Box 492.

92. William H. Rehnquist, Memorandum to the Conference, November 7, 1990, Marshall Papers, Box 524.

93. *In Re* Vey, 117 S. Ct. 1294 (1997).

94. Vey v. Clinton, 117 S. Ct. 1792 (1997).

95. Martin v. District of Columbia Court of Appeals, 506 U.S. 1 (1992). Martin was one of the frequent filers Chief Justice Rehnquist had referred to in his November 1990 memorandum. At that point, Martin had filed forty-three petitions with the Court. Regarding Stevens's position, see also his dissents in, for example, Zatko v. California, 502 U.S. 16, 18 (1991).

96. Harry A. Blackmun, Memorandum to the Conference, September 30, 1986, Marshall Papers, Box 406.

97. See, for example, Abraham, *The Judicial Process*, p. 215 n. 126.

98. John Paul Stevens, Memorandum to the Conference, October 1, 1986, Marshall Papers, Box 407.

99. Abraham, *The Judicial Process*, p. 215 n. 126.

100. Antonin Scalia, Memorandum to the Conference, April 26, 1990, Marshall Papers, Box 493.

101. 494 U.S. 259 (1990).

102. William J. Brennan, Memorandum to the Conference, April 30, 1990, Marshall Papers, Box 493.

103. 494 U.S. at 274 (emphasis added).

104. See William H. Rehnquist, Memoranda to the Conference, April 27, 30, 1990, Marshall Papers, Box 493.

105. See, for example, Marshall Papers, Boxes 452, 570.

106. For a summary of the controversy, see O'Brien, *Storm Center*, pp. 150–52.

107. Sheryl Farmer, Memorandum to the Chief Justice, June 12, 1987, Marshall Papers, Box 408; Kathleen Arberg, Memorandum to the Chief Justice, June 12, 1987, Marshall Papers, Box 408.

108. John Paul Stevens to William H. Rehnquist, June 12, 1987, Marshall Papers, Box 408.

109. William J. Brennan to William H. Rehnquist, June 12, 1987, Marshall Papers, Box 408.

110. Harry A. Blackmun to William H. Rehnquist, June 12, 1987, Marshall Papers, Box 408.

111. Antonin Scalia to William H. Rehnquist, June 15, 1987, Marshall Papers, Box 408.

112. Byron R. White to William H. Rehnquist, June 15, 1987, Marshall Papers, Box 408.

113. Thurgood Marshall, Memorandum to Law Clerks, May 17, 1989, Marshall Papers, Box 463.

114. Tim O'Brien to William H. Rehnquist, August 6, 1987, Marshall Papers, Box 408.

115. William H. Rehnquist to Tim O'Brien, August 20, 1987, Marshall Papers, Box 408.

116. William H. Rehnquist, Memorandum to the Conference and Court Officers, August 5, 1987, Marshall Papers, Box 408.

117. William H. Rehnquist to Steven York, June 11, 1987, Marshall Papers, Box 408.

118. William H. Rehnquist to Ward Chamberlin, January 25, 1988, Marshall Papers, Box 435.

119. Ron Nessen to William H. Rehnquist, February 9, 1988, Marshall Papers, Box 435; William H. Rehnquist to Ron Nessen, February 11, 1988, Marshall Papers, Box 435; William H. Rehnquist, Memorandum to the Conference, February 10, 1988, Marshall Papers, Box 435.

120. John Paul Stevens to William H. Rehnquist, February 11, 1988, Marshall Papers, Box 435.

121. John Paul Stevens, Memoranda to the Conference, September 18, 19, 1991, Marshall Papers, Box 535.

122. Harry A. Blackmun to William H. Rehnquist, September 19, 1991, Marshall Papers, Box 525.

123. Antonin Scalia to William H. Rehnquist, September 18, 1991, Marshall Papers, Box 525. For reactions of other justices, see Marshall Papers, Box 525.

124. William H. Rehnquist, Memorandum to the Conference, September 19, 1991, Marshall Papers, Box 525.

125. 487 U.S. 654 (1988); William H. Rehnquist, Memorandum to the Conference, April 7, 1988, Marshall Papers, Box 435.

126. 492 U.S. 490 (1989); William H. Rehnquist to Robin V. Sproul, April 14, 1989, Marshall Papers, Box 463.

127. Toni House, Memorandum to the Chief Justice, March 1, 1989, Marshall Papers, Box 462.

128. Thurgood Marshall to William H. Rehnquist, March 2, 1989, Marshall Papers, Box 462.

129. Antonin Scalia to William H. Rehnquist, March 2, 1989, Marshall Papers, Box 462.

130. William H. Rehnquist to Mary Y. Steinbauer, May 10, 1991, Marshall Papers, Box 525.

131. William J. Brennan, Memorandum to the Conference, December 19, 1990, Marshall Papers, Box 524.

132. Mary M. Elmore, secretary to William J. Brennan, to Tinsley E. Yarbrough, May 29, 1997, author's files. The policy has been continued following Justice Brennan's death in 1997.

133. Thurgood Marshall to John Hope Franklin, April 10, 1986, Marshall Papers, Box 574.

134. A draft of Marshall's remarks is in his papers, Box 574.

135. Calhoun Marshall III to Thurgood Marshall, May 16, 1987, Marshall Papers, Box 35; Ernest W. Higgins to Thurgood Marshall, September 14, 1987, Marshall Papers, Box 36; Thurgood Marshall to Ernest W. Higgins, September 25, 1987, Marshall Papers, Box 36.

136. Rehnquist's letter and excerpts from the agreement are reprinted in *New York Times,* May 26, 1993.

137. *New York Times,* May 24, 26, 1993.

138. *Washington Post,* May 25, 1993; Carl T. Rowan, *Dream Makers, Dream Breakers: The World of Justice Thurgood Marshall* (Boston: Little, Brown, 1994).

139. *New York Times,* May 27, 1993.

140. *New York Times,* May 25, 27, 1993.

141. *New York Times,* May 27, 1993.

142. Ibid.

143. New York Times Co. v. United States, 403 U.S. 713, 729 (1971) (Stewart, J., concurring).

Chapter Three

1. William H. Rehnquist to Robert W. Kastenmeier, December 2, 1987, Thurgood Marshall Papers, Library of Congress, Box 435.

2. For a commentary, see Bennett Boskey and Eugene Gressman, "The Supreme Court Bids Farewell to Mandatory Appeals," 109 S. Ct. 109–26 (1989).

3. Ibid., p. 109. Somewhat arbitrarily, I have omitted discussion of the Rehnquist Court's largely uneventful use of standing and related essentially prudential considerations to avoid deciding particular questions or the claims of particular litigants. In Walter L. Nixon v. United States, 506 U.S. 224 (1993), for example, the Court, speaking through the chief justice, concluded that a federal district judge's challenge to Senate proceedings employed in his impeachment trial raised nonjusticiable political questions.

4. See, for example, Linkletter v. Walker, 381 U.S. 618 (1965).

5. See, for example, Desist v. United States, 394 U.S. 244, 256–59 (1969) (Harlan, J., dissenting).

6. 489 U.S. 288 (1989).

7. Ibid., p. 307.

8. Ibid., p. 309.

9. See, for example, Butler v. McKellar, 494 U.S. 407 (1990); Caspari v. Bohlen, 114 S. Ct. 948 (1994).

10. 494 U.S. 407.

11. 451 U.S. 477 (1981).

12. 486 U.S. 675 (1988).

13. 494 U.S. at 415.

14. Ibid., pp. 417–18.

15. 512 U.S. 154 (1994).

16. 117 S. Ct. 1969 (1997).

17. Ibid., p. 1980.

18. Gardner v. Florida, 430 U.S. 349 (1977).

19. 476 U.S. 1 (1986).

20. 117 S. Ct. at 1983.

21. 113 S. Ct. 1745 (1993).

22. 428 U.S. 465 (1976).

23. 113 S. Ct. at 1753.

24. Ibid., p. 1765.

25. Ibid., p. 1770.

26. 499 U.S. 467 (1991).

27. Wainwright v. Sykes, 433 U.S. 72 (1977); Sanders v. United States, 373 U.S. 1 (1963).

28. 499 U.S. at 507.

29. Felker v. Turpin, 116 S. Ct. 2333 (1996).

30. 28 U.S.C. sec. 1651.

31. 116 S. Ct. at 2342 (footnote omitted).

32. Lindh v. Murphy, 117 S. Ct. 2059 (1997). In O'Sullivan v. Boerckel (1999) (slip opinion), the Court further limited federal habeas review of state defendants' convictions when it held that a defendant who asserted a constitutional claim in a lower state court, but failed to raise it in the state supreme court, thereby had forfeited his right to federal court review of the claim.

33. Hess v. Port Authority Trans-Hudson Corp., 115 S. Ct. 394 (1994).

34. Blatchford v. Native Village of Noatak, 501 U.S. 775, 779 (1991).

35. Dan M. Kahan to Thurgood Marshall, undated, Marshall Papers, Box 533.

36. 116 S. Ct. 1114 (1996).

37. Pennsylvania v. Union Gas Co., 491 U.S. 1 (1989).

38. 134 U.S. 1 (1890).

39. Ibid. at 1135, 1134.

40. Alden v. Maine (1999) (slip opinion). The Florida cases are Florida Prepaid Postsecondary Education Expense Board v. College Savings Bank (1999) (slip opinion), and College Savings Bank v. Florida Prepaid Postsecondary Education Expense Board (1999) (slip opinion). In West v. Gibson (1999) (slip opinion), a five-four majority construed a 1991 amendment to Title VII of the Civil Rights Act of 1964 as authorizing the

Equal Employment Opportunity Commission (EEOC) to award compensatory damages in federal government employment discrimination cases. While conceding that the law permitted court action seeking such damages, the four dissenters, speaking through Justice Kennedy, joined by Chief Justice Rehnquist and Justices Scalia and Thomas, contended that the majority's finding of a like authority on the part of the EEOC was not based on the sort of clear and unequivocal statutory language traditionally required for waivers of federal sovereign immunity.

41. In Wade v. Hunter, 336 U.S. 684 (1949), the Court did hold that the Fifth Amendment guarantee against double jeopardy applies to military courts-martial; in United States v. Tempia, 16 U.S.C.M.A. 629 (1967), the Court of Military Appeals construed the Uniform Code of Military Justice to impose the *Miranda* warnings on military interrogation of suspects.

42. Reid v. Covert, 351 U.S. 487 (1956); Kinsella v. Krueger, 354 U.S. 1 (1957); Kinsella v. United States *ex rel.* Singleton, 361 U.S. 234 (1960).

43. United States *ex rel.* Toth v. Quarles, 350 U.S. 11 (1955).

44. 395 U.S. 258 (1969).

45. 420 U.S. 738 (1975).

46. See, for example, Relford v. U.S. Disciplinary Commandant, 401 U.S. 355 (1971).

47. 420 U.S. at 762.

48. Ibid., p. 764.

49. 483 U.S. 435 (1987).

50. Lewis F. Powell, Jr., Papers, conference notes, Box 281, Washington and Lee University, Lexington, Virginia.

51. Sandra Day O'Connor to William H. Rehnquist, April 6, 1987, Marshall Papers, Box 419; Lewis F. Powell, Jr., to William H. Rehnquist, April 4, 1987, Marshall Papers, Box 419.

52. 483 U.S. at 451 (footnote omitted).

53. Margaret Raymond, Bench Memorandum, February 23, 1987, Marshall Papers, Box 399.

54. William J. Brennan to Thurgood Marshall and Harry Blackmun, March 9, 1987, Box 419, and Marshall's handwritten reply.

55. 483 U.S. at 454.

56. Ibid., pp. 454–55, quoting 395 U.S. at 272–73 (footnote omitted).

57. 24 How. 66 (1861).

58. Puerto Rico v. Branstad, 483 U.S. 219 (1987).

59. See, for example, FDIC v. Meyer, 114 S. Ct. 996 (1994); Siegert v. Gilley, 500 U.S. 226

(1991); Hunter v. Bryant, 502 U.S. 224 (1991); Jett v. Dallas Independent School Dist., 491 U.S. 701 (1989); Westfall v. Erwin, 484 U.S. 292 (1988); Anderson v. Creighton, 483 U.S. 635 (1987); United States v. Stanley, 483 U.S. 669 (1987).

60. McMillan v. Monroe County, Ala., 117 S. Ct. 1734 (1997) (Ginsburg, J., dissenting).

61. 457 U.S. 731 (1982).

62. Ibid., pp. 751–52 (footnote omitted).

63. 117 S. Ct. 1636 (1997).

64. 457 U.S. at 752.

65. 438 U.S. 478 (1978).

66. Ibid., p. 529.

67. Ibid., pp. 526–27.

68. 457 U.S. at 764–65.

69. Ibid., p. 765.

70. Ibid., p. 759.

71. 117 S. Ct. at 1636.

72. Ibid., p. 1643.

73. Ibid., p. 1648.

74. Stevens cited Youngstown Co. v. Sawyer, 343 U.S. 579 (1952); United States v. Burr, 25 F. Cas. 30 (C.C. Va., 1807); United States v. Nixon, 418 U.S. 683 (1974), as well as Marbury v. Madison, 1 Cr. 137 (1803).

75. 117 S. Ct. at 1649–50 (footnote omitted).

76. Ibid., p. 1652.

77. Ibid.

78. Ibid., pp. 1652–53.

79. Ibid., p. 1657. Breyer cited, among other cases, Harlow v. Fitzgerald, 457 U.S. 800 (1982), basing qualified immunity for Nixon presidential assistants partly on factors "peculiarly disruptive of effective government."

80. 117 S. Ct. at 1658.

81. 418 U.S. 683 (1974); Vincent Bugliosi, *No Island of Sanity* (New York: Ballantine, 1998).

82. 117 S. Ct. at 1648.

83. Office of the President v. Office of Independent Counsel, 119 S. Ct. 466 (1998); Rubin v. United States, 119 S. Ct. 461 (1998). *In Re* Sealed Case, 124 F. 3d 230 (D.C. Cir., 1997).

84. Swidler & Berlin v. United States, 66 L.W. 4538, 4539 (1998).

85. Ibid., p. 4540.

86. Ibid., p. 4541.

87. Ibid.

88. 408 U.S. 665 (1972).

89. 66 L.W. at 4541.

90. Ibid., pp. 4541–42.

91. Ibid., p. 4542.

92. See Katy J. Harriger, *Independent Justice: The Federal Special Prosecutor in American Politics* (Lawrence: University Press of Kansas, 1992), for a useful history of the independent counsel.

93. 487 U.S. 654 (1988).

94. Ibid., p. 696.

95. Ibid., p. 699.

96. Ibid., p. 703.

97. Ibid., pp. 710–11.

98. Raines v. Byrd, 117 S. Ct. 2312 (1997).

99. Clinton v. City of New York, 66 L.W. 4543 (1998). The next year, the Court avoided a ruling on the constitutionality of congressional legislation that arguably permitted the use of census sampling in determining a state's population for congressional apportionment purposes, the justices concluding that the statute included no such authorization. Department of Commerce v. U.S. House of Representatives, 119 S. Ct. 765 (1999).

100. Ibid., p. 4549.

101. Ibid., quoting INS v. Chadha, 462 U.S. 919, 951 (1983).

102. 143 U.S. 649 (1892).

103. 66 L.W. at 4551, quoting United States v. Curtiss-Wright Corp., 299 U.S. 304, 320 (1936).

104. Ibid.

105. Ibid., pp. 4552–53.

106. Ibid., p. 4553.

107. Ibid., p. 4556.

108. Ibid., p. 4557.

109. Ibid.

110. Ibid., pp. 4558–59.

111. Ibid., p. 4560.

112. Ibid., p. 4566.

113. See, for example, Federal Radio Commission v. Nelson Brothers, 289 U.S. 266 (1933), upholding agency power to issue broadcast licenses only in the "public interest, convenience, or necessity."

114. Panama Refining Co. v. Ryan, 293 U.S. 388 (1935); Schechter Poultry Corp. v. United States, 295 U.S. 495 (1935).

115. Central R. Co. of New Jersey v. Jersey City, 209 U.S. 473 (1908).

116. New Jersey v. New York, 118 S. Ct. 1726 (1998).

117. Ibid., p. 1736.

118. Ibid., p. 1751.

119. Ibid., p. 1757.

120. Ibid., p. 1759.

121. Ibid., p. 1760.

122. Ibid., pp. 1760–61.

123. Williams v. North Carolina, 325 U.S. 226 (1945).

124. Baker by Thomas v. General Motors Corp., 118 S. Ct. 657 (1998).

125. Ibid., p. 668, quoting McElmoyle ex rel. Bailey v. Cohen, 13 Pet. 312, 325 (1839).

126. 118 S. Ct. at 671.

127. *In Re* Griffiths, 413 U.S. 717 (1973).

128. 470 U.S. 274 (1985).

129. 487 U.S. 59 (1988).

130. Barnard v. Thorstenn, 489 U.S. 546 (1989).

131. 487 U.S. at 69.

132. Sandra Day O'Connor to Anthony Kennedy, May 12, 1988, Marshall Papers, Box 408.

133. Harry A. Blackmun to Anthony Kennedy, May 16, 1988, Marshall Papers, Box 408.

134. Sandra Day O'Connor to Anthony Kennedy, May 17, 1988, Marshall Papers, Box 408.

135. Ward v. Maryland, 12 Wall. 418 (1871); Toomer v. Witsell, 334 U.S. 385 (1948).

136. 470 U.S. at 290.

137. He cited Shapiro v. Thompson, 394 U.S. 618 (1969), which struck down a one-year residency requirement for receipt of welfare benefits.

138. Barnard v. Thorstenn, 489 U.S. at 560.

139. 395 U.S. 486 (1969).

140. Ibid., p. 547.

141. U.S. Term Limits v. Thornton, 115 S. Ct. 1842, 1869 (1995).

142. Ibid., p. 1875.

143. Ibid., p. 1889.

144. See, for example, McCulloch v. Maryland, 4 Wheat. 316 (1819); Collector v. Day, 11 Wall. 113 (1871).

145. See, for example, Gillespie v. Oklahoma, 257 U.S. 501 (1922); Panhandle Oil Co. v. Mississippi (1928).

146. Helvering v. Gerhardt, 304 U.S. 405 (1938).

147. Graves v. O'Keefe, 306 U.S. 466 (1939).

148. 485 U.S. 505 (1988).

149. Ibid., p. 531.

150. Davis v. Michigan Dept. of Treasury, 489 U.S. 803 (1989).

151. Ibid., p. 803.

152. Ibid., pp. 821–22. In 1999, the Court turned back a challenge raised by two federal district judges against an Alabama county's ordinance imposing an occupational tax on those not otherwise required to pay a license fee under state law, including federal, state, and county officeholders. Emphasizing the tax's nondiscriminatory character, the Court rejected the judges' contention that it violated intergovernmental tax immunity doctrine. Jefferson County, Alabama v. Acker (1999) (slip opinion).

153. 4 Wheat. at 316.

154. See, for example, Pennsylvania v. Nelson, 350 U.S. 497 (1956); Hines v. Davidowitz, 312 U.S. 52 (1941).

155. See, for example, CSX Transp., Inc. v. Easterwood, 113 S. Ct. 1732 (1993); Cipollone v. Liggett Group, Inc., 112 S. Ct. 2608 (1992); North Dakota v. Dole, 495 U.S. 423 (1990); California v. ARC America Corp., 490 U.S. 93 (1989).

156. 112 S. Ct. at 2608.

157. Ibid., p. 2618.

158. Ibid., p. 2633.

159. Perpich v. Department of Defense, 496 U.S. 334 (1990); Harry A. Blackmun to John Paul Stevens, May 31, 1990, Marshall Papers, Box 509.

160. South Dakota v. Dole, 483 U.S. 203 (1987).

161. Steward Machine Co. v. Davis, 301 U.S. 548 (1937).

162. 483 U.S. at 211.

163. Ibid., p. 213.

164. Ibid., p. 218.

Chapter Four

1. United States v. E.C. Knight Co., 156 U.S. 1 (1895).

2. Gibbons v. Ogden, 9 Wheat. 1 (1824).

3. See, for example, Champion v. Ames, 188 U.S. 321 (1903).

4. Hammer v. Dagenhart, 247 U.S. 251 (1918).

5. Bailey v. Drexel Furniture Co., 259 U.S. 20 (1922).

6. 198 U.S. 45 (1905).

7. 261 U.S. 525 (1923).

8. Morey v. Doud, 354 U.S. 457 (1957); New Orleans v. Dukes, 427 U.S. 297 (1976).

9. NLRB v. Jones & Laughlin Corp., 301 U.S. 1 (1937); Wickard v. Filburn, 317 U.S. 111 (1942).

10. United States v. Darby Lumber Co., 312 U.S. 100 (1941).

11. 426 U.S. 833 (1976).

12. Garcia v. San Antonio Metropolitan Transit Authority, 469 U.S. 528 (1985).

13. 304 U.S. 144 (1938).

14. Ibid., p. 152.

15. Ibid., pp. 152–53 n. 4.

16. 116 S. Ct. 1589 (1996).

17. 9 Wheat. at 1.

18. Wickard v. Filburn, 317 U.S. at 111, 120 (Jackson, J.).

19. 9 Wheat. at 194–95.

20. Ibid., p. 196.

21. Ibid., p. 197 (emphasis added).

22. Ibid.

23. See, for example, New York v. Miln, 36 U.S. 102 (1837); License Cases, 46 U.S. 504 (1847); Passenger Cases, 48 U.S. 283 (1849).

24. 298 U.S. 238 (1936).

25. Ibid., p. 308.

26. Schechter Corp. v. United States, 295 U.S. 495, 546 (1935).

27. 317 U.S. at 120.

28. 312 U.S. at 124 (emphasis added).

29. 317 U.S. at 120.

30. See, for example, Cleveland v. United States, 329 U.S. 14 (1946), upholding the Mann Act prosecutions of a Morman who transported his several wives interstate.

31. Perez v. United States, 402 U.S. 146 (1971).

32. Maryland v. Wirtz, 392 U.S. 183, 192–93 (1968) (Harlan, J.).

33. United States v. Lopez, 115 S. Ct. 1624, 1634 (1995).

34. Ibid.

35. Ibid., p. 1632, quoting 2 F. 3d 1342, 1366 (5 CA, 1993).

36. Ibid., p. 1633, quoting Marbury v. Madison, 1 Cranch 137, 177 (1803) (Marshall, C.J.).

37. Ibid., p. 1633.

38. Ibid., p. 1632.

39. Ibid., p. 1634.

40. Ibid., p. 1637.

41. Ibid., p. 1641.

42. Ibid., p. 1642.

43. Ibid., p. 1642.

44. Ibid., p. 1647.

45. Ibid.

46. Ibid., p. 1651 (asterisk omitted).

47. Ibid.

48. Ibid., p. 1652.

49. Ibid., p. 1656.

50. Ibid., p. 1654.

51. Ibid.

52. Swift & Co. v. United States, 196 U.S. 375, 398 (1905).

53. 115 S. Ct. at 1659.

54. Ibid.

55. 317 U.S. at 120.

56. Breyer cited Perez v. United States, 402 U.S. 146 (1971) (loan sharking); Daniel v. Paul, 395 U.S. 298 (1969) (discrimination in rural amusement park); and Wickard v. Filburn, 317 U.S. at 111 (farmer's consumption of a portion of wheat crop).

57. 115 S. Ct. at 1664.

58. Ibid., p. 1668.

59. Ibid., p. 1651.

60. Hodel v. Va. Surface Min. & Reclam. Ass'n, 452 U.S. 264, 288 (1981).

61. Federal Energy Regulatory Com'n v. Mississippi, 456 U.S. 742 (1982).

62. New York v. United States, 112 S. Ct. 2408, 2435 (1992).

63. Ibid., p. 2446.
64. Ibid., p. 2447.
65. Ibid., p. 2418.
66. 117 S. Ct. 2365 (1997).
67. Ibid., p. 2370.
68. Ibid., p. 2371.
69. Quoted in ibid., p. 2372.
70. Quoted in ibid., p. 2373 (emphasis in original).
71. Ibid., p. 2374.
72. Ibid., p. 2373 (footnote omitted).
73. Ibid., p. 2376.
74. Ibid.
75. Ibid., pp. 2380–81. The cases cited were Testa v. Katt, 380 U.S. 386 (1947), and Federal Energy Regulatory Com'n (FERC) v. Mississippi, 456 U.S. at 742.
76. Ibid., p. 2384.
77. Ibid., p. 2385.
78. Ibid., pp. 2385–86.
79. Ibid., p. 2389, citing *Federalist* No. 27.
80. Ibid., p. 2391.
81. Ibid., p. 2392.
82. Ibid., pp. 2401–2.
83. Ibid., p. 2404.
84. Ibid.
85. Ibid.
86. BMW v. Gore, 116 S. Ct. 1589 (1996). When a five-four majority invoked state sovereign immunity doctrine in 1999 to shield a state from a lawsuit to require it to honor its employees' right to federal overtime benefits, Justice Souter further declared, "The resemblance of today's state sovereign immunity to the *Lochner* era's industrial due process is striking. The Court began this century by imputing immutable constitutional status to a conception of economic self-reliance that was never true to industrial life and grew insistently fictional with the years, and the Court has chosen to close the century by conferring like status on a conception of state sovereign immunity that is true neither in history nor to the structure of the Constitution. I expect the Court's late essay into immunity doctrine will prove the equal of its earlier experiment in laissez-faire, the one being as unrealistic as the other, as indefensible, and probably as fleeting." Alden v. Maine (1999) (slip opinion) (Souter, J., dissenting).
87. National Paint & Coatings Ass'n v. City of Chicago, 835 F. Supp. 421 (N.D. Ill., 1993).
88. 45 F. 3d 1124, 1129 (CA 7, 1995).
89. 116 S. Ct. at 1589.
90. 499 U.S. 1, 38 (1991).
91. Ibid., p. 25.
92. Ibid., p. 18.

93. 113 S. Ct. 2711 (1993).
94. The cases cited were Seaboard Air Line R. Co. v. Seegers, 207 U.S. 73 (1907); St. Louis I.M. & S. R. Co. v. Williams, 251 U.S. 63 (1919); Standard Oil Co. of Indiana v. Missouri, 224 U.S. 270 (1912); Southwestern T & T Co. v. Danaher, 238 U.S. 482 (1915).
95. 113 S. Ct. at 2726–27.
96. 116 S. Ct. at 1611.
97. Ibid., p. 1617.
98. Ibid., p. 1614.
99. Ibid., p. 1616.
100. 113 S. Ct. at 2719.
101. Chicago, B. & Q. RR v. Chicago, 166 U.S. 226 (1897).
102. United States v. Causby, 328 U.S. 256, 264 (1946); Batten v. United States, 371 U.S. 955 (1963).
103. 260 U.S. 393 (1922).
104. Ibid., p. 413.
105. Ibid., p. 415.
106. Miller v. Schoene, 276 U.S. 272 (1928).
107. Euclid v. Ambler Realty Co., 272 U.S. 365 (1926).
108. Nestrow v. Cambridge, 277 U.S. 183 (1928).
109. 369 U.S. 590 (1962).
110. 438 U.S. 104 (1978).
111. Keystone Bituminous Coal Ass'n v. De Benedictis, 480 U.S. 470 (1987).
112. 483 U.S. 825 (1987).
113. Ibid., p. 838.
114. 112 S. Ct. 2886 (1992).
115. Ibid., p. 2893.
116. Ibid., p. 2899 (footnote omitted).
117. Dolan v. City of Tigard, 114 S. Ct. 2309 (1994); City of Monterey v. Del Monte Dunes (1999) (slip opinion). During the 1996 term, the Court reviewed Suitum v. Tahoe Regional Planning Agency, 117 S. Ct. 1659 (1997), in which a landowner claimed that the planning agency's determination that her residential lot was ineligible for development amounted to an unconstitutional taking. The justices, however, merely overturned lower court rulings rejecting Suitum's claim on the ground that she had not yet obtained a final agency decision in her case and her claim was thus not yet "ripe" for review, then remanded the case for further proceedings without reaching the merits of Suitum's constitutional claim. See also Babbitt v. Youpee, 117 S. Ct. 727 (1997), finding a provision of the federal Indian land program in violation of the takings clause.
118. Chicago, B. & Q. RR v. Chicago, 166 U.S. at 226.

119. Dolan v. City of Tigard, 114 S. Ct. at 2327.

120. Ibid.

121. 66 L.W. 4468 (1998).

122. Ibid., p. 4473.

123. Ibid., p. 4472.

124. Ibid., p. 4474.

125. 449 U.S. 155 (1980).

126. 66 L.W. at 4474 (emphasis in original).

127. Ibid., p. 4475.

128. Rehnquist cited primarily Loretto v. Teleprompter Manhattan CATV Corp., 458 U.S. 419 (1982).

129. 66 L.W. at 4475.

130. Boston Chamber of Commerce v. Boston, 217 U.S. 189, 195 (1910).

131. United States v. Chandler-Dunbar Water Power Co., 229 U.S. 53, 75–76 (1913).

132. 66 L.W. 4566 (1998).

133. 66 L.W. at 4576, citing Calder v. Bull, 3 Dall. 386 (1798).

134. 372 U.S. 726 (1963).

135. Williamson v. Lee Optical, 348 U.S. 483 (1955).

136. 66 L.W. at 4579–80. Kennedy cited, among other recent cases, United States v. Carlton, 512 U.S. 26 (1994).

137. 66 L.W. at 4577.

138. Ibid., p. 4581. Stevens cited Davon, Inc. v. Shalala, 75 F. 3d 1114, 1124–25 (CA 7, 1996); *In Re* Blue Diamond Coal Co., 79 F. 3d 516, 522 (CA 6, 1996); and the First Circuit's opinion in *Eastern Enterprises*, 110 F. 3d 150 (1997).

139. 66 L.W. at 4581–82.

140. Ibid., p. 4582 (emphasis in original).

141. Ibid. The cases cited were Connolly v. Pension Benefit Guaranty Corporation, 475 U.S. 211 (1986); Concrete Pipe & Products v. Construction Laborers Pension Trust, 508 U.S. 602 (1993).

142. 66 L.W. at 4582. Breyer cited such language from First English Evangelical Lutheran Church of Glendale v. County of Los Angeles, 482 U.S. 304, 315 (1987).

143. 66 L.W. at 4582.

144. Ibid., p. 4583.

145. See, for example, Wyoming v. Oklahoma, 112 S. Ct. 789 (1992); Chemical Waste Management v. Hunt, 112 S. Ct. 2009 (1992); Fort Gratiot Sanitary Landfill, Inc. v. Mich. Dept. of Nat. Res., 112 S. Ct. 2019 (1992); Oregon Waste Systems v. Dept. of Env. Quality, 114 S. Ct. 1345 (1994).

146. See, for example, West Lynn Creamery, Inc. v. Healey, 114 S. Ct. 2205, 2218 (1994).

147. See, for example, Southern Pacific Co. v. Arizona, 325 U.S. 761, 784 (1945) (Black, J., dissenting); Tinsley E. Yarbrough, *Mr. Justice Black and His Critics* (Durham: Duke University Press, 1988), pp. 44–48.

148. Tyler Pipe Indus. v. Wash. State Dept. of Revenue, 483 U.S. 258, 265 (1987).

Chapter Five

1. 304 U.S. 144 (1938).

2. Hugo L. Black to Harlan F. Stone, April 21, 1938, Harlan F. Stone Papers, Library of Congress, Box 63.

3. Harlan F. Stone to Hugo L. Black, April 22, 1938, Harlan F. Stone Papers, Library of Congress, Box 63.

4. 304 U.S. at 155 (Black, J., concurring and dissenting).

5. Morey v. Doud, 354 U.S. 439 (1957); Skinner v. Oklahoma, 316 U.S. 535 (1942).

6. 372 U.S. 726 (1963).

7. Arthur J. Goldberg to Hugo L. Black, April 18, 1963, Hugo L. Black Papers, Library of Congress, Box 372.

8. Ibid.

9. See, for example, Adamson v. California, 332 U.S. 46, 68 (1947) (Black, J., dissenting); Tinsley E. Yarbrough, *Mr. Justice Black and His Critics* (Durham: Duke University Press, 1988), ch. 3.

10. 262 U.S. 390 (1923).

11. 268 U.S. 510 (1925).

12. See, for example, Gitlow v. New York, 268 U.S. 652 (1925); Near v. Minnesota, 283 U.S. 697 (1931).

13. See, for example, Cantwell v. Connecticut, 310 U.S. 296 (1940); Everson v. Bd. of Education, 330 U.S. 1 (1947).

14. 316 U.S. 535 (1942).

15. 378 U.S. 500 (1964).

16. 378 U.S. at 518.

17. 381 U.S. 479 (1965).

18. Ibid., p. 486.

19. Ibid., p. 486.

20. Ibid., p. 500.

21. Ibid., p. 502.

22. Ibid., p. 509.

23. Ibid., p. 522.

24. Ibid.

25. Stewart, joined by Black, also registered a brief dissent in the case, ibid., p. 527.

26. Harper v. Virginia Bd. of Elections, 383 U.S. 663 (1966).

27. Shapiro v. Thompson, 394 U.S. 618 (1969).

28. San Antonio Indep. School Dist. v. Rodriguez, 411 U.S. 1 (1973).

29. Dandridge v. Williams, 397 U.S. 471 (1970).

30. 405 U.S. 438 (1972).

31. 410 U.S. 113 (1973).

32. Maher v. Roe, 432 U.S. 464 (1977); Harris v. McRae, 448 U.S. 297 (1980).

33. 462 U.S. 416 (1983).

34. Thornburgh v. American College of Obstetricians, 476 U.S. 747 (1986).

35. 492 U.S. 490 (1989).

36. Marshall Papers, Box 554.

37. John Paul Stevens to William H. Rehnquist, May 30, 1989, Marshall Papers, Box 480.

38. 492 U.S. at 518.

39. Thornburgh v. American College of Obstetricians, 476 U.S. at 814 (O'Connor, J., joined by Rehnquist, J., dissenting); City of Akron v. Akron Center for Reproductive Health, 462 U.S. at 452 (O'Connor, J., joined by White and Rehnquist, JJ., dissenting).

40. 492 U.S. at 525–26.

41. Ibid., p. 532.

42. Ibid., p. 534.

43. Ohio v. Akron Center for Reproductive Health, 497 U.S. 502 (1990).

44. Ibid., p. 520.

45. Ibid., pp. 519–20.

46. Ibid., p. 520.

47. 497 U.S. 417 (1990).

48. 497 U.S. at 480.

49. John Paul Stevens to William H. Rehnquist, December 7, 1989, Marshall Papers, Box 500.

50. William J. Brennan, Jr., to Thurgood Marshall, June 13, 1990, Marshall Papers, Box 499. See also William J. Brennan, Jr., to Harry A. Blackmun, June 18, 1990, Marshall Papers, Box 499.

51. 500 U.S. 173 (1991).

52. Ibid., p. 207.

53. Ibid., p. 210.

54. Ibid., p. 207.

55. Harris v. McRae, 448 U.S. 297 (1980); Webster v. Reproductive Services, 492 U.S. at 490. (1989).

56. 500 U.S. at 215.

57. Ibid., p. 216.

58. Ibid., p. 217 (footnote omitted).

59. Ibid., pp. 224–25.

60. Ibid., p. 221.

61. David H. Souter to William H. Rehnquist, April 25, 1991, Marshall Papers, Box 530.

62. William H. Rehnquist to David H. Souter, April 29, 1991, Marshall Papers, Box 530.

63. 112 S. Ct. 2791 (1992).

64. Ibid., p. 2816.

65. Ibid., p. 2843.

66. Ibid., p. 2854.

67. Ibid., pp. 2854–55.

68. Ibid., p. 2855.

69. Ibid., pp. 2855–56.

70. Ibid., p. 2861.

71. Ibid., p. 2884.

72. See, for example, Lambert v. Wicklund, 117 S. Ct. 1169 (1997).

73. Michael H. v. Gerald D., 491 U.S. 110 (1989).

74. DeShaney v. Winnebago County DSS, 489 U.S. 189 (1989).

75. 112 S. Ct. 1061 (1992).

76. 425 U.S. 901 (1976).

77. 478 U.S. 186 (1986).

78. 116 S. Ct. 1620 (1996).

79. Thompson v. Aldredge, 187 Ga. 467 (Ga. S. Ct., 1939).

80. Baker v. Wade, 769 F. 2d 289 (CA 5, 1985); Dronenburg v. Zech, 741 F. 2d 1388 (CA D.C., 1984).

81. 405 U.S. at 465.

82. 410 U.S. at 221.

83. 478 U.S. at 188 n. 1.

84. Ibid., pp. 190–91.

85. Ibid., p. 191.

86. Ibid., pp. 191–92, quoting Palko v. Connecticut, 302 U.S. 319, 325, 326 (1937).

87. Ibid., p. 192, quoting Moore v. East Cleveland, 431 U.S. 494, 503 (1977).

88. Ibid.

89. Ibid., p. 194.

90. Ibid.

91. 394 U.S. 557 (1969).

92. 478 U.S. at 195.

93. Ibid., pp. 195–96.

94. Ibid., p. 196.

95. Ibid.

96. Ibid., p. 197.

97. For a discussion of Powell's consideration of *Bowers*, see John C. Jeffries, Jr., *Justice Lewis F. Powell, Jr.* (New York: Scribners, 1994), pp. 511–30.

98. 478 U.S. at 197.

99. Quoted in Jeffries, *Justice Lewis F. Powell, Jr.*, p. 530.

100. 478 U.S. at 200.

101. Ibid.

102. Ibid., p. 201.

103. Olmstead v. United States, 277 U.S. 438, 478 (1928).

104. 478 U.S. at 206.

105. Ibid., p. 209 n. 3.

106. Ibid., pp. 212–13.

107. Ibid., p. 218.

108. Ibid., pp. 218–19.

109. Ibid., p. 219.

110. Colorado, *Constitution*, art. II, sec. 306.

111. 116 S. Ct. 1620, (1996) 1625.

112. Ibid., p. 1626.

113. Ibid., p. 1628.

114. Ibid.

115. Ibid., quoting Dept. of Agriculture v. Moreno, 413 U.S. 528, 534 (1973).

116. 116 S. Ct. at 1629.

117. Ibid.

118. Ibid.

119. Ibid., pp. 1630–31.

120. Ibid., pp. 1631–32.

121. Ibid., p. 1632.

122. Ibid.

123. Ibid.

124. Ibid., p. 1633.

125. Ibid., p. 1634.

126. Ibid., pp. 1634–35.

127. 133 U.S. 333 (1890).

128. 116 S. Ct. at 1636.

129. Ibid., p. 1637.

130. Loving v. Virginia, 388 U.S. 1 (1967). See, for example, Andrew Koppelman, "Why Discrimination Against Lesbians and Gay Men is Discrimination," *New York University Law Review* 69 (1994): 197; Cass Sunstein, "Homosexuality and the Constitution," *Indiana Law Journal* 70 (1994): 9.

131. Craig M. Bradley, "The Right Not to Endorse Gay Rights: A Reply to Sunstein," *Indiana Law Journal* 70 (winter 1994): 32–34.

132. 388 U.S. at 11 (emphasis added).

133. See, for example, Hunter v. Erickson, 393 U.S. 385 (1969).

134. 116 S. Ct. at 1632.

135. 497 U.S. 261 (1990).

136. 65 L.W. 4669 (1997); 65 L.W. 4695 (1997).

137. 65 L.W. at 4683.

138. Washington v. Glucksberg, 65 L.W. at 4674.

139. Ibid.

140. Ibid., p. 4675.

141. Ibid.

142. Ibid., p. 4676.

143. Ibid.

144. Vacco v. Quill, 65 L.W. at 4695.

145. Washington v. Glucksberg, 65 L.W. at 4678.

146. Ibid.

147. Ibid., p. 4679.

148. Ibid., p. 4701.

149. Ibid., p. 4684.

150. Poe v. Ullman, 367 U.S. 497 (1961).

151. Washington v. Glucksberg, 65 L.W. at 4688.

152. Ibid., p. 4686.

153. Ibid.

154. Ibid., p. 4687.

155. Ibid., p. 4692.

156. Ibid.

157. Ibid., p. 4694.

158. Ibid., p. 4683, quoting Poe v. Ullman, 367 U.S. at 543 (Harlan, J., dissenting).

159. Washington v. Glucksberg, 65 L.W. at 4674.

160. BMW of North America v. Gore, 116 S. Ct. at 1589, 1610 (1996) (Scalia, J. dissenting, joined by Thomas, J.); TXO Production Corp. v. Alliance Resources Corp., 113 S. Ct. 2711, 2726 (1993) (Scalia, J. concurring in judgment, joined by Thomas, J.); Pacific Mut. Life Ins. Co. v. Haslip, 111 S. Ct. 1032, 1046 (1991) (Scalia, J. concurring in judgment). See also U.S. v. Carlton, 114 S. Ct. 2018, 2026 (1994) (Scalia, J. concurring in judgment, joined by Thomas).

161. 111 S. Ct. at 1053.

162. 114 S. Ct. at 2027.

163. 112 S. Ct. at 2874 (footnote omitted).

164. 112 S. Ct. at 2805, quoting 367 U.S. at 543.

165. Washington v. Glucksberg, 65 L.W. at 4678, 4694.

166. 410 U.S. at 173.

167. Washington v. Glucksberg, 65 L.W. at 4674 (Rehnquist, J.).

168. 367 U.S. at 541.

169. Dred Scott v. Sandford, 19 How. 393 (1857).

170. 112 S. Ct. at 2885.

171. City of Chicago v. Morales (1999) (slip opinion).

172. Saenz, Director, California Department of Social Services v. Roe (1999) (slip opinion). See Colgate v. Harvey, 296 U.S. 404 (1935), overruled by Madden v. Kentucky, 309 U.S. 83 (1940).

Chapter Six

1. Everson v. Board of Education, 330 U.S. 1 (1947); Cantwell v. Connecticut, 310 U.S. 296 (1940).

2. Bowen v. Kendrick, 487 U.S. 589 (1988).

3. County of Allegheny v. ACLU, 492 U.S. 573 (1989).

4. Westside Community Schools v. Mergens, 496 U.S. 226 (1990).

5. Zobrest v. Catalina Foothills School District, 509 U.S. 1 (1993).

6. Agostini v. Felton, 117 S. Ct. 1997 (1997).

7. Lambís Chapel v. Center Moriches Union Free School District, 113 S. Ct. 2141 (1993).

8. Lee v. Weisman, 112 S. Ct. 2649 (1992).

9. Board of Education of Kiryas Joel v. Grumet, 114 S. Ct. 2481 (1994).

10. O'Lone v. Shabazz, 482 U.S. 342 (1987).

11. Lyng v. Northwest Indian Cemetery Protective Association, 485 U.S. 439 (1988).

12. Hernandez v. Commissioner, 490 U.S. 680 (1989).

13. Employment Division v. Smith, 494 U.S. 872 (1990).

14. Hobbie v. Unemployment Appeals Commission, 480 U.S. 136 (1987).

15. Frazee v. Illinois Department of Employment Security, 489 U.S. 829 (1989).

16. Church of Lukumi Babalu Aye v. City of Hialeah, 508 U.S. 502 (1993).

17. 117 S. Ct. at 1997.

18. Aguilar v. Felton, 473 U.S. 402 (1985); School District of Grand Rapids v. Ball, 473 U.S. 373 (1985).

19. 494 U.S. 872 (1990).

20. 374 U.S. 398 (1963).

21. City of Boerne v. Flores, 117 S. Ct. 2157 (1997).

22. 403 U.S. 602 (1971).

23. 403 U.S. at 612–13.

24. 330 U.S. at 1.

25. Thomas Jefferson, *The Writings of Thomas Jefferson,* ed. H. A. Washington, vol. 8 (New York: H. W. Derby, 1861), p. 113.

26. Ibid., p. 16.

27. 403 U.S. at 612.

28. 330 U.S. at 16–17.

29. 374 U.S. 203 (1963).

30. Ibid., p. 222.

31. Walz v. Tax Commission, 397 U.S. 664, 674 (1970) (Burger, C.J.).

32. 330 U.S. at 18.

33. Ibid., p. 4 n. 2.

34. Ibid., p. 18.

35. McCollum v. Board of Education, 333 U.S. 203 (1948).

36. 343 U.S. 306 (1952).

37. Ibid., p. 318 (Black, J., dissenting). Justices Frankfurter and Jackson filed separate dissents, based essentially on this same rationale.

38. Board of Education v. Allen, 392 U.S. 236 (1968).

39. 333 U.S. at 239.

40. Ibid., p. 244.

41. Ibid., p. 256.

42. 370 U.S. 421 (1962).

43. Ibid., p. 446.

44. Ibid., pp. 445–46.

45. Earley v. Dicenso and Robinson v. Dicenso.

46. 403 U.S. at 668.

47. 472 U.S. 60 (1985).

48. Ibid., p. 63.

49. Ibid., p. 106.

50. Ibid., p. 92.

51. Ibid.

52. Ibid.

53. Everson v. Board of Education, 330 U.S. at 12.

54. Ralph Ketcham, *James Madison: A Biography* (Charlottesville, Va.: University Press of Virginia, 1990), p. 163.

55. 472 U.S. at 93.

56. Ibid., p. 98.

57. Ibid., p. 93.

58. Ibid., p. 98.

59. Ibid., p. 94, quoting U.S. Congress, *Annals of Congress,* vol. 1, p. 731 (emphasis added).

60. 472 U.S. at 94, quoting U.S. Congress, *Annals of Congress,* vol. 1, p. 434.

61. 472 U.S. at 98–99.

62. Ibid., p. 99.

63. Ibid., p. 100.

64. Ibid., p. 101, quoting Thomas Tucker, U.S. Congress, *Annals of Congress,* vol. 1, p. 915.

65. 472 U.S. at 103, quoting Thomas Jefferson, *The Writings of Thomas Jefferson,* ed. Andrew A. Lipscomb, vol. II (Washington, D.C.: Thomas Jefferson Memorial Association, 1904), p. 429.

66. 472 U.S. at 108.

67. Ibid.

68. Ibid.

69. Ibid., p. 109.

70. Ibid., pp. 109–110.

71. Ibid., pp. 110–11 (footnotes omitted). Rehnquist cited Board of Education v. Allen, 392 U.S. 236 (1968); Meek v. Pittenger, 421 U.S. 349 (1974); Wolman v. Walter, 433 U.S. 229 (1977); Everson v. Board of Education, 330 U.S. at 1; Committee for Public Education and Religious Liberty v. Regan, 444 U.S. 646 (1980); Levitt v. Committee for Public Education and Religious Liberty, 413 U.S. 472 (1973); McCollum v. Board of Education, 333 U.S. at 203; Zorach v. Clauson, 343 U.S. 306 (1952).

72. 472 U.S. at 112.

73. Ibid., p. 113.

74. Ibid., pp. 113–14.

75. Ibid., p. 91.

76. Lamb's Chapel v. Center Moriches School District, 113 S. Ct. at 2149–50 (Scalia, J.,

concurring). See also, for example, Lee v. Weisman, 112 S. Ct. 2649, 2678 (1992) (Scalia, J., dissenting); Edwards v. Aguillard, 482 U.S. 578, 610 (1987) (Scalia, J., dissenting).

77. 112 S. Ct. at 2649.

78. 492 U.S. 573 (1989).

79. Ibid., p. 649 (footnote omitted).

80. Douglas Laycock, "'Nonpreferential' Aid to Religion: A False Claim About Original Intent," *William and Mary Law Review* 27 (1986): 875, 882–83.

81. See Abington v. Schempp, 374 U.S. at 294–304 (Brennan, J., concurring).

82. 463 U.S. 783 (1983).

83. Ibid., p. 792.

84. Ibid., p. 796.

85. 374 U.S. at 299–300.

86. 463 U.S. at 814–15.

87. See Elizabeth Fleet, "Madison's 'Detached Memoranda,'" *William and Mary Quarterly* 3 (1946): 534, 558.

88. 463 U.S. at 815.

89. 112 S. Ct. at 2675 (Souter, J., concurring).

90. See Fleet, "Madison's 'Detached Memoranda,'" p. 560.

91. 472 U.S. at 98.

92. Ibid., p. 93.

93. Ibid., pp. 93–94.

94. Ibid., p. 98.

95. Ketcham, *James Madison*, p. 291.

96. Ibid., p. 290.

97. 370 U.S. 421 (1962).

98. Ibid., p. 427.

99. Ibid., p. 432.

100. See, for example, ibid., p. 436, quoting "Madison's Remonstrance," *The Writings of James Madison*, ed. Gaillard Hunt, vol. 2 (New York: Putnam's, 1900–10), pp. 183, 185.

101. 465 U.S. 668, 687 (1984).

102. Ibid., p. 691.

103. Ibid., pp. 691–92.

104. Walz v. Tax Commission, 397 U.S. 664 (1970).

105. McGowan v. Maryland, 366 U.S. 420 (1961).

106. Zorach v. Clauson, 343 U.S. 306 (1952).

107. 465 U.S. at 692.

108. Ibid.

109. 472 U.S. at 76 (O'Connor, J., concurring).

110. Ibid., p. 83.

111. County of Allegheny v. American Civil Liberties Union, 492 U.S. at 627 (O'Connor, J., concurring).

112. Ibid., p. 631.

113. See, for example, Donald L. Beschle, "The Conservative as Liberal: The Religion Clauses, Liberal Neutrality, and the Approach of Justice O'Connor," *Notre Dame Law Review* 62 (1987): 151; Comment, "*Lemon* Reconstituted: Justice O'Connor's Proposed Modifications of the *Lemon* Test for Establishment Clause Violations," *Brigham Young University Law Review* 1986 (1986): 465; William P. Marshall, "'We Know It When We See It': The Supreme Court and Establishment," *Southern California Law Review* 59 (1986): 495.

114. See, for example, Steven D. Smith, "Symbols, Perceptions, and Doctrinal Illusions: Establishment Neutrality and the 'No Endorsement' Test," *Michigan Law Review* 86 (1987): 266; Mark Tushnet, "The Constitution and Religion," *Connecticut Law Review* 18 (1986): 701.

115. County of Allegheny v. American Civil Liberties Union, 492 U.S. at 670.

116. Ibid., p. 655.

117. Ibid., p. 656.

118. Ibid., p. 655.

119. Ibid., p. 659.

120. Ibid., pp. 662–63.

121. Ibid., p. 659.

122. 112 S. Ct. 2649 (1992).

123. Ibid., p. 2658.

124. Ibid., p. 2683 (emphasis in original).

125. Ibid., pp. 2683–84.

126. Ibid., p. 2684.

127. 370 U.S. at 430.

128. County of Allegheny v. American Civil Liberties Union, 492 U.S. at 661 n. 1.

129. Engel v. Vitale, 370 U.S. at 431.

130. Ibid.

131. Lee v. Weisman, 112 S. Ct. at 2673.

132. Kiryas Joel Village School District v. Grumet, 114 S. Ct. 2481 (1994).

133. 459 U.S. 116 (1982).

134. 114 S. Ct. at 2509.

135. Ibid., p. 2507.

136. Ibid.

137. Ibid., p. 2515.

138. Ibid.

139. Ibid.

140. Ibid.

141. 63 L.W. 4684 (1995).

142. Ibid., p. 4702.

143. Ibid., p. 4699.

144. 63 L.W. 4702 (1995).

145. 454 U.S. 263 (1981).

146. For example, 113 S. Ct. 2141.

147. 63 L.W. at 4722.

148. 117 S. Ct. 1997 (1997).

149. Aguilar v. Felton, 473 U.S. 402 (1985).

150. Ibid., p. 2016.
151. Ibid., p. 2019.
152. 98 U.S. 145 (1879).
153. Braunfeld v. Brown, 366 U.S. 599 (1961).
154. 374 U.S. 398 (1963).
155. 406 U.S. 205 (1972).
156. 455 U.S. 252 (1982).
157. Ibid., p. 262.
158. 494 U.S. 872 (1990).
159. Ibid., pp. 881–83.
160. Ibid., p. 884.
161. Ibid., p. 885, quoting Reynolds v. United States, 98 U.S. at 167.
162. 494 U.S. at 916.
163. Ibid., p. 917 (footnote omitted).
164. 117 S. Ct. 2157 (1997).
165. Kennedy cited South Carolina v. Katzenbach, 383 U.S. 301 (1966).
166. Church of the Lukumi Babalu Aye v. City of Hialeah, 508 U.S. 502 (1993).
167. Committee for Public Education and Religious Liberty v. Nyquist, 413 U.S. 756 (1973).
168. Ibid., pp. 797–98.

Chapter Seven

1. 394 U.S. 576 (1969).
2. Ibid., p. 610 (emphasis in original).
3. Texas v. Johnson, 491 U.S. 397 (1989); United States v. Eichman, 496 U.S. 310 (1990).
4. 391 U.S. 367 (1968).
5. 491 U.S. at 408.
6. Ibid., p. 409.
7. Ibid., p. 410.
8. Ibid., p. 414.
9. Ibid., pp. 417–18.
10. Ibid., p. 419.
11. Harry A. Blackmun to William J. Brennan, June 19, 1989, Marshall Papers, Box 478.
12. 491 U.S. at 421.
13. Halter v. Nebraska, 205 U.S. 34 (1907).
14. Street v. New York, 394 U.S. 576 (1969); Spence v. Washington, 418 U.S. 405 (1974); Smith v. Goguen, 415 U.S. 566 (1974).
15. San Francisco Arts & Athletics, Inc. v. United States Olympic Committee, 483 U.S. 522, 536 (1987).
16. 315 U.S. 568 (1942).
17. 491 U.S. at 430–31.
18. Ibid., p. 437.
19. Ibid., p. 438.
20. 403 U.S. 15 (1971).
21. United States v. Eichman, 496 U.S. 308 (1990).
22. A copy of the Rehnquist draft, dated May 31, 1990, is in the Marshall Papers, Box 510.
23. William H. Rehnquist, Memorandum to the Conference, June 4, 1990, Marshall Papers, Box 510.
24. 112 S. Ct. 2538 (1992).
25. Ibid., pp. 2547–48.
26. Ibid., p. 2559.
27. Ibid., pp. 2560–61.
28. Ibid., p. 2561.
29. Ibid., p. 2562 (footnote omitted).
30. Ibid., p. 2567.
31. Ibid., p. 2561.
32. 501 U.S. 560 (1991).
33. Ibid., pp. 592–93.
34. Ibid., pp. 595–96.
35. Ibid., p. 575 n. 3.
36. Ibid., p. 596.
37. Ibid., p. 590.
38. Ibid., pp. 576–77.
39. Ibid., p. 579.
40. Tinsley E. Yarbrough, *Mr. Justice Black and His Critics* (Durham: Duke University Press, 1988), ch. 4.
41. 376 U.S. 254 (1964).
42. Hustler Magazine v. Falwell, 485 U.S. 46, 53 (1988).
43. Ibid., p. 55.
44. Ibid.
45. Masson v. New Yorker Magazine, Inc., 501 U.S. 496 (1991).
46. Ibid., p. 526.
47. Ibid., pp. 527–28.
48. Milkovich v. Lorain Journal Co., 497 U.S. 1 (1990).
49. Ibid., p. 24.
50. Ibid., p. 28.
51. Ibid., pp. 35–36, quoting from New York Times v. Sullivan, 371 U.S. 415, 445 (1963).
52. See, for example, Black's separate opinion in New York Times v. Sullivan, 376 U.S. at 722.
53. John Paul Stevens, Memorandum to the Conference, May 11, 1989, Marshall Papers, Box 477.
54. Harte-Hanks Communications v. Connaughton, 491 U.S. 657 (1989). The Court has denied certiorari in a number of libel cases raising interesting issues, including Blatty v. New York Times, 485 U.S. 934 (1988), involving omission of a prominent novelist's latest work from the *Times* best-seller list, and Herceg v. *Hustler* Magazine, 485 U.S. 959 (1988), a suit by relatives and friends of a teenager who hanged himself after reading a *Hustler* article on autoerotic asphyxiation. In a memorandum to his colleagues, Chief Justice Rehnquist had recommended a denial of review in the first case and a grant of certiorari in the second. William H.

Rehnquist, Memorandum to the Conference, February 26, 1988, Marshall Papers, Box 435.

55. 413 U.S. 15 (1973).

56. 481 U.S. 497 (1987).

57. Paris Adult Theatre I v. Slaton, 413 U.S. 49 (1973).

58. 481 U.S. at 507, quoting his opinion in ibid., p. 103.

59. Eben Moglen, bench memo, Pope v. Illinois, February 24, 1987, Marshall Papers, Box 399.

60. 481 U.S. at 512 (footnote omitted).

61. Ibid., p. 513.

62. Ibid., p. 512.

63. Ibid., p. 506.

64. Ibid., pp. 504–5.

65. New York v. Ferber, 458 U.S. 747 (1982).

66. Ginsberg v. New York, 390 U.S. 629 (1968).

67. Stanley v. Georgia, 394 U.S. 557 (1969).

68. 495 U.S. 103 (1990).

69. 458 U.S. at 747.

70. 495 U.S. at 138.

71. Ibid., p. 140.

72. Ibid., p. 141.

73. Massachusetts v. Oakes, 491 U.S. 576, 586 (1989).

74. 421 U.S. 809 (1975).

75. Ibid., p. 818.

76. Ibid., p. 588 n. 1.

77. United States v. X-Citement Video, Inc., 115 S. Ct. 464, 473 (1994).

78. Ibid., p. 475.

79. FW/PBS, Inc. v. City of Dallas, 493 U.S. 215 (1990).

80. Freedman v. Maryland, 380 U.S. 51 (1965).

81. Reno v. American Civil Liberties Union, 117 S. Ct. 2329, 2355 (1997).

82. Ibid., p. 2355.

83. Sable Communications v. FCC, 492 U.S. 115, 135 (1989), quoting Carlin Communications, Inc. v. FCC, 837 F. 2d 546, 555, certiorari denied, 488 U.S. 924 (CA 2, 1988).

84. 492 U.S. at 131; National Endowment for the Arts v. Finley, 118 S. Ct. 2168 (1998).

85. Fort Wayne Books v. Indiana, 489 U.S. 46, 57 (1989).

86. Ibid., p. 61.

87. Ibid., p. 75.

88. Ibid., p. 84.

89. Ibid., p. 85.

90. 283 U.S. 697 (1931).

91. Alexander v. United States, 113 S. Ct. 2766, 2783–84 (1993).

92. 478 U.S. 697 (1986).

93. 113 S. Ct. at 2785.

94. For example, Marcus v. Search Warrant, 367 U.S. 717 (1961); A Quantity of Copies of Books v. Kansas, 378 U.S. 205 (1964).

95. 113 S. Ct. at 2786 (emphasis added).

96. Ibid.

97. See, for example, Virginia Pharmacy Board v. Virginia Consumer Council, 452 U.S. 746 (1976).

98. Central Hudson Gas & Electric Corp. v. Public Service Comm., 447 U.S. 557 (1980).

99. Shapero v. Kentucky Bar Ass'n, 486 U.S. 466 (1988).

100. 44 Liquormart, Inc. v. Rhode Island, 116 S. Ct. 1495 (1996).

101. Greater New Orleans Broadcasting Ass'n v. United States (1999) (slip opinion). United States v. Edge Broadcasting Co., 113 S. Ct. 2696 (1993).

102. 116 S. Ct. at 1515–16.

103. Ibid., p. 1515.

104. Bd. of Trustees v. Fox, 492 U.S. 469, 486 n. 1 (1989).

105. Airport Com'rs of Los Angeles v. Jews for Jesus, 482 U.S. 569 (1987).

106. International Society for Krishna Consciousness v. Lee, 112 S. Ct. 2701 (1992).

107. City of Houston v. Hill, 482 U.S. 451 (1987).

108. Boos v. Barry, 485 U.S. 312 (1988).

109. United States v. Kokinda, 497 U.S. 720 (1990).

110. Forsyth County, Ga. v. Nationalist Movement, 112 S. Ct. 2395 (1992).

111. Ward v. Rock Against Racism, 491 U.S. 781 (1989).

112. City of Cincinnati v. Discovery Network, Inc., 113 S. Ct. 1505 (1993).

113. City of Ladue v. Gilleo, 114 S. Ct. 2038 (1994).

114. Lyng v. International Union, UAW, 485 U.S. 360 (1988).

115. Hurley v. Irish-American Gay Group of Boston, 115 S. Ct. 2338 (1995).

116. Hague v. CIO, 307 U.S. 496 (1939).

117. Perry Education Assn. v. Perry Local Educators' Assn., 460 U.S. 37 (1983).

118. 112 S. Ct. at 2701, 2715.

119. Ibid., p. 2716.

120. Ibid., p. 2717.

121. Ibid.

122. Hudgens v. NLRB, 424 U.S. 507 (1976).

123. For examples of memoranda from the Court marshal regarding arrangements for such Right-to-Life marches, see Alfred Wong, Memorandum to the Conference, January 20, 1988,

Marshall Papers, Box 435, and January 17, 1990, Marshall Papers, Box 492.

124. Frisby v. Schultz, 487 U.S. 474 (1988).

125. See, for example, United States v. Guest, 383 U.S. 745 (1966).

126. Bray v. Alexandria Women's Health Clinic, 113 S. Ct. 753 (1993).

127. National Organization for Women, Inc. v. Scheidler, 114 S. Ct. 798 (1994).

128. 114 S. Ct. 2516 (1994).

129. Ibid., 114 S. Ct. at 2516.

130. Ibid., p. 2524.

131. Ibid., p. 2525.

132. Ibid., p. 2526.

133. Ibid., p. 2531 (footnote omitted). In concurring in the denial of a stay in another abortion protest case, Hirsh v. City of Atlanta, 110 S. Ct. 2163 (1990), it might be further noted, Stevens emphasized the distinction that should be drawn "between injunctive relief imposing time, place, and manner restrictions upon a class of persons who have persistently and repeatedly engaged in unlawful conduct, on the one hand, ... and an injunction that constitutes a naked prior restraint against a proposed march by a group that did not have a similar history of illegal conduct in the jurisdiction where the march was scheduled."

134. 114 S. Ct. at 2538–39. Scalia cited, among other cases, Walker v. City of Birmingham, 388 U.S. 307 (1967).

135. 114 S. Ct. at 2539–40.

136. NAACP v. Claiborne Hardware Co., 458 U.S. 886 (1982).

137. 114 S. Ct. at 2542.

138. Ibid., pp. 2549–50.

139. Schenck v. Pro-Choice Network, 117 S. Ct. 855, 872 (1997) (Scalia, J., concurring and dissenting).

140. 393 U.S. 503 (1969).

141. Bethel School District v. Fraser, 478 U.S. 675 (1986).

142. 484 U.S. 260 (1988).

143. Ibid., p. 284.

144. Ibid., p. 291.

145. 416 U.S. 396 (1974).

146. Pell v. Procunier, 417 U.S. 817, 822 (1974).

147. 482 U.S. 78 (1987).

148. 490 U.S. 401 (1989).

149. Cases cited included Jones v. North Carolina Prisoners' Labor Union, 433 U.S. 119 (1977).

150. 482 U.S. at 89.

151. 490 U.S. at 409–10 (footnote omitted).

152. Ibid., p. 423.

153. Ibid., p. 424.

154. Ibid., p. 427.

155. Ibid., p. 431.

156. 391 U.S. 563 (1968).

157. See, for example, Connick v. Myers, 461 U.S. 138 (1983).

158. 114 S. Ct. 1878 (1994).

159. Ibid., p. 1894.

160. Ibid., p. 1898.

161. Ibid., p. 1900.

162. Elrod v. Burns, 427 U.S. 347 (1976); Branti v. Finkel, 445 U.S. 507 (1980).

163. Rutan v. Republican Party of Illinois, 497 U.S. 62 (1990).

164. Ibid., p. 104.

165. Ibid., p. 80.

166. Rankin v. McPherson, 483 U.S. 378, 394 (1987).

167. Quoted in ibid., p. 394.

168. United States v. National Treasury Employees Union, 115 S. Ct. 1003, 1027 (1995).

169. Federal Election Com'n v. Mass. Citizens for Life, 479 U.S. 238 (1986).

170. Tashjian v. Republican Party of Connecticut, 479 U.S. 208 (1986).

171. Meyer v. Grant, 486 U.S. 414 (1988); Buckley v. American Constitutional Law Foundation, 119 S. Ct. 636 (1999).

172. Eu v. San Francisco Cty. Democratic Cent. Com., 489 U.S. 214 (1989).

173. McIntyre v. Ohio Elections Com'n, 115 S. Ct. 1511 (1995).

174. Munro v. Socialist Workers Party, 479 U.S. 189 (1986).

175. Burdick v. Takushi, 112 S. Ct. 2059 (1992).

176. Burson v. Freeman, 112 S. Ct. 1846 (1992).

177. Timmons v. Twin Cities Area New Party, 117 S. Ct. 1364 (1997).

178. Wisconsin v. Mitchell, 113 S. Ct. 2194 (1993).

179. Meese v. Keene, 481 U.S. 465 (1987).

180. Glickman v. Wileman Bros. & Elliott, 117 S. Ct. 2130 (1997).

181. Cohen v. Cowles Media Company, 501 U.S. 663 (1991).

182. Arkansas Writers' Project v. Ragland, 481 U.S. 221 (1987).

183. Florida Bar v. B.J.F., 491 U.S. 524 (1989).

184. Simon & Schuster v. New York Crime Victims Bd., 502 U.S. 105 (1991).

185. Campbell v. Acuff-Rose Music, Inc., 114 S. Ct. 1164 (1994).

186. Riley v. National Federation of the Blind of N.C., 487 U.S. 781 (1988).

187. Branzburg v. Hayes, 408 U.S. 665 (1972).
188. University of Pennsylvania v. E.E.O.C., 493 U.S. 182 (1990).
189. 481 U.S. at 486.

Chapter Eight

1. Miller v. Florida, 482 U.S. 423 (1987). See also Collins v. Youngblood, 497 U.S. 37 (1990), and California Department of Corrections v. Morales, 115 S. Ct. 1597 (1995).
2. 117 S. Ct. 2072 (1997).
3. Kyles v. Whitley, 115 S. Ct. 1555 (1995).
4. Brady v. Maryland, 373 U.S. 83 (1963); Stricker v. Greene (1999) (slip opinion); Arizona v. Youngblood, 488 U.S. 51 (1989).
5. United States v. Salerno, 481 U.S. 739 (1987).
6. Alabama v. Smith, 490 U.S. 794 (1989), overruling Simpson v. Rice, 395 U.S. 711 (1969).
7. Cage v. Louisiana, 498 U.S. 39 (1990).
8. Victor v. Nebraska, 114 S. Ct. 1239 (1994).
9. Griffin v. United States, 502 U.S. 46 (1991).
10. Doggett v. United States, 112 S. Ct. 2686 (1992).
11. Witte v. United States, 115 S. Ct. 2199 (1995).
12. United States v. Dixon, 113 S. Ct. 2849 (1993).
13. United States v. Felix, 112 S. Ct. 1377 (1992).
14. Ricketts v. Adamson, 483 U.S. 1 (1987).
15. Argersinger v. Hamlin, 407 U.S. 25 (1972).
16. Perry v. Leeke, 488 U.S. 272 (1989).
17. Gentile v. State Bar of Nevada, 501 U.S. 1030 (1991).
18. Mallard v. U.S. Dist. Court, 490 U.S. 196 (1989).
19. 487 U.S. 1012 (1988).
20. Ibid., p. 1016. Drafts of the Brennan draft and Scalia concurrence are in the Marshall Papers, Box 450.
21. 487 U.S. at 1022.
22. 497 U.S. 836 (1990).
23. Ibid., pp. 861–62.
24. Ibid., p. 862.
25. Ibid., p. 865.
26. Ibid., p. 870. On the same day *Craig* was decided, Scalia joined the Court in holding in another case, per Justice O'Connor, that the hearsay statements of a child victim lacked demonstrated trustworthiness required for admission as evidence. Idaho v. Wright, 497 U.S. 805 (1990). For other confrontation decisions,

see, for example, White v. Illinois, 502 U.S. 346 (1992); Michigan v. Lucas, 500 U.S. 145 (1991); Kentucky v. Stincer, 482 U.S. 730 (1987).
27. Hudson v. McMillan, 112 S. Ct. 995 (1992); Lilly v. Virginia (1999) (slip opinion).
28. Whitley v. Albers, 475 U.S. 312 (1986); Wilson v. Seiter, 115 S. Ct. 2320 (1991).
29. 112 S. Ct. at 999.
30. Rhodes v. Chapman, 452 U.S. 337 (1981); Estelle v. Gamble, 429 U.S. 97 (1976).
31. 112 S. Ct. at 1000.
32. Ibid., p. 1009.
33. Ibid., p. 1010. For other suits involving prison conditions, see, for example, Farmer v. Brennan, 114 S. Ct. 1970 (1994); Helling v. McKinney, 113 S. Ct. 2475 (1993).
34. United States v. Bajakajian, 118 S. Ct. 2028 (1998).
35. Ibid., p. 2045.
36. Ibid., p. 2046. Other Rehnquist Court rulings involving disputes over forfeiture provisions include Bennis v. Michigan, 116 S. Ct. 994 (1996), in which a five-four majority upheld forfeiture of a car jointly owned by a husband and wife, based on the husband's conviction for a sexual liaison with a prostitute in the vehicle.
37. Jacobson v. United States, 503 U.S. 540 (1992).
38. Chapman v. California, 386 U.S. 18 (1967).
39. Satterwhite v. Texas, 486 U.S. 249 (1988); Neder v. United States (1999) (slip opinion). See also Jones v. United States (1999) (slip opinion), involving a judge's instructions to the jury in the sentencing phase of a capital case.
40. See, for example, his dissent in Bivens v. Six Unknown Named Agents, 403 U.S. 388 (1971).
41. 367 U.S. 643 (1961).
42. United States v. Calandra, 414 U.S. 338 (1974).
43. United States v. Janis, 428 U.S. 433 (1976).
44. United States v. Leon, 468 U.S. 897 (1984).
45. See, for example, Brennan's dissent, joined by Justice Marshall, in ibid., p. 928.
46. James v. Illinois, 493 U.S. 307, 314 (1990).
47. Ibid., p. 929.
48. Illinois v. Krull, 480 U.S. 340 (1987); Arizona v. Evans, 115 S. Ct. 1185 (1995).
49. See, for example, Stevens's dissent in Arizona v. Evans, 115 S. Ct. at 1195.
50. California v. Ciraolo, 476 U.S. 207 (1986).

51. Florida v. Riley, 488 U.S. 445 (1989).

52. California v. Greenwood, 486 U.S. 35 (1988).

53. United States v. Dunn, 480 U.S. 294 (1987).

54. United States v. Verdugo-Urquidez, 494 U.S. 259 (1990).

55. County of Sacramento v. Lewis, 118 S. Ct. 1708 (1998). See also Michigan v. Chesternut, 486 U.S. 567 (1988).

56. Richards v. Wisconsin, 117 S. Ct. 1416 (1997); Wilson v. Arkansas, 115 S. Ct. 1914 (1995).

57. United States v. Ramirez, 118 S. Ct. 992 (1998). During the 1998–99 term, the Court also concluded that defendants briefly in another person's apartment to package cocaine had no legitimate expectation of privacy there. Minnesota v. Carter, 119 S. Ct. 469 (1998).

58. 392 U.S. 1 (1968).

59. Minnesota v. Dickerson, 113 S. Ct. 2130 (1993).

60. Florida v. Jimeno, 500 U.S. 248 (1991).

61. New York v. Burger, 482 U.S. 691 (1987).

62. United States v. Sokolow, 490 U.S. 1 (1989).

63. Smith v. Ohio, 494 U.S. 541 (1990).

64. Wyoming v. Houghton, 119 S. Ct. 1297 (1999); Maryland v. Buie, 494 U.S. 325 (1990).

65. Knowles v. Iowa, 119 S. Ct. 484 (1999); Florida v. Bostick, 501 U.S. 429 (1991).

66. Ibid., p. 438.

67. See the Souter draft opinion and David H. Souter to Sandra Day O'Connor, March 13, June 17, 1991, Marshall Papers, Box 532.

68. Ibid., p. 447.

69. Ibid., p. 449.

70. Ibid., p. 447.

71. Ibid., p. 450.

72. Adams v. Williams, 407 U.S. 143 (1972); Illinois v. Gates, 462 U.S. 213 (1983).

73. Alabama v. White, 196 U.S. 325 (1990).

74. Soldal v. Cook County, Ill., 113 S. Ct. 538 (1992).

75. 496 U.S. 444 (1990).

76. Delaware v. Prouse, 440 U.S. 648 (1979).

77. 496 U.S. at 462 (footnote omitted).

78. Ulhren v. United States, 116 S. Ct. 1769 (1996).

79. Maryland v. Wilson, 117 S. Ct. 882, 886 (1997) (Stevens, J., joined by Kennedy, J., dissenting).

80. Brower v. County of Inyo, 489 U.S. 593 (1989).

81. County of Sacramento v. Lewis, 118 S. Ct. 1708.

82. California v. Acevedo, 500 U.S. 565 (1991).

83. 267 U.S. 132 (1925).

84. 456 U.S. 798 (1982).

85. 500 U.S. at 574.

86. Ibid., p. 599.

87. South Dakota v. Opperman, 428 U.S. 364 (1976); Illinois v. Lafayette, 462 U.S. 640 (1983).

88. Florida v. Wells, 495 U.S. 1 (1990).

89. Colorado v. Bertine, 479 U.S. 367, 381 (1987).

90. Arizona v. Hicks, 480 U.S. 321 (1987).

91. Coolidge v. New Hampshire, 403 U.S. 443 (1971).

92. Horton v. California, 496 U.S. 128, 144–45 (1990).

93. Murray v. United States, 487 U.S. 533 (1988).

94. Ibid., p. 544.

95. 468 U.S. 796, 817 (1984).

96. 487 U.S. at 551.

97. 489 U.S. 602 (1989).

98. 489 U.S. 656 (1989).

99. Skinner v. Railway Labor Executives' Association, 489 U.S. at 636.

100. Ibid., pp. 638, 637.

101. National Treasury Employees Union v. Von Raab, 489 U.S. at 680–81.

102. Ibid., p. 683.

103. Ibid., p. 687.

104. Veronia School Dist. v. Acton, 115 S. Ct. 2386 (1995).

105. Chandler v. Miller, 117 S. Ct. 1295, 1306 (1997).

106. 384 U.S. 436 (1966).

107. Harris v. New York, 401 U.S. 222 (1971).

108. Michigan v. Tucker, 417 U.S. 433 (1974).

109. Nix v. Williams, 467 U.S. 431 (1984).

110. United States v. Mandujano, 425 U.S. 564 (1976).

111. Thompson v. Keohane, 116 S. Ct. 457, 467 (1995).

112. Arizona v. Fulminante, 499 U.S. 279 (1991).

113. Edwards v. Arizona, 451 U.S. 477 (1981).

114. Minnick v. Mississippi, 498 U.S. 146 (1990).

115. Arizona v. Roberson, 486 U.S. 675 (1988).

116. 445 U.S. 573 (1980).

117. New York v. Harris, 495 U.S. 14, 26 (1990).

118. Duckworth v. Eagan, 492 U.S. 195 (1989).

119. Arizona v. Mauro, 481 U.S. 520 (1987).

120. Colorado v. Spring, 479 U.S. 564 (1987).

121. Connecticut v. Barrett, 479 U.S. 523 (1987).

122. Doyle v. Ohio, 426 U.S. 610 (1976).

123. Greer v. Miller, 483 U.S. 756 (1987).

124. Michigan v. Harvey, 494 U.S. 344 (1990).

125. McNeil v. Wisconsin, 501 U.S. 171 (1991).

126. Illinois v. Perkins, 496 U.S. 292 (1990).

127. United States v. Scheffer, 118 S. Ct. 1261 (1998).

128. Ibid., p. 1269.

129. Washington v. Texas, 388 U.S. 14 (1967).

130. 496 U.S. 582 (1990).

131. See William J. Brennan, Jr., Memorandum to the Conference, May 31, 1990, Marshall Papers, Box 507.

132. Sandra Day O'Connor to William J. Brennan, Jr., June 4, 1990, Marshall Papers, Box 507.

133. William J. Brennan, Jr., to Thurgood Marshall, June 7, 1990, Marshall Papers, Box 507.

134. William J. Brennan, Jr., to Thurgood Marshall, June 13, 1990, Marshall Papers, Box 507.

135. 496 U.S. at 608.

136. See, for example, Strauder v. West Virginia, 100 U.S. 303 (1880); Norris v. Alabama, 294 U.S. 587 (1935).

137. Peters v. Kiff, 407 U.S. 493 (1972).

138. Taylor v. Louisiana, 419 U.S. 522 (1975).

139. 380 U.S. 202 (1965).

140. 476 U.S. 79 (1986).

141. 380 U.S. at 223.

142. See, for example, United States v. Jenkins, 701 F. 2d 850 (CA 10, 1983); United States v. Pearson, 448 F. 2d 1207 (CA 5, 1971).

143. Powell cited Castaneda v. Partida, 430 U.S. 482, 494–95 (1977), and Alexander v. Louisiana, 405 U.S. 625, 631–32 (1972), among other cases.

144. 476 U.S. at 137–38.

145. Ibid., p. 106.

146. Griffith v. Kentucky, 479 U.S. 314 (1987).

147. Edmonson v. Leesville Concrete Co., Inc., 500 U.S. 614 (1991).

148. Georgia v. McCollum, 112 S. Ct. 2348 (1992).

149. Purkett v. Elem, 115 S. Ct. 1769 (1995). See also Hernandez v. New York, 500 U.S. 352 (1991).

150. Holland v. Illinois, 493 U.S. 474 (1990).

151. Singleton v. Wuff, 428 U.S. 106 (1976).

152. Powers v. Ohio, 499 U.S. 400, 424 (1991).

153. 114 S. Ct. 1419 (1994).

154. Ibid., p. 1426.

155. Blackmun cited, for example, Cleburne v. Cleburne Living Center, 473 U.S. 432 (1985), applying rational basis scrutiny to classifications based on mental retardation.

156. 114 S. Ct. at 1419.

157. Ibid., p. 1435, citing Mississippi Univ. for Women v. Hogan, 458 U.S. 718 (1982).

158. 114 S. Ct. at 1435.

159. Ibid., p. 1436.

160. Ibid., p. 1437.

161. Ibid., p. 1438, quoting Lewis v. United States, 146 U.S. 370, 378 (1892); Lamb v. United States, 36 Wis. 424, 427, 426 (1874).

162. Gregg v. Georgia, 428 U.S. 153 (1976).

163. Woodson v. North Carolina, 428 U.S. 280 (1976).

164. Furman v. Georgia, 408 U.S. 238 (1972).

165. Coker v. Georgia, 433 U.S. 584 (1977).

166. Lockett v. Ohio, 438 U.S. 586 (1978).

167. Richmond v. Lewis, 113 S. Ct. 528 (1992); Maynard v. Cartwright, 486 U.S. 356 (1988).

168. For example, Walton v. Arizona, 497 U.S. 639 (1990).

169. Hitchcock v. Dugger, 481 U.S. 393 (1987).

170. Mills v. Maryland, 486 U.S. 367 (1988); see also McKoy v. North Carolina, 494 U.S. 433 (1990).

171. Tison v. Arizona, 481 U.S. 137 (1987).

172. Franklyn v. Lynaugh, 487 U.S. 164 (1988).

173. Thompson v. Oklahoma, 487 U.S. 815 (1988).

174. Ibid., p. 859.

175. Ibid., p. 865.

176. Ibid., p. 868 n. 4.

177. Stanford v. Kentucky, 492 U.S. 361 (1989).

178. Ibid., p. 390.

179. Ibid., p. 399.

180. Ibid., p. 404.

181. 492 U.S. 302 (1989).

182. Jurek v. Texas, 428 U.S. 262 (1976).

183. Perry v. Lynaugh, 492 U.S. at 360.

184. Ibid., pp. 346–47.

185. Ibid., p. 350.

186. 482 U.S. 496 (1987).

187. 490 U.S. 805 (1989).

188. 501 U.S. 808 (1991).

189. 482 U.S. at 503.

190. 501 U.S. at 819.

191. Ibid., p. 824.

192. Ibid., p. 827.

193. For example, Swift & Co. v. Wickham, 382 U.S. 111 (1965); Oregon *ex rel.* State Land Bd. v. Cornvallis Sand & Gravel Co., 429 U.S. 363 (1977).

194. 501 U.S. at 828.
195. Ibid., pp. 834–35.
196. Ibid., pp. 852–53.
197. Ibid., p. 854.
198. Ibid., p. 855.
199. Ibid., p. 856.
200. Ibid., p. 867.
201. McCleskey v. Kemp, 481 U.S. 279, 292 (1987).
202. Ibid., p. 313.
203. Ibid., p. 315.
204. Ibid., p. 316.
205. Ibid., p. 319.
206. Ibid., pp. 324–25.
207. Ibid., p. 365.
208. Ibid., p. 367.
209. 408 U.S. 238 (1972).
210. McGautha v. California, 402 U.S. 183 (1971).
211. Callins v. Collins, 114 S. Ct. 1127, 1134–35 (1994).
212. Ibid., p. 1127.
213. Ibid., p. 1128.

Chapter Nine

1. 347 U.S. 483 (1954); 349 U.S. 294 (1955).
2. Korematsu v. United States, 323 U.S. 214 (1944); Skinner v. Oklahoma, 316 U.S. 535 (1942).
3. Harper v. Virginia Board of Elections, 383 U.S. 663 (1966).
4. Levy v. Louisiana, 391 U.S. 68 (1968).
5. 383 U.S. at 663.
6. Reynolds v. Sims, 377 U.S. 533 (1964).
7. Williams v. Rhodes, 393 U.S. 23 (1968).
8. Shapiro v. Thompson, 394 U.S. 618 (1969).
9. 411 U.S. 1 (1973).
10. Ibid. But see Plyler v. Doe, 457 U.S. 202 (1982).
11. Dandridge v. Williams, 397 U.S. 471 (1970).
12. Graham v. Richardson, 403 U.S. 365 (1971); *In Re* Griffiths, 413 U.S. 717 (1973); Sugarman v. Dougall, 413 U.S. 634 (1973).
13. Foley v. Connelie, 435 U.S. 291 (1978); Ambach v. Norwick, 441 U.S. 68 (1979).
14. Mathews v. Diaz, 426 U.S. 67 (1976).
15. Massachusetts Bd. of Retirement v. Murgia, 427 U.S. 307 (1976).
16. James v. Valtierra, 402 U.S. 137 (1971).
17. City of New Orleans v. Dukes, 427 U.S. 297 (1976).
18. Craig v. Boren, 429 U.S. 190 (1976); Mississippi University for Women v. Hogan, 458 U.S. 718 (1982).

19. Trimble v. Gordon, 430 U.S. 762 (1977).
20. Soenz, Director, California Department of Social Services v. Roe (1999) (slip opinion). Compare Shapiro v. Thompson, 394 U.S. 618 (1969).
21. United States v. Virginia, 116 S. Ct. 2264, 2275, n. 6 (1996).
22. Ibid., p. 2288. For Rehnquist Court review of gender discrimination claims under federal civil rights legislation, see, for example, International Union, UAW v. Johnson Controls, 499 U.S. 187 (1991); Price Waterhouse v. Hopkins, 490 U.S. 228 (1989).
23. Clark v. Jeter, 486 U.S. 456 (1988).
24. Miller v. Allbright, 118 S. Ct. 1428 (1998).
25. 457 U.S. 202 (1982).
26. Kadmas v. Dickinson Public Schools, 487 U.S. 450 (1988).
27. 410 U.S. 719 (1973).
28. 451 U.S. 355 (1981).
29. 491 U.S. 95 (1989).
30. 477 U.S. 57 (1986).
31. Harris v. Forklift Systems, Inc., 114 S. Ct. 367 (1993).
32. 118 S. Ct. 1989 (1998).
33. Cannon v. University of Chicago, 441 U.S. 677 (1979); Franklin v. Gwinnett County Public Schools, 503 U.S. 60 (1992).
34. 118 S. Ct. at 1999.
35. Ibid., p. 2003, n. 8.
36. Ibid., p. 2004.
37. Ibid., pp. 2003–4.
38. Ibid., p. 2003 n. 8.
39. Ibid., p. 2006, citing Franklin v. Gwinnett County Public Schools, 503 U.S. 60 (1992).
40. 118 S. Ct. at 2004.
41. Ibid., p. 2007.
42. 118 S. Ct. 2257 (1998).
43. Ibid., pp. 2272–73.
44. Ibid., p. 2273.
45. Ibid.
46. 118 S. Ct. 2275, 2293 (1998).
47. Davis v. Monroe County Board of Education (1999) (slip opinion).
48. Olmstead v. L.C. (1999) (slip opinion). Justice Thomas cited Printz v. United States, 521 U.S. 898 (1997), and New York v. United States, 505 U.S. 144 (1992). The other ADA cases discussed in this section, listed in order of their examination in the text, are Sutton v. United Airlines (1999) (slip opinion); Murphy v. United Parcel Service (1999) (slip opinion); Albertsons, Inc. v. Kirkingburg (1999) (slip opinion).
49. 491 U.S. 164 (1989).
50. 98 F. Supp. 532 (E.D.S.C., 1951); Tinsley

E. Yarbrough, *A Passion for Justice: J. Waties War-ing and Civil Rights* (New York: Oxford University Press, 1987), pp. 188–90.

51. Briggs v. Elliott, 132 F. Supp. 776, 777 (E.D.S.C., 1955).

52. Shuttlesworth v. Birmingham Board of Education, 162 F. Supp. 372 (N.D. Ala., 1958).

53. 391 U.S. 430 (1968).

54. Ibid., p. 442.

55. 112 S. Ct. 1430 (1992).

56. See also Board of Education of Okla-homa City v. Dowell, 111 S. Ct. 630 (1991).

57. 112 S. Ct. at 1453.

58. 505 U.S. 717 (1992).

59. Ibid., p. 750.

60. Bazemore v. Friday, 478 U.S. 385 (1986).

61. 497 U.S. 547 (1990).

62. Fullilove v. Klutznick, 448 U.S. 448 (1980).

63. 488 U.S. 467 (1989).

64. Ibid., p. 504.

65. Ibid., p. 529.

66. Ibid., p. 544.

67. Ibid., p. 555.

68. Ibid., p. 537.

69. Ibid., p. 538.

70. Ibid., p. 561.

71. Ibid., p. 559.

72. 115 S. Ct. 2097 (1995).

73. Ibid., p. 2111.

74. Ibid., p. 2117.

75. Ibid., pp. 2118–19.

76. Ibid., p. 2119 (asterisk omitted).

77. Ibid.

78. Ibid., p. 2120.

79. Ibid., pp. 2120–21.

80. Ibid., p. 2122; Washington v. Davis, 426 U.S. 229 (1976).

81. 115 S. Ct. at 2122.

82. Ibid., p. 2124, quoting 488 U.S. at 521–22.

83. Regents of the University of California v. Bakke, 438 U.S. 265 (1978).

84. 78 F. 3d 932 (1995).

85. 116 S. Ct. 2581 (1996).

86. Ibid., p. 2582.

87. Piscataway Township Board of Educa-tion v. Taxman, 118 S. Ct. 595 (1997).

88. 113 S. Ct. 2816 (1993).

89. Ibid., p. 2824.

90. 430 U.S. 144 (1977).

91. 113 S. Ct. at 2834.

92. Ibid.

93. Ibid., p. 2838.

94. Ibid., p. 2841.

95. Ibid., p. 2824.

96. Ibid., p. 2825.

97. 115 S. Ct. 2475 (1995).

98. Ibid., pp. 2485–86.

99. 116 S. Ct. 1894 (1996).

100. Ibid., p. 1907.

101. Ibid., p. 1918.

102. Ibid., p. 1919.

103. Ibid., p. 1909. The *Shaw* saga continues. After the district court enjoined a new district-ing plan on a motion for summary judgment, the Supreme Court reversed, Justice Thomas holding for a unanimous tribunal that a hearing was necessary to determine whether the district-ing had an impermissible racial motive or was based on constitutionally permissible political considerations. Hunt v. Cromartie (1999) (slip opinion).

104. 116 S. Ct. 1941 (1996).

105. Ibid., p. 1977.

106. Ibid., p. 2002.

107. 113 S. Ct. at 2827.

108. 116 S. Ct. at 2003.

109. Ibid., p. 2011.

110. Michael Klarman, "An Interpretive His-tory of Modern Equal Protection," *Michigan Law Review* 90 (1991): 213; Eric Schnapper, "Affirma-tive Action and the Legislative History of the Fourteenth Amendment," *Virginia Law Review* 71 (1985): 753.

111. See, for example, Antonin Scalia, "Origi-nalism: The Lesser Evil," *University of Cincinnati Law Review* 57 (1989): 849.

112. Frontiero v. Richardson, 411 U.S. 677 (1973).

113. Loren Beth, *John Marshall Harlan: Last Whig Justice* (Lexington: University Press of Ken-tucky, 1992); Tinsley E. Yarbrough, *Judicial Enig-ma: The First Justice Harlan* (New York: Oxford University Press, 1995).

114. Cumming v. Board of Education, 175 U.S. 528 (1899).

115. Plessy v. Ferguson, 163 U.S. 537, 559 (1896).

116. Ibid.

117. Ibid., p. 557.

118. Ibid., pp. 560–61.

119. Ibid., p. 561.

120. Civil Rights Cases, 109 U.S. 3, 25 (1883).

121. Ibid., p. 61.

Index

313